Literary Experiences

Volume Two

Stories Poems Essays Plays

Literary Experiences

Volume Two

Stories Poems Essays Plays

Iveson   Oster   McClay

PRENTICE-HALL CANADA INC. SCARBOROUGH, ONTARIO

Canadian Cataloguing in Publication Data

Main entry under title:

Literary experiences: volume 2

For use in grade 12.
Includes index.
ISBN 0-13-538158-4

1. Canadian literature (English).* 2. Canadian
literature (English) – 20th century.* 3. English
literature. 4. English literature – 20th century.
5. American literature. 6. American literature –
20th century.   I. Iveson, Margaret L., date.
II. Oster, John Edward., date.   III. McClay, Jill Kedersha,
date.

PN6014.L58 1990   808'.0427   C88-094957-0

Prentice-Hall, Inc., Englewood Cliffs, *New Jersey*
Prentice-Hall International, Inc., *London*
Prentice-Hall of Australia, Pty., Ltd., *Sydney*
Prentice-Hall of India Pvt., Ltd., *New Delhi*
Prentice-Hall of Japan, Inc., *Tokyo*
Prentice-Hall of Southeast Asia (PTE) Ltd., *Singapore*
Editora Prentice-Hall do Brasil Ltda., *Rio de Janeiro*
Prentice-Hall Hispanoamericana, *S.A., Mexico*

ISBN 0-13-538158-4

Acquiring Editors: Dorothy Greenaway and David Steele
Project Editor: Lavinia Inbar
Production Editor: Karyn Goldberger
Production: Lois Enns
Design: David Peden
Composition: Q Composition
Cover photo: Robert Bourdeau
              1985
              Neg. N° 85-57-85
              8½" × 12" (21.5 × 30.5 cm) Print
              Scotland
              Courtesy: Jane Corkin Gallery, Toronto

Printed and bound in Canada by Gagné Printing
1 2 3 4 5 GP 94 93 92 91 90

Table of Contents

UNIT ONE: AN EXCHANGE OF GIFTS

UNIT TWO: INNOCENCE AND EXPERIENCE

UNIT THREE: A SENSE OF PLACE

UNIT FOUR: SEE INTO THE LIFE

Acknowledgments

No literary anthology is solely the work of its editors. The authors whose works are included here really began the process by creating literature which inspires us in our work with students. The students and teachers who responded to early drafts of the manuscript offered interesting and useful suggestions, many of which were incorporated into the final version of the book. Susan Pritchard helped to research and write the biographies. Dorothy Greenaway and David Steele have provided assistance and support throughout this project. Also at Prentice-Hall, editors MaryBeth Leatherdale, Lavinia Inbar and Karyn Goldberger carefully read and edited the drafts. Our families have read and responded to selections. As well, Bob, Bev, and Alec have encouraged and supported our efforts on this project and our work more generally. Earl Buxton's example continues to influence the direction of our thinking about literature. Our thanks to you all.

Margaret L. Iveson

John E. Oster

Jill Kedersha McClay

About the Editors

Margaret L. Iveson, Ph.D., is an Assistant Professor of Secondary Education at the University of Alberta. Previously she was an English teacher, Department Head, and Language Arts Consultant with Edmonton Public Schools. She has also been President of the Alberta Language Arts Council and a member of the Alberta Senior High Language Arts Curriculum Committee.

John E. Oster, Ph.D., is a Professor of Secondary Education at the University of Alberta. He formerly taught in Saskatchewan secondary schools and at the Universities of Saskatchewan and New Brunswick. He has been editor of *Alberta English*, a member of the Alberta Senior High Language Arts Curriculum Committee, and Assistant Dean (Practicum) at the University of Alberta.

Jill Kedersha McClay, B.A. (Honours), M. Ed., is currently a sessional lecturer, faculty consultant, and Ph.D. student in the Department of Secondary Education at the University of Alberta. Previously she taught high-school English in the United States and Mexico.

To the Student

A witty philosopher once observed that "the problem with life is there's no control group." Each of us has to make decisions in life, and we never have a chance to discover what lies down "the road not taken" (to quote Robert Frost). Although each of us as an individual is limited to a single lifetime of experience, through reading literature we can all share in the experiences and see inside the minds of many people, including those from other times and other cultures. The wide variety of literary selections in this anthology provides an opportunity to gain the insights of many writers from Canada and around the world.

Equally important, however, is that in reading these selections you can gain insight into yourself and your relationships with others. Authors contribute part of the meaning of a work of literature by providing the literary text, but readers too are partners in the process of "meaning-making." A work of literature comes alive not on the page but in the mind of a reader. The images, associations and ideas the reader brings to the literary work are important aspects of reading literature. Robert Currie describes the writer-reader partnership metaphorically when he states that his poems are "slim bombs craving explosion . . . awaiting your arrival with a light." When reading the works of literature in this anthology, be an active reader by using your own experience and intellect to help illuminate the literary text. By reflecting on your own ideas and feelings, as well as those of the writers and literary characters, you will find that literature can lead to a deeper understanding of the human condition.

Literature, however, is more than a rich source for psychological and sociological understanding. A piece of literature is a carefully crafted work of art. The form of the work is as essential to it as is the content. We can gain most from a literary work, therefore, when we focus not just on what the writer says, but on how he or she says it. As the poet W.H. Auden has observed, a poem is "a verbal contraption" and the good reader is one who is curious about how the contraption works. Examining the choices writers make and the effects of those choices will help you become a more discerning reader and a more sensitive and accomplished writer.

In this anthology you will encounter literature that explores relationships between creating and responding, innocence and experience, place and personal identity, and appearance and reality. While, of course, no piece of literature is universally appealing, we trust that within these pages you will find many stories, poems, essays and plays that bring you pleasure, touch you personally, cause you to think more deeply and extend your literary horizons.

AN EXCHANGE OF GIFTS

The impulse to create, in one form or another, and to respond
to the creative works of others are important human
attributes. While few of us are creative geniuses, we are all
enriched by the creative output of those individuals who are.
However, even as respondents to the works of other people,
we play an important role in the creative process. As viewers,
readers, and listeners we bring our own attitudes, values and
experiences to works of art. In this way, we shape their meanings for ourselves.

Poems, stories, and essays about creating and responding to
works of art are featured in this unit. The term "art" is used
here in a broad sense to include literature, visual arts, dance,
music, and media. Many writers of selections in this unit
stress that respondents to a work of art are partners in its creation. The Canadian poet Alden Nowlan, for example, refers
to the sharing of a creative work as "An Exchange of Gifts"
between the person who produced it and the person who
responds to it. Perhaps the ultimate response to a work of art,
however, is to carry on the gift-giving tradition by engaging
in one's own artistic creation.

An Exchange of Gifts

Alden Nowlan

As long as you read this poem
I will be writing it.
I am writing it here and now
before your eyes,
although you can't see me.
Perhaps you'll dismiss this
as a verbal trick,
the joke is you're wrong;
the real trick
is your pretending
this is something
fixed and solid,
external to us both.
I tell you better:
I will keep on
writing this poem for you
even after I'm dead.

The Secret

Denise Levertov

Two girls discover
the secret of life
in a sudden line of
poetry.

I who don't know the
secret wrote
the line. They
told me

(through a third person)
they had found it
but not what it was,
not even

what line it was. No doubt
by now, more than a week
later, they have forgotten
the secret,

the line, the name of
the poem. I love them
for finding what
I can't find,

and for loving me
for the line I wrote,
and for forgetting it
so that

a thousand times, till death
finds them, they may
discover it again, in other
lines,

in other
happenings. And for
wanting to know it,
for

assuming there is
such a secret, yes,
for that
most of all.

I Carried With Me Poems

Gail Dusenbery

I carried with me poems, poems which spewed out of
   everything: I saw poems hanging from the clotheslines,
   hanging from the streetlamps: I saw poems glowing
   in the bushes, pushing out of the earth as tulips do;
I felt poems breathe in the dark March night like ghosts
   which squared and wheeled through the air;
I felt poems brushing the tops of chimneys, brushing
   by in the dark; I felt poems being born in the city,
   Venuses breaking through a shattered sea of mirrors;
I felt all the poets of the city straining,
   isolated poets, knowing none of the others, straining;
I felt that some gazed into the March night, looking,
   and finding;
and others were running down the steep streets,
   seeking, and seeking to embrace;
and others stood in empty bookstores turning over pages
   of fellow poets whom they loved but didn't know;
and some pondered over coffee growing cold, in harshly
   lit cafeterias, and gazed at the reflections of the eaters
   in the wall-to-wall mirrors:
some dwelt on what it was to grow old;
some dwelled on love;
some had gone out of time;
some, going out of time, looked back into time, and
   started;

I felt all these lives and existences, all with poems at
    their center;

I knew none of these poets;
but I felt these intimations augured well, for me, and
    for poetry:
and my steps grew big, giant steps, I bounded down
    Park Street,
a tall, taciturn, fast-walking poets' accomplice.

Mending a Sidewalk . . . Making a Poem

Ted Olson

It's simple in theory. Just three ingredients:
something solid, something fluid, some sort of binder.
The mix, though, must be right. The formulas
never quite fit. You keep experimenting:
a cupful, a fistful, a sprinkle. But look out:
a slosh too much and it's ruined.
   Now to work.
They're refractory. They sulk. They don't want to marry.
You thwack, pummel, flail, churn, larrup,
and cuss. You're tempted to say the hell with it.
But somehow finally they cohere into an ugly
coarse gray sludge.
   And that's just the beginning.
The stuff doesn't like being caged. It clots, clogs,
spills over, goes wherever it isn't supposed to.
Matter's contrary. You've got to show it you're boss.
And slowly, ever so slowly, it dociles. You think
By golly, I've got it! But you haven't. Not yet.
It has to jell. Don't try to hurry it. But don't
wait too long. Catch it while it's malleable.

Now to groom and polish. Carefully . . . carefully
until at last the coarse gray-burlap surface
takes on gray-burlap and lustre.
   Stop, now, quick!
Don't let it get too slick!

On Keeping a Notebook

Joan Didion

"'T HAT Woman Estelle,' " the note reads, " 'is partly the reason why George Sharp and I are separated today.' *Dirty crepe-de-Chine wrapper, hotel bar, Wilmington RR, 9:45 a.m. August Monday morning.*"

Since the note is in my notebook, it presumably has some meaning to me. I study it for a long while. At first I have only the most general notion of what I was doing on an August Monday morning in the bar of the hotel across from the Pennsylvania Railroad station in Wilmington, Delaware (waiting for a train? missing one? 1960? 1961? why Wilmington?), but I do remember being there. The woman in the dirty crepe-de-Chine wrapper had come down from her room for a beer, and the bartender had heard before the reason why George Sharp and she were separated today. "Sure," he said, and went on mopping the floor. "You told me." At the other end of the bar is a girl. She is talking, pointedly, not to the man beside her but to a cat lying in the triangle of sunlight cast through the open door. She is wearing a plaid silk dress from Peck & Peck, and the hem is coming down.

Here is what it is: the girl has been on the Eastern Shore, and now she is going back to the city, leaving the man beside her, and all she can see ahead are the viscous summer sidewalks and the 3 a.m. long-distance calls that will make her lie awake and then sleep drugged through all the steaming mornings left in August (1960? 1961?). Because she must go directly from the train to lunch in New York, she wishes that she had a safety pin for the hem of the plaid silk dress, and she also wishes that she could forget about the hem and the lunch and stay in the cool bar that smells of disinfectant and malt and make friends with the woman in the crepe-de-Chine wrapper. She is afflicted by a little self-pity, and she wants to compare Estelles. That is what that was all about.

Why did I write it down? In order to remember, of course, but exactly what was it I wanted to remember? How much of it actually happened? Did any of it? Why do I keep a notebook at all? It is easy to deceive oneself on all those scores. The impulse to write things down is a peculiarly compulsive one, inexplicable to those who do not share it, useful only accidentally, only secondarily, in the way that any compulsion tries to justify itself. I suppose that it begins or does not begin in the cradle. Although I have felt compelled to write things down since I was five years old, I doubt that my daughter ever will, for she is a singularly blessed and accepting child, delighted with life exactly as life presents itself to her, unafraid to go to sleep and unafraid to wake up. Keepers of private notebooks are a different breed altogether, lonely and resistant rearrangers of things, anxious malcontents, children afflicted apparently at birth with some presentiment of loss.

My first notebook was a Big Five tablet, given to me by my mother with the sensible suggestion that I stop whining and learn to amuse myself by writing down my thoughts. She returned the tablet to me a few years ago; the first entry is an account of a woman who believed herself to be freezing to death in the Arctic night, only to find, when day broke, that she had stumbled onto the Sahara Desert, where she would die of the heat before lunch. I have no idea what turn of a five-year-old's mind could have prompted so insistently "ironic" and exotic a story, but it does reveal a certain predilection for the extreme which has dogged me into adult life; perhaps if I were analytically inclined I would find it a truer story than any I might have told about Donald Johnson's birthday party or the day my cousin Brenda put Kitty Litter in the aquarium.

So the point of my keeping a notebook has never been, nor is it now, to have an accurate factual record of what I have been doing or thinking. That would be a different impulse entirely, an instinct for reality which I sometimes envy but do not possess. At no point have I ever been able successfully to keep a diary; my approach to daily life ranges from the grossly negligent to the merely absent, and on those few occasions when I have tried dutifully to record a day's events, boredom has so overcome me that the results are mysterious at best. What is this business about "shopping, typing piece, dinner with E, depressed"? Shopping for what? Typing what piece? Who is E? Was this "E" depressed, or was I depressed? Who cares?

In fact I have abandoned altogether that kind of pointless entry; instead I tell what some would call lies. "That's simply not true," the members of my family frequently tell me when they come up against my memory of a shared event. "The party was *not* for you, the spider was *not* a black widow, *it wasn't that way at all.*" Very likely they are right, for not only have I always had trouble distinguishing between what happened and what merely might have happened, but I remain unconvinced that the distinction, for my purposes, matters. The cracked crab that I recall having for lunch the day my father came home from Detroit in 1945 must certainly be embroidery, worked into the day's pattern to lend verisimilitude; I was ten years old and would not now remember the cracked crab. The day's events did not turn on cracked crab. And yet it is precisely that fictitious crab that makes me see the afternoon all over again, a home movie run all too often, the father bearing gifts, the child weeping, an exercise in family love and guilt. Or that is what it was to me. Similarly, perhaps it never did snow that August in Vermont; perhaps there never were flurries in the night wind, and maybe no one else felt the ground hardening and summer already dead even as we pretended to bask in it, but that was how it felt to me, and it might as well have snowed, could have snowed, did snow.

How it felt to me: that is getting closer to the truth about a notebook. I sometimes delude myself about why I keep a notebook, imagine that some thrifty virtue derives from preserving everything observed. See enough and write it down, I tell myself, and then some morning when the world seems drained of wonder, some day when I am only going through the motions of doing what I am supposed to do, which is write—on that bankrupt morning I will simply open my notebook and there it will all be, a forgotten account with accumulated interest, paid passage back to the world out there: dialogue overheard in hotels and elevators and at the hatcheck counter in Pavillon (one middle-aged man shows his hat check to another and says, "That's my old football number"); impressions of Bettina Aptheker and Benjamin Sonnenberg and Teddy ("Mr. Acapulco") Stauffer; careful *aperçus* about tennis bums and failed fashion models and Greek shipping heiresses, one of whom taught me a significant lesson (a lesson I could have learned from F. Scott Fitzgerald, but perhaps we all must meet the very rich for ourselves) by asking, when I arrived to interview her in her orchid-filled sitting room on the second day of a paralyzing New York blizzard, whether it was snowing outside.

I imagine, in other words, that the notebook is about other people. But of course it is not. I have no real business with what one stranger said to another at the hat-check counter in Pavillon; in fact I suspect that the line "That's my old football number" touched not my own imagination at all, but merely some memory of something once read, probably "The Eighty-Yard Run." Nor is my concern with a woman in a dirty crepe-de-Chine wrapper in a Wilmington bar. My stake is always, of course, in the unmentioned girl in the plaid silk dress. *Remember what it was to be me*: that is always the point.

It is a difficult point to admit. We are brought up in the ethic that others, any others, all others, are by definition more interesting than ourselves; taught to be diffident, just this side of self-effacing. ("You're the least important person in the room and don't forget it," Jessica Mitford's governess would hiss in her ear on the advent of any social occasion; I copied that into my notebook because it is only recently that I have been able to enter a room without hearing some such phrase in my inner ear.) Only the very young and the very old may recount their dreams at breakfast, dwell upon self, interrupt with memories of beach picnics and favorite Liberty lawn dresses and the rainbow trout in a creek near Colorado Springs. The rest of us are expected, rightly, to affect absorption in other people's favorite dresses, other people's trout.

And so we do. But our notebooks give us away, for however dutifully we record what we see around us, the common denominator of all we see is always, transparently, shamelessly, the implacable "I." We are not talking here about the kind of notebook that is patently for public consumption, a structural conceit for binding together a series of graceful *pensées*; we are talking about something private, about bits of the mind's string too short to use, an indiscriminate and erratic assemblage with meaning only for its maker.

And sometimes even the maker has difficulty with the meaning. There does not seem to be, for example, any point in my knowing for the rest of my life that, during 1964, 720 tons of soot fell on every square mile of New York City, yet there it is in my notebook, labeled "FACT." Nor do I really need to remember that Ambrose Bierce liked to spell Leland Stanford's name "£eland $tanford" or that "smart women almost always wear black in Cuba," a fashion hint without much potential for practical application. And does not the relevance of these notes seem marginal at best?:

> In the basement museum of the Inyo County Courthouse in Independence, California, sign pinned to a mandarin coat: "This MANDARIN COAT was often worn by Mrs. Minnie S. Brooks when giving lectures on her TEAPOT COLLECTION."

> Redhead getting out of car in front of Beverly Wilshire Hotel, chinchilla stole, Vuitton bags with tags reading:

> MRS. LOU FOX
> HOTEL SAHARA
> VEGAS

Well, perhaps not entirely marginal. As a matter of fact, Mrs. Minnie S. Brooks and her MANDARIN COAT pull me back into my own childhood, for although I never knew Mrs. Brooks and did not visit Inyo County until I was thirty, I grew up in just such a world, in houses cluttered with Indian relics and bits of gold ore and ambergris and the souvenirs my Aunt Mercy Farnsworth brought back from the Orient. It is a long way from that world to Mrs. Lou Fox's world, where we all live now, and is it not just as well to remember that? Might not Mrs. Minnie S. Brooks help me to remember what I am? Might not Mrs. Lou Fox help me to remember what I am not?

But sometimes the point is harder to discern. What exactly did I have in mind when I noted down that it cost the father of someone I know $650 a month to light the place on the Hudson in which he lived before the Crash? What use was I planning to make of this line by Jimmy Hoffa: "I may have my faults, but being wrong ain't one of them"? And although I think it interesting to know where the girls who travel with the Syndicate have their hair done when they find themselves on the West Coast, will I ever make suitable use of it? Might I not be better off just passing it on to John O'Hara? What is a recipe for sauerkraut doing in my notebook? What kind of magpie keeps this notebook? "*He was born the night the Titanic went down.*" That seems a nice enough line, and I even recall who said it, but is it not really a better line in life than it could ever be in fiction?

But of course that is exactly it: not that I should ever use the line, but that I should remember the woman who said it and the afternoon I heard it. We were on her terrace by the sea, and we were finishing the wine left from lunch, trying to get what sun there was, a California winter sun. The woman whose husband was born the night the *Titanic* went down wanted to rent her house, wanted to go back to her children in Paris. I remember wishing that I could afford the house, which cost $1,000 a month. "Someday you will," she said lazily. "Someday it all comes." There in the sun on her terrace it seemed easy to believe in someday, but later I had a low-grade afternoon hangover and ran over a black snake on the way to the supermarket and was flooded with inexplicable fear when I heard the checkout clerk explaining to the man ahead of me why she was finally divorcing her husband. "He left me no choice," she said over and over as she punched the register. "He has a little seven-month-old baby by her, he left me no choice." I would like to believe that my dread then was for the human condition, but of course it was for me, because I wanted a baby and did not then have one and because I wanted to own the house that cost $1,000 a month to rent and because I had a hangover.

It all comes back. Perhaps it is difficult to see the value in having one's self back in that kind of mood, but I do see it; I think we are well advised to keep on nodding terms with the people we used to be, whether we find them attractive company or not. Otherwise they run up unannounced and surprise us, come hammering on the mind's door at 4 a.m. of a bad night and demand to know who deserted them, who betrayed them, who is going to make amends. We forget all too soon the things we thought we could never forget. We forget the loves and the betrayals alike, forget what we whispered and what we screamed, forget who we were. I have already lost touch with a couple of people I used to be; one of them, a seventeen-year-old, presents little threat, although it would be of some interest to me to know again what it feels like to sit on a river levee drinking vodka-and-orange-juice and listening to Les Paul and Mary Ford and their echoes sing "How High the Moon" on the car radio. (You see I still have the scenes, but I no longer perceive myself among those present, no longer could even improvise the dialogue.) The other one, a twenty-three-year-old, bothers me more. She was always a good deal of trouble, and I suspect she will reappear when I least want to see her, skirts too long, shy to the point of aggravation, always the injured party, full of recriminations and little hurts and stories I do not want to hear again, at once saddening me and angering me with her vulnerability and ignorance, an apparition all the more insistent for being so long banished.

It is a good idea, then, to keep in touch, and I suppose that keeping in touch is what notebooks are all about. And we are all on our own when it comes to keeping those lines open to ourselves: your notebook will never help me, nor mine you. *"So what's new in the whiskey business?"* What could that possibly mean to you? To me it means a blonde in a Pucci bathing suit sitting with a couple of fat men by the pool at the Beverly Hills Hotel. Another man approaches, and they all regard one another in silence for a while. "So what's new in the whiskey business?" one of the fat men finally says by way of welcome, and the blonde stands up, arches one foot and dips it in the pool, looking all the while at the cabana where Baby Pignatari is talking on the telephone. That is all there is to that, except that several years later I saw the blonde coming out of Saks Fifth Avenue in New York with her California complexion and a voluminous mink coat. In the harsh wind that day she looked old and irrevocably tired to me, and even the skins in the mink coat were not worked the way they were doing them that year, not the way she would have wanted them done, and there is the point of the story. For a while after that I did not like to look in the mirror, and my eyes would skim the newspapers and pick out only the deaths, the cancer victims, the premature coronaries, the suicides, and I stopped riding the Lexington Avenue IRT because I noticed for the first time that all the strangers I had seen for years—the man with the seeing-eye dog, the spinster who read the classified pages every day, the fat girl who always got off with me at Grand Central— looked older than they once had.

It all comes back. Even that recipe for sauerkraut: even that brings it back. I was on Fire Island when I first made that sauerkraut, and it was raining, and we drank a lot of bourbon and ate the sauerkraut and went to bed at ten, and I listened to the rain and the Atlantic and felt safe. I made the sauerkraut again last night and it did not make me feel any safer, but that is, as they say, another story.

The Story of Nil

Gabrielle Roy
translated by Alan Brown

Q UITE often I asked my small pupils to sing together. One day, in the midst of their rather colourless voices, I could make out one that was clear, vibrant and astonishingly accurate. I had the group stop and let Nil go on alone. What a ravishing voice, and how precious to me, who had never had much of an ear for music!

From then on I would ask: "Nil, will you give the note?"

He would do so without coaxing and without pride—a child born to sing as others are born to pout.

The rest, my flight of sparrows, took off in his wake, soon following rather well; for besides his rare talent, Nil seemed able to pass it on to the others. We listened to him and believed we too could sing.

My music hour was the envy of the teachers in neighbouring classrooms.

"What's going on? We're getting a concert from your room every day now!"

They couldn't believe it, for I had never before shone as a singing teacher.

Our old inspector was stupefied when he came around.

"What's this? Your children are singing a thousand times better than other years!"

Then he stopped staring suspiciously at me, and asked to have them sing once more; and first thing I knew he was off in a happy reverie in which he seemed not even to remember that he was a school inspector.

Shortly after this visit I had another from our principal, who said in a faintly sarcastic way:

"I understand your children are such fine singers this year. I'm very curious to hear these little angels. Would you ask them to perform for me?"

Our principal was a little man made somewhat taller by his crest of blond hair, combed up in the middle like the picture of Monsieur Thiers in the dictionary. His dress, which was that of our teaching brothers at the time, was also very impressive: a black frock-coat and a white, starched dickey.

I had the pupils come close in a compact group, with Nil, one of the smallest, almost hidden in the middle. I made a little sign to him. He gave the starting tone just loudly enough to be heard by those around him. A wire vibrating harmoniously somewhere near! And the choir took off with such zest and in such perfect unison that I thought: Even the principal must be dazzled by this!

At any rate the mocking smile vanished quickly from his face. In its place appeared, to my amazement, the same expression of happy reverie, as if he had forgotten that he was a manager always busy running his school.

Hands behind his back, he wagged his head gently in rhythm with the tune and even when the song was ended kept on listening to it in his mind a moment longer.

But he had spotted the captivating voice. He brought Nil out of the group, looked long and attentively at him, and patted him on the cheek.

As I accompanied him to the door, he said:

"Well, with your thirty-eight sparrows you've caught a meadowlark this year. Do you know the lark? Let him sing and there's not a heart but is lightened!"

I suppose I was too young myself to know what a lightened heart was. But I soon had some idea of it.

That day had started very badly, under a driving autumn rain. The children arrived at school wet, sniffling and ill-humoured, with enormous muddy feet that soon turned my schoolroom, which I loved to see sparkling clean, into a kind of stable. As soon as I went to pick up a still-intact clod of black earth, two or three children would make a point of crushing others with their toes, scattering them in the aisles, watching me slyly all the while. I hardly recognized my pupils in these little rebels who would have risen against me at the drop of a hat, and perhaps they didn't recognize in me their beloved school mistress of yesterday. What had happened to turn us into something resembling enemies?

Some of our most experienced colleagues blamed the moments before the storm, the children's delicate nerves being strained by the atmospheric tension; and some said it was the long school days following weekends or holidays. After that taste of freedom the return to school was like going back to jail; and they grew quite disobedient, and all the more excitable, fidgety and impossible because they felt in their bones, poor things, that their revolt against the adult world had not the slightest chance of ultimate success.

It was my turn to have one of those dreadful days when the teacher seems to be there to do nothing but scold, and the children to comply, and all the sadness in the world settles into this place which can be so happy at other times.

As the bad weather kept up, instead of working off this excess nervousness in the open air we had to go to the gym in the basement, where shoes were loud on the hard floor. The children fought about nothing. I had to treat split lips and bloody noses.

Afterwards, fresh from a visit to the toilets, the children left their desks one after the other to ask permission to go down again. Impossible to continue with my lesson in that traffic! One would leave, another would just be coming back, the door would open, a draught would blow scribblers to the floor and they'd be picked up covered with dirt, and the door would slam: another child was going out. Suddenly I could take no more. "No! That will do! There's a limit after all."

Now it happened that without thinking, but as if I had done it on purpose, my "no" fell on little Charlie, a gentle child, quite guileless, whom his mother purged two or three times a year with a mixture of sulphur and molasses. Relegated to his desk, Charlie couldn't hold in very long. The odour gave him away to his neighbours, little monsters who pretended to be shocked, and shouted from where they sat, as if it wasn't obvious enough. "Charlie did it in his pants." In haste I had to write a note to his mother whom I knew to be vindictive, while Charlie stood at my desk, his legs apart, whimpering with shame.

I hadn't long to wait for the consequences. Charlie had been gone a half-hour when the principal showed his head in the high glass of the door and gestured that he wanted to speak to me. It was a serious business when he called us out to the corridor. Charlie's mother, he told me, had phoned. She was so furious that he had trouble persuading her not to sue me. Laugh if you please, there was such a thing as parents suing a teacher for less than that, and I was accused of having obliged Charlie's mother to re-wash his underwear, which she had done only yesterday.

I tried to present the facts from my point of view, but the principal remarked with some severity that it was better to let the whole class go to the toilet for nothing than to prevent one child in real need.

Perhaps because I was ashamed of myself, I tried to make the children ashamed at having shown their worst possible side all day. They weren't in the least contrite; quite the contrary—they seemed very pleased with themselves indeed, for the most part.

I went and sat down, completely discouraged. And the future descended on me, making all my years to come resemble this one day. I could see myself in twenty, thirty years, still in the same place, worn down by my task, the very image of the "oldest" of my present colleagues whom I found so pitiful; and thinking of them, my pity turned on myself. It goes without saying that the children took advantage of my dejection to chase each other up and down the aisles and add to the tumult. My glance fell on little Nil. While almost all the children were running amok, he was at his desk, trying to concentrate on his drawing. Apart from singing, what interested him most was to draw a cabin, always the same cabin, surrounded by curious animals, with chickens as tall as his cows.

I called to him, I think as if for help:

"Nil, come here a second."

He came running. He was a funny little manikin and always

oddly dressed. On this day a pair of men's braces, barely shortened, held up pants that were too big, their crotch hanging to his knees. His boots must have been just as oversized, for I heard them clatter as he ran up. With his mop of tow-coloured hair and his square head, flat on the top, he looked like a good little kulak determined to get an education. In fact, when he wasn't singing he was the last one in the class that you'd take for a meadowlark.

He leaned toward me affectionately.

"What do you want?"

"To talk to you. Tell me, who taught you to sing so well?"

"My mother."

I had glimpsed her once when the report cards were given out: a gentle, embarrassed smile, high cheekbones like Nil's, fine, penetrating eyes under her snow-white kerchief, a timid shadow who left as she had come, in silence. Did she know more than a few words apart from her own Ukrainian tongue?

"So she teaches you in Ukrainian?"

"Why, sure!"

"Do you know many Ukrainian songs?"

"Hundreds!"

"So many?"

"Well, at least ten . . . or twelve."

"Would you sing us one?"

"Which one?"

"Any one you like."

He took up a firm stand as if to resist the wind, his feet wide apart, his head thrown back, his eyes already shining, in a transformation more radical than I had ever seen—the first time he had sung at school in his mother's language: a little rustic turned into one possessed by music. His body swayed to a catchy rhythm, his shoulders went up, his eyes flamed, and a smile from time to time parted his slightly fleshy lips. With raised hand he seemed to point with a graceful gesture at some pretty scene in the distance, and you couldn't help following the gesture to see what it was he found so pleasing. I couldn't tell which was better: listening to him with my eyes closed, to enjoy that splendid voice without distraction; or watching him sing, so lively, so playful, as if he were ready to rise from the earth.

When this delightful song was ended we were in another world. The children had gradually gone back to their seats. I was no longer in despair about my future. Nil's singing had turned my heart inside out like a glove. Now I was confident about life.

I asked Nil: "Have you any idea what the song's about?"

"Sure I have!"

"Could you explain it to us?"

He launched into the story:

"There's a tree. It's a cherry tree in bloom. In the country my mother comes from there's lots of them. This cherry tree, it's in the middle of a field. Some young girls are dancing around it. They're waiting for the boys that are in love with them."

"What a lovely story!"

"Yes, but it's going to be sad," said Nil, "for one of the boys was killed in the war."

"Oh, that's too bad!"

"No, because that gives a chance to another fellow who was secretly in love with her, and he's the good guy."

"Oh! Fine! But where did your mother learn these songs?"

"In that country, before they left, when she was a little girl. Now she says that's all we have left from the Ukraine."

"And she's hurrying to get all that into your little head so it's your turn to keep it?"

He looked at me gravely to be very sure of what I had said, then he smiled affectionately.

"I won't lose a one," he said. And then, "Would you like me to sing another one?"

My mother had broken a hip about three months before. She had been immobilized in a plaster corset for a long time. The doctor had finally removed it and asserted that she would be able to walk if she persevered. She made a great effort every day, but couldn't manage to move her bad leg. I had seen her losing hope during the last week or two. I would catch her sitting in her armchair by the window looking at the outdoors with an expression of heart-rending regret. I would scold her so that she wouldn't think I was worried about her. Lively, active and independent as she was, what would her life be if she spent the rest of it a cripple? The horror I had felt one day at the thought of being chained for a lifetime to my teacher's desk gave me a glimpse of her feelings at the prospect of never leaving her prisoner's lookout at the window.

One day I had the notion of bringing Nil home to entertain her, for she found the days "deathly long."

"Would you like to come home, Nil, and sing for *my* mother? She's lost all her songs!"

He had a way of saying yes without a word, placing his little hand in mine as if to tell me: You know very well I'd go to the world's end with you. And it went straight to my heart.

On the way I explained to him that my mother was much older than his, and that it was hard at her age to get back her lost confidence. I still don't know what possessed me to get into explanations of that kind with a child of six and a half. But he listened, deadly serious, trying with all his might to fathom what I expected of him.

When my mother, who had just had a nap, opened her eyes and saw beside her this manikin in his wide braces, she must have thought he was one of the poor kids I had so often brought home so that she could make them a coat or alter one to their size. She said a little bitterly, but more in sadness, I think, at no longer being able to help:

"What's this? You know I can't sew anymore, except little things I can do by hand."

"No, no, it's not that. It's a surprise. Listen."

I made a sign to Nil. He planted himself in front of my mother as if to resist a strong wind, and launched into the happy song of the cherry tree. His body swayed, his eyes sparkled, a smile came to his lips, his little hand rose up to point, far beyond this sickroom, to what? A highway? A plain? Some open landscape, anyway, that he made you want to see.

When he had finished he looked at my mother, who said not a word, hiding her gaze from him. He suggested:

"D'you want to hear another one of my songs?"

My mother, as if from a distance, nodded her head, without showing her face, which stayed hidden behind her hand.

Nil sang another song, and this time my mother held her head high, watching the smiling child; and with his help she too was away, taking flight far above life, on the wings of a dream.

That evening she asked me to bring her a strong kitchen chair with a high back and help her stand up behind it, using it as a support.

I suggested that the chair could slip and pull her forward, so she had me lay a heavy dictionary on it.

With this strange "walker" of her own invention my mother resumed her exercises. Weeks passed and I could see no change. I was growing completely discouraged. My mother too, no doubt, for she seemed to have given up. What I didn't know was that, having realized she was on the point of succeeding, she had decided to go on with her exercises in secret so as to give me a surprise. A surprise it was! I was in the blackest despondency that evening when I heard her shout from her room:

"I'm walking! I can walk!"

I ran to her. My mother, pushing the chair in front of her, was progressing with tiny mechanical steps, like those of a wind-up doll, and she kept up her cry of triumph:

"I can walk! I can walk!"

Of course I don't claim that Nil performed a miracle. But perhaps he gave a little puff at just the right time to the flickering faith of my mother.

However that may be, this experiment gave me the urge to try another.

The previous year I had gone along with one of my colleagues and a group of her pupils who were putting on a little play for the old people in a home in our town.

Of all the prisons that human beings forge for themselves or are forced to suffer, not one, even today, seems as intolerable as the one in which we are confined by age. I had sworn never again to set foot in that home; it had upset me so. Maybe during the year I had made some progress in compassion, for here I was thinking of taking Nil there. He seemed the only one likely to be able to comfort the old people I had seen immured in the institution.

I spoke to the principal who thought for a long time and then said the idea had its good points . . . very good points, but first I'd have to get permission from the mother.

I set about writing a letter to Nil's mother, in which I said something to the effect that the songs she had brought from the Ukraine and passed on to her son seemed to be beneficial to the people here, as perhaps they had been to her own people . . . helping them to live . . . And would she please lend me Nil for an evening that might go on rather late?

I read it to Nil, asking him to get it firmly into his head because he would have to read it at home and give an exact translation to this mother. He listened attentively and as soon as I had finished asked if I'd like him to repeat it word for word, just to be sure that he had memorized it. I said that wouldn't be necessary, that I had faith in his memory.

Next day Nil brought me the reply on a piece of paper cut out from a brown paper bag. It was in telegraphic style:

"We lend Nil to the old people."

It was signed in letters that looked like embroidery:

Paraskovia Galaïda.

"What a beautiful name your mother has!" I said to Nil, trying to read it properly.

And on hearing my odd pronunciation, he burst out laughing in my face.

The old people's home had its own little auditorium, with a platform two steps high lit by a row of weak footlights which isolated it from the audience.

Caught in a beam of golden light, Nil was charming to see with his straw-coloured hair and the Ukrainian blouse with its embroidered collar, which his mother had made him wear. For my own part I missed a little seeing my manikin with the wide braces. On his face with its high cheekbones you could already see the joy he felt at the idea of singing. From my hiding place, where if need be I could prompt him as to what to do, I could see the audience as well as the stage, and it was among them, you might have thought, that the real drama was being played—that of life saying its last word.

In the first row was an old man afflicted with a convulsive palsy, like an apple tree that someone had shaken, still trembling long after its last fruit had fallen. Somewhere someone was breathing with a whistling sound like wind caught inside a hollow tree. Another old man tried to keep up with his lungs in a race with death. Near the middle of the room was one, half paralyzed, whose living eyes in his inert face had an unbearable lucidity. There was a poor woman, swollen to an enormous mass of flesh. And no doubt there were those who were still unscathed, if that happy chance consisted here of simply being worn, wrinkled, shrunken and eroded by some process of unimaginable ferocity. When is old age at its most atrocious: when you are in it, like these people in the home?— or seen from afar, through the eyes of tender youth that could wish for death at the sight?

Then, in that day's end, the clear, radiant voice of Nil rose as if from the shining morning of life. He sang of the flowering cherry tree, of the girls in love dancing their round on the plain, of the expectations of youthful hearts. With a gesture that was charmingly at ease he would raise his hand and point to a distant road to be followed . . . or a far horizon which, from his shining eyes, you imagined must be luminous. At one moment his lips parted in a smile that was so contagious it leapt over the footlights and appeared in all its fresh sweetness on the aged faces. He sang about Petrushka's adventure, and how he was caught by his own trickery. He sang a song that I had never heard, a gentle, melancholy song about the Dnieper River running on and on, bearing laughter and sighs, hopes and regrets, down toward the sea, until at the end everything melts into the eternal waves.

I didn't know the old people; they had changed so. In the dark evening of their lives this ray of morning had broken through to them. The palsied man succeeded in holding still a moment so as to hear more clearly. The eye of the paralytic no longer wandered, searching, calling for help, but turned and fixed upon Nil so as to see him as well as possible. The man who had been chasing his own breathing seemed to be holding his breath with his two hands clasped across his chest in a marvellous respite from his affliction. They all looked happy now, hanging on the next notes from Nil. And the tragic spectacle of the audience ended in a kind of parody, with old men excited as children, some on the verge of laughter, others of tears, because they were rediscovering so vividly in themselves the traces of what was lost.

Then I said to myself that this was, after all, too cruel, and I would never again bring Nil here to sing and re-awaken hope.

How the renown of my little healer of the ills of life began to spread, I have no idea, but soon I was getting requests from all sides.

One day, through the high glass door-panel, the principal made a sign that he wanted to talk to me.

"This time," he said, "it's a psychiatric hospital that's asking for our little Ukrainian lark. This is a serious question, and we must think it over."

Yes, it was serious, but once again, and as if it were beyond my own will, my decision had been made. If Paraskovia Galaïda gave her permission I would go with Nil to see the "madmen," as people called them then.

She agreed, with no trouble. I wonder now if she even worried about where we went. She seemed to have as much confidence in me as Nil did.

In the mental hospital also there was a little auditorium with a low platform, but without any bank of footlights or spots to separate this side from that. Everything was bathed in the same dull, uniform light. If the world of the aged in the home had made me think of tragedy's last act, here I had the impression of an epilogue mimed by shadows that had already passed on to a kind of death.

The patients were seated in docile ranks, most of them apathetic, their eyes bleak, twiddling their thumbs or biting at their lips.

Nil made his entrance on the narrow platform of the stage. There was a rustle of surprise in the audience. A few patients even grew excited at this marvellous apparition—a child, here! One of them, over-agitated, pointed his finger at him in a kind of joyous bewilderment, as if asking others to confirm what his eyes were seeing.

Nil took up his position, his feet apart, a lock of hair hanging over his forehead, his hands on his hips, for he was going to start with "Kalinka" which he had just learned from his mother. He caught its devilish rhythm with fiery charm.

From the very first notes there was a silence such as you

would feel when the forest hushes to hear a birdsong somewhere on a distant branch.

Nil was swaying, filled with an irresistible liveliness, sometimes tracing a gentle curve with his hand, sometimes passionately clapping both hands together. The patients followed his movements in ecstasy. And always this silence, as if in adoration.

"Kalinka" ended. Nil explained in a few words, as I had taught him, the meaning of the next song. He did this with complete ease, no more nervous than if he had been in class among his companions. Then he launched into his music again as if he would never grow tired of singing.

Now the patients were breathing together audibly, like a single, unhappy monster moving in the shadows, dreaming of its own release.

Nil went from one song to another, one sad, the next one gay. He no more saw the madmen than he had seen the aged, the sick, the sorrowful, with their torments of body and soul. He sang of the sweet, lost land of his mother which she had given him to keep, its prairies, its trees, a lone horseman crossing the distant plain. He ended with that gesture of his hand that I never tired of, pointing to a happy road, far away at the end of this world, and tapping the floor with his heel.

At once I was sure the patients were going to eat him alive. The nearest ones tried to reach him when he came down from the little platform. Those in the back pushed at the front ranks, trying to touch him too. A woman patient caught him by the arm and held him for a moment to her breast. Another pulled him away from her and kissed him. They all wanted to take possession of the wonder child, to take him alive, to prevent him at all costs from leaving them.

Nil, who had, without recognizing it, eased so much sadness, took fright at the terrible happiness he had unleashed. His eyes, filled with terror, called to me for help. A guard gently extricated him from the embrace of a sobbing patient:

"Dear child, little nightingale, stay here, stay here with us!"

Toward the back of the room another claimed possession of him, weeping:

"This is my little boy that they stole. Long ago. Give him back. Give me back my life."

He was all trembling when I got him in my arms.

"There, there, it's all finished! You made them too happy, that's all. Too happy!"

We had left the taxi, walking the rest of the way to Nil's house. He seemed to have forgotten the troublesome scene in the hospital, and his first care was to guide me, for as soon as we left the sidewalk I had no idea where I was going.

It was early May. It had rained hard for several days and the fields across which Nil was leading me were a sea of mud, with occasional clumps of low, thorny bushes that caught at my clothing. I could only guess at this strange landscape, for there were no street-lamps here. Not even what you could call a road. Just a vague path where trodden mud made the footing a little more firm than elsewhere. The path wound from one cabin to the next, and the feeble light from windows helped us somewhat. But Nil seemed not to need the light, for he jumped sure-footedly from one fairly dry spot to the next. Then we stood on the edge of a stretch of soft mud that gave off water like a sponge. To cross it there was a walk of planks thrown zig-zag here and there. The gaps were always longer than a single step. Nil would leap across and turn around to give me his hand, encouraging me to spring. He was delighted to bring me to his home; there was not a hint of suspicion in this happy child that I might pity him for living in this zone of the disinherited. It was true that beneath that soaring sky filled with stars, these cabins with their backs to the city, looking out over the free prairie vastness, formed a strangely fascinating shantytown.

From time to time, a fetid smell wafted toward us in waves, spoiling the fresh spring air. I asked Nil where it came from, and at first he didn't know what I was talking about, I suppose the smell was so familiar to him. Then he pointed behind us to a long, dark mass that blocked the horizon.

"The slaughterhouse," he said. "It must be the slaughter-house that stinks."

Now we had crossed the muddy sea and I was fated that night to go from one surprise to the next, for the unpleasant smell suddenly gave way to the good, simple one of wet earth.

Then the perfume of a flower reached me. We were coming close to Nil's house, and this was the powerful odour of a hyacinth in its pot outside near the door, struggling with a force almost equal to the last waves from the abattoir. Another few paces and the hyacinth had won. At the same time, from a nearby pond came a triumphant chorus of hylas.

Paraskovia Galaïda must have been on the lookout for us. She came at a run out of their cabin which was itself, no doubt, made of old bits of plank and waste boards. In the light of a crescent moon filtering through the clouds it seemed to me amazingly pale, as clean and pleasant as if it had just been whitewashed. It stood in a fenced enclosure. A gate opened inwards. So far as I could judge, it was made of nothing less than the foot of an iron bedstead mounted on hinges in the post. They squeaked as Paraskovia Galaïda opened the gate and welcomed us into the perfumed dooryard. The strange light revealed that everything in the place was scrupulously clean.

Paraskovia took my hands and backed toward the house. In front was a rough wooden bench. She made me sit down between Nil and herself. At once the cat of the place left the shadows and leapt to the back of the bench, where he made his narrow bed, content to be one of us, his head between our shoulders, purring.

With Nil's help, I tried to express to Paraskovia Galaïda something of the joy her small son's singing had brought to so many people; and she, with his help, tried to thank me for I wasn't quite sure what. Soon we had given up trying to pour out our feelings by means of words, listening instead to the night.

Then it seemed to me I caught a sign from Paraskovia Galaïda to Nil. Her eyes closed, she gave him a starting note just as he gave it at school. A delicate musical throat vibration sounded. Their voices began together, one a little hesitant at first but quickly convinced by the stronger of the two. Then they flew upward, harmonizing as they rose in a strangely lovely song, one of life as it is lived and life as it is dreamed.

Under that immense sky it took your heart and turned it round and turned it over, as a hand might do, before leaving it an instant, with due gentleness, to the freedom of the air.

Alex

Phyllis Webb

at five o'clock today Alex four years old said
I will draw a picture of you!
at first he gave me no ears and I said
you should give me ears
I would like big ears one on each side
and he added them and three buttons down the front
now I'll make your skirt wide he said and he did
and he put pins in all up and down my ribs and I waited
and he said now I'll put a knife in you
it was in my side and I said does it hurt
and No! he said and we laughed and he said
now I'll put a fire on you and he put male
fire on me in the right place then scribbled me
all into flames shouting FIRE FIRE FIRE
FIRE FIRE FIRE and I said
shall we call the fire engines and he said Yes!
this is where they are and the ladders are bending
and we made siren noises as he drew the engines on
over the page then he said the Hose! and he put
the fire out and that's better I said
and he rolled over laughing like crazy
because it was all on paper

Nine-Year Olds, Meet Monet

Ellen Goodman

S HE was on what the school called a "field trip," as if the fourth graders were anthropologists and the Museum of Fine Arts were a foreign land.

It was, in some ways, a meeting of different cultures. The nine-year-old chatter splintered in huge marble hallways built to echo nineteenth-century discussions of Art. The blue jeans and T-shirts jarred with the gilt frames holding priceless paintings.

The class had gone to meet one of the woman's favorite people—Claude Monet—and so, she had gone along. Not to introduce them, you understand, but to accompany them.

There she was struck, not by the contrasting cultures, but by the contrasting values of one culture. The children had been taken en masse to meet an individualist. They had come, clutching worksheets in one hand and best friends in the other—the channel markers of the social system—to see the work of a man who rebelled against his own artistic system.

Watching them giggling together and sharing answers she thought again: They are becoming socialized, for better and for worse.

The worksheets and friends were, in one way or another, the constraints of society on the ego. How they performed on paper and with each other would inevitably be marked down on the up-to-date report card under the headings "Learning Skills" and "Social Skills." Yet the paintings on the wall were the work of the disciplined but essentially "unsocialized" ego of the artist who believed in the primary value of self-expression.

If, like Monet, they skipped school to go to the sea, or drew cartoons of their teacher, they would be labeled "social problems." If they had the nerve to believe that their own rebellious notions were better than the collected wisdom of the École des Beaux-Arts, they too would be considered antisocial egotists.

The nine-year-olds, scattered around the rooms full of luscious landscapes, were, on the whole, good kids. You didn't have to remind them to keep their hands off. They had been almost civilized out of the real Me-Decade, the first years of life. Totally selfish at one, outrageously self-centered at two, by now the cutting edges of their egos had rubbed off against each other and the adults. They raised their hands and waited their turns and followed directions. They had learned the acts of survival—cooperation, and orderliness, laced with hypocrisy and covered with suppression.

They were becoming socialized. For better and for worse.

She thought of all the conflicting feelings and messages that went into this process. Be yourself but get along with others. Be popular but don't follow the crowd. Write an imaginative story, within these margins and in this time. Paint . . . by numbers.

They say that societies get the children they want. The imaginative three-year-old becomes the reasonable ten-year-old. The nursery-school child who asks, "How do they get the people inside the television set?" becomes the middle-school child who reads the ingredients on the cereal box. The two-year-old exhibitionist becomes the twelve-year-old conformist who won't wear the wrong kind of blue jeans.

As kids grow up, they are less exhausting and less imaginative, less selfish and less creative. They are easier to live with. Their egos come under control. They become socialized, for better and for worse.

We train selfishness out of them. Yet, ironically, some who resist, like the artists, may end up giving the most to others. The product of the most egotistical self-expression may become a generous gift available on the museum wall or the library shelf.

The fourth graders finished their hour with Monet. They were impressed with Impressionism and would, for a while, remember the man they'd met. They left, with their worksheets in one hand and their best friends in the other, still chattering. They passed, in reasonable order, through the doorway and down the massive staircase.

Very few of them had read or understood the words printed on the wall of the exhibit. They were copied from a letter Monet had written to a friend: "Don't you agree that on one's own with nature, one does better? Me, I'm sure of it. . . . What I'm going to do here will at least have the merit of not resembling anyone else, or so I think, because it will be simply the expression of what I myself have felt."

A Work of Art

Anton Chekhov

HOLDING under his arm an object wrapped in a newspaper, Sasha Smirnov, the only son of his mother, walked nervously into the office of Doctor Koshelkov.

"Well, my dear boy," exclaimed the doctor warmly, "how do you feel today? What's the good news?"

Sasha began to blink with his eyes, put his hand over his heart, and stammered nervously:

"My mother sends her regards and begs to thank you . . . I am my mother's only son, and you have saved my life . . . and we both hardly know how to thank you."

"Come, come, my young friend, let us not speak of it," interrupted the doctor, literally melting with pleasure. "I have done what anybody else in my place would have done."

"I am the only son of my mother . . . We are poor people and consequently we are not in a position to pay you for your trouble . . . and it makes it very embarrassing for us, Doctor, although both of us, mother and I, who am the only son of my mother, beg of you to accept from us, a token of our gratitude, this object which . . . is an object of rare worth, a wonderful masterpiece in antique bronze."

The doctor made a grimace.

"Why, my dear friend," he said, "it is entirely unnecessary. Don't need this in the least."

"Oh, no, no," stammered Sasha. "I beg you please accept it!"

He began to unwrap the bundle, continuing his entreaties in the meantime:

"If you do not accept this, you will offend both my mother and myself . . . This is a very rare work of art . . . an antique bronze. It is a relic left by my dead father. We have been prizing it as a very dear remembrance . . . My father used to buy up bronze antiques, selling them to lovers of old statuary . . . And now we continue in the same business, my mother and myself."

Sasha undid the package and enthusiastically placed it on the table.

It was a low candelabrum of antique bronze, a work of real art representing a group: On a pedestal stood two figures of women clad in the costume of Mother Eve and in poses that I have neither the audacity nor the temperament to describe. These figures were smiling coquettishly and in general gave one the impression that, were it not for the fact that they were obliged to support the candlestick, they would lean down from their pedestal and exhibit a performance which . . . my dear reader, I am even ashamed to think of it!

When the doctor espied the present, he slowly scratched his head, cleared his throat and blew his nose.

"Yes, indeed, a very pretty piece of work," he mumbled . . . "But—how shall I say it—not quite . . . I mean . . . rather unconventional . . . not a bit literary, is it? . . . You know . . . the devil knows . . ."

"Why?"

"Beelzebub himself could not have conceived anything more ugly. Should I place such a phantasmagoria upon my table I would pollute my entire home."

"Why, Doctor, what a strange conception you have of art!" cried Sasha in offended tones. "This is a real masterpiece. Just look at it! Such is its harmonious beauty that just to contemplate it fills the soul with ecstasy and makes the throat choke down a sob! When you see such loveliness you forget all earthly things . . . Just look at it! What life, what motion, what expression!"

"I quite understand all this, my dear boy," interrupted the

doctor. "But I am a married man. Little children run in and out of this room and ladies come here continually."

"Of course," said Sasha, "if you look at it through the eyes of the rabble, you see this noble masterpiece in an entirely different light. But you certainly are above all that, Doctor, and especially when your refusal to accept this gift will deeply offend both my mother and myself, who am the only son of my mother . . . You have saved my life . . . and in return we give you our dearest possession and . . . my only regret is that we are unable to give you the mate to this candelabrum."

"Thanks, friend, many thanks . . . Remember me to your mother and . . . But for God's sake! You can see for yourself, can't you? Little children run in and out of this room and ladies come here continually . . . However, leave it here! There's no arguing with you."

"Don't say another word!" exclaimed Sasha joyously. "Put the candelabrum right here, next to the vase. By Jove, but it's a pity that I haven't got the mate to give you. But it can't be helped. Well, good-bye, Doctor!"

After the departure of Sasha the doctor looked for a long time at the candelabrum and scratched his head.

"This is beautiful, all right," he thought. "It would be a pity to throw it away . . . And yet I dare not keep it . . . Hm! . . . Now who in the world is there to whom I can present or donate it?"

After long deliberation he hit upon a good friend of his, the lawyer Ukhov, to whom he was indebted for legal services.

"Fine!" chuckled the doctor. "Being a close friend of his, I cannot very well offer him money, and so I will give him this piece of indecency instead . . . And he's just the man for it . . . single, and somewhat of a gay bird, too."

No sooner thought than done. Dressing himself, the doctor took the candelabrum and went to the home of Ukhov.

"Good morning, old chap!" he said. "I have come here to thank you for your trouble . . . You will not take money, and I will therefore repay you by presenting you with this exquisite masterpiece . . . Now say for yourself, isn't it a dream?"

As soon as the lawyer caught sight of it he was exhilarated with its beauty.

"What a wonderful work of art!" he laughed uproariously. "Ye gods, what conceptions artists will get in their heads! What alluring charm! Where did you get this little dandy?"

But now his exhilaration had oozed away and he became frightened. Looking stealthily toward the door, he said:

"But, I can't accept it, old chap. You must take it right back."

"Why?" asked the doctor in alarm.

"Because . . . because . . . my mother often visits me, my clients come here . . . and besides, I would be disgraced even in the eyes of my servants."

"Don't say another word!" cried the doctor gesticulating wildly. "You simply have got to accept it! It would be rank ingratitude for you to refuse it! Such a masterpiece! What motion, what expression . . . You will greatly offend me if you don't take it!"

"If only this were daubed over or covered with fig leaves . . ."

But the doctor refused to listen to him. Gesticulating even more wildly, he ran out of Ukhov's house in the thought that he was rid of the present.

When the doctor was gone the lawyer carefully examined the candelabrum, and then, just as the doctor had done, he began to wonder what in the world he could do with it.

"O very beautiful object," he thought. "It is a pity to throw it away, and yet it is disgraceful to keep it. I had best present it to someone . . . I've got it! . . . This very evening I'm going to give it to the comedian Shoshkin. The rascal loves such things, and besides, this is his benefit night . . ."

No sooner thought than done. That afternoon the well-packed candelabrum was brought to the comedian Shoshkin.

That whole evening the dressing room of the comedian Shoshkin was besieged by men who hastened to inspect the present. And during all the time the room re-echoed with hilarious laughter which most closely resembled the neighing of horses.

If any of the actresses approached the door and said, "May I enter?" the hoarse voice of Shoshkin was immediately heard to reply:

"Oh, no, no, my darling, you mustn't. I am not dressed!"

After the performance the comedian shrugged his shoulders, gesticulated with his hands and said:

"Now what in the world am I to do with this? I live in a private apartment! I am often visited by actresses! And this isn't a photograph that one could conceal in a drawer!"

"Why don't you sell it?" suggested the wig maker. "There is a certain old woman who buys up antique bronzes . . . Her name is Smirnova . . . You had better take a run over there; they'll show you the place all right, everybody knows her . . ."

The comedian followed his advice . . .

Two days later Koshelkov, his head supported on his hand, was sitting in his office concocting pills. Suddenly the door was opened and into the office rushed Sasha. He was smiling radiantly and his breast heaved with joy . . . In his hands he held something wrapped in a newspaper.

"Doctor!" he cried breathlessly. "Imagine my joy! As luck would have it, I've just succeeded in getting the mate to your candelabrum! Mother is so happy! I am the only son of my mother . . . You have saved my life."

And Sasha, quivering with thankfulness and rapture, placed a candelabrum before the doctor. The latter opened his mouth as if to say something, but uttered not a word . . . His power of speech was gone . . .

Andrea del Sarto

Called "The Faultless Painter"

Robert Browning

But do not let us quarrel any more,
No, my Lucrezia; bear with me for once:
Sit down and all shall happen as you wish.
You turn your face, but does it bring your heart?
I'll work then for your friend's friend, never fear,
Treat his own subject after his own way,
Fix his own time, accept too, his own price,
And shut the money into this small hand
When next it takes mine. Will it? tenderly?
Oh, I'll content him,—but to-morrow, Love!   10
I often am much wearier than you think,
This evening more than usual, and it seems
As if—forgive now—should you let me sit
Here by the window with your hand in mine
And look a half-hour forth on Fiesole,
Both of one mind, as married people use,
Quietly, quietly the evening through,
I might get up to-morrow to my work
Cheerful and fresh as ever. Let us try.
To-morrow, how you shall be glad for this!   20
Your soft hand is a woman of itself,
And mine the man's bared breast she curls inside.
Don't count the time lost, neither; you must serve
For each of the five pictures we require:
It saves a model. So! keep looking so—
My serpentining beauty, rounds on rounds!

—How could you ever prick those perfect ears,
Even to put the pearl there! oh, so sweet—
My face, my moon, my everybody's moon,
Which everybody looks on and calls his   30
And, I suppose, is looked on by in turn,
While she looks—no one's: very dear, no less.
You smile? why, there's my picture ready made,
There's what we painters call our harmony!
A common grayness silvers everything,—
All in a twilight, you and I alike
—You, at the point of your first pride in me
(That's gone you know),—but I, at every point;
My youth, my hope, my heart, being all toned down
To yonder sober pleasant Fiesole.   40
There's the bell clinking from the chapel-top;
That length of convent-wall across the way
Holds the trees safer, huddled more inside;
The last monk leaves the garden; days decrease,
And autumn grows, autumn in everything.
Eh? the whole seems to fall into a shape
As if I saw alike my work and self
And all that I was born to be and do,
A twilight-piece. Love, we are in God's hand.
How strange now looks the life he makes us lead;   50
So free we seem, so fettered fast we are!
I feel he laid the fetter: let it lie!
This chamber for example—turn your head—
All that's behind us! You don't understand
Nor care to understand about my art,
But you can hear at least when people speak:
And that cartoon, the second from the door
—It is the thing, Love! so such things should be—
Behold Madonna!—I am bold to say.
I can do with my pencil what I know,   60
What I see, what at bottom of my heart
I wish for, if I ever wish so deep—

Do easily, too—when I say, perfectly,
I do not boast, perhaps: yourself are judge,
Who listened to the Legate's talk last week,
And just as much they used to say in France.
At any rate, 'tis easy, all of it!
No sketches first, no studies, that's long past:
I do what many dream of all their lives,
—Dream? strive to do, and agonize to do,   70
And fail in doing. I could count twenty such
On twice your fingers, and not leave this town,
Who strive—you don't know how the others strive
To paint a little thing like that you smeared
Carelessly passing with your robes afloat,—
Yet do much less, so much less, Someone says,
(I know his name, no matter)—so much less!
Well, less is more, Lucrezia: I am judged.
There burns a truer light of God in them,
In their vexed beating stuffed and stopped-up brain, 80
Heart, or whate'er else, than goes on to prompt
This low-pulsed forthright craftsman's hand of mine.
Their works drop groundward, but themselves, I know,
Reach many a time a heaven that's shut to me,
Enter and take their place there sure enough,
Though they come back and cannot tell the world.
My works are nearer heaven, but I sit here.
The sudden blood of these men! at a word
Praise them, it boils, or blame them, it boils too.
I, painting from myself, and to myself,   90
Know what I do, am unmoved by men's blame
Or their praise either. Somebody remarks
Morello's outline there is wrongly traced,
His hue mistaken; what of that? or else,
Rightly traced and well ordered; what of that?
Speak as they please, what does the mountain care?
Ah, but a man's reach should exceed his grasp,
Or what's a heaven for? All is silver-gray,

Placid and perfect with my art: the worse!
I know both what I want and what might gain,   100
And yet how profitless to know, to sigh
"Had I been two, another and myself,
Our head would have o'erlooked the world!" No doubt.
Yonder's a work now, of that famous youth
The Urbinate who died five years ago.
('Tis copied, George Vasari sent it me.)
Well, I can fancy how he did it all,
Pouring his soul, with kings and popes to see,
Reaching, that heaven might so replenish him,
Above and through his art—for it gives way;   110
That arm is wrongly put—and there again—
A fault to pardon in the drawing's lines,
Its body, so to speak: its soul is right,
He means right—that, a child may understand.
Still, what an arm! and I could alter it:
But all the play, the insight and the stretch—
Out of me, out of me! And wherefore out?
Had you enjoined them on me, given me soul,
We might have risen to Rafael, I and you!
Nay, Love, you did give all I asked, I think—   120
More than I merit, yes, by many times.
But had you—oh, with the same perfect brow,
And perfect eyes, and more than perfect mouth,
And the low voice my soul hears, as a bird
The fowler's pipe, and follows to the snare—
Had you, with these the same, but brought a mind!
Some women do so. Had the mouth there urged
"God and the glory! never care for gain.
The present by the future, what is that?
Live for fame, side by side with Agnolo!   130
Rafael is waiting: up to God, all three!"
I might have done it for you. So it seems:
Perhaps not. All is as God overrules.
Beside, incentives come from the soul's self;

The rest avail not. Why do I need you?
What wife had Rafael, or has Agnolo?
In this world, who can do a thing, will not;
And who would do it, cannot, I perceive:
Yet the will's somewhat—somewhat, too, the power—
And thus we half-men struggle. At the end,   140
God, I conclude, compensates, punishes.
'Tis safer for me, if the award be strict,
That I am something underrated here,
Poor this long while, despised, to speak the truth.
I dared not, do you know, leave home all day,
For fear of chancing on the Paris lords.
The best is when they pass and look aside;
But they speak sometimes; I must bear it all.
Well may they speak! That Francis, that first time,
And that long festal year at Fontainebleau!   150
I surely then could sometimes leave the ground,
Put on the glory, Rafael's daily wear,
In that humane great monarch's golden look,—
One finger in his beard or twisted curl
Over his mouth's good mark that made the smile,
One arm about my shoulder, round my neck,
The jingle of his gold chain in my ear,
I painting proudly with his breath on me,
All his court round him, seeing with his eyes,
Such frank French eyes and such a fire of souls   160
Profuse, my hand kept plying by those hearts,—
And, best of all, this, this, this face beyond,
This in the background, waiting on my work,
To crown the issue with a last reward!
A good time, was it not, my kingly days,
And had you not grown restless . . . but I know—
'Tis done and past; 'twas right, my instinct said;
Too live the life grew, golden and not gray,
And I'm the weak-eyed bat no sun should tempt
Out of the grange whose four walls make his world.   170

How could it end in any other way?
You called me, and I came home to your heart.
The triumph was, to have ended there; then if
I reached it ere the triumph, what is lost?
Let my hands frame your face in your hair's gold,
You beautiful Lucrezia that are mine!
"Rafael did this, Andrea painted that;
The Roman's is the better when you pray,
But still the other's Virgin was his wife"—
Men will excuse me. I am glad to judge   180
Both pictures in your presence; clearer grows
My better fortune, I resolve to think.
For, do you know, Lucrezia, as God lives,
Said one day Agnolo, his very self,
To Rafael . . . I have known it all these years . . .
(When the young man was flaming out his thoughts
Upon a palace-wall for Rome to see,
Too lifted up in heart because of it)
"Friend, there's a certain sorry little scrub
Goes up and down our Florence, none cares how,   190
Who, were he set to plan and execute
As you are, pricked on by your popes and kings,
Would bring the sweat into that brow of yours!"
To Rafael's!—And indeed the arm is wrong.
I hardly dare . . . yet, only you to see,
Give the chalk here—quick, thus the line should go!
Ay, but the soul! he's Rafael! rub it out!
Still, all I care for, if he spoke the truth,
(What he? why, who but Michel Agnolo?
Do you forget already words like those?)   200
If really there was such a chance, so lost,—
Is, whether you're—not grateful—but more pleased.
Well, let me think so. And you smile indeed!
This hour has been an hour! Another smile?
If you would sit thus by me every night
I should work better, do you comprehend?

I mean that I should earn more, give you more.
See, it is settled dusk now; there's a star;
Morello's gone, the watch-lights show the wall,
The cue-owls speak the name we call them by.   210
Come from the window, love,—come in, at last,
Inside the melancholy little house
We built to be so gay with. God is just.
King Francis may forgive me: oft at nights
When I look up from painting, eyes tired out,
The walls become illumined, brick from brick
Distinct, instead of mortar, fierce bright gold,
That gold of his I did cement them with!
Let us but love each other. Must you go?
That Cousin here again? he waits outside?   220
Must see you—you, and not with me? Those loans?
More gaming debts to pay? you smiled for that?
Well, let smiles buy me! have you more to spend?
While hand and eye and something of a heart
Are left me, work's my ware, and what's it worth?
I'll pay my fancy. Only let me sit
The gray remainder of the evening out,
Idle, you call it, and muse perfectly
How I could paint, were I but back in France,
One picture, just one more—the Virgin's face.   230
Not yours this time! I want you at my side
To hear them—that is, Michel Agnolo—
Judge all I do and tell you of its worth.
Will you? To-morrow, satisfy your friend.
I take the subjects for his corridor,
Finish the portrait out of hand—there, there,
And throw him in another thing or two
if he demurs; the whole should prove enough
To pay for this same Cousin's freak. Beside,
What's better and what's all I care about,   240
Get you the thirteen scudi for the ruff!
Love, does that please you? Ah, but what does he,

The Cousin! what does he to please you more?
I am grown peaceful as old age to-night.
I regret little, I would change still less.
Since there my past life lies, why alter it?
The very wrong to Francis!—it is true
I took his coin, was tempted and complied,
And built this house and sinned, and all is said.
My father and my mother died of want.   250
Well, had I riches of my own? you see
How one gets rich! Let each one bear his lot.
They were born poor, lived poor, and poor they died:
And I have laboured somewhat in my time
And not been paid profusely. Some good son
Paint my two hundred pictures—let him try!
No doubt, there's something strikes a balance. Yes,
You loved me quite enough, it seems to-night.
This must suffice me here. What would one have?
In heaven, perhaps, new chances, one more chance—   260
Four great walls in the new Jerusalem,
Meted on each side by the angel's reed,
For Leonard, Rafael, Agnolo and me
To cover—the three first without a wife,
While I have mine! So—still they overcome
Because there's still Lucrezia,—as I choose.

Again the Cousin's whistle! Go, my Love.

El Greco: Espolio

Earle Birney

The carpenter is intent on the pressure of his hand

on the awl   and the trick of pinpointing his strength
through the awl to the wood   which is tough
He has no effort to spare for despoilings
or to worry if he'll be cut in on the dice
His skill is vital to the scene   and the safety of the
    state
Anyone can perform the indignities   It's his hard arms
and craft that hold the eyes of the convict's women
There is the problem of getting the holes exact
(in the middle of this elbowing crowd)
and deep enough to hold the spikes
after they've sunk through those bared feet
and inadequate wrists he knows are waiting behind him

He doesn't sense perhaps that one of the hands
is held in a curious gesture over him—
giving   or asking   forgiveness?—
but he'd scarcely take time to be puzzled by poses
Criminals come in all sorts
as anyone knows who makes crosses
are as mad or sane as those who decide on their killings
Our one at least has been quiet so far
though they say he talked himself into this trouble
a carpenter's son who got notions of preaching

Well here's a carpenter's son who'll have carpenter sons
God willing   and build what's wanted
temples or tables   mangers or crosses
and shape them decently
working alone in that firm and profound abstraction
which blots out the bawling of rag-snatchers
To construct with hands   knee-weight   braced thigh
keeps the back turned from death

But it's too late now for the other carpenter's boy
to return to this peace before the nails are hammered

Pavlova

Lorna Crozier

Even you, Pavlova, you
with the beautiful feet and arms,
even you did not die
with grace or beauty.
Your last words
Get my swan costume ready
were what we would have written
for you, but death would not
lift you weightless
into the bright air.

You waited
in the shadows of the wings,
moistening your lips,
crossing yourself as you had
a hundred times before.
Should I have had children instead?
Sons and daughters
to show pictures to.
This is the country I left,
see why I weep.

In Russia the snow is falling
as it does in memory, falling
on the backs of horses,
settling in the furs of women
who ride to the concert halls.

In your garden in England
the swan who laid his neck
across your shoulders
and bit your flesh
in his dark unpredictable beak
dreams himself whole again
up to where the sky
was made for swans.

Lonely and sick you lie
in a Dutch hotel.
Your lungs like stones
press you into the bed.
Clutching your husband's hand,
you feel the warmth of the mistress
he left just moments ago,
hear his words
She will not dance tomorrow,
as the doctor cuts
into your ribcage
to drain the pus
and let the breath in.

Fred Astaire

R. Glenn Martin

He was as deft
As birds in flight—
A shooting star
That lit the night.

He danced as breezes
Move in spring
Or as the eagle
Tips its wing.

His movements were
A sleight of hand,
Enchanted steps
In magicland.

No eye could follow
Leaps so fleet—
Prestissimo
With flying feet,

Yet moments later
He could flow
In marvelous
Adagio.

His partners were
Transformed. They all
Experienced
The miracle

That while they danced
With him, they shone
As they had never
Done alone.

The dazzling ease,
The grace, the style,
The humor and
The elfin smile,

The range, the scope,
Poems in air—
No one has done it
Like Astaire.

Others have danced,
But only he
Revised the laws
Of gravity.

Harrison Bergeron

Kurt Vonnegut, Jr.

T HE year was 2081, and everybody was finally equal. They weren't only equal before God and the law. They were equal every which way. Nobody was smarter than anybody else. Nobody was better looking than anybody else. Nobody was stronger or quicker than anybody else. All this equality was due to the 211th, 212th, and 213th Amendments to the Constitution, and to the unceasing vigilance of agents of the United States Handicapper General.

Some things about living still weren't quite right, though. April, for instance, still drove people crazy by not being springtime. And it was in that clammy month that the H-G men took George and Hazel Bergeron's fourteen-year-old son, Harrison, away.

It was tragic, all right, but George and Hazel couldn't think about it very hard. Hazel had a perfectly average intelligence, which meant she couldn't think about anything except in short bursts. And George, while his intelligence was way above normal, had a little mental handicap radio in his ear. He was required by law to wear it at all times. It was tuned to a government transmitter. Every twenty seconds or so, the transmitter would send out some sharp noise to keep people like George from taking unfair advantage of their brains.

George and Hazel were watching television. There were tears on Hazel's cheeks, but she'd forgotten for the moment what they were about.

On the television screen were ballerinas.

A buzzer sounded in George's head. His thoughts fled in panic, like bandits from a burglar alarm.

"That was a real pretty dance, that dance they just did," said Hazel.

"Huh?" said George.

"That dance—it was nice," said Hazel.

"Yup," said George. He tried to think a little about the ballerinas. They weren't really very good—no better than anybody else would have been, anyway. They were burdened with sashweights and bags of birdshot, and their faces were masked, so that no one, seeing a free and graceful gesture or a pretty face, would feel like something the cat dragged in. George was toying with the vague notion that maybe dancers shouldn't be handicapped. But he didn't get very far with it before another noise in his ear radio scattered his thoughts.

George winced. So did two out of the eight ballerinas.

Hazel saw him wince. Having no mental handicap herself, she had to ask George what the latest sound had been.

"Sounded like somebody hitting a milk bottle with a ball peen hammer," said George.

"I'd think it would be real interesting, hearing all the different sounds," said Hazel, a little envious. "All the things they think up."

"Um," said George.

"Only, if I was Handicapper General, you know what I would do?" said Hazel. Hazel, as a matter of fact, bore a strong resemblance to the Handicapper General, a woman named Diana Moon Glampers. "If I was Diana Moon Glampers," said Hazel, "I'd have chimes on Sunday—just chimes. Kind of in honor of religion."

"I could think, if it was just chimes," said George.

"Well—maybe make 'em real loud," said Hazel. "I think I'd make a good Handicapper General."

"Good as anybody else," said George.

"Who knows better'n I do what normal is?" said Hazel.

"Right," said George. He began to think glimmeringly about his abnormal son who was now in jail, about Harrison, but a twenty-one-gun salute in his head stopped that.

"Boy!" said Hazel, "that was a doozy, wasn't it?"

It was such a doozy that George was white and trembling, and tears stood on the rims of his red eyes. Two of the eight ballerinas had collapsed to the studio floor, were holding their temples.

"All of a sudden you look so tired," said Hazel. "Why don't you stretch out on the sofa, so's you can rest your handicap bag on the pillows, honeybunch." She was referring to the forty-seven pounds of birdshot in a canvas bag, which was padlocked around George's neck. "Go on and rest the bag for a little while," she said. "I don't care if you're not equal to me for a while."

George weighed the bag with his hands. "I don't mind it," he said. "I don't notice it any more. It's just a part of me."

"You been so tired lately—kind of wore out," said Hazel. "If there was just some way we could make a little hole in the bottom of the bag, and just take out a few of them lead balls. Just a few."

"Two years in prison and two thousand dollars' fine for every ball I took out," said George. "I don't call that a bargain."

"If you could just take a few out when you came home from work," said Hazel. "I mean—you don't compete with anybody around here. You just set around."

"If I tried to get away with it," said George, "then other people'd get away with it—and pretty soon we'd be right back to the dark ages again, with everybody competing against everybody else. You wouldn't like that, would you?"

"I'd hate it," said Hazel.

"There you are," said George. "The minute people start cheating on laws, what do you think happens to society?"

If Hazel hadn't been able to come up with an answer to this question, George couldn't have supplied one. A siren was going off in his head.

"Reckon it'd fall all apart," said Hazel.

"What would?" said George blankly.

"Society," said Hazel uncertainly. "Wasn't that what you just said?"

"Who knows?" said George.

The television program was suddenly interrupted for a news bulletin. It wasn't clear at first as to what the bulletin was about, since the announcer, like all announcers, had a serious speech impediment. For about half a minute, and in a state of high excitement, the announcer tried to say, "Ladies and gentlemen . . ."

He finally gave up, handed the bulletin to a ballerina to read.

"That's all right . . ." Hazel said of the announcer, "he tried. That's the big thing. He tried to do the best he could with what God gave him. He should get a nice raise for trying so hard."

"Ladies and gentlemen . . ." said the ballerina, reading the bulletin. She must have been extraordinarily beautiful, because the mask she wore was hideous. And it was easy to see that she was the strongest and most graceful of all the dancers, for her handicap bags were as big as those worn by two-hundred-pound men.

And she had to apologize at once for her voice, which was a very unfair voice for a woman to use. Her voice was a warm, luminous, timeless melody. "Excuse me . . ." she said, and she began again, making her voice absolutely uncompetitive.

"Harrison Bergeron, age fourteen," she said in a grackle squawk, "has just escaped from jail, where he was held on suspicion of plotting to overthrow the government. He is a genius and an athlete, is under-handicapped, and should be regarded as extremely dangerous."

A police photograph of Harrison Bergeron was flashed on the screen upside down, then sideways, upside down again, then right side up. The picture showed the full length of Harrison against a background calibrated in feet and inches. He was exactly seven feet tall.

The rest of Harrison's appearance was Halloween and hardware. Nobody had ever borne heavier handicaps. He had outgrown hindrances faster than the H-G men could think them up. Instead of a little ear radio for a mental handicap, he wore a tremendous pair of earphones, and spectacles with thick, wavy lenses. The spectacles were intended to make him not only half blind, but to give him whanging headaches besides.

Scrap metal was hung all over him. Ordinarily, there was a certain symmetry, a military neatness, to the handicaps issued to strong people, but Harrison looked like a walking junkyard. In the race of life, Harrison carried three hundred pounds.

And to offset his good looks, the H-G men required that he wear at all times a red rubber ball for a nose, keep his eyebrows shaved off, and cover his even white teeth with black caps at snaggle-tooth random.

"If you see this boy," said the ballerina, "do not—I repeat, do not—try to reason with him."

There was the shriek of a door being torn from its hinges.

Screams and barking cries of consternation came from the television set. The photograph of Harrison Bergeron on the screen jumped again and again, as though dancing to the tune of an earthquake.

George Bergeron correctly identified the earthquake, and well he might have—for many was the time his own home had danced to the same crashing tune. "My God . . ." said George, "that must be Harrison!"

The realization was blasted from his mind instantly by the sound of an automobile collision in his head.

When George could open his eyes again, the photograph of Harrison was gone. A living, breathing Harrison filled the screen.

Clanking, clownish, and huge, Harrison stood in the centre of the studio. The knob of the uprooted studio door was still in his hand. Ballerinas, technicians, musicians, and announcers cowered on their knees before him, expecting to die.

"I am the Emperor!" cried Harrison. "Do you hear? I am the Emperor! Everybody must do what I say at once!" He stamped his foot and the studio shook.

"Even as I stand here . . ." he bellowed, "crippled, hobbled, sickened . . . I am a greater ruler than any man who ever lived! Now watch me become what I *can* become!"

Harrison tore the straps of his handicap harness like wet tissue paper, tore straps guaranteed to support five thousand pounds.

Harrison's scrap-iron handicaps crashed to the floor.

Harrison thrust his thumbs under the bar of the padlock that secured his head harness. The bar snapped like celery.

Harrison smashed his headphones and spectacles against the wall.

He flung away his rubber-ball nose, revealed a man that would have awed Thor, the god of thunder.

"I shall now select my Empress!" he said, looking down on the cowering people. "Let the first woman who dares rise to her feet claim her mate and her throne!"

A moment passed, and then a ballerina arose, swaying like a willow.

Harrison plucked the mental handicap from her ear, snapped off her physical handicaps with marvellous delicacy. Last of all, he removed her mask.

She was blindingly beautiful.

"Now . . ." said Harrison, taking her hand, "shall we show the people the meaning of the word dance? Music!" he commanded.

The musicians scrambled back into their chairs, and Harrison stripped them of their handicaps, too. "Play your best," he told them, "and I'll make you barons and dukes and earls."

The music began. It was normal at first—cheap, silly, false. But Harrison snatched two musicians from their chairs, waved them like batons as he sang the music as he wanted it played. He slammed them back into their chairs.

The music began again and was much improved.

Harrison and his Empress merely listened to the music for a while—listened gravely, as though synchronizing their heartbeats with it.

They shifted their weights to their toes.

Harrison placed his big hands on the girl's tiny waist, letting her sense the weightlessness that would soon be hers.

And then, in an explosion of joy and grace, into the air they sprang!

Not only were the laws of the land abandoned, but the law of gravity and the laws of motion as well.

They reeled, whirled, swivelled, flounced, capered, gambolled, and spun.

They leaped like deer on the moon.

The studio ceiling was thirty feet high, but each leap brought the dancers nearer to it.

It became their obvious intention to kiss the ceiling.

They kissed it.

And then, neutralizing gravity with love and pure will, they remained suspended in air inches below the ceiling, and they kissed each other for a long, long time.

It was then that Diana Moon Glampers, the Handicapper General, came into the studio with a double-barrelled ten-gauge shotgun. She fired twice, and the Emperor and the Empress were dead before they hit the floor.

Diana Moon Glampers loaded the gun again. She aimed it at the musicians and told them they had ten seconds to get their handicaps back on.

It was then that the Bergerons' television tube burned out.

Hazel turned to comment about the blackout to George. But George had gone out into the kitchen for a can of beer.

George came back in with the beer, paused while a handicap signal shook him up. And then he sat down again. "You been crying?" he said to Hazel.

"Yup," she said.

"What about?" he said.

"I forget," she said. "Something real sad on television."

"What was it?" he said.

"It's all kind of mixed up in my mind," said Hazel.

"Forget sad things," said George.

"I always do," said Hazel.

"That's my girl," said George. He winced. There was the sound of a riveting gun in his head.

"Gee—I could tell that one was a doozy," said Hazel.

"You can say that again," said George.

"Gee . . ." said Hazel, "I could tell that one was a doozy."

Professions for Women

Virginia Woolf

W HEN your secretary invited me to come here, she told me that your Society is concerned with the employment of women and she suggested that I might tell you something about my own professional experiences. It is true I am a woman; it is true I am employed; but what professional experiences have I had? It is difficult to say. My profession is literature; and in that profession there are fewer experiences for women than in any other, with the exception of the stage—fewer, I mean, that are peculiar to women. For the road was cut many years ago—by Fanny Burney, by Aphra Behn, by Harriet Martineau, by Jane Austen, by George Eliot*—many famous women, and many more unknown and forgotten, have been before me, making the path smooth, and regulating my steps. Thus, when I came to write, there were very few material obstacles in my way. Writing was a reputable and harmless occupation. The family peace was not broken by the scratching of a pen. No demand was made upon the family purse. For ten and sixpence one can buy paper enough to write all the plays of Shakespeare—if one has a mind that way. Pianos and models, Paris, Vienna and Berlin, masters and mistresses, are not needed by a writer. The cheapness of writing paper is, of course, the reason why women

---

*British women novelists of the eighteenth and nineteenth centuries.

have succeeded as writers before they have succeeded in the other professions.

But to tell you my story—it is a simple one. You have only got to figure to yourselves a girl in a bedroom with a pen in her hand. She had only to move that pen from left to right— from ten o'clock to one. Then it occurred to her to do what is simple and cheap enough after all—to slip a few of those pages into an envelope, fix a penny stamp in the corner, and drop the envelope into the red box at the corner. It was thus that I became a journalist; and my effort was rewarded on the first day of the following month—a very glorious day it was for me—by a letter from an editor containing a cheque for one pound ten shillings and sixpence. But to show you how little I deserve to be called a professional woman, how little I know of the struggles and difficulties of such lives, I have to admit that instead of spending that sum upon bread and butter, rent, shoes and stockings, or butcher's bills, I went out and bought a cat—a beautiful cat, a Persian cat, which very soon involved me in bitter disputes with my neighbours.

What could be easier than to write articles and to buy Persian cats with the profits? But wait a moment. Articles have to be about something. Mine, I seem to remember, was about a novel by a famous man. And while I was writing this review I discovered that if I were going to review books I should need to do battle with a certain phantom. And the phantom was a woman, and when I came to know her better I called her after the heroine of a famous poem, The Angel in the House. It was she who used to come between me and my paper when I was writing reviews. It was she who bothered me and wasted my time and so tormented me that at last I killed her. You who come of a younger and happier generation may not have heard of her—you may not know what I mean by the Angel in the House. I will describe her as shortly as I can. She was intensely sympathetic. She was immensely charming. She was utterly unselfish. She excelled in the difficult arts of family life. She sacrificed herself daily. If there was chicken, she took the leg; if there was a draught she sat in it—in short she was so constituted that she never had a mind or a wish of her own, but preferred to sympathize always with the minds and wishes of others. Above all—I need not say it—

she was pure. Her purity was supposed to be her chief beauty—her blushes, her great grace. In those days—the last of Queen Victoria—every house had its Angel. And when I came to write I encountered her with the very first words. The shadow of her wings fell on my page; I heard the rustling of her skirts in the room. Directly, that is to say, I took my pen in hand to review that novel by a famous man, she slipped behind me and whispered: "My dear, you are a young woman. You are writing about a book that has been written by a man. Be sympathetic; be tender; flatter; deceive; use all the arts and wiles of our sex. Never let anybody guess that you have a mind of your own. Above all, be pure." And she made as if to guide my pen. I now record the one act for which I take some credit to myself, though the credit rightly belongs to some excellent ancestors of mine who left me a certain sum of money—shall we say five hundred pounds a year?—so that it was not necessary for me to depend solely on charm for my living. I turned upon her and caught her by the throat. I did my best to kill her. My excuse, if I were to be had up in a court of law, would be that I acted in self-defense. Had I not killed her she would have killed me. She would have plucked the heart out of my writing. For, as I found, directly I put pen to paper, you cannot review even a novel without having a mind of your own, without expressing what you think to be the truth about human relations, morality, sex. And all these questions, according to the Angel in the House, cannot be dealt with freely and openly by women; they must charm, they must conciliate, they must—to put it bluntly—tell lies if they are to succeed. Thus, whenever I felt the shadow of her wing or the radiance of her halo upon my page, I took up the inkpot and flung it at her. She died hard. Her fictitious nature was of great assistance to her. It is far harder to kill a phantom than a reality. She was always creeping back when I thought I had despatched her. Though I flatter myself that I killed her in the end, the struggle was severe; it took much time that had better have been spent upon learning Greek grammar; or in roaming the world in search of adventures. But it was a real experience; it was an experience that was bound to befall all women writers at that time. Killing the Angel in the House was part of the occupation of a woman writer.

But to continue my story. The Angel was dead; what then remained? You may say that what remained was a simple and common object—a young woman in a bedroom with an ink-pot. In other words, now that she had rid herself of falsehood, that young woman had only to be herself. Ah, but what is "herself"? I mean, what is a woman? I assure you, I do not know. I do not believe that you know. I do not believe that anybody can know until she has expressed herself in all the arts and professions open to human skill. That indeed is one of the reasons why I have come here—out of respect for you, who are in process of showing us by your experiments what a woman is, who are in process of providing us, by your failures and successes, with that extremely important piece of information.

But to continue the story of my professional experiences. I made one pound ten and six by my first review; and I bought a Persian cat with the proceeds. Then I grew ambitious. A Persian cat is all very well, I said; but a Persian cat is not enough. I must have a motor car. And it was thus that I became a novelist—for it is a very strange thing that people will give you a motor car if you will tell them a story. It is a still stranger thing that there is nothing so delightful in the world as telling stories. It is far pleasanter than writing reviews of famous novels. And yet, if I am to obey your secretary and tell you my professional experiences as a novelist, I must tell you about a very strange experience that befell me as a novelist. And to understand it you must try first to imagine a novelist's state of mind. I hope I am not giving away professional secrets if I say that a novelist's chief desire is to be as unconscious as possible. He has to induce in himself a state of perpetual lethargy. He wants life to proceed with the utmost quiet and regularity. He wants to see the same faces, to read the same books, to do the same things day after day, month after month, while he is writing, so that nothing may break the illusion in which he is living—so that nothing may disturb or disquiet the mysterious nosings about, feelings round, darts, dashes and sudden discoveries of that very shy and illusive spirit, the imagination. I suspect that this state is the same both for men and women. Be that as it may, I want you to imagine me writing a novel in a state of trance. I want you to figure to yourselves a girl sitting with a pen in her hand, which for minutes, and indeed for hours, she never dips into the inkpot. The image that comes to mind when I think of this girl is the image of a fisherman lying sunk in dreams on the verge of a deep lake with a rod held out over the water. She was letting her imagination sweep unchecked round every rock and cranny of the world that lies submerged in the depths of our unconscious being. Now came the experience, the experience that I believe to be far commoner with women writers than with men. The line raced through the girl's fingers. Her imagination had rushed away. It had sought the pools, the depths, the dark places where the largest fish slumber. And then there was a smash. There was an explosion. There was foam and confusion. The imagination had dashed itself against something hard. The girl was roused from her dream. She was indeed in a state of the most acute and difficult distress. To speak without figure she had thought of something, something about the body, about the passions which it was unfitting for her as a woman to say. Men, her reason told her, would be shocked. The consciousness of what men will say of a woman who speaks the truth about her passions had roused her from her artist's state of unconsciousness. She could write no more. The trance was over. Her imagination could work no longer. This I believe to be a very common experience with women writers—they are impeded by the extreme conventionality of the other sex. For though men sensibly allow themselves great freedom in these respects, I doubt that they realize or can control the extreme severity with which they condemn such freedom in women.

These then were two very genuine experiences of my own. These were two of the adventures of my professional life. The first—killing the Angel in the House—I think I solved. She died. But the second, telling the truth about my own experiences as a body, I do not think I solved. I doubt that any woman has solved it yet. The obstacles against her are still immensely powerful—and yet they are very difficult to define. Outwardly, what is simpler than to write books? Outwardly, what obstacles are there for a woman rather than for a man? Inwardly, I think, the case is very different; she still has many ghosts to fight, many prejudices to overcome. Indeed it will be a long time still, I think, before a woman can sit down to write a book without finding a phantom to be slain, a rock to be dashed against. And if this is so in literature, the freest of all professions for women, how is it in the new professions which you are now for the first time entering?

Those are the questions that I should like, had I time, to ask you. And indeed, if I have laid stress upon these professional experiences of mine, it is because I believe that they are, though in different forms, yours also. Even when the path is nominally open—when there is nothing to prevent a woman from being a doctor, a lawyer, a civil servant—there are many phantoms and obstacles, as I believe, looming in her way. To discuss and define them is I think of great value and importance; for thus only can the labour be shared, the difficulties be solved. But besides this, it is necessary also to discuss the ends and the aims for which we are fighting, for which we are doing battle with these formidable obstacles. Those aims cannot be taken for granted; they must be perpetually questioned and examined. The whole position, as I see it—here in this hall surrounded by women practising for the first time in history I know not how many different professions—is one of extraordinary interest and importance. You have won rooms of your own in the house hitherto exclusively owned by men. You are able, though not without great labor and effort, to pay the rent. You are earning your five hundred pounds a year. But this freedom is only a beginning; the room is your own, but it is still bare. It has to be furnished; it has to be decorated; it has to be shared. How are you going to furnish it, how are you going to decorate it? With whom are you going to share it, and upon what terms? These, I think, are questions of the utmost importance and interest. For the first time in history you are able to ask them; for the first time you are able to decide for yourselves what the answers should be. Willingly would I stay and discuss those questions and answers—but not tonight. My time is up; and I must cease.

A Place to Stand On

Margaret Laurence

> The creative writer perceives his own world once and for all in childhood and adolescence, and his whole career is an effort to illustrate his private world in terms of the great public world we all share. Graham Greene, *Collected Essays*

I BELIEVE that Graham Greene is right in this statement. It does not mean that the individual does not change after adolescence. On the contrary, it underlines the necessity for change. For the writer, one way of discovering oneself, of changing from the patterns of childhood and adolescence to those of adulthood, is through the explorations inherent in the writing itself. In the case of a great many writers, this explanation at some point—and perhaps at all points—involves an attempt to understand one's background and one's past, sometimes even a more distant past which one has not personally experienced.

This sort of exploration can be clearly seen in the works of contemporary African writers, many of whom re-create their people's past in novels and plays in order to recover a sense of themselves, an identity and a feeling of value from which they were separated by two or three generations of colonialism and missionizing. They have found it necessary, in other words, to come to terms with their ancestors and their gods in order to be able to accept the past and be at peace with the dead, without being stifled or threatened by their past.

Oddly enough, it was only several years ago, when I began

doing some research into contemporary Nigerian writing and its background, that I began to see how much my own writing had followed the same pattern—the attempt to assimilate the past, partly in order to be freed from it, partly in order to try to understand myself and perhaps others of my generation, through seeing where we had come from.

I was fortunate in going to Africa when I did—in my early twenties—because for some years I was so fascinated by the African scene that I was prevented from writing an autobiographical first novel. I don't say there is anything wrong in autobiographical novels, but it would not have been the right thing for me—my view of the prairie town from which I had come was still too prejudiced and distorted by closeness. I had to get farther away from it before I could begin to see it. Also, as it turned out ultimately, the kind of novel which I can best handle is one in which the fictional characters are very definitely *themselves*, not me, the kind of novel in which I can feel a deep sense of connection with the main character without a total identification which for me would prevent a necessary distancing.

I always knew that one day I would have to stop writing about Africa and go back to my own people, my own place of belonging, but when I began to do this, I was extremely nervous about the outcome. I did not consciously choose any particular time in history, or any particular characters. The reverse seemed to be true. The character of Hagar in *The Stone Angel* seemed almost to choose me. Later, though, I recognized that in some way not at all consciously understood by me at the time I had had to begin approaching my background and my past through my grandparents' generation, the generation of pioneers of Scots-Presbyterian origin, who had been among the first to people the town I called Manawaka. This was where my own roots began. Other past generations of my father's family had lived in Scotland, but for me, my people's real past—my own real past—was not connected except distantly with Scotland; indeed, this was true for Hagar as well, for she was born in Manawaka.

The name Manawaka is an invented one, but it had been in my mind since I was about seventeen or eighteen, when I first began to think about writing something set in a prairie town. Manawaka is not my hometown of Neepawa—it has elements of Neepawa, especially in some of the descriptions of places, such as the cemetery on the hill or the Wachakwa valley through which ran the small brown river which was the river of my childhood. In almost every way, however, Manawaka is not so much any one prairie town as an amalgam of many prairie towns. Most of all, I like to think, it is simply itself, a town of the mind, my own private world, as Graham Greene says, which one hopes will ultimately relate to the outer world which we all share.

When one thinks of the influence of a place on one's writing, two aspects come to mind. First, the physical presence of the place itself—its geography, its appearance. Second, the people. For me, the second aspect of environment is the most important, although in everything I have written which is set in Canada, whether or not actually set in Manitoba, somewhere some of my memories of the physical appearance of the prairies come in. I had, as a child and as an adolescent, ambiguous feelings about the prairies. I still have them, although they no longer bother me. I wanted then to get out of the small town and go far away, and yet I felt the protectiveness of that atmosphere, too. I felt the loneliness and the isolation of the land itself, and yet I always considered southern Manitoba to be very beautiful, and I still do. I doubt if I will ever live there again, but those poplar bluffs and the blackness of that soil and the way in which the sky is open from one side of the horizon to the other—these are things I will carry inside my skull for as long as I live, with the vividness of recall that only our first home can have for us.

Nevertheless, the people were more important than the place. Hagar in *The Stone Angel* was not drawn from life, but she incorporates many of the qualities of my grandparents' generation. Her speech is their speech, and her gods their gods. I think I never recognized until I wrote that novel just how mixed my own feelings were towards that whole generation of pioneers—how difficult they were to live with, how authoritarian, how unbending, how afraid to show love, many of them, and how willing to show anger. And yet, they had inhabited a wilderness and made it fruitful. They were, in the end, great survivors, and for that I love and value them.

The final exploration of this aspect of my background came when I wrote—over the past six or seven years—*A Bird in the House*, a number of short stories set in Manawaka and based upon my childhood and my childhood family, the only semi-autobiographical fiction I have ever written. I did not realize until I had finished the final story in the series how much all these stories are dominated by the figure of my maternal grandfather, who came of Irish Protestant stock. Perhaps it was through writing these stories that I finally came to see my grandfather not only as the repressive authoritarian figure from my childhood, but also as a boy who had to leave school in Ontario when he was about twelve, after his father's death, and who as a young man went to Manitoba by sternwheeler and walked the fifty miles from Winnipeg to Portage la Prairie, where he settled for some years before moving to Neepawa. He was a very hard man in many ways, but he had had a very hard life. I don't think I knew any of this, really knew it, until I had finished those stories. I don't think I ever knew, either, until that moment how much I owed to him. One sentence, near the end of the final story, may show what I mean. "I had feared and fought the old man, yet he proclaimed himself in my veins."

My writing, then, has been my own attempt to come to terms with the past. I see this process as the gradual one of freeing oneself from the stultifying aspect of the past, while at the same time beginning to see its true value—which, in the case of my own people (by which I mean the total community, not just my particular family), was a determination to survive against whatever odds.

The theme of survival—not just physical survival, but the preservation of some human dignity and in the end some human warmth and ability to reach out and touch others—this is, I have come to think, an almost inevitable theme for a writer such as I, who came from a Scots-Irish background of stern values and hard work and puritanism, and who grew up during the drought and depression of the thirties and then the war.

This theme runs through two of my novels other than *The Stone Angel* (in which it is, of course, the dominant theme). In *A Jest of God* and *The Fire-Dwellers*, both Rachel and Stacey are in their very different ways threatened by the past and by the various inadequacies each feels in herself. In the end, and again in their very different ways and out of their very different dilemmas, each finds within herself an ability to survive— not just to go on living, but to change and to move into new areas of life. Neither book is optimistic. Optimism in this world seems impossible to me. But in each novel there is some hope, and that is a different thing entirely.

If Graham Greene is right—as I think he is—in his belief that a writer's career is "an effort to illustrate his private world in terms of the great public world we all share," then I think it is understandable that so much of my writing relates to the kind of prairie town in which I was born and in which I first began to be aware of myself. Writing, for me, has to be set firmly in some soil, some place, some outer and inner territory which might be described in anthropological terms as "cultural background." But I do not believe that this kind of writing needs therefore to be parochial. If Hagar in *The Stone Angel* has any meaning, it is the same as that of an old woman anywhere, having to deal with the reality of dying. On the other hand, she is not an old woman anywhere. She is very much a person who belongs in the same kind of prairie Scots-Presbyterian background as I do, and it was, of course, people like Hagar who created that background, with all its flaws and its strengths. In a poem entitled *Roblin Mills, Circa 1842*, Al Purdy said:

> They had their being once
> and left a place to stand on

They did indeed, and this is the place we are standing on, for better and for worse.

I remember saying once, three or four years ago, that I felt I had written myself out of that prairie town. I know better now. My future writing may not be set in that town—and indeed, my novel, *The Fire-Dwellers*, was set in Vancouver. I may not always write fiction set in Canada. But somewhere, perhaps in the memories of some characters, Manawaka will probably always be there, simply because whatever I am was shaped and formed in that sort of place, and my way of seeing, however much it may have changed over the years, remains in some enduring way that of a small-town prairie person.

Mind Must Be the Firmer

Timothy Findley

> Mind must be the firmer,
> Heart the more fierce,
> Courage the greater
> As our strength diminishes.

THESE are lines from an old English poem that was cherished by Margaret Laurence—cherished, rehearsed over time, and implemented. Wherever she found these words—whenever it was they first refused to go away and leave her alone—that moment must be counted as one of the most important in all the sixty years of her life. As words, as articulation, they became a corner-stone of her resources. They inform not only her writing: they also inform whatever we know of how she lived and how she died.

Margaret Laurence was a great believer in simplicity. She was also one of its greatest practitioners. This is where the *firmness* came in. Firmness, for Margaret Laurence, was one of simplicity's most important synonyms. "I will" and "I won't" were two of her absolutes. She would not and could not tolerate anything less than her full capacity to make words work on paper. Nor would she tolerate anything less than her full capacity to stand for what she believed in.

As time progressed and her capacities expanded, she also progressed from *firm* to *firmer*. If you knew Margaret Laurence, you had to contend with this sometimes difficult part of her will. And if you knew her well, you wished, in a way, you could protect her from it. Part of her firmness and, of course, an extremely potent part of her will was her rejection—which was total—of any kind of safety: personal, intellectual, or physical. She struggled thirty years and more at her table to produce on the page an account of what was in her mind—and that, as any serious writer knows, is a struggle utterly without the benefit of self-preservation. The onslaught of fictional men and women, ideas, and events—all of whom and all of which can achieve their existence only if the writer succeeds at giving them articulation—has a strange, seductive power to suggest that articulation "cannot be achieved." Unless you are firm.

So Margaret Laurence stayed there at her table, no matter how long it took to get things right. And when she rose and when she handed over what she had written, she said: "This is it, the way it should be, the way it must be, the way it is and the way it will stay."

This is it: the way it will stay: *The Stone Angel, A Jest of God, The Fire-Dwellers, A Bird in the House, The Diviners*: firm, firmer, firmest.

The fierceness in her was mighty.

Margaret Laurence had to contend with a body whose nervous system tended to betray her just when she needed it most to be strong. She shook. Her knees gave way. Her hands could be seen from almost any distance, reaching for the backs of chairs and the tops of tables—anything to hold her up and stop her from shaking. Rising to speak—choosing, against all odds, to rise at all—in order to tell what she believed—these were the harshest enemies she had whenever it came to speaking her mind. But speak her mind she must—and fiercely. She said something once that gave the essence of all her beliefs: her certainty that we, her beloved humankind, were capable of wilful, self-determined sanity if only we would *try.* . . . Margaret Laurence believed, with a passion so profound it almost puts me to shame to think of it, that war and hatred must *and can* be put aside. And she devoted, even to the point of exhaustion, all the latter years of her life to activities supporting this belief. But her open espousal of peace through nuclear disarmament brought her, as it must, a host of enemies, name-callers, finger-pointers: people who called her a "fool," a "red," and the word that disturbed her most, "subversive." What Margaret Laurence said to these accusers was said with the kind of ferocity that only absolute certainty can justify. "If the quest for peace," she said, "is subversive, then what, in the name of God, is war?"

Fierce, fiercer, fiercest.

One day the word came that Margaret Laurence was going to die. No backing off, no second chance at survival, nothing to mitigate the certainty. Up to about a year before this day arrived, those of us who knew and loved her had been aware of her struggles to take up the pen again and write. Her last major piece of work had been published in 1974. This was her masterpiece, *The Diviners*. But since that year, her writer's output had been meagre: three books for children and one of essays written in the past. Her time was given over to anti-nuclear and peace activities. She was also—with great success and personal popularity—the chancellor of Trent University. But what she wanted—besides these things—was one more book. And it wouldn't come.

What very few people knew was that, during this time, Margaret Laurence was slowly going blind with cataracts. She couldn't properly wield the pen. She couldn't properly type, though both activities were still producing a vast outpouring of letters to students and fans and friends. And then there was a "miracle." A plastic lens was implanted in one of her eyes—and she began to write again. She could barely believe her good fortune. What she wrote, and what she completed, and what, in a not-too-distant future, will be published was a book devoted to the theme of motherhood: a memoir. She worked on this until the week before she died.

Brave, braver, bravest.

Euripides told us: "Never that which is shall die."

He didn't mean people, I guess. I guess what he meant was ideas and truths and things like that. I think he meant, too, that whatever goes into life—the whole of what is alive— is alive forever. Margaret Laurence is dead. But so—we are told—is Euripides. I'm sure you know exactly what I mean. Goodbye, Margaret Laurence. And thank you.

Sonnet 16

John Milton

When I consider how my light is spent
Ere half my days, in this dark world and wide,
And that one talent which is death to hide
Lodged with me useless, though my soul more bent
To serve therewith my Maker, and present
My true account, lest He returning chide;
"Doth God exact day-labour, light denied?"
I fondly ask. But Patience, to prevent
That murmur, soon replies, "God doth not need
Either man's work or his own gifts. Who best
Bear his mild yoke, they serve him best. His state
Is kingly: thousands at his bidding speed,
And post o'er land and ocean without rest;
They also serve who only stand and wait."

Ode on a Grecian Urn

John Keats

Thou still unravished bride of quietness,
   Thou foster-child of silence and slow time,
Sylvan historian, who canst thus express
   A flowery tale more sweetly than our rhyme:
What leaf-fringed legend haunts about thy shape
   Of deities or mortals, or of both,
      In Tempe or the dales of Arcady?
   What men or gods are these? What maidens loath?
What mad pursuit? What struggle to escape?
     What pipes and timbrels? What wild ecstasy?

Heard melodies are sweet, but those unheard
   Are sweeter; therefore, ye soft pipes, play on;
Not to the sensual ear, but, more endeared,
   Pipe to the spirit ditties of no tone:
Fair youth, beneath the trees, thou canst not leave
   Thy song, nor ever can those trees be bare;
     Bold Lover, never, never canst thou kiss,
Though winning near the goal—yet, do not grieve;
    She cannot fade, though thou hast not thy bliss,
   For ever wilt thou love, and she be fair!

Ah, happy, happy boughs! that cannot shed
   Your leaves, nor ever bid the Spring adieu;
And, happy melodist, unwearied,
   For ever piping songs for ever new;
More happy love! more happy, happy love!

For ever warm and still to be enjoy'd,
   For ever panting and for ever young;
All breathing human passion far above,
  That leaves a heart high-sorrowful and cloy'd,
    A burning forehead, and a parching tongue.

Who are these coming to the sacrifice?
  To what green altar, O mysterious priest,
Lead'st thou that heifer lowing at the skies,
  And all her silken flanks with garlands drest?
What little town by river or sea-shore,
  Or mountain-built with peaceful citadel,
    Is emptied of this folk, this pious morn?
And, little town, thy streets for evermore
  Will silent be; and not a soul to tell
    Why thou art desolate, can e'er return.

O Attic shape! Fair attitude! with brede
  Of marble men and maidens overwrought,
With forest branches and the trodden weed;
  Thou, silent form, dost tease us out of thought
As doth eternity: Cold Pastoral!
  When old age shall this generation waste,
    Thou shalt remain, in midst of other woe
  Than ours, a friend to man, to whom thou say'st,
"Beauty is truth, truth beauty,"—that is all
    Ye know on earth, and all ye need to know.

Anecdote of the Jar

Wallace Stevens

I placed a jar in Tennessee,
And round it was, upon a hill.
It made the slovenly wilderness
Surround that hill.

The wilderness rose up to it,
And sprawled around, no longer wild.
The jar was round upon the ground
And tall and of a port in air.

It took dominion everywhere.
The jar was gray and bare.
It did not give of bird or bush,
Like nothing else in Tennessee.

Works of the Imagination

Gina Berriault

T HE silent train ascended through forest and alongside a torrent so cold and so swift the water was white, and small white birds flew up like spray. On a bridge undergoing repairs the train came to a halt. Just outside Thomas Lang's window, a workman in a black knit cap was hammering at a railing, and the silence all around isolated each ring of the hammer.

Lang arrived in Grindelwald in the evening, coming from Bern where, contrary to his intention to call on a friend from the States and tell him about the insoluble task his memoirs had become, he had stayed only half-a-day and called on no one. In the early night he wandered along a path on the outskirts of the town. The day was a national holiday, and fireworks opened in languid sprays all around in the dusk, and the boom of fireworks echoed against the mountains. Someone approached him on the path, a figure twice as tall as himself. Closer, he saw it was a little girl, half as tall as himself, carrying a long stick covered with tallow, the torch at its tip casting around her a high, black figure of shadows. Up on the dark mountains small lights burned here and there, far, far apart—fires perched on the night itself. In the morning a snowy mountain stood just outside his hotel window, brought closer by the sun almost to within reach of his hand.

On a small, quiet train he went higher, up to Kleine Scheidegg, up to an old hotel where twelve years ago he had stayed a few days in winter, and not alone. The mountains had impressed him then as a phenomenon on display, but now he was shocked by their immensity, hypnotized by their beauty and crystal silence. Cowbells and voices rang in the silence with an entrancingly pure pitch, and the density of the stone was silence in another guise.

The elderly, elegant manager registered him at the desk in the small lobby. A very tall, strong man, also elderly, in a dark green apron, whom Lang had observed carrying up four suitcases at a time, carried up his two, while another assistant, also in a green apron, a slight, dark man, surely Spanish, graciously shy, stepped in a lively way to the foot of the wide, curving staircase and gestured for him to go up. Lang climbed the stairs with his hand on the rail. He had not often assisted himself that way and had no need to now. He was an erect, lean and healthy sixty, and why, then, was his hand on the banister?

The silence in the room was like an invasion, a possession by the great silent mountains. The cloth on the walls, a print of pastoral scenes with amorous couples, flute players, and lambs, roused a memory of another room, somewhere else in this hotel, where he had lain in an embrace with a woman who, at the time, was very dear. All that he remembered of the previous visit were the three persons he had been traveling with—the woman, a close friend, and the friend's wife—all now no longer in touch with him and perhaps not with one another. They had come to watch a movie being made of a novel of his. In the novel there had been only a brief mention of the Alps, but the movie director and the script writer had worked out a counterfeit scene from that remark, and he had watched, amused and apart.

Once in the night he was wakened by his heart's terror. His heart always wakened him in time for him to witness his own dying, and he waited now with his hand over his heart. When the terror subsided he took his notebook from the bedside table and fumbled to uncap his pen. Through the translucent curtains the sky and the white mountains gave him enough light to write by, but his hand was given no reason to write. Was this another place he would leave, his notebook empty? Traveling all spring and into the summer, he had found no place where he could begin his memoirs. If one place had been so full of the sound of the ocean—not just the waves, whose monotonous beat often went unheard, but the threat in the depths—another place was too full of the sounds of the city— insane noises. And in quiet places he heard, in memory, the voices of his healers back in the States, men who had never truly known just what it was he had lost, and gave the loss such facile names—confidence, faith, whatever—and the names of several persons who had been dear to him and were lost to him. These healers had promised him his completed memoirs, and other novels in the future, if only he would begin, because, they said, work itself wrought miracles and brought the spirit back from the grave. But there was a loss beyond their probing, a loss they were unwilling to accept as the finality he knew it was, a loss, a failing, that might even be commonplace and yet was a terrible sacrilege. It was indifference, like a deep, drugged sleep, to everyone else on earth. Ah, how could that change have come about in himself when his very reason for being had been the belief that each human life was sacred?

He got up and drew aside the mist-like curtains. The train station was dimly lit, the awning rippling a little in the night wind. Out on the dark hills a few hazy lights burned through the night, miles apart. And beyond and all around, the luminous mountains. When he was inside the hotel their unseen presence warned him of his breath's impending abeyance, but now, gazing out at them, he felt his chest deepen to take in their cold breath across the distance, a vast breath as necessary to him as his own.

The day brought hikers up from the cities, way below. They came up in the small, silent trains, and wore big boots, thick socks, and knapsacks, as if bound for a climb of several days. But they roamed over the grassy hills for an hour or so and converged at the tables below the hotel's lower windows. They sat under colored umbrellas and under the windows' reflections of the mountains, and ate what appeared to be savory food. He kept a distance from them. There was room enough.

The only guests in the spacious parlor were far off, a family group playing cards at a table covered with green felt. On the parquetry floors lay rich, red Persian rugs, and the many couches and chairs of antique beauty took up only small space in the large room. A long and narrow glassed-in sunporch with an abundance of wicker chairs adjoined the parlor, and he paced along its length, remembering the hotel in winter, the parlor's black-and-white marble fireplace ablaze, the pleasurable jostling and agitation of the many guests, and the hieroglyphs of distant, dark figures against the snow. He settled himself at a large table in a corner of the parlor, but all he could do was trace the glow and grain of the wood around his empty notebook.

On his way down the hall, restless, wondering if he would move on the next day, he paused before the first of several framed photographs along the wall, an early one of four climbers assembled in the photographer's studio against a backdrop of a painted mountain, all in hats and ties and heavy boots, with pots, picks, a goat. Few attempted the scaling of mountains in these years; now climbers were swarming up every mountain on earth. Farther along, he stopped before a photograph of *Der Eiger*, the mountain looming up over this hotel and over the town, miles below, a sheer, vertical face of stone. White lines were painted on the photograph, marking the ascents to the top, and at the base were the names of the fallen, preceded by white crosses. He passed along before the faces of the triumphant ones, a row of them, all young, and spent a longer time before a couple from Germany, a man and a woman, she a strongly smiling blond and he a curly-haired handsome fellow, the kind who would take a woman along.

Then he went out, keeping apart from the many hikers who walked in a line toward Eiger as if on a pilgrimage. He strode over the lush grass, over the rise and fall of the hills, and on the crest of a hill he halted to take a look at the great stone's face. Two figures were slowly, slowly climbing. His vision lost them in an instant and it took him some time to locate them again, so small were they and at the mercy of the atmosphere, appearing and disappearing. He sat down on the grass to watch them, his hand above his eyes to prevent the sun from playing tricks on him. The roar of an avalanche shocked him, convincing him that a mountain was collapsing, and then he saw the source of the thunder—a small fall of snow, far, far away. Somewhere he had read that the Alps had moved one hundred miles from their original location in Italy, and he wondered if the move had been centuries long, or cataclysmic, in a time when there were no human beings around to be terrified and obliterated. When his eyes began to ache from the searching, from the finding and losing of the specks that were his climbers, he returned to his room and lay down, his hand over his stone-struck eyes.

Toward twilight, when no one sat under the mountains' reflections, when they had all gone down on the trains, he went out again, strolling to higher ground over patches of tiny wildflowers that were like luminous rugs on the grass. Up near the entrance to the train tunnel that cut through stone to the top of the Jungfrau, he came to a large, heavy-wire pen where several restless dogs roved. The dogs resembled wolves, tawny with black markings, and their wild intelligent Mongol faces reminded him of the faces of nineteenth century Russian writers. It was a comparison against his will, yet he was amused by it and felt lightheaded over it. They paused to look into his face and into his eyes, slipped by along the fence, then returned, curious about him as he was about them. Soon in the darkening air he felt he was gazing at Gogol, at Tolstoy, at Chekhov, their faces intent on each human soul.

Stumbling a time or two, he made his way back down to the hotel that stood in a nimbus of its own lights. Before he went in he took a last look at the great stone. No fire burned anywhere on its enormous expanse. The climbers had made a bivouac for the night on a ledge and were already asleep.

Once in the night he was wakened by a deep wondering about the couple on the ledge. The fact of their lying on a ledge somewhere on that great stone stirred in him a concern for all persons he had ever loved. Then he slept again, and the couple was lying somewhere on the cold vastness of the night, on no ledge.

In the morning he went out under an overcast sky, before any hikers appeared. The stone was monstrous. Each sight of it failed to diminish, by repetition, the shock of it. So steep was the north side, the mountain must have been split down the very center, and the other half was a hundred miles away. The climbers were not yet halfway up the wall. Often, as before, he lost sight of them, found one again and not the other, and then found the other after losing the first. After a time he covered his eyes to rest them. If they fell, would the silence and the distance deny to him their terror? He lowered his hand, searched again, and found one dark figure on a snowy ledge. The figure fell the instant he found it. It fell so fast he was unable to trace its fall and unable to find it on a lower ledge or at the base. Nowhere, now, was the other climber. Then both had fallen, and their terror entered into his heart without his expecting it. It was the same terror that wakened him in the night at the last moment so that he might witness his own dying. It was the same kind of moment now, under the sun. With his hand over his heart he went back over the hills to the hotel.

No one was at the desk in the lobby, neither the manager nor one or the other of his assistants in their green aprons. One of them would confirm the tragedy. Somewhere, back in an office, there must be a radio voice informing everyone of the climbers' fate. Outside, the murmur of the crowd under the umbrellas and the fitful, labored music of an accordion were like the sounds the deaf make, that are unheard by them. In the parlor he found the shy assistant passing through, the one he was convinced had been a child refugee from the Spanish Civil War.

"El hombre y la mujer en la montana, ellos se cayeron?"

The man smiled sadly, graciously, implying with his smile that if he did not understand Spanish at least he understood the importance of the question for the one who asked it.

With faltering German he tried to repeat the question, but a strong resistance, following disappointment, whisked away his small vocabulary. He went back to the lobby.

The manager, wearing a fine suit the same gray as his hair, was now standing at the desk, glancing through some papers. A fire wavered in the small fireplace.

"The couple on Eiger, they fell?"

The manager's brow, high, smooth for a man his age, underwent a brief overcast. "May I ask who?"

"The couple on Eiger."

"Ah yes, the photographs in the corridor? Only those who succeeded. Only those."

"The couple up there now," he said.

"There is no one climbing now."

"Then they fell?"

"No one is climbing and no one is falling."

Lang went up the stairs, hand on the rail, a weakness in his legs from the terror of the lives lost, no matter if they were specks, motes, undulations of the atmosphere. Up in his room he sat down at the desk, opened his notebook, and wrote the first word on the first of the faint lines that he likened now to infinitely fine, blue veins.

The Camel Dances

Arnold Lobel

T HE Camel had her heart set on becoming a ballet dancer.

"To make every movement a thing of grace and beauty," said the Camel. "That is my one and only desire."

Again and again she practiced her pirouettes, her relevés and her arabesques. She repeated the five basic positions a hundred times each day. She worked for long months under the hot desert sun. Her feet were blistered, and her body ached with fatigue, but not once did she think of stopping.

At last the Camel said, "Now I am a dancer." She announced a recital and danced before an invited group of camel friends and critics. When her dance was over, she made a deep bow.

There was no applause.

"I must tell you frankly," said a member of the audience, "as a critic and spokesman for this group, that you are lumpy and humpy. You are baggy and bumpy. You are, like the rest of us, simply a camel. You are not and never will be a ballet dancer!"

Chuckling and laughing, the audience moved away across the sand.

"How very wrong they are!" said the Camel. "I have worked hard. There can be no doubt that I am a splendid dancer. I will dance and dance just for myself."

That is what she did. It gave her many years of pleasure.

MORAL: Satisfaction will come to those who please themselves.

The Thought-Fox

Ted Hughes

I imagine this midnight moment's forest:
Something else is alive
Beside the clock's loneliness
And this blank page where my fingers move.

Through the window I see no star:
Something more near
Though deeper within darkness
Is entering the loneliness:

Cold, delicately as the dark snow,
A fox's nose touches twig, leaf;
Two eyes serve a movement, that now
And again now, and now, and now

Sets neat prints into the snow,
Between trees, and warily a lame
Shadow lags by stump and in hollow
Of a body that is bold to come

Across clearings, an eye,
A widening deepening greenness,
Brilliantly, concentratedly,
Coming about its own business

Till, with a sudden sharp hot stink of fox
It enters the dark hole of the head.
The window is starless still; the clock ticks,
The page is printed.

Les petites villes

Anne Hébert

Je te donnerai de petites villes
De toutes petites villes tristes.

Les petites villes dans nos mains
Sont plus austères que des jouets
Mais aussi faciles à manier.

Je joue avec les petites villes,
Je les renverse
Pas un homme ne s'en échappe
Ni une fleur ni un enfant.

Les petites villes sont désertes
Et livrées dans nos mains.

J'écoute, l'oreille contre les portes
J'approche une à une toutes les portes,
De mon oreille.

Les maisons ressemblent à des coquillages muets
Qui ne gardent dans leurs spirales glacées
Aucune rumeur de vent
Aucune rumeur d'eau.

Les parcs et les jardins sont morts
Les jeux alignés
Ainsi que dans un musée.

Je ne sais pas où l'on a mis
Les corps figés des oiseaux.

Les rues sont sonores de silence.
L'écho du silence est lourd
Plus lourd
Qu'aucune parole de menace ou d'amour.

Mais voici qu'à mon tour
J'abandonne les petites villes de mon enfance.
Je te les offre
Dans la plénitude
De leur solitude.

Comprends-tu bien le présent redoutable?
Je te donne d'étranges petites villes tristes,
Pour le songe.

The Little Towns

Anne Hébert
translated by Peter Miller

I shall give you some little towns
Some quite little sad towns.

The little towns in our hands
Are more austere than toys
But just as easy to handle.

I play with the little towns.
I overturn them
Not a man escapes from them
Nor a flower nor a child.

The little towns are deserted
And delivered into our hands.

I listen, my ear against the doors
One by one to all the doors
I bend my ear.

The houses are like mute shells
That keep in their icy spirals
No whisper of wind
No whisper of water.

The parks and the gardens are dead
The playgrounds lined up
As in a museum.

I do not know where have been placed
The congealed bodies of the birds.

The streets are sonorous with silence.
The echo of the silence is heavy
More heavy
Than any word of menace or of love

But see, here in my turn
I abandon the little towns of my childhood.
I offer them to you
In the fullness
Of their solitude.

Do you understand well the redoubtable present?
I give you some strange little sad towns,
For a dream.

The Little Towns

Anne Hébert
translated by John Glassco

I shall give you the little towns
The poor sad little towns,

The little towns cupped in our palms
More exigent than toys
As easy to the hand.

I play with the little towns
I turn them over
Never a man escapes them
No flower, no child.

The little towns are empty—
Given into our hands.

I listen, my ear to the doors
I lean to the doors, one by one,
With my ear . . .

O the houses are dumb sea-shells—
No longer in the frozen spiral
Any sound of the wind
Any sound of water.

Dead, the parks and the gardens
The games are all put to sleep
In a dead museum.

I cannot tell where they have put
The deathstill bodies of the birds.

The streets resound with silence
The echo of their silence is a weight of lead
More leaden
Than any words of menace or of love.

And here am I too, in my turn
Forsaking the little towns of my childhood . . .
I offer them to you
In all the infinite depth
Of their loneliness.

Now do you grasp the dangerous gift?
I have given you the strange sad little towns
For your own imagining.

The House was Quiet and the World was Calm

Wallace Stevens

The house was quiet and the world was calm.
The reader became the book; and summer night

Was like the conscious being of the book.
The house was quiet and the world was calm.

The words were spoken as if there was no book,
Except that the reader leaned above the page,

Wanted to lean, wanted much most to be
The scholar to whom his book is true, to whom

The summer night is like a perfection of thought.
The house was quiet because it had to be.

The quiet was part of the meaning, part of the mind:
The access of perfection to the page.

And the world was calm. The truth in a calm world,
In which there is no other meaning, itself

Is calm, itself is summer and night, itself
Is the reader leaning late and reading there.

UNIT 2

INNOCENCE AND EXPERIENCE

Our experience, or lack of experience, shapes our actions, knowledge, and beliefs—in other words, the way we conduct our lives. Acquiring experience is an inevitable result of living, but whether it leads to wisdom or cynicism, to open-mindedness or bigotry, to callousness or compassion is dependent on many factors. Some individuals may emerge from personal tragedy or the horror of warfare strengthened as human beings; others may suffer extreme psychological damage. Not all experience, of course, is unpleasant or traumatic. Falling in love, becoming a parent, learning about different cultures are just a few examples of experiences that may be very positive.

In some ways each of us is naive; in other ways, each is experienced. Literature, however, offers all of us a chance to acquire vicariously a wide range of experience. Many writers have examined how loss of innocence and acquisition of experience shape and change the lives of individuals. This unit presents an opportunity for the reader to explore this theme from a wide variety of perspectives.

Lies

Yevgeny Yevtushenko
translated by Robin Milner-Gulland and Peter Levi, S.J.

Telling lies to the young is wrong.
Proving to them that lies are true is wrong.
Telling them that God's in his heaven
and all's well with the world is wrong.
The young know what you mean. The young are people.
Tell them the difficulties can't be counted,
and let them see not only what will be
but see with clarity these present times.
Say obstacles exist they must encounter
sorrow happens, hardship happens.
The hell with it. Who never knew
the price of happiness will not be happy.
Forgive no error you recognize,
it will repeat itself, increase,
and afterwards our pupils
will not forgive in us what we forgave.

Boys and Girls

Alice Munro

M Y father was a fox farmer. That is, he raised silver foxes, in pens; and in the fall and early winter, when their fur was prime, he killed them and skinned them and sold their pelts to the Hudson's Bay Company or the Montreal Fur Traders. These companies supplied us with heroic calendars to hang, one on each side of the kitchen door. Against a background of cold blue sky and black pine forests and treacherous northern rivers, plumed adventurers planted the flags of England or of France; magnificent savages bent their backs to the portage.

For several weeks before Christmas, my father worked after supper in the cellar of our house. The cellar was whitewashed, and lit by a hundred-watt bulb over the worktable. My brother Laird and I sat on the top step and watched. My father removed the pelt inside-out from the body of the fox, which looked surprisingly small, mean and rat-like, deprived of its arrogant weight of fur. The naked, slippery bodies were collected in a sack and buried at the dump. One time the hired man, Henry Bailey, had taken a swipe at me with this sack, saying, "Christmas present!" My mother thought that was not funny. In fact she disliked the whole pelting operation—that was what the killing, skinning, and preparation of the furs was called—and wished it did not have to take place in the house. There was the smell. After the pelt had been stretched inside-out on a long board my father scraped away delicately, removing the little clotted webs of blood vessels, the bubbles of fat; the smell of blood and animal fat, with the strong primitive odour of the fox itself, penetrated all parts of the house. I found it reassuringly seasonal, like the smell of oranges and pine needles.

Henry Bailey suffered from bronchial troubles. He would cough and cough until his narrow face turned scarlet, and his light blue, derisive eyes filled up with tears; then he took the lid off the stove, and, standing well back, shot out a great clot of phlegm—hsss—straight into the heart of the flames. We admired him for this performance and for his ability to make his stomach growl at will, and for his laughter, which was full of high whistlings and gurglings and involved the whole faulty machinery of his chest. It was sometimes hard to tell what he was laughing at, and always possible that it might be us.

After we had been sent to bed we could still smell fox and still hear Henry's laugh, but these things, reminders of the warm, safe, brightly lit downstairs world, seemed lost and diminished, floating on the stale cold air upstairs. We were afraid at night in the winter. We were not afraid of *outside* though this was the time of year when snowdrifts curled around our house like sleeping whales and the wind harassed us all night, coming up from the buried fields, the frozen swamp, with its old bugbear chorus of threats and misery. We were afraid of *inside*, the room where we slept. At this time the upstairs of our house was not finished. A brick chimney went up one wall. In the middle of the floor was a square hole, with a wooden railing around it; that was where the stairs came up. On the other side of the stairwell were the things that nobody had any use for any more—a soldiery roll of linoleum, standing on end, a wicker baby carriage, a fern basket, china jugs and basins with cracks in them, a picture of the Battle of Balaclava, very sad to look at. I had told Laird, as soon as he was old enough to understand such things, that bats and skeletons lived over there; whenever a man escaped from the county jail, twenty miles away, I imagined that he had somehow let himself in the window and was hiding behind the linoleum. But we had rules to keep us safe. When the light was on, we were safe as long as we did not step off the square of worn carpet which defined our bedroom-space; when the light was off no place was safe but the beds themselves. I had to turn out the light kneeling on the end of my bed, and stretching as far as I could to reach the cord.

In the dark we lay on our beds, our narrow life rafts, and fixed our eyes on the faint light coming up the stairwell, and sang songs. Laird sang "Jingle Bells," which he would sing any time, whether it was Christmas or not, and I sang "Danny Boy." I loved the sound of my own voice, frail and supplicating, rising in the dark. We could make out the tall frosted shapes of the windows now, gloomy and white. When I came to the part, *When I am dead, as dead I well may be*—a fit of shivering caused not by the cold sheets but by pleasurable emotion almost silenced me. *You'll kneel and say, an Ave there above me*—What was an Ave? Every day I forgot to find out.

Laird went straight from singing to sleep. I could hear his long, satisfied, bubbly breaths. Now for the time that remained to me, the most perfectly private and perhaps the best time of the whole day, I arranged myself tightly under the covers and went on with one of the stories I was telling myself from night to night. These stories were about myself, when I had grown a little older; they took place in a world that was recognizably mine, yet one that presented opportunities for courage, boldness and self-sacrifice, as mine never did. I rescued people from a bombed building (it discouraged me that the real war had gone on so far away from Jubilee). I shot two rabid wolves who were menacing the schoolyard (the teachers cowered terrified at my back). I rode a fine horse spiritedly down the main street of Jubilee, acknowledging the townspeople's gratitude for some yet-to-be-worked-out piece of heroism (nobody ever rode a horse there, except King Billy in the Orangemen's Day parade). There was always riding and shooting in these stories, though I had only been on a horse twice—bareback because we did not own a saddle—and the second time I had slid right around and dropped under the horse's feet; it had stepped placidly over me. I really was learning to shoot, but I could not hit anything yet, not even tin cans on fence posts.

Alive, the foxes inhabited a world my father made for them. It was surrounded by a high guard fence, like a medieval town,

with a gate that was padlocked at night. Along the streets of
this town were ranged large, sturdy pens. Each of them had a
real door that a man could go through, a wooden ramp along
the wire, for the foxes to run up and down on, and a kennel—
something like a clothes chest with airholes—where they slept
and stayed in winter and had their young. There were feeding
and watering dishes attached to the wire in such a way that
they could be emptied and cleaned from the outside. The dishes
were made of old tin cans, and the ramps and kennels of odds
and ends of old lumber. Everything was tidy and ingenious;
my father was tirelessly inventive and his favourite book in the
world was Robinson Crusoe. He had fitted a tin drum on a
wheelbarrow, for bringing water down to the pens. This was
my job in summer, when the foxes had to have water twice
a day. Between nine and ten o'clock in the morning, and again
after supper, I filled the drum at the pump and trundled it
down through the barnyard to the pens, where I parked it, and
filled my watering can and went along the streets. Laird came
too, with his little cream and green gardening can, filled too
full and knocking against his legs and slopping water on his
canvas shoes. I had the real watering can, my father's, though
I could only carry it three-quarters full.

The foxes all had names, which were printed on a tin plate
and hung beside their doors. They were not named when they
were born, but when they survived the first year's pelting and
were added to the breeding stock. Those my father had named
were called names like Prince, Bob, Wally and Betty. Those
I had named were called Star or Turk, or Maureen or Diana.
Laird named one Maud after a hired girl we had when he was
little, one Harold after a boy at school, and one Mexico, he
did not say why.

Naming them did not make pets out of them, or anything
like it. Nobody but my father ever went into the pens, and he
had twice had blood-poisoning from bites. When I was bringing them their water they prowled up and down on the paths
they had made inside their pens, barking seldom—they saved
that for nighttime, when they might get up a chorus of community frenzy—but always watching me, their eyes burning,
clear gold, in their pointed, malevolent faces. They were beautiful for their delicate legs and heavy, aristocratic tails and

the bright fur sprinkled on dark down their backs—which gave them their name—but especially for their faces, drawn exquisitely sharp in pure hostility, and their golden eyes.

Besides carrying water I helped my father when he cut the long grass, and the lamb's quarter and flowering money-musk, that grew between the pens. He cut with the scythe and I raked into piles. Then he took a pitch-fork and threw fresh-cut grass all over the top of the pens, to keep the foxes cooler and shade their coats, which were browned by too much sun. My father did not talk to me unless it was about the job we were doing. In this he was quite different from my mother, who, if she was feeling cheerful, would tell me all sorts of things—the name of a dog she had had when she was a little girl, the names of boys she had gone out with later on when she was grown up, and what certain dresses of hers had looked like—she could not imagine now what had become of them. Whatever thoughts and stories my father had were private, and I was shy of him and would never ask him questions. Nevertheless I worked willingly under his eyes, and with a feeling of pride. One time a feed salesman came down into the pens to talk to him and my father said, "Like to have you meet my new hired man." I turned away and raked furiously, red in the face with pleasure.

"Could of fooled me," said the salesman. "I thought it was only a girl."

After the grass was cut, it seemed suddenly much later in the year. I walked on stubble in the earlier evening, aware of the reddening skies, the entering silences, of fall. When I wheeled the tank out of the gate and put the padlock on, it was almost dark. One night at this time I saw my mother and father standing talking on the little rise of ground we called the gangway, in front of the barn. My father had just come from the meathouse; he had his stiff bloody apron on, and a pail of cut-up meat in his hand.

It was an odd thing to see my mother down at the barn. She did not often come out of the house unless it was to do something—hang out the wash or dig potatoes in the garden. She looked out of place, with her bare lumpy legs, not touched by the sun, her apron still on and damp across the stomach from the supper dishes. Her hair was tied up in a kerchief, wisps of it falling out. She would tie her hair up like this in the morning, saying she did not have time to do it properly, and it would stay tied up all day. It was true, too; she really did not have time. These days our back porch was piled with baskets of peaches and grapes and pears, bought in town, and onions and tomatoes and cucumbers grown at home, all waiting to be made into jelly and jam and preserves, pickles and chili sauce. In the kitchen there was a fire in the stove all day, jars clinked in boiling water, sometimes a cheesecloth bag was strung on a pole between two chairs, straining blue-black grape pulp for jelly. I was given jobs to do and I would sit at the table peeling peaches that had been soaked in the hot water, or cutting up onions, my eyes smarting and streaming. As soon as I was done I ran out of the house, trying to get out of earshot before my mother thought of what she wanted me to do next. I hated the hot dark kitchen in summer, the green blinds and the flypapers, the same old oilcloth table and wavy mirror and bumpy linoleum. My mother was too tired and preoccupied to talk to me, she had no heart to tell about the Normal School Graduation Dance; sweat trickled over her face and she was always counting under her breath, pointing at jars, dumping cups of sugar. It seemed to me that work in the house was endless, dreary and peculiarly depressing; work done out of doors, and in my father's service, was ritualistically important.

I wheeled the tank up to the barn, where it was kept, and I heard my mother saying, "Wait till Laird gets a little bigger, then you'll have a real help."

What my father said I did not hear. I was pleased by the way he stood listening, politely as he would to a salesman or a stranger, but with an air of wanting to get on with his real work. I felt my mother had no business down here and I wanted him to feel the same way. What did she mean about Laird? He was no help to anybody. Where was he now? Swinging himself sick on the swing, going around in circles, or trying to catch caterpillars. He never once stayed with me till I was finished.

"And then I can use her more in the house," I heard my mother say. She had a dead-quiet, regretful way of talking about me that always made me uneasy. "I just get my back turned and she runs off. It's not like I had a girl in the family at all."

I went and sat on a feedbag in the corner of the barn, not wanting to appear when this conversation was going on. My mother, I felt, was not to be trusted. She was kinder than my father and more easily fooled, but you could not depend on her, and the real reasons for the things she said and did were not to be known. She loved me, and she sat up late at night making a dress of the difficult style I wanted, for me to wear when school started, but she was also my enemy. She was always plotting. She was plotting now to get me to stay in the house more, although she knew I hated it (*because* she knew I hated it) and keep me from working for my father. It seemed to me she would do this simply out of perversity, and to try her power. It did not occur to me that she could be lonely, or jealous. No grown-up could be; they were too fortunate. I sat and kicked my heels monotonously against a feedbag, raising dust, and did not come out till she was gone.

At any rate, I did not expect my father to pay any attention to what she said. Who could imagine Laird doing my work— Laird remembering the padlock and cleaning out the watering-dishes with a leaf on the end of a stick, or even wheeling the tank without it tumbling over? It showed how little my mother knew about the way things really were.

I have forgotten to say what the foxes were fed. My father's bloody apron reminded me. They were fed horsemeat. At this time most farmers still kept horses, and when a horse got too old to work, or broke a leg or got down and would not get up, as they sometimes did, the owner would call my father, and he and Henry went out to the farm in the truck. Usually they shot and butchered the horse there, paying the farmer from five to twelve dollars. If they had already too much meat on hand, they would bring the horse back alive, and keep it for a few days or weeks in our stable, until the meat was needed. After the war the farmers were buying tractors and gradually getting rid of horses altogether, so it sometimes happened that we got a good healthy horse, that there was just no use for any more. If this happened in the winter we might keep the horse in our stable till spring, for we had plenty of hay and if there was a lot of snow—and the plow did not always get our road cleared—it was convenient to be able to go to town with a horse and cutter.

The winter I was eleven years old we had two horses in the stable. We did not know what names they had had before, so we called them Mack and Flora. Mack was an old black workhorse, sooty and indifferent. Flora was a sorrel mare, a driver. We took them both out in the cutter. Mack was slow and easy to handle. Flora was given to fits of violent alarm, veering at cars and even at other horses, but we loved her speed and high-stepping, her general air of gallantry and abandon. On Saturdays we went down to the stable and as soon as we opened the door on its cosy, animal-smelling darkness Flora threw up her head, rolled her eyes, whinnied despairingly and pulled herself through a crisis of nerves on the spot. It was not safe to go into her stall; she would kick.

This winter also I began to hear a great deal more on the theme my mother had sounded when she had been talking in front of the barn. I no longer felt safe. It seemed that in the minds of the people around me there was a steady undercurrent of thought, not to be deflected, on this one subject. The word *girl* had formerly seemed to me innocent and unburdened, like the word *child*; now it appeared that it was no such thing. A girl was not, as I had supposed, simply what I was; it was what I had to become. It was a definition, always touched with emphasis, with reproach and disappointment. Also it was a joke on me. Once Laird and I were fighting, and for the first time ever I had to use all my strength against him; even so, he caught and pinned my arm for a moment, really hurting me. Henry saw this, and laughed, saying, "Oh, that there Laird's gonna show you, one of these days!" Laird was getting a lot bigger. But I was getting bigger too.

My grandmother came to stay with us for a few weeks and I heard other things. "Girls don't slam doors like that." "Girls keep their knees together when they sit down." And worse still, when I asked some questions, "That's none of girls' business." I continued to slam the doors and sit as awkwardly as possible, thinking that by such measures I kept myself free.

When spring came, the horses were let out in the barnyard. Mack stood against the barn wall trying to scratch his neck and haunches, but Flora trotted up and down and reared at the fences, clattering her hooves against the rails. Snow drifts dwindled quickly, revealing the hard grey and brown earth, the familiar rise and fall of the ground, plain and bare after the fantastic landscape of winter. There was a great feeling of opening-out, of release. We just wore rubbers now, over our shoes; our feet felt ridiculously light. One Saturday we went out to the stable and found all the doors open, letting in the unaccustomed sunlight and fresh air. Henry was there, just idling around looking at his collection of calendars which were tacked up behind the stalls in a part of the stable my mother had probably never seen.

"Come to say goodbye to your old friend Mack?" Henry said. "Here, you give him a taste of oats." He poured some oats into Laird's cupped hands and Laird went to feed Mack. Mack's teeth were in bad shape. He ate very slowly, patiently shifting the oats around in his mouth, trying to find a stump of a molar to grind it on. "Poor old Mack," said Henry mournfully. "When a horse's teeth's gone, he's gone. That's about the way."

"Are you going to shoot him today?" I said. Mack and Flora had been in the stable so long I had almost forgotten they were going to be shot.

Henry didn't answer me. Instead he started to sing in a high, trembly, mocking-sorrowful voice, *Oh, there's no more work, for poor Uncle Ned, he's gone where the good darkies go.* Mack's thick, blackish tongue worked diligently at Laird's hand. I went out before the song was ended and sat down on the gangway.

I had never seen them shoot a horse, but I knew where it was done. Last summer Laird and I had come upon a horse's entrails before they were buried. We had thought it was a big black snake, coiled up in the sun. That was around in the field that ran up beside the barn. I thought that if we went inside the barn, and found a wide crack or a knothole to look through, we would be able to see them do it. It was not something I wanted to see; just the same, if a thing really happened, it was better to see it, and know.

My father came down from the house, carrying the gun.

"What are you doing here?" he said.

"Nothing."

"Go on up and play around the house."

He sent Laird out of the stable. I said to Laird. "Do you want to see them shoot Mack?" and without waiting for an answer led him around to the front door of the barn, opened it carefully, and went in. "Be quiet or they'll hear us," I said. We could hear Henry and my father talking in the stable, then the heavy, shuffling steps of Mack being backed out of his stall.

In the loft it was cold and dark. Thin, crisscrossed beams of sunlight fell through the cracks. The hay was low. It was a rolling country, hills and hollows, slipping under our feet. About four feet up was a beam going around the walls. We piled hay up in one corner and I boosted Laird up and hoisted myself. The beam was not very wide; we crept along it with our hands flat on the barn walls. There were plenty of knot-holes, and I found one that gave me the view I wanted—a corner of the barnyard, the gate, part of the field. Laird did not have a knothole and began to complain.

I showed him a widened crack between two boards. "Be quiet and wait. If they hear you you'll get us in trouble."

My father came in sight carrying the gun. Henry was leading Mack by the halter. He dropped it and took out his cigarette papers and tobacco; he rolled cigarettes for my father and himself. While this was going on Mack nosed around in the old, dead grass along the fence. Then my father opened the gate and they took Mack through. Henry led Mack away from the path to a patch of ground and they talked together, not loud enough for us to hear. Mack again began searching for a mouthful of fresh grass, which was not to be found. My father walked away in a straight line, and stopped short at a distance which seemed to suit him. Henry was walking away from Mack too, but sideways, still negligently holding on to the halter. My father raised the gun and Mack looked up as if he had noticed something and my father shot him.

Mack did not collapse at once but swayed, lurched sideways and fell, first on his side; then he rolled over on his back and, amazingly, kicked his legs for a few seconds in the air. At this Henry laughed, as if Mack had done a trick for him. Laird, who had drawn a long, groaning breath of surprise when the shot was fired, said out loud, "He's not dead." And it seemed to me it might be true. But his legs stopped, he rolled on his side again, his muscles quivered and sank. The two men walked over and looked at him in a businesslike way; they bent down and examined his forehead where the bullet had gone in, and now I saw his blood on the brown grass.

"Now they just skin him and cut him up," I said. "Let's go." My legs were a little shaky and I jumped gratefully down into the hay. "Now you've seen how they shoot a horse," I said in a congratulatory way, as if I had seen it many times before. "Let's see if any barn cat's had kittens in the hay." Laird jumped. He seemed young and obedient again. Suddenly I remembered how, when he was little, I had brought him into the barn and told him to climb the ladder to the top beam. That was in the spring, too, when the hay was low. I had done it out of a need for excitement, a desire for something to happen so that I could tell about it. He was wearing a little bulky brown and white checked coat, made down from one of mine. He went all the way up, just as I told him, and sat down on the top beam with the hay far below him on one side, and the barn floor and some old machinery on the other. Then I ran screaming to my father, "Laird's up on the top beam!" My father came, my mother came, my father went up the ladder talking very quietly and brought Laird down under his arm, at which my mother leaned against the ladder and began to cry. They said to me, "Why weren't you watching him?" but nobody ever knew the truth. Laird did not know enough to tell. But whenever I saw the brown and white checked coat hanging in the closet, or at the bottom of the rag bag, which was where it ended up, I felt a weight in my stomach, the sadness of unexorcized guilt.

I looked at Laird who did not even remember this, and I did not like the look on his thin, winter-pale face. His expression was not frightened or upset, but remote, concentrating. "Listen," I said, in an unusually bright and friendly voice, "you aren't going to tell, are you?"

"No," he said absently.

"Promise."

"Promise," he said. I grabbed the hand behind his back to make sure he was not crossing his fingers. Even so, he might have a nightmare; it might come out that way. I decided I had better work to get all thoughts of what he had seen out of his mind—which, it seemed to me, could not hold very many things at a time. I got some money I had saved and that afternoon we went into Jubilee and saw a show, with Judy Canova, at which we both laughed a great deal. After that I thought it would be all right.

Two weeks later I knew they were going to shoot Flora. I knew from the night before, when I heard my mother ask if the hay was holding out all right, and my father said, "Well, after to-morrow there'll just be the cow, and we should be able to put her out to grass in another week." So I knew it was Flora's turn in the morning.

This time I didn't think of watching it. That was something to see just one time. I had not thought about it very often since, but sometimes when I was busy, working at school, or standing in front of the mirror combing my hair and wondering if I would be pretty when I grew up, the whole scene would flash into my mind: I would see the easy, practised way my father raised the gun, and hear Henry laughing when Mack kicked his legs in the air. I did not have any great feeling of horror and opposition, such as a city child might have had; I was too used to seeing the death of animals as a necessity by which we lived. Yet I felt a little ashamed, and there was a new wariness, a sense of holding-off, in my attitude to my father and his work.

It was a fine day, and we were going around the yard picking up tree branches that had been torn off in winter storms. This was something we had been told to do, and also we wanted to use them to make a teepee. We heard Flora whinny, and then my father's voice and Henry's shouting, and we ran down to the barnyard to see what was going on.

The stable door was open. Henry had just brought Flora out, and she had broken away from him. She was running free in the barnyard, from one end to the other. We climbed up on the fence. It was exciting to see her running, whinnying, going up on her hind legs, prancing and threatening like a horse in a Western movie, an unbroken ranch horse, though she was just an old driver, an old sorrel mare. My father and Henry ran after her and tried to grab the dangling halter. They tried to work her into a corner, and they had almost succeeded when she made a run between them, wild-eyed, and disappeared around the corner of the barn. We heard the rails clatter down as she got over the fence, and Henry yelled, "She's into the field now!"

That meant she was in the long L-shaped field that ran up by the house. If she got around the center, heading towards the lane, the gate was open; the truck had been driven into the field this morning. My father shouted to me, because I was on the other side of the fence, nearest the lane, "Go shut the gate!"

I could run very fast. I ran across the garden, past the tree where our swing was hung, and jumped across a ditch into the lane. There was the open gate. She had not got out, I could not see her up on the road; she must have run to the other end of the field. The gate was heavy. I lifted it out of the gravel and carried it across the roadway. I had it half-way across when she came in sight, galloping straight towards me. There was just time to get the chain on. Laird came scrambling through the ditch to help me.

Instead of shutting the gate, I opened it as wide as I could. I did not make any decision to do this, it was just what I did. Flora never slowed down; she galloped straight past me, and Laird jumped up and down, yelling, "Shut it, shut it!" even after it was too late. My father and Henry appeared in the field a moment too late to see what I had done. They only saw Flora heading for the township road. They would think I had not got there in time.

They did not waste any time asking about it. They went back to the barn and got the gun and the knives they used, and put these in the truck; then they turned the truck around and came bouncing up the field toward us. Laird called to them, "Let me go too, let me go too!" and Henry stopped the truck and they took him in. I shut the gate after they were all gone.

I supposed Laird would tell. I wondered what would happen to me. I had never disobeyed my father before, and I could not understand why I had done it. Flora would not really get away. They would catch up with her in the truck. Or if they did not catch her this morning somebody would see her and telephone us this afternoon or tomorrow. There was no wild country here for her to run to, only farms. What was more, my father had paid for her, we needed the meat to feed the foxes, we needed the foxes to make our living. All I had done was make more work for my father who worked hard enough already. And when my father found out about it he was not going to trust me any more; he would know that I was not entirely on his side. I was on Flora's side, and that made me no use to anybody, not even to her. Just the same, I did not regret it; when she came running at me and I held the gate open, that was the only thing I could do.

I went back to the house, and my mother said, "What's all the commotion?" I told her that Flora had kicked down the fence and got away. "Your poor father," she said, "now he'll have to go chasing over the countryside. Well, there isn't any use planning dinner before one." She put up the ironing board. I wanted to tell her, but thought better of it and went upstairs and sat on my bed.

Lately I had been trying to make my part of the room fancy, spreading the bed with old lace curtains, and fixing myself a dressing-table with some leftovers of cretonne for a skirt. I planned to put up some kind of barricade between my bed and Laird's, to keep my section separate from his. In the sunlight, the lace curtains were just dusty rags. We did not sing at night any more. One night when I was singing Laird said, "You sound silly," and I went right on but the next night I did not start. There was not so much need to anyway, we were no longer afraid. We knew it was just old furniture over there, old jumble and confusion. We did not keep to the rules. I still stayed awake after Laird was asleep and told myself stories, but even in these stories something different was happening, mysterious alterations took place. A story might start off in the old way, with a spectacular danger, a fire or wild animals, and for a while I might rescue people; then things would change around, and instead, somebody would be rescuing me. It might be a boy from our class at school, or even Mr. Campbell, our teacher, who tickled girls under the arms. And at this point the story concerned itself at great length with what I looked like, how long my hair was, and what kind of dress I had on; by the time I had these details worked out the real excitement of the story was lost.

It was later than one o'clock when the truck came back. The tarpaulin was over the back, which meant there was meat in it. My mother had to heat dinner up all over again. Henry and my father had changed from their bloody overalls into ordinary working overalls in the barn, and they washed their arms and necks and faces at the sink, and splashed water on their hair and combed it. Laird lifted his arm to show off a streak of blood. "We shot old Flora," he said, "and cut her up in fifty pieces."

"Well I don't want to hear about it," my mother said. "And don't come to my table like that."

My father made him go and wash the blood off.

We sat down and my father said grace and Henry pasted his chewing-gum on the end of his fork, the way he always did; when he took it off he would have us admire the pattern. We began to pass the bowls of steaming, overcooked vegetables. Laird looked across the table at me and said proudly, distinctly, "Anyway it was her fault Flora got away."

"What?" my father said.

"She could of shut the gate and she didn't. She just open' it up and Flora run out."

"Is that right?" my father said.

Everybody at the table was looking at me. I nodded, swallowing food with great difficulty. To my shame, tears flooded my eyes.

My father made a curt sound of disgust. "What did you do that for?"

I did not answer. I put down my fork and waited to be sent from the table, still not looking up.

But this did not happen. For some time nobody said anything, then Laird said matter-of-factly, "She's crying."

"Never mind," my father said. He spoke with resignation, even good humour, the words which absolved and dismissed me for good. "She's only a girl," he said.

I didn't protest that, even in my heart. Maybe it was true.

Remembering Kevan MacKenzie

Henry Taylor

Once upon a time I spent a summer
At a camp for children far from here,
Teaching riding to young boys and girls.
I taught them to make a horse go straight,
The way to make a horse stand still.
They grew and danced like weeds before my eyes.

Now there remains in my mind's eye
One face of all the faces of that summer;
It smiles at me, and I sit here
Wondering what's become of all the girls
That Kevan MacKenzie hounded straight
To earth, and may be chasing still.

Every week there was a dance, and still
I can recall the roll of those girls' eyes
As they hunted love, the first of summer:
Kevan, refusing to dance, stood straight
By the wall and dared the girls
To rout him from his sanctuary here.

Later he began to dress with care, and here
I remember the guarded gleam in his eye
As he came through the door and went straight
For the oldest and prettiest girl,
While with that stare that disturbs me still
The young girls hunted the first love of summer.

In the arms of that tall breath of summer
He danced, and looked her waist in the eye.
I whispered then, "Be cheerful, girls,
The sunshine boys are here."
When the music at last grew still,
The tall girl smiled, once more stood straight.

The days of dancing and love rode straight
To the last long week of that summer.
When I said goodbye to my boys and girls
I stood among them with tears in my eyes,
While Kevan MacKenzie, smiling still,
Said, "You must be glad to get out of here."

Now I sit here in another summer
And rising straight in my mind's eye
Kevan and his girls are dancing still.

Children's Camp

Dorothy Livesay

Call it safety—
That cool island where
No headlines glare
No rumour of the world
Disturbs the ear;
Boys' arms and legs
Are fancy-free
To spin like catherine wheels
Through hours of play
Until, at night
With campfire at the throat
Their hearts sing out, sing out
They chant their way and float
To airy sleep.

Though gongs awaken
Summer is a season of high bells
Rung in the skies, and shaken
Through green leaves calling out a dance,
Sun's baton striking time:
So bells ring out all day!
But clock's invisible
And day moves into week
Unchained by calendar or season;
Hours need no rhyme
And summer needs no reason.

Call it safety
That island where
No motors hum
No planes drone
No bombs loom—
Here childhood is miraged,
Anchored in dream
A cordon against sound.

Call it safety, where
Under the tall star
And the cedar bough
A dream takes form.

Childhood Is the Kingdom
Where Nobody Dies

Edna St. Vincent Millay

Childhood is not from birth to a certain age and at a
    certain age
The child is grown, and puts away childish things.
Childhood is the kingdom where nobody dies.

Nobody that matters, that is. Distant relatives of course
Die, whom one never has seen or has seen for an hour,
And they gave one candy in a pink-and-green striped
    bag, or a jack-knife
And went away, and cannot really be said to have lived
    at all.

And cats die. They lie on the floor and lash their tails,
And their reticent fur is suddenly all in motion
With fleas that one never knew were there,
Polished and brown, knowing all there is to know,
Trekking off into the living world.
You fetch a shoe-box, but it's much too small, because
    she won't curl up now:
So you find a bigger box, and bury her in the yard, and
    weep.

But you do not wake up a month from then, two
    months,
A year from then, two years, in the middle of the night

And weep, with your knuckles in your mouth, and
    say Oh, God! Oh, God!
Childhood is the kingdom where nobody dies that mat-
    ters,—mothers and fathers don't die.

And if you have said, "For heaven's sake, must you
    always be kissing a person?"
Or, "I do wish to gracious you'd stop tapping on the
    window with your thimble!"
Tomorrow, or even the day after tomorrow if you're
    busy having fun,
Is plenty of time to say, "I'm sorry, mother."

To be grown up is to sit at the table with people who
    have died, who neither listen nor speak;
Who do not drink their tea, though they always said
Tea was such a comfort.

Run down into the cellar and bring up the last jar of
    raspberries; they are not tempted.
Flatter them, ask them what was it they said exactly
That time, to the bishop, or to the overseer, or to Mrs.
    Mason;
They are not taken in.
Shout at them, get red in the face, rise.
Drag them up out of their chairs by their stiff shoulders
    and shake them and yell at them;
They are not startled, they are not even embarrassed;
    they slide back into their chairs.

Your tea is cold now.
You drink it standing up,
And leave the house.

Bears

Adrienne Rich

Wonderful bears that walked my room all night,
Where have you gone, your sleek and fairy fur,
Your eyes' veiled and imperious light?

Brown bears as rich as mocha or as musk,
White opalescent bears whose fur stood out
Electric in the deepening dusk,

And great black bears that seemed more blue than
    black,
More violet than blue against the dark—
Where are you now? Upon what track

Mutter your muffled paws that used to tread
So softly, surely, up the creakless stair
While I lay listening in bed?

When did I lose you? Whose have you become?
Why do I wait and wait and never hear
Your thick nocturnal pacing in my room?
My bears, who keeps you now, in pride and fear?

Simple Arithmetic

Virginia Moriconi

Geneva, January 15

D EAR Father,
Well, I am back in School, as you can see, and
the place is just as miserable as ever. My only friend,
the one I talked to you about, Ronald Fletcher, is not coming
back any more because someone persuaded his mother that
she was letting him go to waste, since he was extremely pho-
togenic, so now he is going to become a child actor. I was very
surprised to hear this, as the one thing Ronnie liked to do
was play basketball. He was very shy.

The flight wasn't too bad. I mean nobody had to be carried
off the plane. The only thing was, we were six hours late and
they forgot to give us anything to eat, so for fourteen hours
we had a chance to get quite hungry but, as you say, for the
money you save going tourist class, you should be prepared to
make a few little sacrifices.

I did what you told me, and when we got to Idlewild I paid
the taxi driver his fare and gave him a fifty-cent tip. He was
very dissatisfied. In fact he wouldn't give me my suitcase. In
fact I don't know what would have happened if a man hadn't
come up just while the argument was going on and when he
heard what it was all about he gave the taxi driver a dollar and
I took my suitcase and got to the plane on time.

During the trip I thought the whole thing over. I did not
come to any conclusion. I know I have been very extravagant
and unreasonable about money and you have done the best

you can to explain this to me. Still, while I was thinking about it, it seemed to me that there were only three possibilities. I could just have given up and let the taxi driver have the suitcase, but when you realise that if we had to buy everything over again that was in the suitcase we would probably have had to spend at least five hundred dollars, it does not seem very economical. Or I could have gone on arguing with him and missed the plane, but then we would have had to pay something like three hundred dollars for another ticket. Or else I could have given him an extra twenty-five cents which, as you say, is just throwing money around to create an impression. What would you have done?

Anyway I got here, with the suitcase, which was the main thing. They took two week-end privileges away from me because I was late for the opening of School. I tried to explain to M. Frisch that it had nothing to do with me if the weather was so bad that the plane was delayed for six hours, but he said that prudent persons allow for continjensies of this kind and make earlier reservations. I don't care about this because the next two week-ends are skiing week-ends and I have never seen any point in waking up at six o'clock in the morning just to get frozen stiff and endure terrible pain, even if sports are a part of growing up, as you say. Besides, we will save twenty-seven dollars by having me stay in my room.

In closing I want to say that I had a very nice Christmas and I apreciate everything you tried to do for me and I hope I wasn't too much of a bother. (Martha explained to me that you had had to take time off from your honeymoon in order to make Christmas for me and I am very sorry even though I do not think I am to blame if Christmas falls on the twenty-fifth of December, especially since everybody knows that it does. What I mean is, if you had wanted to have a long honeymoon you and Martha could have gotten married earlier, or you could have waited until Christmas was over, or you could just have told me not to come and I would have understood.)

I will try not to spend so much money in the future and I will keep accounts and send them to you. I will also try to remember to do the eye exercises and the exercises for fallen arches that the doctors in New York prescribed.

Love,
Stephen

Dear Stephen,

Thank you very much for the long letter of January fifteenth. I was very glad to know that you had gotten back safely, even though the flight was late. (I do not agree with M. Frisch that prudent persons allow for "continjensies" of this kind, now that air travel is as standard as it is, and the service usually so good, but we must remember that Swiss people are, by and large, the most meticulous in the world and nothing offends them more than other people who are not punctual.)

In the affair of the suitcase, I'm afraid that we were both at fault. I had forgotten that there would be an extra charge for luggage when I suggested that you should tip the driver fifty cents. You, on the other hand, might have inferred from his argument that he was simply asking that the tariff—i.e. the fare, plus the overcharge for the suitcase—should be paid in full, and regulated yourself accordingly. In any event you arrived, and I am only sorry that obviously you had no time to learn the name and address of your benefactor so that we might have paid him back for his kindness.

I will look forward to going over your accounting and I am sure you will find that in keeping a clear record of what you spend you will be able to cut your cloth according to the bolt, and that, in turn, will help you to develop a real regard for yourself. It is a common failing, as I told you, to spend too much money in order to compensate oneself for a lack of inner security, but you can easily see that a foolish purchase does not insure stability, and if you are chronically insolvent you can hardly hope for peace of mind. Your allowance is more than adequate and when you learn to make both ends meet you will have taken a decisive step ahead. I have great faith in you and I know you will find your anchor to windward in your studies, in your sports, and in your companions.

As to what you say about Christmas, you are not obliged to "apreciate" what we did for you. The important thing was that you should have a good time, and I think we had some wonderful fun together, the three of us, don't you? Until your mother decides where she wants to live and settles down, this is your *home* and you must always think of it that way. Even though I have remarried, I am still your father, first and last, and Martha is very fond of you too, and very understanding about your problems. You may not be aware of it but in fact she is one of the best friends you have. New ideas and new stepmothers take a little getting used to, of course.

Please write to me as regularly as you can, since your letters mean a great deal to me. Please try too, at all times, to keep your marks up to scratch, as college entrance is getting harder and harder in this country, and there are thousands of candidates each year for the good universities. Concentrate particularly on spelling. "Contingency" is difficult, I know, but there is no excuse for only one "p" in "appreciate"! And *do* the exercises.

Love,

Father

Geneva, January 22

Dear Mummy,

Last Sunday I had to write to Father to thank him for my Christmas vacation and to tell him that I got back all right. This Sunday I thought I would write to you even though you are on a cruze so perhaps you will never get my letter. I must say that if they didn't make us write home once a week I don't believe that I would ever write any letters at all. What I mean is that once you get to a point like this, in a place like this, you see that you are supposed to have your life and your parents are supposed to have their lives, and you have lost the connection.

Anyway I have to tell you that Father was wonderful to me and Martha was very nice too. They had thought it all out, what a child of my age might like to do in his vacation, and sometimes it was pretty strenuous, as you can imagine. At the end the School sent the bill for the first term, where they charge you for the extras which they let you have here and it seems that I had gone way over my allowance and besides I had signed for a whole lot of things I did not deserve. So there was a terrible scene and Father was very angry and Martha cried and said that if Father always made such an effort to consider me as a person I should make an effort to consider him as a person too and wake up to the fact that he was not Rockefeller and that even if he was sacrificing himself so that I could go to one of the most expensive schools in the world it did not mean that I should drag everybody down in the mud by my reckless spending. So now I have to turn over a new leaf and keep accounts of every penny and not buy anything which is out of proportion to our scale of living.

Except for that one time they were very affectionate to me and did everything they could for my happiness. Of course it was awful without you. It was the first time we hadn't been together and I couldn't really believe it was Christmas.

I hope you are having a wonderful time and getting the rest you need and please write me when you can.

All my love,
Stephen

Geneva, January 22

Dear Father,

Well it is your turn for a letter this week because I wrote to Mummy last Sunday. (I am sure I can say this to you without hurting your feelings because you always said that the one thing you and Mummy wanted was a civilised divorce so we could all be friends.) Anyway Mummy hasn't answered my letter so probably she doesn't aprove of my spelling any more than you do. I am beginning to wonder if maybe it wouldn't be much simpler and much cheaper to if I didn't go too college after all. I really don't know what this education is for in the first place.

There is a terrible scandal here at School which has been very interesting for the rest of us. One of the girls, who is only sixteen, has gotten pregnant and everyone knows that it is all on account of the science instructer, who is a drip. We are waiting to see if he will marry her, but in the meantime she is terrifically upset and she has been expelled from the School. She is going away on Friday.

I always liked her very much and I had a long talk with her last night. I wanted to tell her that maybe it was not the end of the world, that my stepmother was going to have a baby in May, although she never got married until December, and the sky didn't fall in or anything. I thought it might have comforted her to think that grown-ups make the same mistakes that children do (if you can call her a child) but then I was afraid that it might be disloyal to drag you and Martha into the conversation, so I just let it go.

I'm fine and things are just the same.

Love,

Stephen

New York, February 2

Dear Stephen,

It would be a great relief to think that your mother did not "aprove" of your spelling either, but I'm sure that it's not for that reason that you haven't heard from her. She was never any good as a correspondent, and now it is probably more difficult for her than ever. We did indeed try for what you call a "civilised divorce" for all our sakes, but divorce is not an easy thing for any of the persons involved, as you well know, and if you try to put yourself in your mother's place for a moment, you will see that she is in need of time and solitude to work things out for herself. She will certainly write to you as soon as she has found herself again, and meanwhile you must continue to believe in her affection for you and not let impatience get the better of you.

Again, in case you are really in doubt about it, the purpose of your education is to enable you to stand on your own feet when you are a man and make something of yourself. Inaccuracies in spelling will not *simplify* anything.

I can easily see how you might have made a parallel between your friend who has gotten into trouble, and Martha who is expecting the baby in May, but there is only a superficial similarity in the two cases.

Your friend is, or was, still a child, and would have done better to have accepted the limitations of the world of childhood—as you can clearly see for yourself, now that she is in this predicament. Martha, on the other hand, was hardly a child. She was a mature human being, responsible for her own actions and prepared to be responsible for the baby when it came. Moreover I, unlike the science "instructer" am not a drip, I too am responsible for *my* actions, and so Martha and I are married and I will do my best to live up to her and the baby.

Speaking of which, we have just found a new apartment because this one will be too small for us in May. It is right across the street from your old school and we have a kitchen, a dining alcove, a living room, two bedrooms—one for me and Martha, and one for the new baby—and another room which will be for you. Martha felt that it was very important for you to feel that you had a place of your own when you came home to us, and so it is largely thanks to her that we have taken such a big place. The room will double as a study for me when you are not with us, but we will move all my books and papers and paraphernalia whenever you come, and Martha is planning to hang the Japanese silk screen you liked at the foot of the bed. Please keep in touch, and *please* don't forget the exercises.

> Love,
> Father

Geneva, February 5

Dear Father,

There is one thing which I would like to say to you which is that if it hadn't been for you *I* would never had heard of a "civilised divorce," but that is the way you explained it to me. I always thought it was crazy. What I mean is, wouldn't it have been better if you had said, "I don't like your mother any more and I would rather live with Martha," instead of insisting that you and Mummy were always going to be the greatest friends? Because the way things are now Mummy probably thinks that you still like her very much, and it must be hard for Martha to believe that she was chosen, and I'm pretty much confused myself, although it is really none of my business.

You will be sorry to hear that I am not able to do any of the exercises any longer. I cannot do the eye exercises because my room-mate got so fassinated by the stereo gadget that he broke it. (But the School Nurse says she thinks it may be just as well to let the whole thing go since in her opinion there was a good chance that I might have gotten more cross-eyed than ever, fidgeting with the viewer.) And I cannot do the exercises for fallen arches, at least for one foot, because when I was decorating the Assembly Hall for the dance last Saturday, I fell off the stepladder and broke my ankle. So now I am in the Infirmary and the School wants to know whether to send the doctor's bill to you or to Mummy, because they had to call in a specialist from the outside, since the regular School Doctor only knows how to do a very limited number of things. So I have cost a lot of money again and I am very very sorry, but if they were half-way decent in this School they would pay to have proper equipment and not let the students risk their lives on broken stepladders, which is something you could write to the Bookkeeping Department, if you felt like it, because I can't, but you could, and it might do some good in the end.

The girl who got into so much trouble took too many sleeping pills and died. I felt terrible about it, in fact I cried when I heard it. Life is very crewel, isn't it?

I agree with what you said, that she was a child, but I think she knew that, from her point of view. I think she did what she did because she thought of the science instructer as a grown-up, so she imagined that she was perfectly safe with him. You may think she was just bad, because she was a child and should have known better, but I think that it was not entirely her fault since here at School we are all encouraged to take the teachers seriously.

I am very glad you have found a new apartment and I hope you won't move all your books and papers when I come home, because that would only make me feel that I was more of a nuisance than ever.

> Love,
> Stephen

New York, February 8

Dear Stephen,

This will have to be a very short letter because we are to move into the new apartment tomorrow and Martha needs my help with the packing.

We were exceedingly shocked by the tragic death of your friend and very sorry that you should have had such a sad experience. Life can be "crewel" indeed to the people who do not learn how to live it.

When I was exactly your age I broke my ankle too—I wasn't on a defective stepladder, I was playing hockey—and it hurt like the devil. I still remember it and you have all my sympathy. (I have written to the School Physician to ask how long you will have to be immobilised, and to urge him to get you back into the athletic program as fast as possible. The specialist's bill should be sent to me.)

I have also ordered another stereo viewer because, in spite of the opinion of the School Nurse, the exercises are most important and you are to do them *religiously*. Please be more careful with this one no matter how much it may "fassinate" your room-mate.

Martha sends love and wants to know what you would like for your birthday. Let us know how the ankle is mending.

Love,
Father

Geneva, February 12

Dear Father,

I was very surprised by your letter. I was surprised that you said you were helping Martha to pack because when you and Mummy were married I do not ever remember you packing or anything like that so I guess Martha is reforming your charactor. I was also surprised by what you said about the girl who died. What I mean is, if anyone had told me a story like that I think I would just have let myself get a little worked up about the science instructer because it seems to me that he was a villan too. Of course you are much more riserved than I am.

I am out of the Infirmary and they have given me a pair of crutches, but I'm afraid it will be a long time before I can do sports again.

I hope the new apartment is nice and I do not want anything for my birthday because it will seem very funny having a birthday in School so I would rather not be reminded of it.

Love,
Stephen

New York, February 15

Dear Stephen,

This is not an answer to your letter of February twelfth, but an attempt to have a serious discussion with you, as if we were face to face.

You are almost fifteen years old. Shortly you will be up against the stiffest competition of your life when you apply for college entrance. No examiner is going to find himself favourably impressed by "charactor" or "instructer" or "villan" or "riserved" or similar errors. You will have to face the fact that in this world we succeed on our merits, and if we are unsuccessful, on account of sloppy habits of mind, we suffer for it. You are still too young to understand me entirely, but you are not too young to recognise the importance of effort. People who do not make the grade are desperately unhappy all their lives because they have no place in society. If you do not pass the college entrance examinations simply because you are unable to spell, it will be nobody's fault but your own, and you will be gravely handicapped for the rest of your life.

Every time you are in doubt about a word you are to look it up in the dictionary and *memorise* the spelling. This is the least you can do to help yourself.

We are still at sixes and sevens in the new apartment but when Martha accomplishes all she has planned it should be very nice indeed and I think you will like it.

Love,

Father

Geneva, February 19

Dear Father,

I guess we do not understand each other at all. If you immagine for one minute that just by making a little effort I could imaggine how to spell immaggine without looking it up and finding that actually it is "imagine," then you are all wrong. In other words, if you get a letter from me and there are only two or three mistakes well you just have to take my word for it that I have had to look up practically every single word in the dictionary and that is one reason I hate having to write you these letters because they take so long and in the end they are not at all spontainious, no, just wait a second, here it is, "spontaneous," and believe me only two or three mistakes in a letter from me is one of the seven wonders of the world. What I'm saying is that I am doing the best I can as you would aggree if you could see my dictionary which is falling apart and when you say I should *memmorise* the spelling I can't because it doesn't make any sence to me and never did.

Love,
Stephen

New York, February 23

Dear Stephen,

It is probably just as well that you have gotten everything off your chest. We all need to blow up once in a while. It clears the air.

Please don't ever forget that I am aware that spelling is difficult for you. I know you are making a great effort and I am very proud of you. I just want to be sure that you *keep trying*.

I am enclosing a small cheque for your birthday because even if you do not want to be reminded of it I wouldn't want to forget it and you must know that we are thinking of you.

Love,
Father

Geneva, February 26

Dear Father,

We are not allowed to cash personal cheques here in the School, but thank you anyway for the money.

I am not able to write any more because we are going to have the exams and I have to study.

Love,
Stephen

New York, March 2

NIGHT LETTER

BEST OF LUCK STOP KEEP ME POSTED EXAM RESULTS

LOVE,
FATHER

Geneva, March 12

Dear Father,

Well, the exams are over. I got a C in English because aparently I do not know how to spell which should not come as too much of a surprise to you. In Science, Mathematics, and Latin I got A, and in French and History I got a B plus. This makes me first in the class, which doesn't mean very much since none of the children here have any life of the mind, as you would say. I mean they are all jerks, more or less. What am I supposed to do in the Easter vacation? Do you want me to come to New York, or shall I just stay here and get a rest, which I could use?

Love,
Stephen

New York, March 16

Dear Stephen,

I am *immensely* pleased with the examination results. Congratulations. Pull up the spelling and our worries are over.

Just yesterday I had a letter from your mother. She has taken a little house in Majorca, which is an island off the Spanish coast as you probably know, and she suggests that you should come to her for the Easter holidays. Of course you are always welcome here—and you could rest as much as you wanted— but Majorca is very beautiful and would certainly appeal to the artistic side of your nature. I have written to your mother, urging her to write to you immediately, and I enclose her address in case you should want to write yourself. Let me know what you would like to do.

Love,
Father

Geneva, March 19

Dear Mummy,

Father says that you have invited me to come to you in Majorca for the Easter vacation. Is that true? I would be very very happy if it were. It has been very hard to be away from you for all this time and if you wanted to see me it would mean a great deal to me. I mean if you are feeling well enough. I could do a lot of things for you so you would not get too tired.

I wonder if you will think that I have changed when you see me. As a matter of fact I have changed a lot because I have become quite bitter. I have become bitter on account of this School.

I know that you and Father wanted me to have some expearience of what the world was like outside of America but what you didn't know is that Geneva is not the world at all. I mean, if you were born here, then perhaps you would have a real life, but I do not know anyone who was born here so all the people I see are just like myself, we are just waiting not to be lost any more. I think it would have been better to have left me in some place where I belonged even if Americans are getting very loud and money conscious. Because actually most of the children here are Americans, if you come right down to it, only it seems their parents didn't know what to do with them any longer.

Mummy I have written all this because I'm afraid that I have spent too much money all over again, and M. Frisch says that Father will have a crise des nerfs when he sees what I have done, and I thought that maybe you would understand that I only bought these things because there didn't seem to be anything else to do and that you could help me somehow or other. Anyway, according to the School, we will have to pay for all these things.

Concert, Segovia (Worth it)	16.00	(Swiss francs)
School Dance	5.00	
English Drama (What do they mean?)	10.00	
Controle de l'habitant (?)	9.10	
Co-op purchases	65.90	
Ballets Russes (Disappointing)	47.00	
Librairie Prior	59.30	
Concert piano (For practicing)	61.00	
Teinturie (They ruined everything)	56.50	
Toilet and Medicine	35.00	
Escalade Ball	7.00	
Pocket Money	160.00	
77 Yoghurts (Doctor's advice)	42.40	
Book account	295.70	
Total	869.90	(Swiss francs)

Now you see the trouble is that Father told me I was to spend about fifty dollars a month, because that was my allowance, and that I was not to spend anything more. Anyway, fifty dollars a month would be about two hundred and ten Swiss francs, and then I had fifteen dollars for Christmas from Granny, and when I got back to School I found four francs in the pocket of my leather jacket and then I had seventy-nine cents left over from New York, but that doesn't help much, and then Father sent me twenty-five dollars for my birthday but I couldn't cash the cheque because they do not allow that here in School, so what shall I do?

It is a serious situation as you can see, and it is going to get a lot more serious when Father sees the bill. But whatever you do I imploar you not to write to Father because the trouble seems to be that I never had a balance foreward, and I am afraid that it is impossible to keep accounts without a balance foreward, and even more afraid that by this time the accounts have gone a little bizerk.

Do you want me to take a plane when I come to Majorca? Who shall I say is going to pay for the ticket?

Please do write me as soon as you can, because the holidays begin on March 30 and if you don't tell me what to do I will be way out on a lim.

Lots and lots of love,
Stephen

Geneva, March 26

Dear Father,

I wrote to Mummy a week ago to say that I would like very much to spend my Easter vacation in Majorca. So far she has not answered my letter, but I guess she will pretty soon. I hope she will because the holidays begin on Thursday.

I am afraid you are going to be upset about the bill all over again, but in the Spring term I will start anew and keep you in touch with what is going on.

Love,
Stephen

P.S. If Mummy doesn't write what shall I do?

A Boy's Will

Janet Frame

ALL the wild summer holidays Peter was angry. The rain came down heavily almost every day but it was not the rain that angered, it was people—family, visitors, neighbours who moved judging, complaining in their subtropical sweat and steam with their damp skin clinging to the new plastic-covered chairs in the sitting room and their voices tired and their eyes puzzled when they looked at him, as if they did not understand; and then he grew puzzled too for he did not know what they were trying to understand.

He wanted to be left alone. His fourteen years belonged to him like trophies. He sensed that this, his fifteenth year, would be so much prized by himself and others that he would need to fight to preserve it for himself. Everyone had suddenly become intensely interested, seeming to want to share him and explore him. In the first week of the holidays when in answer to his mother's question, "Where have you been?" he said, "Nowhere," his aunt Lily who had come to stay began to chant with an inexplicable triumph in her thick country throat, "Where have you been?—Nowhere.—What did you do?— Nothing."

"It's begun, Cara," she said softly. She was standing by the telephone pressing her hand gently upon the cradle, circling her index finger on the black polished curves.

"It's begun, Cara."

Her hand quivered as she spoke.

What did she mean by her chant? "Nowhere, nothing, no-one?"

Why did everyone know so much about him? About his future too, what he would become, where he would live, how he would feel in his most secret self?

His aunt had said,

"In a few years, Cara, he'll want to break away. You can see the signs already."

His mother replied.

"As I've told you, Lily, it's a scientific career for him. With his I.Q."

His I.Q. was high. He'd heard them say it was so high it couldn't be marked. His mother had said in tones of awe as if she had been describing an elusive beast instead of his intelligence that it was so high it had "gone off the page," while Aunt Lily had replied in a sour dry voice,

"These tests are not as reliable as they were once thought to be." Then his aunt Lily sighed as if she wanted something that would never be given to her and though he possessed skates, a transistor, a half-share with his brother Paul in a dinghy and there were few things he wanted desperately, he identified the feeling Aunt Lily had and he felt sorry for her with her hairy chin and her footballer's legs. When she came to stay everyone always told her, "You're one of the family, Lil, you're one of the family," but it was said so often that nobody seemed to believe it any more and she was really not one of the family, she laughed too loudly and her clothes were funny and she was just a woman living by herself in a room, in Wellington: in a room, not even in a house. It was when she came to stay that Peter's mother talked about him and Paul and their young sister Emily, describing what they had said or done, how from the very first he'd shown signs of exceptional intelligence, how he'd skipped classes at school, had learned to play the piano and was now on to Chopin Waltzes and Beethoven's Moonlight Sonata.

When Aunt Lily arrived Peter had to play all his music to her.

"Play the Beethoven," his mother said, closing her eyes and humming, "De-De-De, De-De-De, De-De-De. . . ."

"Now the Minute Waltz again, Peter. (He does this well because it ties in with his mathematics.)"

Peter felt his fingers moving stiffly. He'd been shirking his practice. His aunt murmured in her sour dry voice,

"He's good technically but he thumps."
He heard his mother's quick intake of breath and her protective,

"He hasn't always thumped. He hasn't been practising. You should have heard him . . ."
and his aunt's cold reply,

"Anyone really interested in music practises all the time."
His mother sighed then.

"There are so many demands made on him, with his intelligence. . . ."

He played his pieces, too, when a family friend arrived by plane from America, and though the friend had been flying all night and his eyes were dark with wanting to sleep he sat on one of the new plastic-covered chairs listening to the messy blurr of notes made by Peter's unpractised fingers.

The expression masked on his face he said calmly,

"That's all right."
Peter saw his mother frown, searching the remark for the comforting word "brilliant". Not finding it, she looked lonely and Peter, turning and seeing her face and knowing what she wanted, felt miserable. He finished in a hurried swallow of notes banging the final chords down like a window sash and taking the kid's toy, an American police car, the visitor had given him he escaped through the kitchen and downstairs to the garage where, his misery giving way to anger, he leapt up and down on the lid of an applebox until it snapped beneath him, sharply, satisfyingly.

Auckland this summer was a factory of storms. Lightning, thunder, rain swept from West to East, Tasman to Pacific, rolling big smoke-white clouds like a bushfire in the sky with tongues of lightning darting and stabbing and the thunder exploding and more rain like sheets of aluminium falling. Peter dealt with each storm by recording it, calculating, experimenting. He collected and measured the rain in his rain-gauge, he read his barometer, his maximum and minimum thermometer, and then after such close disciplined reading he spent hours reading the sky, in agreeable free translation. His teacher had written on his School Report, "What has happened to Peter's reading? Must read more." Peter had not explained that he suddenly found clouds more interesting than words. Clouds,

light, heat, sound. On their Christmas trip round the East
Coast in the family car he carried his barometer like a book on
his lap, reading it.

"He'll be a meteorologist," his mother said, almost destroy-
ing his new passion with the weight of her tomorrow.
He made a sundial too and set it on one of the fenceposts but
there had been so much rain and so little sun that its applebox
surface was sodden. Only once or twice at the beginning of
the holidays he had been able to read the time by the shadow
but now, when the holidays were nearly over, that time seemed
so long ago, a time when he had not been angry, when his
anger did not seize him so completely that he threw things or
slapped his young sister, prompting his mother's cry,

"Peter, stop bullying. Remember you're fourteen to her
eleven. Be your age."

His brother Paul, two years older, had a job for the holidays
and would let no-one forget that he earned five pounds a week
and was grown up. He was studying photography, too, and
spent his spare time shut in the downstairs bathroom with a
sheet of cardboard over the window and the slit under the door
sealed with newspaper, developing and enlarging films. With
his savings and his earnings he'd bought himself an enlarger,
all the James Bond paperbacks, two books of science fiction,
a bottle of Cedar Wood pre-electric shave lotion, and he'd had
his trousers tapered. One Saturday early in the holidays he'd
gone with Peter for a train-ride to Swanson where they sat in
the Domain sheltering under the macrocarpa trees, licking
icecreams, jelly-tipped on sticks, and reading comics bought
at the railway bookstall. It rained, they came home early, and
on the way home Paul made it clear that he hadn't gone out
with Peter for the day that he'd *taken* Peter, and as they loitered
up the drive, preparing answers to embarrassing questions
they might be asked, Paul said, "I'll never go anywhere with
you again. You act like a kid."
Now, in the weekends, Paul went to the pictures with a girl-
friend and Peter saw little of him except when they watched
television.

There had been a fuss about that too. His aunt Lily nearly
died when she saw the new television set. She had cried out as
if she were in danger.

"What about the children? For their sake. . . ."

Peter's mother flushed.

"Ted and I made the decision. It's easy for you as you've no children."

Aunt Lily nodded meekly.

"I just hoped," she said quietly, "that it wouldn't draw the children too much."

Draw? Once when he had a boil on his neck his mother had put a poultice on it, as she said, to "draw" it. She had burned the poultice in the oil drum at the back of the section.

Certainly they watched television at first. They enjoyed the easy programmes, those with the laughs, and escaped when the serious news appeared showing jungle warfare, poverty, disease, famine. But that, too, had been at the beginning of the holidays before Peter began to get angry. Now he seldom watched except for the programme starring the cowboy who gambled. Peter knew all the poker terms. I'll raise you, he'd say coolly to an imaginary opponent. He'd seen a programme, too, about the chances of a fly settling on a certain lump of sugar and he'd worked out the probability and had even snared Paul's interest in this, though what was the use when all their windows and doors had insect screens and flies never landed on the sugar?

It was just before he began to make his kite that he heard his mother saying to Aunt Lily,

"Do you notice how impatient he's getting? His intelligence will be no use if he has no patience. Paul is the one who perseveres. Paul will go far."

"You mean he's the plodding type?"

Peter saw his mother's shocked face as she absorbed all that plodding implied. Oh no, her children were bright, quick, surely they would never plod.

"I think *persevere* is the word. Peter will find life hard if he has no patience. He's grown so quick-tempered!"

Peter pulled a face to himself. Who did they think they were to try to live his life for him?

"This interest in the weather. It could be permanent. I rang up the Department."

He heard his aunt's manuka-stick voice,

"The experts now say. . . ."

He did not wait to hear what the experts now said. He escaped from the top of the stairs down to the garage and ten minutes later Emily came upstairs crying.

"Peter thumped me!"

Peter sat on an upturned applebox in the garage. He could imagine his mother's exclamation,

"Thumped you!"

And her tender admonition afterwards,

"Peter, you must be kind to your little sister. Boys must be gentle with girls."

How could he explain that the thumping had been Emily's fault? They'd all watched a programme on television the night before where there was an old woman, so old and tired that she had to be moved from her little house to be put among the old people, and the film showed her arriving with the few belongings she'd been allowed to bring with her, and one was a photograph of herself as a young girl, and just when she was deciding where to hang it in her new bedroom, a big nurse in a white fly-a-way hat had rushed into the room, admired the photograph, said the woman had not grown a day older, then she'd seized the photograph and the old woman stood looking unhappy and lonely with her arms dangling and her hands empty. But that had been last night on television. Now, this morning, Emily had taken an open page of Peter's Boy's Book of Outdoor Hobbies and drawn a picture of the old woman clinging to her treasure while the nurse tried to take it from her. Peter had no quarrel with Emily's drawing. The programme had frightened him, too, for old age was part of tomorrow and tomorrow was like one of those tools that clamped down and screwed tight, permanently fixing every-thing beneath it. But Emily had drawn the picture where she shouldn't have, over the diagram of the kite that Peter planned to make, and surely a thump was small punishment for such a crime?

The Boy's Book of Outdoor Hobbies was one of the few conso-lations Peter had during the holidays. He had worked carefully through it, making the sundial, the wind gauge, other inter-esting items not connected with the weather. He had skipped the chapter on Photography and Radio for these were Paul's interests and it was better, at this stage, to know nothing about them than try to compete with Paul's accurate detailed knowledge. With an elder brother in the family it was a case of the younger taking the leftovers or perishing in the comparisons that would follow.

"When Paul takes photographs he——"

"Paul knows how to fix the tv when it breaks down—"
Peter had decided, therefore, as his next project, to make a box kite.

He rubbed angrily at the pencilled lines of the old woman and the photograph and the wicked nurse. Emily ought to have known better. The figures quite covered his diagram and measurements. And even if he managed to decipher them and make his kite would the weather be clear for kite-flying? Rain steamed in the sky, the leaves of the big subtropical flowers grew glossy, their stems grew tall, the bush on the hills had a milky green appearance as if rain and milk had fallen together from the sky.
Peter found paste, bamboo sticks, string, a roll of blue and white crepe paper left over from someone's attempt at fancy dress, and forgetting about Emily and the old woman and thumping and the weather and his future he began to make his kite.
Just then he heard his mother and aunt coming downstairs.

"In this gap between showers I'll show you the passion fruit growing by Emily's playhouse."
His mother looked into the garage.
"What are you doing, Peter? Oh, making a kite."
She turned apologetically to Aunt Lily.
"I suppose it's a childish thing for him to make. For all his intelligence he's young for his age."
"All normal boys like kites," Aunt Lily said smoothly.
They crossed the lawn to the playhouse where Emily with the innocent gaze of one who has been thumped and avenged peeped out at them.

"Aren't they big? It will be ages before they ripen. I've always wanted to grow passion fruit."

"I love passion fruit."
They were coming back across the lawn. Peter's mother seized the opportunity to scold him for his treatment of Emily.

"We can't have these rages, Peter."

He heard her saying with sadness in her voice as they climbed the stairs,

"Though he has always played the piano best when he's been angry. I'm sorry he's giving it up. Ted's sorry too. I don't know what's come over the boy these holidays. There was a drop in his school work, too, at the end of last year. The teacher remarked on it. He doesn't seem to have the patience."

"You have to have patience," Aunt Lily said, snapping shut the insect-screen door.

It took Peter several hours to make his kite. He knew he was perhaps the only boy in the street making a kite; he knew also that as soon as it was launched everyone would be flying kites and no doubt some would break the rules, flying theirs in forbidden places like the street where entanglement in the wires would cause electrocution and death. Peter had been warned. There was not much his mother and his father and his teachers had not warned him about. When he thought of his kite as an instrument of death he began to breathe quickly and his hands grew cold and he could not believe that anything so beautiful could help to destroy. It was a box kite, blue and white, as light as a bird's wing on bamboo-stick bones. None of the other boys in the street would make a box kite; theirs would be the usual kind, flat, a skeleton cross of sticks fleshed with brown paper or plastic with a sharp nose and tail and though it would fly the flight would be a plunging swooping movement as if it were not at home in the sky and longed to descend to earth whereas the box kite, Peter knew, would float and drift without panic or restlessness, like a cloud. To Peter, the clouds that passed overhead during all the wild stormy rainy holidays had been unlike any others he had known; or perhaps his feeling for them had changed. In a mysterious way they seemed to contain promises of a wall or window opening beyond into the light. Sometimes in the evening the sun setting in secret appeared to grow so full of light that it could not contain itself and burst through, suddenly, thrusting like a shaft through the big soft clouds down, down into the earth. Watching, Peter knew a feeling of strength, of himself powered by light, of a discovery that he could not understand or control. He felt after closely reading, translating the sky day after day night after night (the "holiday

reading" *Under the Greenwood Tree, Great Expectations*, lay unopen-
ed on his bookshelf) that the clouds in their lightness would
offer no resistance when the time came for the moment, *his*
moment, to burst through. Without being able to articulate
his dream he thought that the moment might come when he
flew his blue and white box kite.

When that evening he drew aside the curtains in the sitting
room he could not suppress his joy when he saw the clear
bright sky.

"Ooh Mum, it'll be fine tomorrow. Isn't the sky lovely?" he
called.

He frowned when he heard her comment.

"Come and look at the sky everyone. Peter says come and
look at the sky."

And her loudly whispered aside to his father.

"It's the poet in him, Ted. Peter's discovered the wonders
of Nature."

Peter felt the rage growing in him. It was *his* sky, *his* light,
his clouds. He had impulsively let others intrude to claim
them.

Before the whole family could surge about the drawn curtain
he swung it back across the window.

"It's gone now," he said sullenly.

"Will you fly your new kite tomorrow?" his mother asked,
and turning to his father said proudly,

"Peter made such a beautiful kite today. Not the ordinary
sort of kite, either."

And then turning to Aunt Lily,

"He's clever with his hands as well."

Peter decided then that he would not make an event of the
flight. If the next day were fine he would sneak out, launch
the kite, fly it to his satisfaction, then come home without any
of the family knowing what had happened. At the back of the
house there was a playground as big as two paddocks where
the Catholic children played games and where during the holidays the grass had grown as tall as wheat and had browned
without sun as everyone's skin, too, had turned brown in the
humid sunless weather. Day by day the rain lashed the grass
and the strong winds rippled it and the cloud-shapes twisted
across it in plaited shadows. It was an ideal place to fly a kite.

Peter dreamed of it as he lay in bed. He would run through the grass with his kite flying behind and above him. He would not feel any more the irritating rage and impatience that kept overwhelming him for there would be nothing to rage over, then, flying his kite, with his face looking up at the clouds and the sky that swung like a vast ship's deck under the surge of the sky's waves. He could almost feel that he might be standing in the sky, sailing through it, steering his path on a voyage of discovery.

The day was fine, the sky clear except for cottontails of cloud and rather more wind than Peter had hoped for. He did not hurry to get up. He sneaked a plate of Weetabix from the kitchen to his bedroom, ate most of it, then lay waiting for Paul and his father to go to work and for Emily to go about her recent domestic craze of making clothes for her teenage doll. Then, when Peter was sure the coast was clear he made ready his kite but his plans for secrecy were destroyed when he met his mother by the kitchen door. She was standing, waiting, while the washing eddied in its white machine. Did all mothers know how to destroy in such subtle ways? Surely she too had not been thinking all night of whether today would be fine for kite-flying? Surely mothers had other things to think of besides their children and their abilities, their intelligence, and what the future held for them in such proud frightening store?

"A nice day to fly your kite, Peter."

He grunted. Then, remembering his manners, he said,

"I think I'll try it in the Catholic playground."

"Good!" his mother said, seeming to think, but not saying, that once he had flown his kite he might go on to activities more suited to his intelligence. Her eyes as she looked at him were heavy as if his future lay inside them like a dark stone.

He climbed through the fence and ran into the playground. The kite obeyed at a touch, stumbled in a jaggling way, at first, over the long grass until it caught and was caught by the passing wind when it began to float like a feather then to turn and swim lightly like a fish in buoyant air, while Peter ran, his feet and legs soaked in the long wet grass, the grass-seeds like clusters of shot stinging his knees; feeling the kitestring as if, tied to himself, it were a part of his own body. He knew a pleasurable feeling at once of lightness and of anchorage, as if his fastrunning legs were tangled for ever in the twisted stems of grass while another part of himself were floating lightly up near the shredded white clouds; then suddenly he found himself out of breath, with running and flying, and he was sobbing with his eyes full of stinging tears, and he stopped running and stood still while the kite jerked and laboured above him, no longer flying with freedom and grace. He felt the tears falling down his face. He was aghast at his weeping but he could not stop it, and all the while he clung fast to the kite string feeling the weight like that of a restless wing upon his arm. It was then that a stronger gust of wind came buffeting, gashing the fragile blue and white crepe paper body, and as the kite drifted down the blue and white paper trailed behind it like shreds of skin. It fell a few yards from where Peter was standing. For a moment he stood still. Then slowly he wound the string and calmly picked up the broken kite. He felt no rage at its breaking. He carried it over the playground, through the gap in the back fence and was crossing the lawn when his mother, hanging out the washing, saw him and cried out, her face full of sympathy,

"Oh Peter, your lovely kite! What happened to it?"
Peter's voice was calm.

"The wind was too strong."

"What a shame!"
His mother spoke into the white flapping sheets. He knew that when she went upstairs she would say to Aunt Lily who would be reading her share of the morning paper,

"Peter's kite is broken, his lovely kite!"
Perhaps she might also say,

"More tantrums, I suppose. That boy. For all his intelligence, that boy. . . ."
That boy. He was that boy. He was intelligent. He had been in the Silver class at Intermediate and his brother, for all his photography and repairing of radios, had been in the Bronze, and his sister—well, sisters were not the same.
That boy.

Immune, he went to the garage. He understood now what the television preachers meant when they insisted the skies had opened. He believed them. He saw his mother with a stone in her eyes and a bone in her throat. Stone and bone were his future and she could never remove them nor perhaps would he want her to. He did not want her to grow old, or go to an institution and have her treasure snatched from her. He felt suddenly protective towards her. He looked at her standing passively on the lawn while the flying sheets and towels slapped at her face and he felt a surge inside him as if he still anchored the blue and white kite and the kite itself flew on towards the hidden sun.

"Now keep your temper, Peter. Just because your kite's broken don't go throwing things around or interfering with Emily's playhouse!"

Shrugging his shoulders as he'd seen his father do, Peter laid the kite gently on the garage floor. Then taking the remaining whole pieces of crepe paper he began patiently to renew and repair the broken body.

Darcy in the Land of Youth

Frank O'Connor

One

DURING the War when he was out of a job Mick Darcy went to England as clerk in a factory. He found the English as he had always supposed them to be: people with a great welcome for themselves and very little for anyone else.

Besides, there were the air-raids, which the English pretended not to notice. In the middle of the night Mick would be wakened by the wail of a siren and the thump of faraway guns, like all the windowpanes of heaven rattling. The thud of artillery, growing louder, accompanied a faint buzz like a cat's purring that seemed to rise out of a corner of the room and mount the wall to the ceiling, where it hung, breathing in steady spurts, exactly like a cat. Pretending not to notice things like that struck Mick as a bit ostentatious: he would rise and dress himself and sit lonesome by the gasfire, wondering what on earth had induced him to leave home.

The daytime wasn't much better. The works were a couple of miles outside the town, and he shared an office with a woman called Penrose and a Jew called Isaacs. Penrose addressed him as "Mr Darcy" and when he asked her to call him "Mick" she affected not to hear. Isaacs was the only one in the works who called him "Mick", but it soon became plain that he only wanted Mick to join the Communist Party.

"You don't want to be a fellow traveller," he said.

"No," said Mick. "I don't want to be a traveller at all."

On his afternoons off, he took long, lonesome country walks, but there was nothing there you could describe as country either; only red-brick farms and cottages with crumpled oak frames and high, red-tiled roofs, big, sickly-looking fields divided by low neat hedges that made them look as though they all called one another by their surnames, and handsome-looking pubs named like The Star and Garter or The Shoulder of Mutton that were never open when you wanted them. No wonder he pined for Cork, his girl, Ina, and his great friend, Chris.

But it is amazing the effect even one girl can have on a feeling of home-sickness. Janet Fuller in Personnel was a tall, thin, fair-haired girl with a quick-witted laughing air. When Mick talked to her she listened with her head forward and her eyebrows raised expectantly. There was nothing in the least alarming about Janet, and she didn't seem to want to convert him to anything, so he asked her to have a drink with him. She even called him "Mick" without being asked.

It was a great comfort. Now he had someone to talk to in his spare time, and he no longer felt scared of the country or the people. Besides, he had begun to master his job, and this always gave him a feeling of self-confidence. He even began to surprise the others at the factory. One day a group of them, including Janet, had broken off work for a chat when they heard the boss and scattered—even Janet said "Goodbye" hastily. But Mick just gazed out of the window, his hands still in his trousers pockets, and when the boss came in, he saluted him over his shoulder. "Settling in, Darcy?" the boss said in a friendly tone. "Just getting the hang of things," Mick replied modestly. Next day the boss sent for him, but it was only to ask his advice about something, and Mick gave it in his forthright way. If Mick had a weakness, it was that he liked to hear himself talk.

But he still continued to get shocks. One evening he had supper in the flat that Janet shared with a girl called Fanny, who was an analyst in one of the factories. Fanny was a good-looking dark haired girl with a tendency to moodiness. She asked how Mick was getting on with Mrs Penrose.

"Oh," said Mick, "she still calls me 'Mr Darcy'."

"I suppose that's only because she expects to be calling you something else before long," said Fanny gloomily.

"Oh, no, Fanny," said Janet. "You wouldn't know Penrose now. She's a changed woman. With her husband in Egypt, Peter posted to Yorkshire, and no one to play with but George, she's begun to talk about the simple pleasures of life. Penrose and primroses, you know."

"Penrose?" Mick exclaimed incredulously. "I never thought she was that sort. Are you sure, Janet? I'd have thought she was an iceberg."

"An iceberg!" Janet said gleefully, rubbing her hands. "Oh, boy! A blooming fireship!"

Going home that night through the pitch-dark streets, Mick really felt at home for the first time. He had made friends with two of the nicest girls you could wish for—fine, broad-minded girls you could speak to as you'd speak to a man. He had to step into the roadway to make room for two other girls, flicking their torches on and off before them—school-girls, to judge by their voices. "Of course, he's married," one of them said as they passed, and then went off into a rippling scale of laughter that sounded almost unearthly in the silence and darkness.

A bit too broad-minded at times, perhaps, thought Mick, coming to himself. For a while he did not feel quite so much at home.

Two

In the spring evenings Janet and himself cycled off into the nearby villages and towns for their drinks. Janet wanted him to see the country. Sometimes Fanny came too, but she did not seem so keen on it. It was as though she felt herself in the way, yet when she did refuse to accompany them, she looked after them with such a reproachful air that it seemed to make Janet feel guilty.

One Sunday evening they went to church together. It seemed to surprise Janet that Mick went to Mass every Sunday. She went with him once and clearly it did not impress her. Her own religion seemed a bit mixed. Her father had been a Baptist lay preacher and her mother a Methodist, but Janet herself had fallen in love with a parson at the age of eleven and remained Church till she joined the Socialist Party at the age of eighteen. Most of the time she did not seem to Mick to have any religion at all. She said that you just died and rotted, and that was all anyone knew about it, and this seemed to be the general view. There were any amount of religions, but no beliefs you could put your finger on.

Janet was so eager that he should go to church with her that he agreed, though it was against his principles. It was a little town ten miles from where they lived. Inside the church was a young sailor playing the organ while another turned over for him. The parson rang the bell himself, and only three women turned up. The service itself was an awful sell. The parson turned his back on them and read prayers at the east window; the organist played a hymn, which the three women and Janet joined in, and then the parson read more prayers. However, it seemed to get Janet all worked up.

"Pity about Fanny," she said when they were drinking beer in the inn yard later. "We could be very comfortable in the flat only for her. Haven't you a friend who'd take her off our hands?"

"Only in Ireland."

"Tell him I'll get him a job here. Say you've a nice girl for him as well. She really *is* nice, Mick."

"Oh, I know," said Mick. "But hasn't she a fellow already?"

"Getting a fellow for Fanny is the great problem of my life," Janet said ruefully.

"I wonder if she'd have him," said Mick, thinking how nice it would be to have a friend as well as a girl. Janet was as good as gold, but there were times when Mick pined for masculine companionship.

"If he's anything like you, she'd jump at him," said Janet.

"Oh, there's no resemblance," said Mick who had never before been flattered like this and loved it. "Chris is a holy terror."

"A holy terror is what Fanny needs," Janet said grimly.

It was only as time went by that he realized she was not exaggerating. Fanny was jealous; there was no doubt of that. She didn't intend to be rude, but she watched his plate as

Janet filled it, and he saw that she grudged him even the food he ate. There wasn't much, God knows, and what there was, Janet gave him the best of, but all the same it was embarrassing. Janet did her best by making her feel welcome to join them, but Fanny only grew moodier.

"Oh, come on, Fanny!" Janet said one evening. "I only want to show Mick the Plough in Alton."

"Well, who'd know it better?" Fanny asked darkly, and Janet's temper blazed up.

"There's no need to be difficult," she said.

"Well, it's not my fault if I'm inhibited, is it?" asked Fanny with a cowed air. Mick saw with surprise that she was terrified of Janet in a tantrum.

"I didn't say you were inhibited," Janet replied in a stinging voice. "I said you were difficult."

"Same thing from your point of view, isn't it?" Fanny asked. "Oh, I suppose I was born that way. You'd better let me alone."

All the way out Janet was silent, and Mick saw she was still mad, though he couldn't guess why. He didn't know what Fanny meant when she said she was inhibited, or why she seemed to speak about it as if it were an infectious disease. He only knew that Janet had to be smoothed down.

"We'll have to get Chris for Fanny all right," he said. "An exceptional girl like that, you'd think she'd have fellows falling over her."

"I don't think Fanny will ever get a man," Janet said in a shrill, scolding voice. "I've thrown dozens of them at her head, but she won't even make an effort to be polite. I believe she's one of those women who go through life without even knowing what it's about. She's just a raging mass of inhibitions."

There it was again! Prohibitions, exhibitions, inhibitions! Mick wished to God Janet would use simple words. He knew what exhibitions were from one old man in the factory who had gone to gaol because of them, but if inhibitions meant the opposite, what was there to grouse about?

"Couldn't we do something about them?" he asked helpfully.

"Yes, darling," she replied mockingly. "Take her away to hell and give her a good roll in the hay. Then bring her back to me, human."

Mick was so shocked he did not reply. By this time he was used to English dirty jokes, but he knew this wasn't just one of them. No doubt Janet was joking about the roll in the hay—though he wasn't too sure she was joking about that either—but she wasn't joking about Fanny. She really meant that all that was wrong with Fanny was that she was still a virgin, and that this was a complaint she did not suffer from herself.

The smugness of it horrified him as much as the savagery. Put in a certain way, it might be understandable and even forgivable. Girls of Janet's kind were known at home as "damaged goods" but Mick had never permitted the expression to pass. He had a strong sense of justice and always took the side of the underdog. Some girls hadn't the same strength of character as others, he supposed; some were subjected to great temptations. He had never met any, to his knowledge, but he was quite sure that if he had he would have risen to the occasion. But a girl of that kind standing up and denouncing another girl's strength as weakness was too much for him altogether. It was like being asked to stand on his head.

Having got rid of her tantrum, Janet cheered up. "This is wonderful," she sighed with a tranquil pleasure as they floated downhill to Alton and the Plough—a pleasant little inn, standing by the bridge. Mick didn't feel it was so very wonderful. He had begun to wonder what Fanny had meant by asking who would know it better than Janet, and why Janet had lost her temper so badly. It sounded to him as though there had been some dirty work in connexion with it.

While Janet sat in the garden, he went to the bar for beer and stood there for a while unnoticed. There was a little group at the bar: a bald, fat man in an overcoat, smoking a pipe; a good-looking young man with a fancy waistcoat, and a local with a face like a turnip. The landlord, a man of about fifty, had a long, haggard face and wore horn-rimmed glasses; his wife, apparently twenty years younger, was a good-looking woman with bangs and a Lancashire accent. They never noticed Mick while they discussed a death in the village.

"I'm not against religion," the man with the turnip face spluttered excitedly. "I'm chapel myself, but I never tried to force my own views on people. All the months poor Harry was paralysed his wife and daughter never so much as wet his lips. That idn't right, is it? That idn't religion."

"No, Bill," said the landlord, shaking his head. "Going too far, I call that."

"That's fanaticism," said the man with the pipe.

"Everyone is entitled to his own views, but them weren't old Harry's views, were they?" asked the man with the turnip face.

"No, Bill, they certainly weren't," the landlord's wife said sadly.

"I'm for freedom, myself," Bill said, tapping his chest. "The night before he died, I come in here and got a quart of mild and bitter. Didn't I, Joe?"

"Mild, wadn't it, Bill?" the publican asked anxiously.

"No, Joe, mild and bitter was always Harry's drink."

"Don't you remember, Joe?" the landlord's wife asked.

"Funny," her husband replied sadly. "I could have sworn it was mild."

"Anyhow, I said to Millie and Sue, 'All right,' I said. 'You run along to chapel, or wherever you want to go. I'll sit up with old Harry.' Then I took out the bottle. His poor eyes lit up. Couldn't move, couldn't speak, but I shall never forget how he looked at that bottle. I had to hold his mouth open"— Bill threw back his head and pulled down one side of his mouth with his thumb—"and let it trickle down. And was I pleased when he died next morning? I said to myself, 'That man might have gone into his grave without a drink.' No, if that's religion give me beer!"

"Wonder where old Harry is now," the fat man said, removing his pipe reverently. "Mystery, Joe, i'nt it?"

"Shocking!" the landlord said, shaking his head.

"We don't know, do we, Charles?" the landlady said sadly.

"Nobody knows," Bill bawled scornfully as he took up his pint again. "How could they? Parson pretends to know, but he don't know any more than you and me. Shove you in the ground and let the worms have you—that's all anybody knows."

Mick was struck by the similarity of Janet's views with those of the people in the pub, and he felt you really couldn't expect much from any of them.

"Isn't it lovely here?" she said when he brought out the drinks.

"Very nice," Mick said without much enthusiasm. You couldn't feel very enthusiastic about a place while you were wondering who else had been there with your girl.

"We must come and spend a few days here some time," she said, and it made him more depressed than ever. "You don't think I'm too bitchy about Fanny, do you, Mick?"

"It's not that," he said. "I wasn't thinking about Fanny in particular. Just about the way everybody in the factory seems to behave—fellows and girls going off together, as if they were going to a dance."

"Having seen the factory, can you wonder?" she asked, and took a long drink of her beer.

"And when they get tired of one another they go off with someone else," he said dryly. "Or back to the number they started with. Like Hilda in the packing shed. She's tired of knocking round with Dorman, and when her husband comes back she's going to drop him. At least, she says she will."

"Isn't that how these things usually end?" she asked.

"Oh, come on, Janet!" he said scornfully. "You're not going to pretend there's nothing else to it."

"I suppose like everything else, it's just what you choose to make it," she said with a shrug.

"That isn't making much of it," he said, beginning to grow heated. "If it's only a roll in the hay, as you call it, there's nothing in it for anybody."

"And what do you think it should be?" she asked with a frosty politeness that seemed to be the equivalent of his heat. He realized that he wasn't really keeping to the level of a general discussion. He could distinctly hear how common his accent had become, but excitement and a feeling of injury carried him away. He sat back stubbornly with his hands in his trousers pockets.

"But look here, Janet, learning to live with somebody isn't a thing you can pick up in a weekend. It's not a part-time job. You wouldn't take up a job somewhere in the middle, expecting to like it, and intending to drop it in a few months' time if you didn't."

"Oh, Mick, don't tell me you have inhibitions too!" she said in mock distress.

"I don't know what they are and I don't care," retorted Mick, growing commoner as he descended further from the heights of abstract discussion. "And most of the people who use words like that have no idea of their meaning either."

"Scruples, shall we say, so?" she asked, yielding the point.

"Well, we can agree on what they are," he said.

"But after all, Mick, you've had affairs yourself, haven't you?" she added.

Now, this was a question Mick dreaded to answer, because, owing to a lack of suitable opportunities for which he was in no way to blame, he had not. For the matter of that, so far as he knew, none of his friends had either. But coming from a country where men's superiority—affairs or no affairs—was unchallenged, he did not like to admit that, so far as experience went, Fanny and he were in the one boat. He was even beginning to understand why poor Fanny felt such a freak.

"I'm not pretending I haven't," he said casuistically.

"But then there's no argument, Mick," she said with all the enthusiasm of a liberal mind discovering common ground with an opponent.

"No argument, maybe, but there are distinctions," he said knowingly.

"Such as?"

"Oh, between playing the fool and being in love," he replied as though he could barely bother to explain such matters to one as inexperienced as herself.

"The combination isn't altogether unknown either, is it?"

"The distinction seems to be, quite a bit," he replied. "To me, Penrose is one thing and you're another. Maybe I wouldn't mind having an affair with Penrose. God knows it's about all she's good for."

"But you would with me?" she said, growing red.

"I would," Mick said, realizing that the cat was out of the bag at last. "I suppose it's a matter of responsibilities. If I make a friend, I don't begin by thinking what use I can make of him. If I fall in love with a girl I'm not going to begin calculating how cheap I can get her. I don't want anything cheap," he added earnestly. "I'm not going to rush into anything till I know the girl well enough to try and make a decent job of it. Is that plain?"

"Remarkably plain," she said icily. "You mean you're not that sort of man. Let me buy you a drink."

"No, thanks."

"Then I think we'd better be getting back," she said, rising and looking like the wrath of God.

Mick, crushed and humiliated, followed her at a slouch, his hands still in his pockets. It wasn't good enough. At home a girl would have gone on with an argument like that till one of them fell unconscious, and in an argument Mick had real staying power, so he felt that she was taking an unfair advantage. Of course, he saw that she had some reason. However you looked at it, she had more or less told him she expected him to be her lover, and he had more or less told her that he was not that sort of man, and he had a suspicion that this was an entirely new experience for Janet. She might well feel mortified.

But the worst of it was that thinking it over, he realized that even then, he had not been quite honest. In fact, he had not been honest at all. He had not told her that he already had a girl at home. He believed all he had said, but he didn't believe it quite so strongly as all that—not so as to make exceptions. Given time, he might easily have made an exception of Janet. She was the sort of girl most men made an exception of. It was the shock that had made him express himself so bluntly; the shock of realizing that a girl he cared for had been the mistress of other men. He had reacted that way more in protest against them than against her.

But the real shock had been the discovery that he cared so much what she was.

Three

They never resumed the discussion openly, on those terms at least, and it seemed at times as though Janet had forgiven him, but only just. The argument was always there beneath the surface, ready to break out again if either lost his temper. It flared up for a moment whenever she mentioned Fanny—
"I suppose one day she'll meet an Irishman, and they'll spend

the rest of their lives discussing their inhibitions." And when she mentioned other men she had known, like Bill, with whom she had spent a holiday in Dorset, and an American called Tom, with whom she had gone to the Plough in Alton, she seemed to be contrasting a joyous past with a dreary present, and became cold and insolent.

Mick, of course, gave as good as he got. He had a dirty tongue when he chose to use it, and he had considerably more ammunition than she had. The canteen was always full of gossip about who was living with whom, and whose wife (or husband) had returned and found him (or her) in bed with somebody else, and he passed it on with an air of amused contempt. The first time she said "Good!" in a ringing voice: afterwards, she contented herself with a shrug. Mick suggested helpfully that perhaps it took all those religions to deal with as many scandals, and she retorted that, no doubt, one religion would be more than enough for Ireland.

All the same, he could not help feeling that it wasn't nice. He remembered what Fanny had said about the Plough. Really, really, it wasn't nice! It seemed to show a complete lack of sensibility in Janet to bring him to a place where she had stayed with another man, and it made him suspicious of every other place she brought him.

Still, he could not do without her, nor, apparently, could she do without him. They met every evening after work, went off together on Saturday afternoons, and even went to Mass together on Sunday mornings.

As a result, before he went home on leave, everything seemed to have changed between them. She no longer made snooty remarks about Fanny's virginity and ceased to refer to Bill and Tom altogether. Indeed, from her conversation it would have been hard to detect that she had ever known such men, much less been intimate with them. Mick wondered whether it wasn't possible for a woman to be promiscuous and yet remain innocent, and decided regretfully that it wasn't. But no wife or sweetheart could have shown more devotion in the last week before his holiday, and when they went to the station together and walked arm-in-arm to the end of the long draughty platform, she was stiff with unspoken misery. She seemed to feel it was her duty to show no sign of emotion, either.

"You will come back, Mick, won't you?" she asked.

"Why?" Mick replied banteringly. "Do you think you can keep off Americans for a fortnight?"

Janet spat out a horrible word that showed only too clearly her familiarity with Americans and others. It startled and shocked Mick. It seemed that the English had strong ideas about when you could joke and when you couldn't, and this was apparently not a time for joking. To his surprise, he found her trembling all over.

At any other time he would have argued with her, but already he was, in spirit at least, halfway home. Beyond the end of the line was Cork, and meat and butter and nights of unbroken sleep. When he leaned out of the window to wave goodbye she was standing like a statue, looking curiously desolate.

He didn't reach home until the following evening. Since he had told no one of his arrival he came in an atmosphere of sensation. He shaved, and, without waiting for more than a cup of tea, set off down the road to Ina's. Ina was the youngest of a large family, and his arrival there created a sensation too. Elsie, the eldest, a fat jolly girl just home from work, shouted with laughter at him.

"He smelt the sausages!" she said.

"You can keep your old sausages," Mick said scornfully. "I'm taking Ina out to dinner."

"You're what?" asked Elsie. "You have high notions like the goats in Kerry."

"But I have to make my little brothers' supper, honey," Ina said laughingly, smoothing his hair. She was a slight, dark, radiant girl with a fund of energy.

"Tell them to make it themselves," said Mick.

"Tell them, you!" cried Elsie. "Someone should have told them years ago, the caubogues! They're thirty, and they have no more intention of marrying than of flying. Have you e'er an old job for us over there? I'm damned for want of a man."

Ina, surprised at Mick's firmness, rushed upstairs to change. Her two brothers came in, expressed astonishment at Mick's arrival, satisfaction at his promotion, incredulity at his opinion that the English were not beaten already, and consternation that their supper was not on the table. They began hammering together with their knives and forks.

"Supper up!" shouted the elder. "We can't wait all night. Where the hell is Ina?"

"Coming out to dinner with me," Mick said with a sniff, feeling that for once he was uttering a curtain line.

They called for Chris—an undersized lad with a pale face like a fist and a voice like melted butter. He expressed great pleasure at seeing them, but gave no sign of it, because it was part of Chris's line not to be impressed by anything. He had always regarded Mick as a bit of a softy because of Ina. For himself, he would never keep a girl for more than a month because it gave her ideas.

"Ah, what do you want going to town for supper for?" he drawled incredulously, as if this were only another indication that Mick was not quite right in the head. "Can't ye have it at home? 'Twon't cost ye anything."

"You didn't change much anyway," Mick said dryly. "Hurry up, or we won't get anything at all."

Next morning, in bed, Mick got a letter from Janet that must have been written while he was still on the train. She said that trying to face things without him was like trying to get used to an amputated limb: she kept on making movements before realizing that it wasn't there. At that point, Mick dropped the letter with a sigh. He wished English people wouldn't write like that. It sounded so unreal.

He wished he could remain at home, but didn't see how he could do it, without a job. Instead, he started to coax Chris into coming back with him. He knew that his position in the factory would guarantee a job for anyone who did. Besides, he had grown tired of Ina's brothers telling him how the Germans would win the war. He had never been very interested in the war or who won it, and was surprised to hear himself replying in Chris's cynical drawl, "They will, and what else?" Ina's brothers were equally surprised. They had not expected Mick to turn his coat so quickly.

"People here never seem to talk of anything only religion

and politics," he said one night to Chris as they were walking up the Western Road.

"And what better could they talk about?" asked Chris. "Damn glad you were to get back to them! You can get a night's rest anyway."

"There's no one to stop you," Mick said.

Chris stared at him, uncertain whether or not Mick meant what he seemed to mean. Like most other friends, they had developed throughout the years along a pattern of standard reaction in which Mick had played the innocent, Chris the worldly one. Now, Mick seemed to be developing out of his knowledge entirely.

"Go on!" he said with a cautious grin. "Are they as good-natured as that?"

"I didn't want to say it," said Mick modestly. "But I've the very girl for you."

"You don't say so!" Chris exclaimed, with a smile of a child who has ceased to believe in Santa Claus but likes to hear about it just the same.

"Grand-looking girl with a good job and a flat of her own," said Mick. "What more do you want?"

Chris suddenly beamed.

"I wouldn't let Ina hear me talking like that if I was you," he said. "Some of them quiet-looking girls are a terrible hand with a hatchet."

At that moment it struck Mick with cruel force how little Ina or anybody else had to reproach him with. They were passing by the college, and groups of clerks and servant girls were strolling by, whistling and calling. He was sure there wasn't another man in Ireland who would have behaved as stupidly as he had done. He remembered Janet at the railway station with her desolate air, and her letter, which he had not answered, and which, perhaps, she had really meant. A bloody fool!

Suddenly everything seemed to turn upside down on him. He was back in the bar in Alton, listening to the little group discussing the dead customer while he waited to carry the drinks out to Janet on the rustic seat in the garden, feeling that she was unreal and faithless. Now, it wasn't she who

seemed unreal, but the Western Road and the clerks and servant girls who just didn't know what they wanted. They were
a dream from which he had wakened; a dream from which he
had wakened before without even realizing that he was awake.

He was so shaken that he almost told Chris about Janet,
but he knew that Chris wouldn't understand him any more
than he had understood himself. Chris would talk sagaciously
of "damaged goods", as if there were only one way a woman
could be damaged.

"I have to go back to town, Chris," he said, stopping. "I
just remembered a telephone call I have to make."

"Fair enough," Chris said, with an understanding that surprised him. "I suppose you might as well tell her I'm coming
too."

Four

Outside, against the clear summer sky, shadowy figures moved
with pools of light at their feet and searchlights flickered like
lightning over the battlements of the castle. Chris groaned and
Mick gripped his arm confidently.

"This is nothing," he said. "Probably only a scouting plane.
You get lots of them around here. Wait till they start dropping a few wagons of high explosive!"

It was a real pleasure to Mick to hear himself talk in that
way. He seemed to have become forceful and cool all at once.
It had something to do with Chris's being there, as though
this had given his protective instincts full scope. But there was
something else as well; something he could not have believed
possible. It was almost as though he were arriving home.
Home, he felt, was a funny thing for him to think of at a time
like that.

There was no raid, so he brought Chris round to the girls'
flat, and Chris groaned again at the channel of star-shaped
traffic signals that twinkled between the black cliffs of houses,
whose bases opened so mysteriously to reveal pale stencilled
signs or caverns of smoky light.

Janet opened the door, gave one hasty, incredulous glance
at Chris, and then hurled herself at Mick. Chris opened his
eyes with a start—he later admitted to Mick that he had never

before seen a doll so quick off the mark—but Mick no longer minded what he saw. While Chris and Fanny were in the throes of starting a conversation, he followed Janet into the kitchen, where she was recklessly tossing a week's rations into the frying pan. She was hot and excited, and she used two dirty words in succession, but they did not disturb him either. He leaned against the kitchen wall with his hands in his trousers pockets and smiled at her.

"Glad to see me?" he said.

"You should try this god-damn grease!" she said, rubbing her hand.

"I'm afraid you'll find I've left my principles behind me this time," he said.

"Oh, good!" she said, not as enthusiastically as you might expect, but Mick put that down to the burn.

"What do you think of Chris?"

"A bit quiet, isn't he?" she asked doubtfully.

"Scared," said Mick with a sniff. "So would you be if your first glimpse of a country was in the middle of an alert. He'll get over that. Should we go off somewhere for the weekend?"

"Next weekend?"

"Or the one after. I don't mind."

"You are in a hurry, aren't you?"

"So would you be, too, if you'd spent a fortnight in Cork."

"And Fanny as well?"

"Why not? The more the merrier. Let's go somewhere really good. Take the bikes and make a proper tour of it. I'd like Chris to see a bit of the real country."

It certainly did make a difference, having someone else there to think for. And a fortnight later, the four of them set off on bicycles out of town. Landscape and houses gradually changed about them, and old brick and flint gave place to houses of small yellow stones, tinted with golden moss. Out of the woven pullovers of wall rose gables with coifs of tile. It all came over Mick in a rush; the company of a friend and of his girl and a country he felt he had mastered. This was what it really meant to feel at home. When the others sat on a bench outside a country public-house, Mick brought out the beer and smiled with the pride of ownership.

"Good?" he asked Chris.

"The beer isn't much, if that's what you mean," said Chris, who still specialized in not being impressed.

In the late evening they reached their destination, and dismounted in the cobbled yard of an inn where, according to Janet, Queen Elizabeth was supposed to have stayed. At either end of the dining room there was an oak dresser full of willow-ware, with silvery sauceboats on the shelves and brass pitchers on top.

"You'd want to mind your head in this hole," Chris said resentfully.

"But this place is four hundred years old, man," said Mick.

"You think in that time they'd make enough to rebuild it," said Chris.

He was still acting in character, but Mick was just a little disappointed in him. Fanny had been thrown into such a panic that she was prepared to hit it off with anybody, but Chris seemed to have lost a lot of his dash. Mick was not quite sure yet that he would not take fright before Fanny, but he would certainly do so if he knew what a blessed innocent she was. Whenever Mick looked at her, her dark sullen face broke into a wistful smile that made him think of a Christian martyr's first glimpse of the lion.

After supper Janet showed them round the town and finally led them to a pub that was on no street at all but was approached by a complicated system of alleyways. The little bar room was full, and Janet and he were crowded into the yard, and sat there on a bench in the starlight. Behind the clutter of old tiled roofs a square battlements tower rose against the sky.

"You're certain Fanny will be all right with Chris?" Janet asked anxiously.

"Oh, certain!" said Mick, wondering if his troops had opened negotiations with the enemy behind his back. "Why? Did she say anything?"

"No, but she's in a flat spin," Janet said, clucking with mother solicitude. "I've told her everything I could think of, but she's still afraid she's got it wrong. If anyone could, that damn girl will. He does understand how innocent she is, doesn't he?"

"Oh, perfectly," said Mick, feeling that his troops were already sufficiently out of hand. If Janet started giving them orders, they would undoubtedly cut and run.

Back in the bedroom, Chris was so depressed that it came almost as a relief to Mick, because he had no time to worry about himself. Then the handle of the door turned softly, and Janet tiptoed in in her bathing-wrap, her usual, competent, cool self as though arriving in men's bedrooms at that hour of night were second nature to her. "Ready, Chris?" she whispered. Chris was a lad of great principle and Mick could not help admiring his spirit. With a face like death on him he went out, and Janet cautiously closed the door behind him. Mick listened to make sure he didn't hide in the lavatory. Then Janet switched off the light, drew back the black-out curtain, and shivering slightly, opened the window on the dark inn yard.

Five

When Mick woke up and realized where he was he felt an extraordinary peace. It was as though he had laid down some heavy burden he had been carrying all his life. The pleasantest part of it was that the burden was quite unnecessary, and that he had lost nothing by laying it down.

With a clarity that seemed to be another part of his happy state, he realized that all the charm of the old town had only been a put-up job of Janet's. Clearly, she had been here already with another man. He should have known it when she took them to the pub. That, too, was her reason for choosing this pleasant old inn. She had stayed there with someone else. It was probably the American, and it might well be the same bed. Women had no interest in scenery or architecture unless they had been made love to in them, and this showed a certain amount of good sense. They brought one man there because they had been happy with another there. Happiness— that was the secret the English had and the Irish lacked.

He didn't feel quite so sure of this when he realized that what had waked him was Janet's weeping. There she was, crying quietly beside him in the bed. It alarmed him, because he knew that in his innocence he might easily have done something wrong.

"What is it, Jan?" he asked at last.

"Oh, nothing," she said, dabbing her nose viciously with her handkerchief. "Go to sleep!"

"But how can I with you like that?" he asked plaintively. "Was it something I did?"

"No, of course not, Mick. I'm just a fool, that's all."

The wretchedness in her voice made him forget his doubts of himself and think of her worries. Being a man of the world was all right, but Mick would always be more at home with other people's troubles. He put his arm round her and she sighed and threw a bare leg over him. It embarrassed him, but he reminded himself that he was now a man of the world.

"Tell me," he said as though he were talking to a child.

"Oh, it's only what you said that night at the Plough," she sobbed.

"The Plough?"

"The Plough at Alton."

Mick found it impossible to remember what he had said at the Plough, except that it was probably something silly; but he was used to the way women had of remembering things some man had said and forgotten, and which he would be glad if they had forgotten too.

"Remind me," he said.

"Oh, when you said that love was a matter of responsibility."

"Oh, yes, I remember," he said, but he didn't. What he remembered mostly was that she had more or less told him about the other men and he had been hurt and angry. Now that he was no longer hurt and angry he didn't want to be reminded of what he had said. "But you shouldn't take it so seriously, Jan."

"What else could I do but take it seriously?" she asked fiercely. "Of course I was mad with you for telling me the truth about myself, but I knew you were right. That was the way I'd always felt myself, only I blinded myself, just as you said; taking up love like a casual job I could drop when I pleased. Now I'm well paid for my bloody stupidity."

She began to sob again, bitterly. Mick felt completely lost. If only the damn situation would stay steady long enough for him to get used to it! He had felt he understood this strange country, and now he realized he hadn't understood it at all. He had accepted all it had to teach him, and now all he got for his pains was to be told that he had been right all the time, and had only made a fool of himself in changing.

"Oh, of course, that's all perfectly true, Janet, but you can take it to the fair," he said weakly. "You should see some of the things I've seen at home in the last couple of weeks." He hadn't really seen anything, and he knew he was making it up, but the warmth of his feelings made it seem as though he had seen nightmares. "People brought up to look at the physical facts of love as something inhuman and disgusting! If they must believe in some sort of nonsense, it would be better for them to believe in the fairies, as they used to do."

"Yes, but if I had a daughter, I'd prefer to bring her up like that than in the way I was brought up, Mick. At least, she'd be capable of being serious about something. What can I be serious about? I made fun of Fanny because she didn't sleep round like the rest of us, but if Fanny falls for Chris, the joke will be on me."

"You don't mean you didn't want to come, all the time?" he asked in consternation.

"It's not that," she said, beating her forehead with her fist. "But can't you see that I wanted to prove to myself that I could be a decent girl for you, and that I wasn't one of the factory janes you made fun of? All right. You're not like the others, but how am I to show you? How do you know I won't be back here with another fellow in a couple of weeks time? I wanted to give you something worth while, and now I have nothing to give you."

"I wouldn't say that, you know," Mick said in embarrassment, but he really didn't know what else to say. Clearly this was another of these extraordinary occasions when the aeroplane you had been travelling so comfortably in turned upside down, and you were hanging on to your seat for fear of going through the roof. Here he had been for a glorious hour or so, feeling himself the hell of a fellow, and now he was back where he started, a plain, dull, decent lad again. He did not want to say it, but he knew he was going to say it anyway, and he did.

"We can always get married, you know."

This threw Janet into something like convulsions, because if she did marry him she would never have the opportunity of showing him what she was really like, and it took him a long time to persuade her that he had never thought of her as anything but a serious-minded girl—most of the time, anyhow. Then she gave a deep sigh and fell asleep in the most awkward manner on his chest. Outside, the dawn was painting the old roofs and walls in the stiff artless colours of a child's paint-box. He felt a little bit lonely, a little bit sorry for himself. He knew that Chris would be furious and with good reason. As a man of the world he was a complete wash-out. He would have liked to remain a man of the world at least for a few months until it came natural to him, and he could scoff at conventions and pretensions from some sort of background of experience.

But it wasn't in his character, and you couldn't escape your character wherever you were or whatever you did. Marriage, it seemed, came more natural to him.

A Celebration of the Emotions

Ellen Goodman

THIS week, when madness came east in repeated bulletins, like weather reports of a western blizzard, something happened here at home so benign as to seem hardly newsworthy at all. Two of my closest friends had a baby.

The arrival of Julia was a personal, almost selfish pleasure, the kind that comes when another small person joins the cast of characters and enters the circle of those to care about, wonder about and watch.

But there was more than that. Talking with my friend about the specifics—the 9 pounds and 1 ounce, the 21 inches and 12 hours—it occurred to me that this birth was the only thing that had happened this week that made me celebrate the emotions. I felt again some pleasure toward—rather than simply fear and horror of—the irrational side of human nature.

You see, they were the second set of my friends to have a baby within the past month. They belong in fact to a whole category of people who have had their first children in their thirties, thereby creating a slight boom—a pop perhaps—in the birth curve. They are, as Nora Ephron ruefully described herself, "a trend."

This population is of course portrayed as a prototype of the New Planned Parents. We are told that they are the ones who waited, the ones who carefully resolved the restlessness of their youth and the direction of their careers before they had children.

In some crucial way they are regarded as the first generation to make a rational decision to have children in an era when parenting is defined as an option, even a lifestyle. These Planned Parents are the ones who weighed the claims of parenting and nonparenting. They are heralded now as the Parents of the Age of Reason.

Well, as Margaret Mead would have said, "Piffle." Piffle to the human conceit of rational childbearing. Reason may determine the timing of children and the number of children, but I think it has less to do with the decision to have a baby— before or after thirty—than with the decision to fall in love.

After all, reason is only an early warning system and a safety checklist. Rationally these new and older parents had seen more, seen every pitfall and peril of parenting among their friends. At thirty or thirty-seven, they knew the slim margins of error and the wide probability of making an error. If reason is statistical, then to any rational person, the numbers would suggest the difficulty of being better at this job than any other parent, even their own.

Reason advises people to reduce the risks of their life. Reason is cautious in the face of change. Reason cannot really imagine the depths of feeling and connection that come with childbirth, the way in which the palette of human emotions opens up from primary colors to a vast and subtle rainbow. Reason can only think of diapers.

These trendy parents, the Age of Reason people, go now into the family business in a milieu which overestimates the pains and underestimates the pleasures of children. If they were truly rational, even sensible, surely they would have remained childless.

But the fact is that after all the parent tests are taken, after all the pros and cons are calibrated, after all the timers are set, the desire for children is fundamentally and humanly that. A desire. As Nora Ephron explained her maternity, in this peer group, "I wanted to have a baby."

If it is reason that inhibits us, it is desire that impels us, and we are hardly immune to that at thirty or thirty-seven. It's desire that makes us believe that we can do it right and desire that urges us to take the risk.

What is that desire? A biological urge to reproduce? Surely

in part. But I think there is also the impulse to share in the most natural of human experiences, to find meaning in the most fundamental of human tasks and to find a connection in the most primal of human relationships.

Let others praise the rational parent. I find it peculiarly reassuring, at least in this tragic week, when Julia was born, to remember that some of our most primitive, deepest instinctual human emotions also give life.

December 1978

Holy Thursday

William Blake

'Twas on a Holy Thursday, their innocent faces clean,
The children walking two & two, in red & blue &
    green,
Grey-headed beadles walk'd before, with wands as white
    as snow,
Till into the high dome of Paul's they like Thames'
    waters flow.

O what a multitude they seem'd, these flowers of Lon-
    don town!
Seated in companies they sit with radiance all their
    own.
The hum of multitudes was there, but multitudes of
    lambs,
Thousands of little boys & girls raising their innocent
    hands.

Now like a mighty wind they raise to heaven the voice
    of song,
Or like harmonious thunderings the seats of Heaven
    among.
Beneath them sit the aged men, wise guardians of the
    poor;
Then cherish pity, lest you drive an angel from your
    door.

Holy Thursday

William Blake

Is this a holy thing to see
In a rich and fruitful land,
Babes reduc'd to misery,
Fed with cold and usurous hand?

Is that trembling cry a song?
Can it be a song of joy?
And so many children poor?
It is a land of poverty!

And their sun does never shine,
And their fields are bleak & bare,
And their ways are fill'd with thorns:
It is eternal winter there.

For where-e'er the sun does shine,
And where-e'er the rain does fall,
Babe can never hunger there,
Nor poverty the mind appall.

The Chimney Sweeper

William Blake

When my mother died I was very young,
And my father sold me while yet my tongue
Could scarcely cry " 'weep! 'weep! 'weep! 'weep!"
So your chimneys I sweep, & in soot I sleep.

There's little Tom Dacre, who cried when his head,
That curl'd like a lamb's back, was shav'd: so I said
"Hush, Tom! never mind it, for when your head's bare
You know that the soot cannot spoil your white hair."

And so he was quiet, & that very night,
As Tom was a-sleeping, he had such a sight!—
That thousands of sweepers, Dick, Joe, Ned, & Jack,
Were all of them lock'd up in coffins of black.

And by came an Angel who had a bright key,
And he open'd the coffins & set them all free;
Then down a green plain leaping, laughing, they run,
And wash in a river, and shine in the Sun.

Then naked & white, all their bags left behind,
They rise upon clouds and sport in the wind;
And the Angel told Tom, if he'd be a good boy,
He'd have God for his father, & never want joy.

And so Tom awoke; and we rose in the dark,
And got with our bags & our brushes to work.
Tho' the morning was cold, Tom was happy & warm;
So if all do their duty they need not fear harm.

The Chimney Sweeper

William Blake

A little black thing among the snow,
Crying " 'weep! 'weep!" in notes of woe!
"Where are thy father & mother? say?"
"They are both gone up to the church to pray.

"Because I was happy upon the heath,
And smil'd among the winter's snow,
They clothed me in the clothes of death,
And taught me to sing the notes of woe.

"And because I am happy & dance & sing,
They think they have done me no injury,
And are gone to praise God & his Priest & King,
Who make up a heaven of our misery."

Arms and the Boy

Wilfred Owen

Let the boy try along this bayonet-blade
How cold steel is, and keen with hunger of blood;
Blue with all malice, like a madman's flash;
And thinly drawn with famishing for flesh.

Lend him to stroke these blind, blunt bullet-leads
Which long to nuzzle in the hearts of lads,
Or give him cartridges of fine zinc teeth,
Sharp with the sharpness of grief and death.

For his teeth seem for laughing round an apple.
There lurk no claws behind his fingers supple;
And God will grow no talons at his heels,
Nor antlers through the thickness of his curls.

Picnic on the Battlefield

Fernando Arrabal

CHARACTERS

ZAPO, *a soldier*
MONSIEUR TÉPAN, *the soldier's father*
MADAME TÉPAN, *the soldier's mother*
ZÉPO, *an enemy soldier*
FIRST CORPSMAN
SECOND CORPSMAN

Scene: A battlefield. Barbed wire stretches from one end of the stage to the other, with sandbags piled against it. Battle is in full swing. We hear bombs bursting, rifle shots and machine-gun fire. Alone on stage, hidden flat on his belly among the sandbags, ZAPO is very frightened. The fighting stops. Silence. From a knitting-bag, ZAPO takes out a ball of wool, knitting needles, and starts knitting a sweater that is already quite well along. The field telephone beside him suddenly rings.

ZAPO: Hello . . . hello . . . yes, sir,
Captain. . . . Yes, this is the sentry in
Section 47. . . . Nothing new,
Captain. . . . Excuse me, Captain, when
are we going to start fighting again? . . .
And what am I supposed to do with the
grenades? Should I send them on up
front or to the rear? . . . Don't get

annoyed, I didn't say that to upset you. . . . And, Captain, I'm really feeling pretty lonesome. Couldn't you send me a companion out here? . . . Even the goat. [*Evidently the Captain gives him a good dressing down.*] Yes sir, Captain, yes sir! [ZAPO *hangs up. We hear him grumbling to himself. Silence.*]

[*Enter* MONSIEUR *and* MADAME TÉPAN, *carrying baskets as though they are off on a picnic. Their son, who is sitting with his back turned, does not see them arriving.*]

M. TÉPAN: [*ceremoniously*] My boy, get up and kiss your mother on the forehead.

[*Taken by surprise,* ZAPO *gets up and, with a great deal of respect, gives his mother a kiss on the forehead. He is about to speak, but his father beats him to it.*]

Now give *me* a kiss.

ZAPO: My dear sweet parents, how did you ever dare come all the way out to a dangerous spot like this? You must leave here right away.

M. TÉPAN: Are you trying to tell your father what war and danger are all about? For me, all this is only a game. How many times do you think I've jumped off the subway while it was still moving?

MME TÉPAN: We thought you were probably bored, so we came to pay you a little visit. After all, this war business must get pretty tiresome.

ZAPO: It all depends.

M. TÉPAN: I know perfectly well what goes on. In the beginning it's all new and exciting. You enjoy the killing and throwing grenades and wearing a helmet; it's quite the thing, but you end up bored as hell. In my day, you'd have really seen something. Wars were a lot livelier, much more colorful. And then best of all, there were horses, lots of horses. It was real pleasure: if the captain said "Attack!" before you could shake a stick we were all assembled on horseback in our red uniforms. That was something to see. And then we'd go galloping forward, sword in hand, and suddenly find ourselves hard against the enemy. And they'd be at their finest too, with their horses—there were always loads and loads of beautifully round-bottomed horses and their polished boots, and their green uniforms.

MME TÉPAN: No, the enemy uniform wasn't green. It was blue. I remember perfectly well it was blue.

M. TÉPAN: And I say it was green.

MME TÉPAN: When I was little I went out on the balcony any number of times to watch the battle, and I'd say to the little boy next door, "I'll bet you a gumdrop the Blues win." And the Blues were our enemies.

M. TÉPAN: All right, so you win.

MME TÉPAN: I always loved battles. When I was little, I always said that when I grew up I wanted to be a Colonel in the Dragoons. But Mama didn't want me to. You know what a stickler she is.

M. TÉPAN: Your mother's a real nincompoop.

ZAPO: Forgive me, but you've got to leave. You can't go walking into a war when you're not a soldier.

M. TÉPAN: I don't give a damn. We're here to have a picnic with you in the country and spend a nice Sunday.

MME TÉPAN: I even made a lovely meal. Sausage, hard-boiled eggs, I know how much you like them! Ham sandwiches, red wine, some salad and some little cakes.

ZAPO: O.K., we'll do whatever you say. But if the Captain comes along he'll throw a fit. Plus the fact that he doesn't go for the idea of visiting the battlefront. He keeps telling us: "War calls for discipline and grenades, but no visits."

M. TÉPAN: Don't you worry about it, I'll have a few words with your Captain.

ZAPO: And what if we have to start fighting again?

M. TÉPAN: You think that scares me, I've seen worse. Now if it was only cavalry battles! Times have changed, that's something you don't understand. [A pause.] We came on motorcycle. Nobody said anything.

ZAPO: They probably thought you were arbitrators.

M. TÉPAN: We did have some trouble getting through, though. With all those jeeps and tanks.

MME TÉPAN: And the very minute we arrived, you remember that bottleneck because of the cannon?

M. TÉPAN: During wartime, you've got to be prepared for anything. Everybody knows that.

MME TÉPAN: Well now, we're ready to start eating.

M. TÉPAN: Right you are, I could eat a horse. It's the smell of gunpowder that does it.

MME TÉPAN: We'll eat sitting down on the blanket.

ZAPO: All right to eat with my rifle?

MME TÉPAN: Let your rifle alone. It's bad manners to bring your rifle to the table. [A pause.] Why, child, you're filthy as a little pig. How did you manage to get in such a mess? Let's see your hands.

ZAPO: [*Ashamed, he shows them.*] I had to crawl along the ground during maneuvers.

MME TÉPAN: How about your ears?

ZAPO: I washed them this morning.

MME TÉPAN: That should do then. Now how about your teeth? [*He shows them.*] Very good. Now who's going to give his little boy a great big kiss for brushing his teeth so nicely? [*To her husband.*] Well, give your son a kiss for brushing his teeth so nicely. [M. TÉPAN *gives his son a kiss.*] Because, you know, one thing I just won't allow is not washing, and blaming it on the war.

ZAPO: Yes, Mama.
[*They eat.*]

M. TÉPAN: Well, my boy, have you been keeping up a good shooting score?

ZAPO: When?

M. TÉPAN: Why, the last few days.

ZAPO: Where?

M. TÉPAN: Right here and now. After all, you *are* fighting a war.

ZAPO: No, no great shakes. I haven't kept up a very good score. Practically no bull's-eyes.

M. TÉPAN: Well, what have you been scoring best with in your shooting, enemy horses or soldiers?

ZAPO: No, no horses. There aren't any horses any more.

M. TÉPAN: Well, soldiers then?

ZAPO: Could be.

M. TÉPAN: Could be? Aren't you sure?

ZAPO: It's just that I . . . I fire without taking aim [*a pause*] and when I fire I say an *Our Father* for the guy I shot.

M. TÉPAN: You've got to show more courage. Like your father.

MME TÉPAN: I'm going to put a record on the phonograph. [*She puts on a record: a Spanish
pasodoble. Sitting on the ground, they all
three listen.*]

M. TÉPAN: Now that's real music. Yes, ma'am. I
tell you. *Olé* !

[*As the music continues, an enemy soldier,* ZÉPO *enters. He is dressed
like* ZAPO. *Only the color of his uniform is different.* ZÉPO *wears
green;* ZAPO *wears gray. Standing unseen behind the family, his
mouth agape,* ZÉPO *listens to the music. The record comes to an end.*
ZAPO, *getting up, spots* ZÉPO. *Both raise their hands in the air,
while* M. *and* MME TÉPAN *look at them startled.*]

M. TÉPAN: What's going on?

[ZAPO *seems about to act, but hesitates. Then, very decisively, he
points his rifle at* ZÉPO.]

ZAPO: Hands up!

[ZÉPO, *more terrified than ever, raises his hands still higher.* ZAPO
doesn't know what to do. All of a sudden, he hurriedly runs toward
ZÉPO *and taps him gently on the shoulder, saying*]

ZAPO: You're it! [*Pleased as punch, to his father.*]
There you are! A prisoner!

M. TÉPAN: That's fine. Now what are you going to
do with him?

ZAPO: I don't know. But could be they'll make
me a corporal.

M. TÉPAN: In the meantime, tie him up.

ZAPO: Tie him up? What for?

M. TÉPAN: That's what you do with prisoners, you
tie 'em up!

ZAPO: How?

M. TÉPAN: By his hands.

MME TÉPAN: Oh yes, you've definitely got to tie his
hands. That's the way I've always seen it
done.

ZAPO: All right. [*To the prisoner.*] Please put
your hands together.

ZÉPO: Don't do it too hard.

ZAPO: Oh, no.

ZÉPO: Ouch! You're hurting me.

M. TÉPAN: Come on now, don't mistreat your prisoner.

MME TÉPAN: Is that the way I brought you up? Haven't I told you over and over again that you've got to be considerate of your fellow man?

ZAPO: I didn't do it on purpose. [*To* ZÉPO.] Does it hurt the way it is now?

ZÉPO: No, like this it doesn't hurt.

M. TÉPAN: Speak right up and tell him if it does. Just pretend we're not here.

ZÉPO: This way it's O.K.

M. TÉPAN: Now his feet.

ZAPO: His feet too? How long does this go on?

M. TÉPAN: Didn't they teach you the rules?

ZAPO: Sure.

M. TÉPAN: Well?

ZAPO: [*to* ZÉPO, *very politely*] Would you kindly be good enough to please sit down on the ground?

ZÉPO: All right, but don't hurt me.

MME TÉPAN: See! Now he's taking a dislike to you.

ZAPO: No. No he's not. I'm not hurting you, am I?

ZÉPO: No, this is fine.

ZAPO: [*out of nowhere*] Papa, suppose you took a snapshot with the prisoner down there on the ground and me standing with my foot on his stomach?

M. TÉPAN: Say, yes! That'll look classy.

ZÉPO: Oh, no you don't. Not that!

MME TÉPAN: Let him. Don't be so stubborn.

ZÉPO: No. I said no and mean no.

MME TÉPAN: Just a little old snip of a snapshot. What difference could that possibly make to you? Then we could put it in the dining room right next to the Lifesaving Certificate my husband got thirteen years ago.

ZÉPO: No, you'll never talk me into it.

ZAPO: But why should you refuse?

ZÉPO: I've got a fiancée. And if she ever sees the snapshot, she'll say I don't know how to fight a war.

ZAPO: No, all you have to do is tell her it isn't you at all, it's a panther.

MME TÉPAN: C'mon, say yes.

ZÉPO: All right, but I'm only doing it to please you.

ZAPO: Stretch all the way out.

[ZÉPO *stretches all the way out.* ZAPO *puts one foot on his stomach and grabs his rifle with a military air.*]

MME TÉPAN: Throw your chest out more.

ZAPO: Like this?

MME TÉPAN: Yes, that's it. Don't breathe.

M. TÉPAN: Make like a hero.

ZAPO: How do you mean a hero, like this?

M. TÉPAN: It's a cinch. Make like the butcher when he was telling us what a lady-killer he is.

ZAPO: Like so?

M. TÉPAN: Yes, that's it.

MME TÉPAN: Just be sure your chest is puffed way out, and don't breathe.

ZÉPO: Are you about finished?

M. TÉPAN: Have a little patience. One . . . two . . . three.

ZAPO: I hope I'll come out all right.

MME TÉPAN: Oh yes, you looked very military.

M. TÉPAN: You were fine.

MME TÉPAN: That makes me want to have my picture taken, too.

M. TÉPAN: Now there's a good idea.

ZAPO: All right. I'll take it if you want me to.

MME TÉPAN: Give me your helmet so I'll look like a soldier.

ZÉPO: I don't want any more pictures. Even one was too much.

ZAPO: Don't feel that way. Come right down
to it, what difference could it make?

ZÉPO: That's my final say.

M. TÉPAN: [*to his wife*] Don't push him. Prisoners
are always very touchy. If we keep it up,
he'll get mad and spoil all our fun.

ZAPO: Well now, what are we going to do with
him?

MME TÉPAN: We could ask him to eat with us. What
do you think?

M. TÉPAN: I don't see any reason why not.

ZAPO: [*to* ZÉPO] All right then, how'd you like
to eat with us?

ZÉPO: Uh . . .

M. TÉPAN: We brought along a nice bottle of wine.

ZÉPO: Well, in that case O.K.

MME TÉPAN: Make yourself right at home. Don't be
afraid to ask for things.

ZÉPO: Fine.

M. TÉPAN: Well now, how about you, have you
been keeping up a good shooting score?

ZÉPO: When?

M. TÉPAN: Why, the last few days.

ZÉPO: Where?

M. TÉPAN: Right here and now. After all, you *are*
fighting a war.

ZÉPO: No, no great shakes. I haven't kept up a
very good score. Practically no bull's-
eyes.

M. TÉPAN: Well, what have you been scoring best
with in your shooting, enemy horses
or soldiers?

ZÉPO: No, no horses. There aren't any horses
any more.

M. TÉPAN: Well, soldiers then?

ZÉPO: Could be.

M. TÉPAN: Could be? Aren't you sure?

ZÉPO: It's just that I . . . I fire without taking
aim [*a pause*] and when I fire I say a
Hail Mary for the guy I shot.

ZAPO:	A *Hail Mary?* I'd have thought you'd say an *Our Father.*
M. TÉPAN:	Come, my boy, you have to be courageous.
ZÉPO:	No. Always a *Hail Mary.* [*A pause.*] It's shorter.
MME TÉPAN:	[*to* ZÉPO] If you like, we can untie you.
ZÉPO:	No, leave me this way. It doesn't matter.
M. TÉPAN:	You're not going to start putting on airs with us? If you want us to untie you, just say the word.
MME TÉPAN:	Please feel free.
ZÉPO:	Well, if you really mean it, untie my feet. But it's just to please you people.
M. TÉPAN:	Zapo, untie him. [ZAPO *unties him.*]
MME TÉPAN:	Well now, feel better?
ZÉPO:	Sure do. But listen, maybe I'm causing you too much trouble.
M. TÉPAN:	Not at all. Make yourself right at home. And if you want us to undo your hands, just say so.
ZÉPO:	No, not my hands, too. I don't want to overdo it.
M. TÉPAN:	Not at all, my boy, not at all. I tell you, you don't disturb us one bit.
ZÉPO:	All right, go ahead and untie my hands then. But just while we eat, huh? I don't want you to think when you give me an inch I'm going to take a mile.
M. TÉPAN:	Untie his hands, sonny.
MME TÉPAN:	Well, since our honorable prisoner is so nice, we're going to have a lovely day here in the country.
ZÉPO:	Don't call me "honorable" prisoner. Just say "prisoner" plain and simple.
MME TÉPAN:	You're sure that won't make you feel bad?
ZÉPO:	No, not at all.

M. TÉPAN: Well, you're certainly unpretentious, anyway.

[*Sound of airplanes.*]

ZAPO: Airplanes. They're going to bomb us for sure.

[ZAPO *and* ZÉPO *dive for the sandbags and hide.*]

ZAPO: [*to his parents*]. Run for cover! The bombs are going to land right on you.

[*The sound of the planes drowns out everything. Immediately bombs start falling. Shells explode nearby. Deafening racket.* ZAPO *and* ZÉPO *are crouching among the sandbags.* M. TÉPAN *goes on calmly talking to his wife, who answers him with equal calm. Because of the bombardment we cannot hear their conversation.*
MME TÉPAN *heads for one of the picnic baskets, from which she takes an umbrella. She opens it. The* TÉPANS *take shelter under the umbrella as though it were raining. Standing there, they shift from one foot to the other, in rhythm, all the while discussing personal matters. The bombardment continues. At last, the airplanes take off. Silence.*
M. TÉPAN *stretches one arm out from under the umbrella to make certain there is no longer anything coming down from the sky.*]

M. TÉPAN: You can close your umbrella now.

[MME TÉPAN *closes it. Together they go over to their son and prod him on the behind a couple of times with the umbrella.*]

M. TÉPAN: All right, come on out. The bombing's over.

[ZAPO *and* ZÉPO *come out of their hiding place.*]

ZAPO: They didn't get you?
M. TÉPAN: You don't expect anything to happen to your father, do you? [*Proudly.*] Little bombs like that? Don't make me laugh.

[*From the left, a pair of Red Cross* CORPSMEN *enter, carrying a stretcher.*]

FIRST CORPSMAN:	Any bodies?
ZAPO:	No, none here.
FIRST CORPSMAN:	You're sure you took a good look?
ZAPO:	Absolutely.
FIRST CORPSMAN:	And there's not one single body?
ZAPO:	Didn't I just say so?
FIRST CORPSMAN:	Not even someone wounded?
ZAPO:	Not even.
SECOND CORPSMAN:	Well, we're really up the creek! [*To* ZAPO, *persuasively.*] Take a good look all around here, see if you don't turn up a stiff someplace.
FIRST CORPSMAN:	Don't press the issue. They told you once and for all there aren't any.
SECOND CORPSMAN:	What a lousy deal!
ZAPO:	I'm really very sorry. I swear I didn't plan it that way.
SECOND CORPSMAN:	That's what they all say. That there aren't any corpses, and that they didn't plan it that way.
FIRST CORPSMAN:	So let the man alone!
M. TÉPAN:	[*obligingly*] If we can help you at all, we'd be delighted to. At your service.
SECOND CORPSMAN:	Well, I don't know. If we keep on like this, I really don't know what the Captain's going to say to us.
M. TÉPAN:	What seems to be the trouble?
SECOND CORPSMAN:	Just that the others are all getting sore wrists carrying out the dead and wounded, while we still haven't come up with anything? And it's not because we haven't been looking.
M. TÉPAN:	I see. That really is a bore. [*To* ZAPO.] You're quite sure there are no corpses?
ZAPO:	Obviously, Papa.
M. TÉPAN:	You looked under the sandbags?
ZAPO:	Yes, Papa.
M. TÉPAN:	[*angrily*] Why don't you come right out and say you don't want to have any part in helping these good gentlemen?

FIRST CORPSMAN:	Don't jump on him like that. Leave him alone. We'll just hope we have better luck in some other trench where maybe everybody'll be dead.
M. TÉPAN:	I'd be delighted for you.
MME TÉPAN:	So would I. Nothing pleases me more than to see people who take their work seriously.
M. TÉPAN:	[*indignantly, to anyone within hearing*]. Well, isn't anyone going to do anything for these gentlemen?
ZAPO:	If it was up to me, it'd be good as done.
ZÉPO:	Same here.
M. TÉPAN:	Look here now, isn't one of you at least wounded?
ZAPO:	[*ashamed*]. No, not me.
M. TÉPAN:	[*to* ZÉPO] What about you?
ZÉPO:	[*ashamed*] Me either. I never was lucky.
MME TÉPAN:	[*delighted*] I just remembered! This morning, while I was peeling onions, I cut my finger. How's that?
M. TÉPAN:	Why of course! [*Really in the swing of things.*] They'll put you on the stretcher and carry you right off!
FIRST CORPSMAN:	Sorry, it's no good. Women don't count.
M. TÉPAN:	Well, that didn't get us anywhere.
FIRST CORPSMAN:	It doesn't matter.
SECOND CORPSMAN:	Maybe we can get our fill in the other trenches. [*They start to go off.*]
M. TÉPAN:	Don't you worry, if we find a corpse, we'll hang onto it for you. There's not a chance we'd give it to anybody but you.
SECOND CORPSMAN:	Thank you very much, sir.
M. TÉPAN:	It's nothing, my boy. It's the very least I could do.

[*The* CORPSMEN *make their goodbyes. All four of the others reply in kind. The* CORPSMEN *exit.*]

MME TÉPAN:	That's what's so pleasant about spending Sunday out in the battlefield. You always

run into such nice folks. [*A pause.*] Come to think of it, why is it you're enemies?

ZÉPO: I don't know. I'm not too well educated.

MME TÉPAN: I mean is it from birth, or did you become enemies after?

ZÉPO: I don't know. I don't know a thing about it.

M. TÉPAN: Well then, how did you come to go to war?

ZÉPO: One day I was home fixing my mother's iron and a man came by and said to me: "Are you Zépo?" . . . "Yes." . . . "Good, you've got to go to war." So I asked him, "What war?" And he said to me: "Don't you read the newspapers? You are a hick!" So I told him yes I did, but not all that war stuff . . .

ZAPO: That's just what happened to me; exactly what happened to me.

M. TÉPAN: Sure, they came after you, too.

MME TÉPAN: No, it's not the same. You weren't fixing the iron that day, you were repairing the car.

M. TÉPAN: I was talking about the rest of it. [*To* ZÉPO]. Go on. Then what happened?

ZÉPO: Well, then I told him that I had a fiancée, and if I didn't take her to the movies on Sunday, she wouldn't know what to do with herself. He said that that didn't matter.

ZAPO: Same as me. Exactly the same as me.

ZÉPO: Well, then my father came down and he said I couldn't go to war because I didn't have a horse.

ZAPO: Like my father said.

ZÉPO: The man said they didn't use horses any more, and I asked him if I could take along my fiancée. He said no. Then I asked him could I take along my aunt to

	make me custard every Thursday. I like custard.
MME TÉPAN:	[*realizing that she has forgotten something*]. Oh! The custard!
ZÉPO:	Again he said no.
ZAPO:	The way he did to me.
ZÉPO:	And ever since then, here I am, nearly always all alone in the trench here.
MME TÉPAN:	As long as you're so much alike, and both so bored, I think you and your honorable prisoner might play together this afternoon.
ZAPO:	Oh no, Mama! I'm too scared. He's an enemy.
M. TÉPAN:	Oh come on now, don't be scared.
ZAPO:	If you knew what the general told us about the enemy.
MME TÉPAN:	What did he tell you?
ZAPO:	He said the enemy soldiers are very mean. When they take prisoners, they put pebbles in their socks so it hurts when they walk.
MME TÉPAN:	How horrible! What savages!
M. TÉPAN:	[*indignantly, to* ZÉPO] Aren't you ashamed to be part of an army of criminals?
ZÉPO:	I didn't do anything. I'm not mad at anybody.
MME TÉPAN:	He's trying to put one over on us, acting like a little saint.
M. TÉPAN:	We should never have untied him. Probably all we have to do is have our backs turned for him to go putting pebbles in our socks.
ZÉPO:	Don't be so mean to me.
M. TÉPAN:	How do you expect us to be? I'm shocked. I know just what I'm going to do. I'm going to find the Captain and ask him to let me go into battle.

ZAPO: He won't let you. You're too old.

M. TÉPAN: Well then I'll go buy a horse and a saber and I'll go to war on my own.

ZÉPO: Please, madame, don't treat me like this. Besides, I was just going to tell you, *our* general said the same thing about you people.

MME TÉPAN: How could he dare tell such a lie?

ZAPO: The very same thing, honest?

ZÉPO: Yes, the very same thing.

M. TÉPAN: Maybe it's the same one who talked to both of you.

MME TÉPAN: Well, if it is the same general, the least he could do is use a different speech. Imagine telling everybody the same thing.

M. TÉPAN: [*to* ZÉPO, *changing his tone*] Can I fill your glass again?

MME TÉPAN: I hope you enjoyed our little lunch.

M. TÉPAN: It was better than Sunday, anyway.

ZÉPO: What happened then?

M. TÉPAN: Well, we went out to the country and laid all our chow out on the blanket. While we had our backs turned, a cow came along and ate the whole lunch, including the napkins.

ZÉPO: What a glutton, that cow!

M. TÉPAN: Yes, but then to get even, we ate the cow.
[*They laugh.*]

ZAPO: [*to* ZÉPO] I bet they weren't hungry after that.

M. TÉPAN: To your health!
[*They all drink.*]

MME TÉPAN: [*to* ZÉPO] Tell me something, what do you do for amusement in the trenches?

ZÉPO: Just to pass the time and keep myself amused, I take odds and ends of rags and make little flowers out of them. See, I get bored a lot.

MME TÉPAN:	And what do you do with these rag flowers?
ZÉPO:	At first I used to send them to my fiancée, but one day she told me that the cellar and the greenhouse were already filled with them, that she didn't know what to do with them any more, and would I mind sending her something else for a change?
MME TÉPAN:	And what did you do?
ZÉPO:	I tried learning something else, but I couldn't do it. So, to pass the time, I just go on making my rag flowers.
MME TÉPAN:	And then do you throw them away?
ZÉPO:	No, now I've found a way to make use of them: I furnish one flower for each of my buddies who dies. That way, I know that even if I make a whole lot, there'll never be enough.
M. TÉPAN:	You found a good way out.
ZÉPO:	[timidly] Yes.
ZAPO:	Well, you know what I do so's not to get bored is knit.
MME TÉPAN:	But tell me, do all the soldiers get bored the way you two do?
ZÉPO:	That depends on what they do for relaxation.
ZAPO:	Same thing over on our side.
M. TÉPAN:	Well then, let's stop the war.
ZÉPO:	But how?
M. TÉPAN:	Very easy. You tell your buddies that the enemy doesn't want to fight, and you tell the same thing to your comrades. And everybody goes home.
ZAPO:	Terrific.
MME TÉPAN:	That way you can finish fixing the iron.
ZAPO:	How come nobody ever thought of that before?
MME TÉPAN:	It takes your father to come up with ideas like that. Don't forget he's a

	Normal School graduate, and a philatelist, too.
ZÉPO:	But what will all the field-marshals and the corporals do?
M. TÉPAN:	We'll give 'em guitars and castanets to keep 'em quiet.
ZÉPO:	Excellent idea.
M. TÉPAN:	See how easy it is? It's all settled.
ZÉPO:	We'll wow 'em.
ZAPO:	Boy, will my buddies be glad!
MME TÉPAN:	What do you say we celebrate and put on that pasodoble we were listening to before?
ZÉPO:	Wonderful!
ZAPO:	Yes, put on the record, Mama.

[MME TÉPAN *puts on the record. She winds the phonograph and waits. Not a sound is heard.*]

M. TÉPAN:	You can't hear anything.
MME TÉPAN:	[*going to the phonograph*] Oh! . . . I made a boo-boo! Instead of putting on a record, I put on a beret.

[*She puts the record on. A lively pasodoble is heard.* ZAPO *dances with* ZÉPO; MME TÉPAN *with her husband.*
The field telephone rings. None of the group hears it. They go on dancing in a lively manner.
The phone rings again. The dancing continues. Battle breaks out once more with a great din of bombs, rifle fire and the crackle of machine-guns. Having noticed nothing, the two couples keep on dancing gaily. A sudden machine-gun blast mows them all down. They fall to the ground, stone dead. One bullet seems to have nicked the phonograph: the music keeps repeating the same strain over and over, like a record with a scratch in it. We hear this repeated strain for the remainder of the play.
From the left, the two CORPSMEN *enter, carrying the empty stretcher.*]

FAST CURTAIN

From Dakto to Detroit: Death of a Troubled Hero

Jon Nordheimer

A FEW tenants living in the E. J. Jeffries Homes, a dreary public housing project in Corktown, an old Detroit neighborhood, can still remember Dwight Johnson as a little boy who lived in one of the rust-brown buildings with his mother and baby brother. They think it strange, after all that has happened to Dwight, to remember him as a gentle boy who hated to fight.

Dwight Johnson died one week from his 24th birthday, shot and killed as he tried to rob a grocery store a mile from his home. The store manager later told the police that a tall Negro had walked in shortly before midnight, drawn a revolver out of his topcoat and demanded money from the cash register.

The manager pulled his own pistol from under the counter and the two men struggled. Seven shots were fired.

Four and one-half hours later, on an operating table at Detroit General Hospital, Dwight (Skip) Johnson died from five gunshot wounds.

Ordinarily, the case would have been closed right there, a routine crime in a city where there were 13,583 armed robberies last year.

But when the detectives went through the dead man's wallet for identification, they found a small white card with its edges rubbed thin from wear. "Congressional Medal of Honor Society

—United States of America," it said. "This certifies that Dwight H. Johnson is a member of this society."

The news of the death of Sergeant Dwight Johnson shocked the black community of Detroit. Born out of wedlock when his mother was a teenager and raised on public welfare, he had been the good boy on his block in the dreary housing project, an altar boy and Explorer Scout, one of the few among the thousands of poor black youngsters in Detroit who had struggled against the grinding life of the ghetto and broken free, coming home from Vietnam tall and strong and a hero.

The story of Dwight Johnson and his drift from hero in Dakto, Vietnam, to villain in Detroit is a difficult one to trace. The moments of revelation are rare. There were, of course, those two brief episodes that fixed public attention on him: 30 minutes of "uncommon valor" one cold morning in combat that earned him the nation's highest military decoration, and the 30-second confrontation in the Detroit grocery that ended his life.

Oddly, they are moments of extreme violence, and everyone who knew Dwight Johnson—or thought he did—knew he was not a violent man.

Now that the funeral is over and the out-of-town relatives have gone home and the family conferences that sought clues to explain Dwight's odd behavior have ended in bitter confusion, his mother can sit back and talk wistfully about the days when Skip was a skinny kid who was chased home after school by the Corktown bullies.

"Mama," he would ask, "what do I do if they catch me?" His mother would place an arm around his thin shoulders and draw him close. "Skip," she would say, "don't you fight, honey, and don't let them catch you." The boy would look downcast and worried. "Yes, Mama," he'd say.

"Dwight was a fabulous, all-around guy, bright and with a great sense of humor," reflected Barry Davis, an auburn-haired Californian who flew with his wife to Detroit when he heard on a news report that Dwight had been killed. Three others who had served with him in Vietnam, all of them white, also came, not understanding what aberration had led to his death.

"I can remember our first day at Fort Knox and Dwight was the only colored guy in our platoon," Barry Davis recalled.

"So we're in formation and this wise guy from New Jersey says to Dwight, 'Hey, what's the initials N.A.A.C.P. stand for?'

"And Dwight says, 'The National Association for the Advancement of Colored People.'

"And this wise guy from New Jersey says, 'Naw, that ain't it. It stands for Niggers Acting As Colored People.'

"And I said to myself, 'Wow, those are fighting words,' but Dwight just laughed. From then on he was just one of the guys. As it turned out, Dwight liked this wise guy from New Jersey in the end as much as he liked anybody."

Most of the men who served with Sergeant Dwight Johnson remembered him that way—easy-going, hard to rattle, impossible to anger.

But Stan Enders remembers him another way. Stan was the gunner in Skip's tank that morning in Vietnam three years ago, during the fighting at Dakto.

"No one who was there could ever forget the sight of this guy taking on a whole battalion of North Vietnamese soldiers," Stan said as he stood in the sunshine outside Faith Memorial Church in Corktown three weeks ago, waiting for Skip's funeral service to begin.

Their platoon of four M-48 tanks was racing down a road toward Dakto, in the Central Highlands near the Cambodian border and the Ho Chi Minh Trail, when it was ambushed. Communist rockets knocked out two of the tanks immediately, and waves of foot soldiers sprang out of the nearby woods to attack the two tanks still in commission.

Skip hoisted himself out of the turret hatch and manned the mounted .50-caliber machine gun. He had been assigned to this tank only the night before. His old tank, and the crew he had spent 11 months and 22 days with in Vietnam and had never seen action before, was 60 feet away, burning.

"He was really close to those guys in that tank," Stan said. "He just couldn't sit still and watch it burn with them inside."

Skip ran through heavy crossfire to the tank and opened its hatch. He pulled out the first man he came across in the turret, burned but still alive, and got him to the ground just as the tank's artillery shells exploded, killing everyone left inside.

"When the tank blew up Dwight saw the bodies all burned and black, well, he just sort of cracked up," said Stan.

For 30 minutes, armed first with a .45-caliber pistol and then with a submachine gun, Skip hunted the Vietnamese on the ground, killing from five to 20 enemy soldiers, nobody knows for sure. When he ran out of ammunition, he killed one with the stock of the machine gun.

At one point he came face to face with a Communist soldier who squeezed the trigger on his weapon aimed pointblank at him. The gun misfired and Skip killed him. But the soldier would come back to haunt him late at night in Detroit, in those dreams in which that anonymous soldier stood in front of him, the barrel of his AK-47 as big as a railroad tunnel, his finger on the trigger, slowly pressing it.

"When it was all over," Stan said, walking up the church steps as the funeral service got under way, "it took three men and three shots of morphine to hold Dwight down. He was raving. He tried to kill the prisoners we had rounded up. They took him away to a hospital in Pleiku in a straight-jacket."

Stan saw Skip the next day. He had been released from the hospital, and came by to pick up his personal gear. His Vietnam tour was over and he was going home.

No one there would know anything about Dakto until 10 months later, at the White House Medal of Honor Ceremony.

Sergeant Johnson returned home in early 1968, outwardly only little changed from the quiet boy named Skip who had grown up in Detroit and been drafted. Even when he and other black veterans came home and could not find a job, he seemed to take it in stride.

He had been discharged with $600 in his pocket, and it was enough to buy cigarettes and go out at night with his cousin, Tommy Tillman, and with Eddie Wright, a friend from the Jefferies Homes, and make the rounds to the Shadowbox or the Little Egypt, to drink a little beer and have a few dates.

And at home no one knew about the bad dreams he was having. They would have to learn about that later from an Army psychiatrist.

If anyone asked him about Vietnam, he would just shake his head, or laugh and say, "Aw, man, nothing happened," and he would change the subject and talk about the girls in Kuala Lumpur where he went for R and R, or the three-day pass he spent in Louisville, Ky., drinking too much whisky for the first time in his life and ending up in jail.

He returned home just as the Communist Tet offensive erupted in Vietnam, and everyone talked about how lucky he had been to get out before things got hot. They teased him then about his lackluster military career.

"When he came home from Vietnam he was different, sure, I noticed it, all jumpy and nervous and he had to be doing something all the time, it seems," said Eddie Wright. "But mostly he was the same fun-time guy."

Carmen Berry, a close friend of Katrina May, the girl Skip started dating after his discharge, thought she detected nuances of change she attributed to the same mental letdown she had seen in other Vietnam veterans.

"They get quiet," she said, "It's like they don't have too much to say about what it was like over there. Maybe it's because they've killed people and they don't really know why they killed them."

"The only thing that bugged me about Skip then," reflected his cousin Tommy, "and the one thing I thought was kind of strange and unlike him, was the pictures he brought back. He had a stack of pictures of dead people, you know, dead Vietnamese. Color slides."

In the fall he started looking for a job, along with Tommy Tillman.

"We'd go down to the state employment agency every day and take a look at what was listed," his cousin recalled. "Skip was funny; he wouldn't try for any of the hard jobs. If we wrote down the name of a company that had a job that he didn't feel qualified for, he wouldn't even go into the place to ask about it. He'd just sit in the car while I went in.

"Or if he did go in someplace, he'd just sit and mumble a few words when they'd ask him questions. It was like he felt inferior. He'd give a terrible impression. But once we got back in the car, it was the same old Skip, laughing and joking."

One day in October two military policemen came to his house. His mother saw the uniforms and before opening the door whispered urgently, "What did you do?"

"I didn't do nothing, honest, Ma," he answered.

The M.P.'s asked Skip a few questions. They wanted to know what he was doing and if he had been arrested since his discharge. Fifteen minutes after they left, the telephone rang. It was a colonel, calling from the Department of Defense in Washington. Sergeant Johnson was being awarded the Medal of Honor, he said. Could he and his family be in Washington on November 19 so President Johnson could personally present the award?

One week later, on November 19, 1968, they were all there in the White House, Skip tall and handsome in his dress-blue uniform, his mother, Katrina and Tommy Tillman. The President gave a little speech. The national election was over, the Democrats had lost, but there were signs of movement at the Paris peace talks.

> "Our hearts and our hopes are turned to peace as we assemble here in the East Room this morning," the President said. "All our efforts are being bent in its pursuit. But in this company we hear again, in our minds, the sound of distant battles."

Five men received the Medal of Honor that morning. And when Sergeant Johnson stepped stiffly forward and the President looped the pale blue ribbon and sunburst medal around his neck, a citation was read that described his valor.

Later, in the receiving line, when his mother reached Skip, she saw tears streaming down his face.

"Honey," she whispered, "what are you crying about? You've made it back."

After he officially became a hero, it seemed that everyone in Detroit wanted to hire Dwight Johnson, the only living Medal of Honor winner in Michigan. Companies that had not been interested in a diffident ex-G.I. named Johnson suddenly found openings for Medal of Honor Winner Johnson.

Among those who wanted him was the United States Army.

"The brass wanted him in the Detroit recruiting office because—let's face it—here was a black Medal of Honor winner, and blacks are our biggest manpower pool in Detroit," said an Army employee who had worked with Skip after he rejoined the service a month after winning the medal. "Personally, I think a lot of promises were made to the guy that couldn't be kept. You got to remember that getting this guy back into the Army was a feather in the cap of a lot of people."

Events began moving quickly then for Skip. He married Katrina in January (the Pontchartrain Hotel gave the couple its bridal suite for their wedding night), and the newlyweds went to Washington in January as guests at the Nixon inaugural. Sergeant Johnson began a long series of personal appearances across Michigan in a public relations campaign mapped by the Army.

In February, 1,500 persons paid $10 a plate to attend a testimonial dinner for the hero in Detroit's Cobo Hall, co-sponsored by the Ford Motor Company and the Chamber of Commerce. A special guest was General William C. Westmoreland, Army Chief of Staff and former commander of United States forces in Vietnam.

"Dwight was a hot property back in those days," recalled Charles Bielak, a civilian information officer for the Army's recruiting operations in Detroit. "I was getting calls for him all over the state. Of course, all this clamor didn't last. It reached a saturation point somewhere along the way and tapered off."

But while it lasted, Skip's life was frenetic. Lions Clubs . . . Rotary . . . American Legion. Detroit had a new hero. Tiger Stadium and meet the players. Sit at the dais with the white politicians. Be hailed by the black businessmen who would not have bothered to shake his hand before. Learn which fork to use for the salad. Say something intelligent to the reporters. Pick up the check for dinner for friends. Live like a man who had it made.

But Leroy May, the hero's father-in-law, could still see the child behind the man.

"Dwight and Katrina were a perfect match—they both had a lot of growing up to do," he said. "They didn't know how to handle all the attention they got in those early days. They'd go out to supper so much Katrina complained she couldn't eat any more steak. I had to take them out and buy them hot dogs and soda pop. They were just like a couple of kids."

Bills started piling up. "They were in over their heads as soon as they were married," Mr. May said.

Everyone extended credit to the Medal of Honor winner. Even when he bought the wedding ring, the jeweler would not take a down payment. Take money from a hero? Not then.

Later, the Johnsons discovered credit cards.

At first they lived in an $85-a-month apartment. But Katrina wanted a house. Skip signed a mortgage on a $16,000 house on the west side of Detroit. Monthly payments were $160.

In the spring of 1970, he wrote a bad check for $41.77 at a local market. The check was made good by a black leader in Detroit who was aghast that the Medal of Honor winner had gotten himself into a financial hole.

"I went to see him and told him he couldn't go on like this," said the man, a lawyer who asked to remain anonymous. "I said he was young and black and had the Medal of Honor. He could do anything he wanted. I tried to get him to think about college and law school. The black businessmen would pick up the tab. He wouldn't have any part of it."

Looking back on this meeting, the lawyer said he suspected Skip was burdened by a "ghetto mentality" that limited his horizons. His world had been a public housing project and schools a few blocks away. Now, suddenly, events had thrust him outside the security of his boyhood neighborhood into a world dominated by whites.

He was paralyzed, the lawyer speculated, by an inability to formulate a plan of action in this alien culture that he had been transported to by something that happened on the other side of the globe.

"What does he do when he's introduced to Bunkie Knudsen, the president of Ford?" asked the lawyer. "Does he come across strong and dynamic because he knows there is a $75,000-a-year job waiting for him if he makes a good impression? And what happens to him when he just stands there and fumbles and doesn't know if he should shake hands or just nod his head? He was forced to play a role he was never trained for and never anticipated."

Tommy Tillman remembers how Skip would take several friends downtown to the Pontchartrain Hotel for an expensive meal and sit fumbling with the silverware, watching the others to see what fork to use first. "I'd say to him, 'Shoot, man, what do you care? Go ahead and use anything you want.'

"I wondered how he must feel when he's the guest of honor at one of those fancy meetings he was all the time going to."

It was about this time that the stomach pains started.

"It was all that rich food he was eating," said his father-in-law. His mother recalled that "Skip always did have a nervous stomach."

He began staying away from his job as a recruiter, missed appointments and speaking engagements. "It got so bad I had to pick him up myself and deliver him to a public appearance," said Mr. Bielak. "I had to handcuff myself to the guy to get him someplace. It was embarrassing. I couldn't understand his attitude."

Last summer it was decided that Sergeant Johnson should report to Selfridge Air Force Base, not far from Detroit, for diagnosis of stomach complaints.

From Selfridge he was sent in September to Valley Forge Army Hospital in Pennsylvania. An Army psychiatrist later mulled over his notes on the patient and talked about them.

> Maalox and bland diet prescribed. G.I. series conducted. Results negative. Subject given 30-day convalescent leave 16 October 1970. Absent without leave until 21 January 1971 when subject returned to Army hospital on own volition. Subsequent hearing recommended dismissal of A.W.O.L. charge and back pay reinstated. Subject agreed to undergo psychiatric evaluation. In cognizance of subject's outstanding record in Vietnam, the division's chief psychiatrist placed in charge of the case. Preliminary analysis: Depression caused by post-Vietnam adjustment problem.

In February, Eddie Wright bumped into Skip on a Detroit street.

"Hey, man, where've you been?"

"I just got out of Valley Forge on a pass."

"How things going there?"

"They got me in the psycho ward."

"Huh, you got to be kidding."

"No, man, they think I'm crazy."

During the convalescent leave, Sergeant Johnson borrowed $4,992 from a Detroit credit union. In his wallet he had a cashier's check for $1,500, the back pay the Army had awarded him. Most of his time he spent at home on the pass but when he went out he would drive to the Jeffries Homes and play basketball with the teenagers after school.

"He was a big man down there with the kids," recalled his cousin. "We had all lived in the project and had been on welfare, just like these kids there today, and we were like heroes because we had broken out of there. We had made it to the outside world, and to them we were big successes. We had made it.

"Skip was something special. He had that medal, and they were proud of him. He'd be down there five minutes and the kids would come around and say, 'Hey man, ain't you Dwight Johnson?' "

Back in Detroit on leave on one occasion, his mother asked him to drive her to a doctor's appointment. In the office, an off-duty black Detroit policeman, Ronald Turner, recognized the Medal of Honor winner. When he asked for an account of his experience in Vietnam, Skip replied: "Don't ask me anything about the medal. I don't even know how I won it."

Later, the policeman reported, Skip complained that he had been exploited by the Army. He told him that ever since he won the medal he had been set on a hero's path as an inspiration to black kids.

Others recalled how upset he had become when his recruiting talks at some black high schools in Detroit had been picketed by militants who called him an "electronic nigger," a robot the Army was using to recruit blacks for a war in Asia.

With his psychiatrist, he began to discuss his deeper anxieties.

> Since coming home from Vietnam the subject has had bad dreams. He didn't confide in his mother or wife, but entertained a lot of moral judgment as to what had happened at Dakto. Why had he been ordered to switch tanks the night before? Why was he spared and not the others? He experienced guilt about his survival. He wondered if he was sane. It made him sad and depressed.

Skip signed out of the hospital on March 28 on a three-day pass to Philadelphia. The next day the newspapers and television were filled with reports of the conviction of First Lieut. William L. Calley, Jr., on charges of murdering Vietnamese civilians. Skip turned up in Detroit a few days later and never returned to the Army hospital.

He settled in at home once again and dodged the telephone calls from the Army.

"How can you take punitive action against a Medal of Honor holder?" asked a major at the hospital who tried to convince him to return.

The Army did contact the Ford Motor Company, however, which had been letting Skip use a Thunderbird for the past two years. Ford picked up the car on the theory that without it he might be inconvenienced enough to return to the hospital. Instead, he cashed the cashier's check for $1,500, his Army back pay, and bought a 1967 Mercury for $850. He changed his unlisted phone number to avoid the Army callers and a growing number of bill collectors.

By April, his house mortgage had not been paid for the previous nine months, and foreclosing proceedings had been started. He owed payments on his credit union loan.

The car had to go into a garage for brake repairs on Wednesday, April 28, and Skip was told that it would cost $78.50 to get it out. The same day, Katrina entered a hospital for removal of an infected cyst, and he told the admitting office clerk he would pay the $25 deposit the next day.

His old high school crowd was concerned about some of his new friends, though. "They were strung out on drugs, and they just seemed to be hanging around Skip for his money," said his mother. "I asked him one night if he was taking anything, and he rolled up his sleeves and showed me there were no tracks [needle marks]. 'Ma,' he said, 'I'm not taking a thing.' "

On his return to the hospital, he began analysis with the chief attending psychiatrist.

Subject is bright. His Army G.T. rating is equivalent of 120 I.Q. In first interviews he does not volunteer information. He related he grew up in a Detroit ghetto and never knew his natural father. He sort of laughed when he said he was a "good boy" and did what was expected of him. The only time he can remember losing his temper as a youth was when neighborhood bullies picked on his younger brother. He was so incensed grownups had to drag him off the other boys. In general, there is evidence the subject learned to live up to the expectations of others while there was a build-up of anger he continually suppressed.

The Army hospital is actually in Phoenixville, Pa., several miles from Valley Forge. It is the principal treatment center for psychiatric and orthopedic patients in the Northeast, with 1,200 beds now occupied.

Because of the large number of amputees and wheelchair patients, the hospital has only two floors and is spread over several acres. Long oak-floored corridors run in all directions, connected by covered walkways and arcades. Someone once measured the hospital and found there were seven miles of corridors in a maze-like jumble. To prevent patients from losing their way, wards are painted different colors.

Dressed in hospital blue denims, the warrior-hero walked the labyrinth late at night, wrestling with the problems that tormented his mind and drained his spirit.

"The first day Dwight arrived here, the hospital's sergeant major brought him to us," said Spec. 6 Herman Avery, a tall Negro with a flat face and close-set eyes, who was master of the ward Dwight was first assigned to at the hospital. "It was the first time the sergeant major ever did that. We got the message. This guy was something special.

"Well, practically the first night he's here they dress him up and take him over to the Freedoms Foundation in Valley Forge to shake hands. When he got back he told me that if they ever did that again he would go A.W.O.L."

There was further psychiatric evaluation.

> Subject expressed doubts over his decision to re-enter the Army as a recruiter. He felt the Army didn't honor its commitment to him. The public affairs were satisfactory to him at first, but he started to feel inadequate. People he would meet would pump his hand and slap his back and say, "Johnson, if you ever think about getting out of the Army, come look me up." On several occasions he contacted these individuals and they didn't remember him. It always took several minutes to remind them who he was.

Lonely and depressed at home, Skip telephoned his cousin. "Let's go out and grab some beers," he said. But his cousin was busy.

He made another phone call that night and spoke to a friend in the Army. "I have a story I'm writing and I want you to peddle it for me," he said. "It starts out like this:

"Sgt. Dwight Johnson is dead and his home has been wiped out . . . "

On April 30, Skip visited Katrina at the hospital. She said they were asking about the hospital deposit. He left at 5:30, promising to return later that evening with her hair curlers and bathrobe.

"He was just the same old Dwight, just kidding and teasing," his wife recalled. "When he was going, he said, 'Ain't you going to give me a little kiss good-by?' He said it like a little boy with his thumb in his mouth. So I kissed him and he went."

When Eddie Wright got home from work that night about 9 o'clock, he got a call from Skip. He said he needed a ride to pick up some money someone owed him and wanted to know if Eddie could get his stepfather to drive him. He said he would pay $15 for the ride.

Around 11 o'clock, Eddie, his mother and his stepfather picked up Skip at his home. At his direction they drove west for about a mile to the corner of Orangelawn and Prest.

"Stop here," Skip told him, getting out of the car. "This guy lives down the street and I don't want him to see me coming."

The family waited in the car for 30 minutes. They became nervous, parked in a white neighborhood, and as Eddie explained later to the police, it may have looked odd for a car filled with blacks to be parked on a dark street. "So we pulled the car out under a street light so everybody could see us," he said.

At about 11:45 a police car pulled up sharply and two officers with drawn pistols got out. "What are you doing here?" they asked.

"We're waiting for a friend."

"What his name?"

"Dwight Johnson."

"Dwight Johnson's on the floor of a grocery store around the corner," the officers said. "He's been shot."

"I first hit him with two bullets," the manager, Charles Landeghem, said later. "But he just stood there, with the gun in his hand, and said, 'I'm going to kill you . . . '

"I kept pulling the trigger until my gun was empty."
Skip's psychiatrist recalled one of the interviews with him.

> The subject remembered coming face to face with a Viet-
> namese with a gun. He can remember the soldier squeez-
> ing the trigger. The gun jammed. The subject has since
> engaged in some magical thinking about this episode. He
> also suffers guilt over surviving it and later winning a high
> honor for the one time in his life when he lost complete
> control of himself. He asked: "What would happen if I lost
> control of myself in Detroit and behaved like I did in Viet-
> nam?" The prospect of such an event apparently was deeply
> disturbing to him.

The burial at Arlington National Cemetery took place on a
muggy and overcast day. The grave, on a grassy slope about
200 yards east of the Kennedy Memorial, overlooks the Poto-
mac and the Pentagon, gray and silent, to the south.

The Army honor guard, in dress blues, carried out its
assignment with precision, the sixth burial of the day for the
eight-man unit, while tourists took photographs at a discreet
distance from the grieving family.

For a few days after the burial, the family weighed the
possibility that Skip had been taking narcotics in the last few
months of his life and the demands of drugs had sent him into
the grocery store with a gun. But the autopsy turned up no
trace of narcotics.

Eddie Wright and his family were released by homicide
detectives after questioning, even after Eddie could not produce
any plausible reason why his best friend had carried out a
bizarre crime and implicated him at the same time.

The dead man's mother was the only one who uttered the
words that no one else dared to speak.

"Sometimes I wonder if Skip tired of this life and needed
someone else to pull the trigger," she said late one night in
the living room of her home, her eyes fixed on a large color
photograph of her son, handsome in his uniform, with the pale
blue ribbon of his country's highest military honor around his
neck.

My Father

Doris Lessing

WE use our parents like recurring dreams, to be entered into when needed; they are always there for love or for hate; but it occurs to me that I was not always there for my father. I've written about him before, but novels, stories, don't have to be "true." Writing this article is difficult because it has to be "true." I knew him when his best years were over.

There are photographs of him. The largest is of an officer in the 1914–18 war. A new uniform—buttoned, badged, strapped, tabbed—confines a handsome, dark young man who holds himself stiffly to confront what he certainly thought of as his duty. His eyes are steady, serious, and responsible, and show no signs of what he became later. A photograph at sixteen is of a dark, introspective youth with the same intent eyes. But it is his mouth you notice—a heavily-jutting upper lip contradicts the rest of a regular face. His moustache was to hide it: "Had to do something—a damned fleshy mouth. Always made me uncomfortable, that mouth of mine."

Earlier a baby (eyes already alert) appears in a lace waterfall that cascades from the pillowy bosom of a fat, plain woman to her feet. It is the face of a head cook. "Lord, but my mother was a practical female—almost as bad as you!" as he used to say, or throw at my mother in moments of exasperation. Beside her stands, or droops, arms dangling, his father, the source of the dark, arresting eyes, but otherwise masked by a long beard.

The birth certificate says: Born 3rd August, 1886, Walton Villa, Creffield Road, S. Mary at the Wall, R.S.D. Name, Alfred Cook. Name and surname of Father: Alfred Cook Tayler. Name and maiden name of Mother: Caroline May Batley. Rank or Profession: Bank Clerk. Colchester, Essex.

They were very poor. Clothes and boots were a problem. They "made their own amusements." Books were mostly the Bible and *The Pilgrim's Progress*. Every Saturday night they bathed in a hip-bath in front of the kitchen fire. No servants. Church three times on Sundays. "Lord, when I think of those Sundays! I dreaded them all week, like a nightmare coming at you full tilt and no escape." But he rabbited with ferrets along the lanes and fields, bird-nested, stole fruit, picked nuts and mushrooms, paid visits to the blacksmith and the mill and rode a farmer's carthorse.

They ate economically, but when he got diabetes in his forties and subsisted on lean meat and lettuce leaves, he remembered suet puddings, treacle puddings, raisin and currant puddings, steak and kidney puddings, bread and butter pudding, "batter cooked in the gravy with the meat," potato cake, plum cake, butter cake, porridge with treacle, fruit tarts and pies, brawn, pig's trotters and pig's cheek and home-smoked ham and sausages. And "lashings of fresh butter and cream and eggs." He wondered if this diet had produced the diabetes, but said it was worth it.

There was an elder brother described by my father as: "Too damned clever by half. One of those quick, clever brains. Now I've always had a slow brain, but I get there in the end, damn it!"

The brothers went to a local school and the elder did well, but my father was beaten for being slow. They both became bank clerks in, I think, the Westminster Bank, and one must have found it congenial, for he became a manager, the "rich brother," who had cars and even a yacht. But my father did not like it, though he was conscientious. For instance, he changed his writing, letter by letter, because a senior criticised it. I never saw his unregenerate hand, but the one he created was elegant, spiky, careful. Did this mean he created a new personality for himself, hiding one he did not like, as he hid his "damned fleshy mouth"? I don't know.

Nor do I know when he left home to live in Luton or why. He found family life too narrow? A safe guess—he found everything too narrow. His mother was too down-to-earth? He had to get away from his clever elder brother?

Being a young man in Luton was the best part of his life. It ended in 1914, so he had a decade of happiness. His reminiscences of it were all of pleasure, the delight of physical movement, of dancing in particular. All his girls were "a beautiful dancer, light as a feather." He played billiards and ping-pong (both for his county); he swam, boated, played cricket and football, went to picnics and horse races, sang at musical evenings. One family of a mother and two daughters treated him "like a son only better. I didn't know whether I was in love with the mother or the daughters, but oh I did love going there; we had such good times." He was engaged to one daughter, then, for a time, to the other. An engagement was broken off because she was rude to a waiter. "I could not marry a woman who allowed herself to insult someone who was defenceless." He used to say to my wryly smiling mother: "Just as well I didn't marry either of *them*; they would never have stuck it out the way you have, old girl."

Just before he died he told me he had dreamed he was standing in a kitchen on a very high mountain holding X in his arms. "Ah, yes, that's what I've missed in my life. Now don't you let yourself be cheated out of life by the old dears. They take all the colour out of everything if you let them."

But in that decade—"I'd walk 10, 15 miles to a dance two or three times a week and think nothing of it. Then I'd dance every dance and walk home again over the fields. Sometimes it was moonlight, but I liked the snow best, all crisp and fresh. I loved walking back and getting into my digs just as the sun was rising. My little dog was so happy to see me, and I'd feed her, and make myself porridge and tea, then I'd wash and shave and go off to work."

The boy who was beaten at school, who went too much to church, who carried the fear of poverty all his life, but who nevertheless was filled with the memories of country pleasures;

the young bank clerk who worked such long hours for so little money, but who danced, sang, played, flirted—this naturally vigorous, sensuous being was killed in 1914, 1915, 1916. I think the best of my father died in that war, that his spirit was crippled by it. The people I've met, particularly the women, who knew him young, speak of his high spirits, his energy, his enjoyment of life. Also of his kindness, his compassion and—a word that keeps recurring—his wisdom. "Even when he was just a boy he understood things that you'd think even an old man would find it easy to condemn." I do not think these people would have easily recognised the ill, irritable, abstracted, hypochondriac man I knew.

He "joined up" as an ordinary soldier out of a characteristically quirky scruple: it wasn't right to enjoy officers' privileges when the Tommies had such a bad time. But he could not stick the communal latrines, the obligatory drinking, the collective visits to brothels, the jokes about girls. So next time he was offered a commission he took it.

His childhood and young man's memories, kept fluid, were added to, grew, as living memories do. But his war memories were congealed in stories that he told again and again, with the same words and gestures, in stereotyped phrases. They were anonymous, general, as if they had come out of a communal war memoir. He met a German in no-man's-land, but both slowly lowered their rifles and smiled and walked away. The Tommies were the salt of the earth, the British fighting men the best in the world. He had never known such comradeship. A certain brutal officer was shot in a sortie by his men, but the other officers, recognising rough justice, said nothing. He had known men intimately who saw the Angels at Mons. He wished he could force all the generals on both sides into the trenches for just one day, to see what the common soldiers endured—*that* would have ended the war at once.

There was an undercurrent of memories, dreams, and emotions much deeper, more personal. This dark region in him, fate-ruled, where nothing was true but horror, was expressed inarticulately, in brief, bitter exclamations or phrases of rage, incredulity, betrayal. The men who went to fight in that war believed it when they said it was to end war. My father believed it. And he was never able to reconcile his belief in his country with his anger at the cynicism of its leaders. And the anger, the sense of betrayal, strengthened as he grew old and ill.

But in 1914 he was naïve, the German atrocities in Belgium inflamed him, and he enlisted out of idealism, although he knew he would have a hard time. He knew because a fortune-teller told him. (He could be described as uncritically superstitious or as psychically gifted.) He would be in great danger twice, yet not die—he was being protected by a famous soldier who was his ancestor. "And sure enough, later I heard from the Little Aunties that the church records showed we were descended the backstairs way from the Duke of Wellington, or was it Marlborough? Damn it, I forget. But one of them would be beside me all through the war, she said." (He was romantic, not only about his solicitous ghost, but also about being a descendant of the Huguenots, on the strength of the "e" in Tayler; and about "the wild blood" in his veins from a great uncle who, sent unjustly to prison for smuggling, came out of a ten-year sentence and earned it, very efficiently, along the coasts of Cornwall until he died.)

The luckiest thing that ever happened to my father, he said, was getting his leg shattered by shrapnel ten days before Passchendaele. His whole company was killed. He knew he was going to be wounded because of the fortuneteller, who had said he would know. "I did not understand what she meant, but both times in the trenches, first when my appendix burst and I nearly died, and then just before Passchendaele, I felt for some days as if a thick, black velvet pall was settled over me. I can't tell you what it was like. Oh, it was awful, awful, and the second time it was so bad I wrote to the old people and told them I was going to be killed."

His leg was cut off at mid-thigh, he was shell-shocked, he was very ill for many months, with a prolonged depression afterwards. "You should always remember that sometimes people are all seething underneath. You don't know what terrible things people have to fight against. You should look at a person's eyes, that's how you tell. . . . When I was like that, after I lost my leg, I went to a nice doctor man and said I was going mad, but he said, don't worry, everyone locks up things like that. You don't know—horrible, horrible, awful things. I was afraid of myself, of what I used to dream. I wasn't myself at all."

In the Royal Free Hospital was my mother, Sister McVeagh. He married his nurse which, as they both said often enough (though in different tones of voice), was just as well. That was 1919. He could not face being a bank clerk in England, he said, not after the trenches. Besides, England was too narrow and conventional. Besides, the civilians did not know what the soldiers had suffered, they didn't want to know, and now it wasn't done even to remember "The Great Unmentionable." He went off to the Imperial Bank of Persia, in which country I was born.

The house was beautiful, with great stone-floored high-ceilinged rooms whose windows showed ranges of snow-streaked mountains. The gardens were full of roses, jasmine, pomegranates, walnuts. Kermanshah he spoke of with liking, but soon they went to Teheran, populous with "Embassy people," and my gregarious mother created a lively social life about which he was irritable even in recollection.

Irritableness—that note was first struck here, about Persia. He did not like, he said, "the graft and the corruption." But here it is time to try and describe something difficult—how a man's good qualities can also be his bad ones, or if not bad, a danger to him.

My father was honourable—he always knew exactly what that word meant. He had integrity. His "one does not do that sort of thing," his "no, it is *not* right," sounded throughout my childhood and were final for all of us. I am sure it was true he wanted to leave Persia because of "the corruption." But it was also because he was already unconsciously longing for something freer, because as a bank official he could not let go into the dream-logged personality that was waiting for him. And later in Rhodesia, too, what was best in him was also what prevented him from shaking away the shadows: it was always in the name of honesty or decency that he refused to take this step or that out of the slow decay of the family's fortunes.

In 1925 there was leave from Persia. That year in London there was an Empire Exhibition, and on the Southern Rhodesian stand some very fine maize cobs and a poster saying that fortunes could be made on maize at 25/– a bag. So on an impulse, turning his back forever on England, washing his hands of the corruption of the East, my father collected all his capital, £800, I think, while my mother packed curtains from Liberty's, clothes from Harrods, visiting cards, a piano, Persian rugs, a governess and two small children.

Soon, there was my father in a cigar-shaped house of thatch and mud on the top of a kopje that overlooked in all directions a great system of mountains, rivers, valleys, while overhead the sky arched from horizon to empty horizon. This was a couple of hundred miles south from the Zambesi, a hundred or so west from Mozambique, in the district of Banket, so called because certain of its reefs were of the same formation as those called *banket* on the Rand. Lomagundi— gold country, tobacco country, maize country—wild, almost empty. (The Africans had been turned off it into reserves.) Our neighbours were four, five, seven miles off. In front of the house . . . no neighbours, nothing; no farms, just wild bush with two rivers but no fences to the mountains seven miles away. And beyond these mountains and bush again to the Portuguese border, over which "our boys" used to escape when wanted by the police for pass or other offences.

And then? There was bad luck. For instance, the price of maize dropped from 25/– to 9/– a bag. The seasons were bad, prices bad, crops failed. This was the sort of thing that made it impossible for him ever to "get off the farm," which, he agreed with my mother, was what he most wanted to do.

It was an absurd country, he said. A man could "own" a farm for years that was totally mortgaged to the Government and run from the Land Bank, meanwhile employing half-a-hundred Africans at 12/– a month and none of them knew how to do a day's work. Why, two farm labourers from Europe could do in a day what twenty of these ignorant black savages would take a week to do. (Yet he was proud that he had a name as a just employer, that he gave "a square deal.") Things got worse. A fortuneteller had told him that her heart ached when she saw the misery ahead for my father: this was the misery.

But it was my mother who suffered. After a period of neurotic illness, which was a protest against her situation, she became brave and resourceful. But she never saw that her husband was not living in a real world, that he had made a captive of her common sense. We were always about to "get off the farm." A miracle would do it—a sweepstake, a goldmine, a legacy. And then? What a question! We would go to England where life would be normal with people coming in for musical evenings and nice supper parties at the Trocadero after a show. Poor woman, for the twenty years we were on the farm, she waited for when life would begin for her and for her children, for she never understood that what was a calamity for her was for them a blessing.

Meanwhile my father sank towards his death (at 61). Everything changed in him. He had been a dandy and fastidious, now he hated to change out of shabby khaki. He had been sociable, now he was misanthropic. His body's disorders—soon diabetes and all kinds of stomach ailments—dominated him. He was brave about his wooden leg, and even went down mine shafts and climbed trees with it, but he walked clumsily and it irked him badly. He greyed fast, and slept more in the day, but would be awake half the night pondering about. . . .

It could be gold divining. For ten years he experimented on private theories to do with the attractions and repulsions of metals. His whole soul went into it but his theories were wrong or he was *unlucky*—after all, if he had found a mine he would have had to leave the farm. It could be the relation between the minerals of the earth and of the moon; his decision to make infusions of all the plants on the farm and drink them himself in the interests of science; the criminal folly of the British Government in not realising that the Germans and the Russians were conspiring as Anti-Christ to . . . the inevitability of war because no one would listen to Churchill, but it would be all right because God (by then he was a British Israelite) had destined Britain to rule the world; a prophecy said 10 million dead would surround Jerusalem—how would the corpses be cleared away?; people who wished to abolish flogging should be flogged; the natives understood nothing but a good beating; hanging must not be abolished because the Old Testament said "an eye for an eye and a tooth for a tooth. . . ."

Yet, as this side of him darkened, so that it seemed all his thoughts were of violence, illness, war, still no one dared to make an unkind comment in his presence or to gossip. Criticism of people, particularly of women, made him more and more uncomfortable till at last he burst out with: "It's all very well, but no one has the right to say that about another person."

In Africa, when the sun goes down, the stars spring up, all of them in their expected places, glittering and moving. In the rainy season, the sky flashed and thundered. In the dry season, the great dark hollow of night was lit by veld fires: the mountains burned through September and October in chains of red fire. Every night my father took out his chair to watch the sky and the mountains, smoking, silent, a thin shabby fly-away figure under the stars. "Makes you think—there are so many worlds up there, wouldn't really matter if we did blow ourselves up—plenty more where we came from."

The Second World War, so long foreseen by him, was a bad time. His son was in the Navy and in danger, and his daughter a sorrow to him. He became very ill. More and more often it was necessary to drive him into Salisbury with him in a coma, or in danger of one, on the back seat. My mother moved him into a pretty little suburban house in town near the hospitals, where he took to his bed and a couple of years later died. For the most part he was unconscious under drugs. When awake he talked obsessively (a tongue licking a nagging sore place) about "the old war." Or he remembered his youth. "I've been dreaming—Lord, to see those horses come lickety-split down the course with their necks stretched out and the sun on their coats and everyone shouting. . . . I've been dreaming how I walked along the river in the mist as the sun was rising. . . . Lord, lord, lord, what a time that was, what good times we all had then, before the old war."

Desert Places

Robert Frost

Snow falling and night falling fast, oh, fast
In a field I looked into going past,
And the ground almost covered smooth in snow,
But a few weeds and stubble showing last.

The woods around it have it—it is theirs.
All animals are smothered in their lairs.
I am too absent-spirited to count;
The loneliness includes me unawares.

And lonely as it is that loneliness
Will be more lonely ere it will be less—
A blanker whiteness of benighted snow
With no expression, nothing to express.

They cannot scare me with their empty spaces
Between stars—on stars where no human race is.
I have it in me so much nearer home
To scare myself with my own desert places.

Acquainted with the Night

Robert Frost

I have been one acquainted with the night.
I have walked out in rain—and back in rain.
I have outwalked the furthest city light.

I have looked down the saddest city lane.
I have passed by the watchman on his beat
And dropped my eyes, unwilling to explain.

I have stood still and stopped the sound of feet
When far away an interrupted cry
Came over houses from another street,

But not to call me back or say good-by;
And further still at an unearthly height,
One luminary clock against the sky

Proclaimed the time was neither wrong nor right.
I have been one acquainted with the night.

The Road Not Taken

Robert Frost

Two roads diverged in a yellow wood,
And sorry I could not travel both
And be one traveler, long I stood
And looked down one as far as I could
To where it bent in the undergrowth;

Then took the other, as just as fair,
And having perhaps the better claim,
Because it was grassy and wanted wear;
Though as for that the passing there
Had worn them really about the same,

And both that morning equally lay
In leaves no step had trodden black.
Oh, I kept the first for another day!
Yet knowing how way leads on to way,
I doubted if I should ever come back.

I shall be telling this with a sigh
Somewhere ages and ages hence:
Two roads diverged in a wood, and I—
I took the one less traveled by,
And that has made all the difference.

The Dead Child

Gabrielle Roy

translated by Joyce Marshall

W HY then did the memory of that dead child seek me out in the very midst of the summer that sang?

When till then no intimation of sorrow had come to me through the dazzling revelations of that season.

I had just arrived in a very small village in Manitoba to finish the school year as replacement for a teacher who had fallen ill or simply, for all I know, become discouraged.

The principal of the Normal School had called me to his office towards the end of my year's study. "Well," he said, "there's a school available for the month of June. It's not much but it's an opportunity. When the time comes for you to apply for a permanent position, you'll be able to say you've had experience. Believe me, it's a help."

And so I found myself at the beginning of June in that very poor village—just a few shacks built on sand, with nothing around it but spindly spruce trees. "A month," I asked myself, "will that be long enough for me to become attached to the children or for the children to become attached to me? Will a month be worth the effort?"

Perhaps the same calculation was in the minds of the children who presented themselves at school that first day of June—"Is this teacher going to stay long enough to be worth the effort?"—for I had never seen children's faces so dejected, so apathetic, or perhaps sorrowful. I had had so little experience. I myself was hardly more than a child.

Nine o'clock came. The room was hot as an oven. Sometimes in Manitoba, especially in the sandy areas, an incredible heat settles in during the first days of June.

Scarcely knowing where or how to begin, I opened the attendance book and called the roll. The names were for the most part very French and today they still return to my memory, like this, for no reason: Madeleine Bérubé, Josephat Brisset, Emilien Dumont, Cécile Lépine. . . .

But most of the children who rose and answered "Present, mamzelle," when their names were called had the slightly narrowed eyes, warm colouring and jet black hair that told of métis blood.

They were beautiful and exquisitely polite; there was really nothing to reproach them for except the inconceivable distance they maintained between themselves and me. It crushed me. "Is this what children are like then," I asked myself with anguish, "untouchable, barricaded in some region where you can't reach them?"

I came to the name Yolande Chartrand.

No one answered. It was becoming hotter by the minute. I wiped a bit of perspiration from my forehead. I repeated the name and, when there was still no answer, I looked up at faces that seemed to me completely indifferent.

Then from the back of the classroom, above the buzzing of flies, there arose a voice I at first couldn't place. "She's dead, mamzelle. She died last night."

Perhaps even more distressing than the news was the calm level tone of the child's voice. As I must have seemed unconvinced, all the children nodded gravely as if to say, "It's true."

Suddenly a sense of impotence greater than any I can remember weighed upon me.

"Ah," I said, lost for words.

"She's already laid out," said a boy with eyes like coals. "They're going to bury her for good tomorrow."

"Ah," I repeated.

The children seemed a little more relaxed now and willing to talk, in snatches and at long intervals.

A boy in the middle of the room offered, "She got worse the last two months."

We looked at one another in silence for a long time, the children and I. I now understood that the expression in their eyes that I had taken for indifference was a heavy sadness. Much like this stupefying heat. And we were only at the beginning of the day.

"Since Yolande . . . has been laid out," I suggested, "and she was your schoolmate . . . and would have been my pupil . . . would you like . . . after school at four o'clock . . . for us to go and visit her?"

On the small, much too serious faces there appeared the trace of a smile, wary, still very sad but a sort of smile just the same.

"It's agreed then, we'll go to visit her, her whole class."

From that moment, despite the enervating heat and the sense that haunted us all, I feel sure, that human efforts are all ultimately destined to a sort of failure, the children fixed their attention as much as possible on what I was teaching and I did my best to rouse their interest.

At five past four I found most of them waiting for me at the door, a good twenty children but making no more noise than if they were being kept in after school. Several of them went ahead to show me the way. Others pressed around me so closely I could scarcely move. Five or six of the smaller ones took me by the hand or the shoulder and pulled me forward gently as if they were leading a blind person. They did not talk, merely held me enclosed in their circle.

Together, in this way, we followed a track through the sand. Here and there thin spruce trees formed little clumps. The air was now barely moving. In no time the village was behind us—forgotten, as it were.

We came to a wooden cabin standing in isolation among the little trees. Its door was wide open, so we were able to see the dead child from quite far off. She had been laid out on rough boards suspended between two straight chairs set back to back. There was nothing else in the room. Its usual contents must have been crowded into the only other room of the house for, besides a stove and table and a few pots on the floor, I could see a bed and a mattress piled with clothes. But no chairs. Clearly the two used as supports for the boards on which the dead child lay were the only ones in the house.

The parents had undoubtedly done all they could for their child. They had covered her with a clean sheet. They had given her a room to herself. Her mother, probably, had arranged her hair in the two very tight braids that framed the thin face. But some pressing need had sent them away: perhaps the purchase of a coffin in town or a few more boards to make her one themselves. At any rate, the dead child was alone in the room that had been emptied for her—alone, that is to say, with the flies. A faint odour of death must have attracted them. I saw one with a blue body walk over her forehead. I immediately placed myself near her head and began to move my hand back and forth to drive the flies away.

The child had a delicate little face, very wasted, with the serious expression I had seen on the faces of most of the children here, as if the cares of the adults had crushed them all too early. She might have been ten or eleven years old. If she had lived a little longer, I reminded myself, she would have been one of my pupils. She would have learned something from me. I would have given her something to keep. A bond would have been formed between me and this little stranger—who knows, perhaps even for life.

As I contemplated the dead child, those words "for life"—as if they implied a long existence—seemed to me the most rash and foolish of all the expressions we use so lightly.

In death the child looked as if she were regretting some poor little joy she had never known. I continued at least to prevent the flies from settling upon her. The children were watching me. I realized that they now expected everything from me, though I didn't know much more than they and was just as confused. Still I had a sort of inspiration.

"Don't you think Yolande would like to have someone with her always till the time comes to commit her to the ground?"

The faces of the children told me I had struck the right note.

"We'll take turns then, four or five around her every two hours, until the funeral."

They agreed with a glow in their dark eyes.

"We must be careful not to let the flies touch Yolande's face."

They nodded to show they were in agreement. Standing around me, they now felt a trust in me so complete it terrified me.

In a clearing among the spruce trees a short distance away, I noticed a bright pink stain on the ground whose source I didn't yet know. The sun slanted upon it, making it flame, the one moment in this day that had been touched by a certain grace.

"What sort of girl was she?" I asked.

At first the children didn't understand. Then a boy of about the same age said with tender seriousness, "She was smart, Yolande."

The other children looked as if they agreed.

"And did she do well in school?"

"She didn't come very often this year. She was always being absent."

"Our teacher before last this year said Yolande could have done well."

"How many teachers have you had this year?"

"You're the third, mamzelle. I guess the teachers find it too lonesome here."

"What did Yolande die of?"

"T.B., mamzelle," they replied with a single voice, as if this was the customary way for children to die around here.

They were eager to talk about her now. I had succeeded in opening the poor little doors deep within them that no one perhaps had ever much wanted to see opened. They told me moving facts about her brief life. One day on her way home from school—it was in February; no, said another, in March— she had lost her reader and wept inconsolably for weeks. To study her lesson after that, she had to borrow a book from one of the others—and I saw on the faces of some of them that they'd grudged lending their readers and would always regret this. Not having a dress for her first communion, she entreated till her mother finally made her one from the only curtain in the house: "the one from this room . . . a beautiful lace curtain, mamzelle."

"And did Yolande look pretty in her lace curtain dress?" I asked.

They all nodded deeply, in their eyes the memory of a pleasant image.

I studied the silent little face. A child who had loved books, solemnity and decorous attire. Then I glanced again at that astonishing splash of pink in the melancholy landscape. I realized suddenly that it was a mass of wild roses. In June they open in great sheets all over Manitoba, growing from the poorest soil. I felt some alleviation.

"Let's go and pick some roses for Yolande."

On the children's faces there appeared the same slow smile of gentle sadness I had seen when I suggested visiting the body.

In no time we were gathering roses. The children were not yet cheerful, far from that, but I could hear them at least talking to one another. A sort of rivalry had gripped them. Each vied to see who could pick the most roses or the brightest, those of a deep shade that was almost red.

From time to time one tugged at my sleeve, "Mamzelle, see the lovely one I've found!"

On our return we pulled them gently apart and scattered petals over the dead child. Soon only her face emerged from the pink drift. Then—how could this be?—it looked a little less forlorn.

The children formed a ring around their schoolmate and said of her without the bitter sadness of the morning, "She must have got to heaven by this time."

Or, "She must be happy now."

I listened to them, already consoling themselves as best they could for being alive.

But why, oh why, did the memory of that dead child seek me out today in the very midst of the summer that sang?

Was it brought to me just now by the wind with the scent of roses?

A scent I have not much liked since the long ago June when I went to that poorest of villages—to acquire, as they say, experience.

A Cultural Exchange

Gail Godwin

ONCE I was twenty-one and terrified I would not get the most out of life. I wanted to marry, to travel, to be a writer. Not in that order; not in any order. Perhaps I could bring everything about simultaneously, without having to make any bridge-burning choices. The truth was, I was a person who had spacious ideals, but who was rather timid when it came to facing unknown space.

I went to Copenhagen on a freighter. It was October, the worst month for storms, and I stayed flat on my back in my cabin for most of the trip. The stewardess brought me oranges, and, in my good moments, I sat up and continued work on the long letter I was writing to the man I intended to marry one of these days.

After a week in Copenhagen, I decided to stay for the winter. I wrote to Barney, my intended, that I had "fallen in love with the Danes." Let him worry a little about the ambiguous plural. The real reason, though I couldn't have told you then, was that traveling wearied and depressed me. I found it hard to concentrate on the pure experience of another culture, when I was feeling self-conscious about eating alone, or trying to dissolve little grains of Woolite in a hotel basin that leaked, or constantly being surprised by one more expense I hadn't counted on.

I went to the American Embassy, and the cultural attaché gave me the name of a widower in Klampenborg, who took out a lot of books on American culture from the USIS library. "He's not running a boardinghouse or anything, mind you, but he did once say that his family has shrunk and he has too much space, and he had been entertaining the thought of taking into the house a well-behaved young person, someone who could help improve his son's English."

And so, one Sunday afternoon, I found myself aboard the electric train, shuttling outward from the city. A rush of cold air came in at each stop: Nordhavn, Svanemøllen, Hellerup, Charlottenlund, Ordrup . . . The names of these suburbs vibrated with the secrets of the country I was now going to discover. Secure that I was being met at the end of the line, I could concentrate on the essences along the way.

I saw him before he saw me. He was clearly a gentleman in the old tradition, the way he stood on the station platform, proud and rather aloof, in his chesterfield, his gray-gloved hands on his walking stick. A real patriarch. My fatherless imagination appropriated his image at once. Then I shrank back as he scanned the windows of my car. But not before I caught the naked wistfulness that played across his features. "We shall look each other over," he had said on the phone, in precise Oxford English. But I had seen, in that eager, lonely look, a predisposition to welcome whatever stepped off the train.

I did just that, pulling up the collar of my polo coat to have something to do with my hands. There was no point in pretending to look up and down the platform, for he was the only person waiting. "Mr. Engelgard? I'm Amanda Sloane. How nice of you to meet me at the station." (". . . *a well-behaved young person*")

"Rolf Engelgard. It is my pleasure." I could see he was as pleased with my appearance as I had been with his. "I live only there, but first we shall walk a little." He pointed to some white apartment buildings on the slope of a hill. Beyond their flat roofs stretched the glassy gray smoothness of the sea, its horizon topped by a small, misty slice of Sweden. "Are you hungry?" he asked. "Maybe you would like to eat first."

"Oh, I had a late breakfast."

"In that case, we shall wait a little. Would you like a ride into Dryehavn, the king's deer park and hunting lodge? It is lovely just now, before the frost comes. We will lunch after. How would you like that?"

"I'd love it, but I hadn't meant to take up your entire Sunday afternoon."

"Time is something of which I have plenty," he said, taking my arm. "So! First a ride into the park, then lunch at Ryttergarten, then I show you my big old flat. Have you learned any Danish yet?"

"Just *tak*. And *tak for sidst*, and *tusind tak*, and *mange tak*. The people here all speak such good English that it makes me shy. Nevertheless, I'd like to try to learn enough to make myself understood . . ."

He stopped suddenly. We were mounting a rather steep cement upgrade, away from the Klampenborg station into a leaf-strewn park. His handsome old face went very pale. "I am sorry," he said, breathing very fast. "Last winter I had a little bronchial ailment and still find myself short of breath. It is such a nuisance." He spoke lightly, with an ironic lilt, but his blue eyes were hard with fury. He stood for several minutes, leaning heavily on his stick, glaring at the clean October sky, as if cursing some Viking deity up there.

"We're not in any hurry," I said tactfully. "That's why I like it here. Everyone takes his time."

"The Danes are downright lazy." He started to walk again. "I am a Norwegian. My parents came here when I was a boy."

"What are Norweigans like, then?" I wanted to win his approval.

"Fierce, proud, hardworking. The Danes have a sense of humor, but the Norwegians work harder. My elder son, for example, is Norwegian to the core. My younger, who lives with me, is typical Danish. Almost thirty and still a student."

"And what does your older son do?"

"A lawyer in Copenhagen. We don't speak of him, please."

"Of course," I agreed, embarrassed by the unexpected rebuff. "Where is your car parked?"

"I have no car. They are very dear in this country. I always ride a bicycle until this drat illness."

"Oh, I thought you said something about a ride in the deer park." *Eccentric*, I was thinking; *a bit senile . . .* ?

"Ah!" he now smiled broadly for the first time, "we are in the deer park. Look." He pointed with his stick toward a hill crowned by a small castle, behind which the early winter sun was already setting at half past one. "We *shall* ride to the king's hunting lodge." He looked down at me, quite pleased with himself. "You wait here, please." He crossed the road and spoke in Danish to a hack driver who stood beside his horses, drinking a bottle of beer.

Soon we were sitting side by side in the open carriage, our legs wrapped in tartan rugs. The driver trotted his pair of bays along the curving path of the woods, where deer grazed close enough for us to see their eyes blink. Engelgard was watching my face avidly for every reaction. "I am so interested to know what you think, all your impressions, Amanda. May I call you Amanda? This will be a new experience for me, too. I have never taken in a lodger. Ever since my wife died, Lars—that is the son who lives with me—has been urging me to let one of our unused rooms. It is such a big flat. It contained twenty-one years of our busy married life, the growing of two boys. I told Lars, 'Whoever comes to live here, *if* I shall find such a person, shall be treated like family.' I could not have it any other way. I wanted a young person. They are more adaptable and straightforward. You come from the southern part of the United States. Wait, let me guess where. One of the Carolinas."

"North Carolina," I said, amazed, "but how could you tell?"

He smiled radiantly. I suddenly saw how good-looking he must have been as a young man. "I was not manager of Thomas Cook and Sons for thirty years without knowing some Americans. Also I have made a study of American dialects. Languages are my hobby. I speak twelve. Would you like to bet: before you leave us, I shall be able to speak like a—what would you call a native of North Carolina?"

"Well, a lot of people say Tarheel."

"Tarheel! How delightful! And what is the origin of the term?"

"I'm ashamed to say I don't know."

"Never mind, we shall find out. We have plenty of time during these long winter months. I must teach you about North Carolina; you shall show me the Danes." He rubbed his gloved hands together and chuckled. "It will be so good to have interesting conversations with someone young and vital.

Poor Lars is at the university all day."

The horses had slowed at the top of a hill. The driver turned to Engelgard and said something in Danish. He replied. When speaking the Scandinavian tongue, his deep voice went up a pitch; he glided softly over the diphthongs, as if he were afraid of mashing them with his strength. *Wait a minute, wait a minute*, the Voice of Experience was warning me, though I hardly ever listened in those days. *Having a fatherly, interpretative landlord your first uncertain winter abroad is one thing; getting involved in the needs of a lonely, authoritative old widower, whose moods go up and down like a seesaw, is something else.*

"Look there, Tarheel. Have you ever seen so many deer in one place?"

I was already phrasing its beauty in a letter to Barney: the tough, bare lines of the royal hunting lodge, the vast and peaceful sward where hundreds of deer grazed within touching distance of the Sunday strollers; the whole thing bathed in the russet glow of this uncanny early sunset. I was so excited about being somewhere foreign, at last, and how I would write about it, that I grabbed Mr. Engelgard and committed myself in a rush of exuberant gratitude.

"You certainly do know how to give things a lovely beginning," I said.

He looked studiously at the crowds of deer and people. A tear detached itself from his eye and rolled down his bony cheek.

"How many deer are there in all, I wonder?" I went on, pretending I hadn't seen.

"The guidebooks say two thousand," replied the ironic, lilting voice, "But I should think many more than that, myself."

I moved into the enormous, rather dark old flat on Wednesday. Its one advantage was its view of the sea. My room had been Mrs. Engelgard's studio, where she did illustrations for women's magazines. Framed originals of these hung three and four deep on every wall. They showed people wearing slightly out-of-style clothes kissing under leafy trees, little children sitting alone in corners, a girl in an evening dress running away from a gloomy old house, her evening cloak streaming behind her.

Mr. Engelgard had spent all of Monday and Tuesday going through the big oak wardrobe, transferring her things into cardboard boxes. The project was still unfinished when I arrived in the taxi.

The old man had taken the train to town, to do some shopping. It was Lars, the perennial-student son, who helped me settle in.

"All these clotheses shall go away," he said, removing from the floor of the wardrobe several pairs of small walking shoes with mud still caked to the heels. He dropped them gently into the cardboard box. "Poor Father. He worked all day and didn't get nowhere. He spend all the time looking at the things. He loved her so much."

Lars was not a bit like his father. He was short and round, like a troll, and had bright red cheeks and a scruffy red beard. His English was as rapid as it was incorrect, for he never paused to search for a word, simply filled in the nearest thing handy. He had switched majors several times and was now in zoology at the University of Copenhagen. "I should have finished my *examen* last year, but father went poor and I stay back and take care of him."

"He said he'd been sick." I began hanging my miracle-fiber outfits in Mrs. Engelgard's wardrobe. I decided to keep Lars's physical description vague in my letter to Barney.

"At night, you hear him. He searches for breath. It break your heart. I sleep in the bed with him. He is unwilling to sleep alone since she die. We hope you shall join us for our supper tonight. Gudrun will cook yellow bean soup. It is gorgeously good, I can tell you. Gudrun is our housekeeper. She is a jolly tart. In the evening she works under the bar at the hotel across the street."

"You mean behind the bar, I hope."

"Behind the bar. You will help my English. It is killing Father. Only, if I wait till I have the right word I never get my thing said. Is better to crash on, don't you think? He who hesitates is last."

"Lost," I corrected, laughing. He would be the brother I never had.

"Lost. Oh, you will be wonderful to have around. And look you—" He walked briskly across the cluttered room to the

French doors and pointed proudly to a slab of frozen earth outside. Several twiglike plants, quite dead, stood stiffly erect. "Our garden. In spring, you shall have vegetables and flowers rising out there."

"But I'll be gone by then. I'll go to Paris in the spring."

"Ah, Paris. Yes. But now we enjoy the long Danish winter."

Mr. Engelgard came home long after dark, his arms full of parcels and books checked out of the USIS library. He breathed as though he might collapse any minute. Lars and I were sitting on the old horsechair sofa in the living room, looking at their family album. "Welcome to our house, Amanda," he said. Then, when he caught his breath, "What did the governor of North Carolina say to the governor of South Carolina?"

"At least I know that one. 'It's a long time between drinks.' "

"Right you are. But watch out: in future they shall not be so easy. I have been to your embassy and wiped out the Carolina shelf." He dropped a package as he was trying to show me a book and cursed in Danish. "Lars, do you think you might help me?" he said petulantly to his son.

Lars jumped up at once and took all the parcels. The cork of a wine bottle poked out of one. "Luckily *that* did not drop," he said roguishly, and disappeared into the kitchen.

"Well, now," said Engelgard, slumping heavily into an armchair, "has Lars shown you where to find things? I see he has lost no time in dragging out the family album. Actually I planned to show you it myself, a bit later on, after dinner some night, when you know us better and the pictures mean something. Poor Lars lacks a sense of occasion, but he means well. Do you like your room? It was my wife's studio."

"I love it. All those paintings. The sea outside. All I need now is a typewriter."

"Yes, you are going to begin your writing career. I shall call a man I know about renting you a machine. My wife worked long hours in that room. Late into the night sometimes. Of course, you must feel free to change things around, though personally, I think everything looks so appropriate as it is."

"Oh, I wouldn't dream of changing anything," I heard myself declare. All afternoon I had been looking for drawers and corners where I could stash the cactus plants and odd knickknacks whose value must lie in personal meanings for some family member.

"No, I thought you wouldn't," he said, rewarding me with his smile. "Ah, Lars, my boy, here you are. I thought of a perfect nickname for you today, since we will all be speaking more English in this house now."

"What is the name, Father?" Lars asked cheerfully, entering with a tray of drinks. There were two whiskies and some strange, yellowish, oily mixture in a wineglass, on whose bottom bounced a disconsolate black olive. "I have made Amanda a martini, just like in America, so she feels at home."

" 'Frowsy' is the name I have chosen," said Engelgard. He turned his head at such an angle that his son could not see his broad wink to me.

"Hmm. It sounds all right. What do it mean?"

"What *does* it mean. Well, the nearest translation would be . . ." He was shaking with barely suppressed mirth. "Let's see, Amanda, wouldn't you say the nearest translation of 'Frowsy' would be 'an American nobleman'?" The old blue eyes coaxed me to be an accomplice.

"Well, yes. I guess that's as good as any," I said. I took a sip of my "martini." Lars had made it with sweet vermouth.

"Frowsy," repeated Lars, rather pleased. "I am Frowsy. How is your martini, the way you like it?"

"Let us drink a toast to the newest member of our family," said Engelgard, raising his own glass, sparing me the necessity of speaking a second untruth.

The next morning, Mr. Engelgard picked up the telephone and spoke familiarly in his musical Danish, and within a few hours a blue portable typewriter was delivered to the flat. We set it up on a large table in the center of my room, and drank a toast to it from Engelgard's schnapps bottle. "When you are a famous writer and they are giving you a cocktail party in a New York skyscraper, go to the window and look out and remember the day we launched your career with a rented typewriter," said the old man. "And remember me a little." Then out he tiptoed, ceremoniously, making way for the muse, and I rolled two sheets and a carbon into the machine and began typing rapidly, knowing he would be listening in the next room.

"Your move, my dear," said Engelgard. It was Saturday night.

Apathetically I moved my queen into the diagonal line of fire from his bishop. My head hurt. *Jeg har en dundrende Hŏvedpine*, according to my Danish phrase book, which was the last thing I needed with eloquent Mr. Engelgard. *I have a splitting headache.* Outside the ocean crashed. Frowsy had telephoned from town to say he had run into his brother, Palle, in the bookstore and they would dine together. Engelgard had been in the bathroom having a coughing fit when the call came and I had to relay the message. He glared at the telephone, then smiled dotingly and asked would I like a game of chess. I had thought of going into Copenhagen on the train, sitting for an hour or so in a place where students hung out. But somehow I had slipped into this role of the dutiful daughter, so of course I couldn't go. He'd feel so abandoned, with Frowsy gone as well, to eat with the son of whom we didn't speak.

"Amanda, you aren't keeping your mind on. the game. Is something the matter? I never saw you give up your queen without a bloodbath."

"Sorry. I think I'm coming down with something. Do you hear a sort of echo in the room? When I woke up today, my throat was kind of scratchy."

"Why did you not say something?" He came around and felt my forehead. He cursed in Danish. "But, my child, you have a fever! We shall have to move quickly if we are to rout this Danish cold. He hangs on and on and sucks your vitality. That is how my illness began. You must go to bed this minute. That is orders." He looked almost pleased.

"But we haven't finished our game," I said, torn between wanting the eventfulness of a sickbed bustle and feeling trapped, here in this overcrowded flat, with a lonely, autocratic old nurse whose dead wife's apron still hung on the hook behind the kitchen door.

"I would have demolished you in three more moves. See? I take your queen and that leaves your castle defenseless. He cannot budge because he is blocked by your pawn. I take your castle and what stands between me and your king?"

True to his diagnosis, I had contracted the genuine Danish cold. For three days I perspired under the eiderdown, feverishly imagining what kind of stories had gone with the framed illustrations on my walls, sneezing into Mr. Engelgard's best silk handkerchiefs, which he then boiled, along with the ones he coughed into, in a cooking pot on the back burner of the stove. I ate the oysters he ordered from the hotel across the street. I drank his toddies of whiskey, sugar, and hot water. I slept and dreamed of North Carolina and woke to hear the Danish wind howling and the waves lashing against the strand. Mr. Engelgard pulled up a chair, propped his feet on the foot of my bed, and told stories about the German occupation of Denmark: how, just here, on Strandvej, the Underground had smuggled their Jewish population in fishing boats over to Sweden; how every Danish wife practiced passive resistance by staring at the crotch of every German soldier she passed. And he told me how he and his wife had ridden their bicycles to Rungsted to have tea with Baroness Blixen.

"You had tea with Isak Dinesen!"

"Certainly. My wife illustrated some of her work. If you are a good girl, Amanda, and write very hard, I shall take you to visit her in the spring."

In those days, I kept carbons of all the letters I wrote. I found I could express things in the unselfconscious flow of a letter that simply evaporated when I sat down, consciously, to write a story. But as I reread these carbons now, in my study in upstate New York, I find that I was then so busy creating experiences that I missed the reality.

Dear Barney (Barney's sons in North Carolina must be teenagers by now),

Outside: the howling northern wind. Four hours of daylight. But how I love it, here among the lovable Danes, fantastic schizophrenic race of Peter Pans, telling macabre jokes one minute and shooting themselves the next. (Who on earth was I referring to?) For $25 a month (I'm sure it must have been more) I have a perfect setup, a beautiful room overlooking the sea (well, their living room did) very near to Isak Dinesen's house. My landlord is a very close friend of hers and we will dine there next week. Engelgard is a real aristocrat, but he hates being old. His son Lars is a very attractive Dane (don't worry, my American heart belongs to you—eventually). Lars, who is something in the zoology dept. at the University of Copenhagen, was showing me the Engelgard family album and there was this picture, browning at the edges, of Mr. E. as a young skier, framed against a Norwegian slope. He was incredibly handsome, a Viking Romeo, cheekbones like brackets (they still are) and a wonderful rakish grin.

After supper the first night I came here, my proud silver-haired host arises from the table (we had yellow bean soup, fried octopus, and Liebfraumilch in my honor) and goes over to the old upright piano with his dead wife's picture on top and proceeds to play and sing in a deep, rich baritone, pausing, however, for shortness of breath, "Nothing could be finer than to be in Carolina in the mor-or-or-ning . . ." I almost cried. And did you know (I didn't) that the reason we are called Tarheels is that General Lee said of the N.C. Regiment, "Oh, they'll stick. They've got tar on their heels."

"I think I'll get dressed and take a walk down Strandvej," I said, on the second day I had been out of bed. We were having the lunch he'd made: black broth, sardines on toast, and Carlsberg Elephant beer.

"You'll do nothing of the kind," snapped Engelgard.

I burst into tears. It was partly out of frustration over being cooped up so long. But also I knew that my own fear of his displeasure was creating a formidable barrier to my freedom.

"Amanda! Dear me!" He came to me quickly, laid his trembling hand against my face. "Oh, I am sorry. I did not think. Maybe I am so afraid of losing things that I hold on too fiercely. You are of course free to walk at any time you wish. I know what, we will go together. I, too, could use some fresh air. This musty old flat. I could show you the fishing boats, then we will have a little something at the hotel. But you must bundle up snugly. Wear those long black stockings I teased you about."

It was a release to be outside, chaperoned or not. How much I'd missed the sense of just going someplace. The sea was calm and Sweden was clear today. We walked slowly, because of his shortness of breath. Gulls dipped, squeaking, up and down in the sky.

"Are things okay between us, Tarheel?" He looked very fit,

wearing his chesterfield and a dark blue woolen scarf knotted high on his neck. His cheeks were pink. Since I had been ill, he seemed to have gained in strength.

"Of course." Tomorrow I would get up early, take the train into Copenhagen, spend the day on my own. It seemed a point of honor to do this, even if, when tomorrow came, I wanted to snuggle in bed. If I didn't get out and go somewhere, I would have nothing to write about.

Sitting in our usual corner in the hotel bar, we drank hot rum. Outside the picture window, the early afternoon sun was setting. "So you don't think I am a mean old man," said Engelgard.

I said don't be silly.

"Palle, my older boy, the lawyer, you know—" he began suddenly, wiping his lips with the napkin, "—after my wife died, I became very morbid. Possibly a bit irritable and demanding. I felt Palle neglected me. He would arrive only to change into clean clothes, then back into town. Sometimes he stayed out all night! One day, we had showdown. I don't wish to hold a post-mortem, but I said, As long as you live in my home you behave like a proper son and show some consideration. He said, Very well, Father, I will not live anymore in your home. And he was gone. He packed his things and moved out the very same night! It shows a certain strength of character, don't you agree?, but also a hardness of heart. I haven't seen him since. I keep thinking for a while that perhaps he would ring me up on the telephone. He did not ring. I send Frowsy to find out if he was all right. They have dinner in town now and then. Frowsy will not say if he speaks of me. Sometimes, I confess it, I feel downright sorry for myself and get a bit crotchety. You do forgive me, won't you, for today? You are free to come and go as you please."

"There's nothing to forgive. You were concerned about me. I appreciate having you in my life."

"Honestly?" he asked eagerly.

"Honestly. I'm sure he'll come around. You'll make up."

His face went hard. "You mistake me. It is too late. He will be sorry one day, possibly, but it is over for me."

I took the ten o'clock train to Copenhagen next day. Mr. Engelgard said, "I think I might straighten out your bookshelf while you are in town. You can't want all these dusty foreign books. I shall leave you some space to put in your own, as you buy them."

I nodded agreeably, rather than say I had no intention of accumulating a lot of heavy books to cart around Europe when I went on the road again.

As I crossed the big square in the center of Copenhagen, in bright winter sunshine, I felt like a racehorse being given his head after weeks inside a stable. I strolled down Stroget and looked in the shops. I bought some stretch ski pants for myself, a package of Viennese coffee (his favorite) for Mr. Engelgard, and a new science-fiction anthology for Frowsy. Then I wandered down to Nyhavn, to the port area, and watched the fishwives scream their wares. At a fruit stand I bought a red apple which I ate ceremoniously while exploring the narrow streets and feeling superconscious of being in Copenhagen. I played a favorite game with myself, in which I imagined my every action being observed by some person at home. Today it was Barney who watched me munching the apple and trailing my fingers along old walls.

In the late afternoon, I came across a restaurant on the corner of two streets. It was crammed with young people. I went in and ordered a beer and looked helplessly around for somewhere to sit. A handsome young Dane with gold hair and the proverbial sucked-in cheeks waved at me, as though I'd been expected. I sat down with him and his friend, a black man in a dapper tweed suit. Their names were Niels and Jean. Niels was a painter, Jean was a journalist from Marseille. Their English was rudimentary, but they shared what they had with me; every now and then, some enthusiasm would get the better of them and away they would go, into a fluid, gesticulating French. Niels said he had met lots of American girls seeing the world. "Why you all the time climbing for something?" he asked. "Why is American women so—" he erupted into French, gesticulating to Jean, who supplied him with the word he wanted, "—ambitious? You are never in the place where you are, always looking into distance of where you aren't."

"I'm not like that," I said, remembering my pure present-time joy of walking in Nyhavn with my apple.

"May we buy you another beer?" asked Jean, in heavily accented English.

After several more beers, it became easier to communicate. We gestured and laughed a lot and language seemed a silly barrier. We were all young, that was the point. Then we were in another restaurant and I was insisting on buying them all supper, for Niels had explained they could not afford to have more than soup. I told them they could take me to see Christiansborg Castle in return; I was afraid to go by myself in the dark. Then, magically, we were there, a sliver of moon tipped over our heads, our giggling ringing out over the silent battlements and turrets. A palace guard appeared out of the shadows and told us we had to leave. We went to another place and drank more beer and I missed the last train to Klampenborg. I thought this was funny, but Niels and Jean exchanged a look of irritation. "Well, I guess you stay at my place and go first thing tomorrow," said Niels. Our comradery was strangely muted as we went through the cobbled streets to Niels's place. Jean and Niels slept on the floor of the living room, giving the bedroom over to me. The sheets were not clean. I heard them giggling together during the early hours of the morning. I slept badly, dreaming that Mr. Engelgard came with the police and dragged me into the public square where two fishwives dressed like Nazis flayed me with wet flounders.

When I returned to the flat in Klampenborg, I found it ominously silent. The door to the bedroom Mr. Engelgard shared with his son was closed. As was the door to the living room, where I had spent so much time with the two of them. I went into my room and dropped the packages on the bed. The bookcase had been straightened and some Penguin paperbacks put in. On the table, next to the blue typewriter, was a note from Frowsy.

> Dear Little Sister
> If you look you out of the window you shall see a little some thing that look like *oil* on the sea, around the edge. That is ICE!!! Father is not himself today and if I was in your shoe I would leave him be. He is an old man and his moods are his privaledge. He worried for you all the night and

though I say dont wait up he must. I come and explain this
evening.

I did not see Mr. Engelgard for one week. He stayed out of
my way and I stayed out of his. Frowsy would come to my
room after supper (I was no longer invited to share their meal
with them) and we would read our separate books (he was
studying for his exams) and talk, after his father had gone to
bed early.

"But he said I was free to come and go as I pleased," I
protested. "It's unfair! I am an adult, not a child." I told
Frowsy the truth, how I had missed the train. For some reason,
I felt it necessary to clear my virtue. "Those two weren't even
interested in me!" I said.

"Then they was fools," said Frowsy humorously. "I understand perfectly, but Father is the older generation and also
Norwegian. That make a difference. We just have to wait till
he get over his fury."

I gave him the Viennese coffee to give to his father. Later I
saw it, still sealed, placed on my new kitchen "shelf." For,
now, by decree relayed by a reluctant Frowsy, I was no longer
welcome in the living room, that was for "family." One night,
when brewing coffee for myself in the kitchen, I discovered
I'd run out of sugar. Furtively, I reached for their sugar on the
next shelf. Old Engelgard had forseen this. Their package had
a homemade label scotch-taped to it. *Engelgard. Do not use!*
How small-minded could you get, I thought, outraged. I do
not have to be a paying prisoner here.

I went into town to American Express and signed up for a
bus tour leaving for Spain the week after Christmas. Meanwhile
I would sweat out my exile. My rent was paid for the rest of
November, and I couldn't leave Denmark till Christmas,
because my mother was sending a Christmas box and she'd be
hurt if there was no place to send it.

I took long walks in the deer park during the day, to avoid
bumping into Mr. Engelgard in the hallway. But the deer
were gone. Then I'd come back, furtively make myself a sandwich, and slip off to my room, where, behind the closed door,
I would type madly: letters to my mother, to Barney, to old

school friends, sometimes just tirades against "the old tyrant," which I would later tear up. Let him think I was writing a great novel. I knew he could hear me. I could hear him, coughing in the next room.

A week before Christmas, he was listening to some carols on the radio. I was in my room, waiting for his next cough. It came. Suddenly, I coughed, too, after he'd finished. I heard him turn down the volume of the carols. He coughed again. I coughed back. Then he called out tentatively, "Amanda?" I combed my hair and went at once to knock on the living room door.

"Come in."

I opened the door. He was sitting in his chair by the fire, his Norwegian blanket wrapped about his legs. He was holding out his arms to me. I went to him and knelt down beside him and bowed my head in his lap. I cried loudly and he raked my hair with his fingers.

"Oh, no, it is not easy, loving people," he said. "Look, Tarheel, can you forgive a selfish old creature?"

"Me, me," I sobbed. "I'm the one. I should have telephoned. But then it was so late. Oh it was so sordid. I had to spend the night with awful people."

"Yes," he crooned, some of the old authoritativeness creeping back into his voice. "You *should* have called. I was worried sick. If you are going to be a great writer, little Amanda, you must learn to imagine the feelings of others."

> Dearest Barney,
> This will be the last communication from Denmark. Friday I take the sollebus (means "sun bus") bound for Barcelona via Hamburg, Strasbourg, Colmar, Besançon, Valence, Provence, and the Pyrenees. . . . Christmas among the Danes was the best ever. We stuffed ourselves and lay about in alcoholic good will. Father Engelgard had placed the almond in my dish of rice porridge and so I got the *Mandelgave* (almondgift): an aquamarine pendant, set in antique gold. It belonged to his wife. I have not had the heart to tell him I'm leaving yet, but I must do it tonight. It will make him sad and that will make me sad.

"What clever clotheses you Americans have." Frowsy was

helping me pack. "In and out of suitcases, yet they never bend."

"Wrinkle," I corrected, pinching him playfully.

"Wrinkle. You have been a good thing for me and my English. But why did you wait so long to tell us you were going?"

"I thought it would be easier."

"Easier for you, maybe. For me, I don't mind. But older people need time to make their brains say yes. It is exactly the way Palle left. Goodbye. Crash. You should have said sooner."

"Oh, dear. I've done the wrong thing again." I was angry at Engelgard for refusing to come out of his room and making me feel guilty. "I hate myself," I added, wanting to be told I shouldn't.

"Oh, you are young. You live a little more and change."

Later that morning, the morning I was to leave, a man with a mop bucket and rags and brushes arrived at the flat. He wore white overalls and went straight to work, cleaning.

"Who on earth is that funny little man in the kitchen?" I asked Frowsy.

"Oh, it's Jacobsen. Father ask me to call him for this morning. He comes sometimes when Father wants to spring-clean."

"But it's not spring."

There was an hour to go before my taxi came. Engelgard's bedroom door was shut. When Jacobsen had finished with the bathroom, I went in and took a long bath, soaking and steaming, wanting to be gone. There was still the painful goodbye to have out with old Engelgard.

I had dressed in the pants and sweater I would wear for traveling, and was crouching before Mrs. Engelgard's too-low mirror, combing my hair, when Mr. Engelgard knocked once on the door and called my name. This was it. We would probably both bawl. I opened the door, smiling sadly.

He was dressed in the suit he'd worn the first day we'd met. I had my mouth open to compliment him on his sense of occasion. How nice he looked, with the dark ascot tucked inside his woolen shirt.

"I will appreciate it," he said in his Oxford English, pointing across the hall, "if you will return to my bathroom and wash away the ring you left in my bathtub. I do not feel I should have to do that for you. Especially when the place has just been cleaned by Jacobsen. I want every trace gone, please."

Then he turned and walked back to his room and slammed the door. I never saw him again.

For several Christmases, Frowsy and I exchanged cards. The Christmas after I left, he became engaged to a fellow student named Birgit. The next Christmas, Birgit had found another. And the following Christmas he wrote, "Father did not make it this year."

Barney also found another, and, I must say, reading over those old carbons, I don't blame him. I also found somebody, and lost him, and found another. Fifteen years passed and my husband and I were staying at the finest hotel in Copenhagen. I am sure the basin did not leak when one tried to dissolve Woolite; I was not there long enough to find out. I looked in the phonebook and there was the name, ENGELGARD, and the same address my mother and Barney had written to, during that other winter.

When I said, "Lars?" he didn't know who I was, but when I said, "Frowsy," he cursed in Danish and said, "Amanda, you come out here at once! This minute, do you hear me?" My husband and I took the train through the autumn suburbs and I found my way from Klampenborg station to the flat as if I'd been gone but a few hours.

The man who opened the door was neither short nor round. He no longer looked like a clown. He had shaved the furry red beard and his hair was golder than I remembered. How could he have grown taller? He had been thirty when we met. Then I realized it was because he no longer stood next to his father. At first he was terribly nervous. When he handed us our coffee cups, his hands shook. For the first half-hour, he addressed all his remarks to my husband. But then he saw me looking around and he said, "You like the way I have decorated. After Father died, I got rid of the old things." He had a slim brown cat who arched her back as he stroked her. "Father would never let us have animals," he said. "One of these days, I may get myself a wife, too, who knows?" Then he laughed like the old Frowsy.

The three of us drove in his new car to Rungsted, along the road that runs by the sea. "So," he said to me, obviously enjoying himself behind the wheel of this sleek machine, "you have become a writer, Amanda, and I have become a zoologist." To my husband he said, "Do you know, if it had not been for your wife, I would have failed those exams. My father was ill and I could not study in bed beside him, and she let me use the table in her room and made coffee when I became sleepy. She rehearsed with me all the bones in the body of a dog, sometimes till three or four in the morning."

"How funny!" I said. "I had forgotten completely about all that. I have been telling Jim what an awful spoiled thing I was."

"Amanda is frequently too hard on herself," said Jim.

We walked through the woods to visit Isak Dinesen's grave. The long, rectangular stone was set flat, under a very old and noble tree. Some beechnuts had fallen on it, near where her name was carved—*Karen Blixen*—and I put them in my pocket as talismans to make my own writing nobler.

"I tell you something funny," said the handsome Dane, who had at last come to look like my false descriptions of him in letters to Barney. "I don't mean it is funny, but it is typical of Father. The only time he ever mentioned you again was when she died. When he saw it in the newspaper, he got very pink—you know how he went, Amanda, when he began to be furious—and he said, 'Good, good, that will show her. It will be in their newspapers, too, and she will read it and regret she was a poor Tarheel who could not stick and will never meet the greatest writer in Denmark. She will be good and sorry.' I hope you don't mind this little anecdote."

"How could I mind," I said, "when it is so like him?" And with love's delayed reaction, I wished with all my heart that the old man could hear me say it: "I am sorry."

"It is the quirks we come to miss most in our dead," mused our host philosophically, as we walked through the sun-touched woods, back to the car. "I wonder why that is?"

I wondered if I should tell him how much better his English was.

The Love Song of J. Alfred Prufrock

T.S. Eliot

S'io credessi che mia risposta fosse
A persona che mai tornasse al mondo,
Questa fiamma staria senza più scosse.
Ma per ciò che giammai di questo fondo
Non tornò viva alcun, s'i'odo il vero,
Senza tema d'infamia ti rispondo.

Let us go then, you and I,
When the evening is spread out against the sky
Like a patient etherised upon a table;
Let us go, through certain half-deserted streets,
The muttering retreats
Of restless nights in one-night cheap hotels
And sawdust restaurants with oyster-shells:
Streets that follow like a tedious argument
Of insidious intent
To lead you to an overwhelming question . . .   10
Oh, do not ask, "What is it?"
Let us go and make our visit.

   In the room the women come and go
Talking of Michelangelo.

   The yellow fog that rubs its back upon the window-
     panes,

The yellow smoke that rubs its muzzle on the window-
  panes
Licked its tongue into the corners of the evening,
Lingered upon the pools that stand in drains,
Let fall upon its back the soot that falls from chimneys,
Slipped by the terrace, made a sudden leap,   20
And seeing that it was a soft October night,
Curled once about the house, and fell asleep.

  And indeed there will be time
For the yellow smoke that slides along the street
Rubbing its back upon the window-panes;
There will be time, there will be time
To prepare a face to meet the faces that you meet;
There will be time to murder and create,
And time for all the works and days of hands
That lift and drop a question on your plate;   30
Time for you and time for me,
And time yet for a hundred indecisions,
And for a hundred visions and revisions,
Before the taking of a toast and tea.

  In the room the women come and go
Talking of Michelangelo.

  And indeed there will be time
To wonder, "Do I dare?" and, "Do I dare?"
Time to turn back and descend the stair,
With a bald spot in the middle of my hair—   40
[They will say: "How his hair is growing thin!"]
My morning coat, my collar mounting firmly to the
  chin,
My necktie rich and modest, but asserted by a simple
  pin—
[They will say: "But how his arms and legs are thin!"]
Do I dare

Disturb the universe?
In a minute there is time
For decisions and revisions which a minute will reverse.

For I have known them all already, known them all—
Have known the evenings, mornings, afternoons,   50
I have measured out my life with coffee spoons;
I know the voices dying with a dying fall
Beneath the music from a farther room.
    So how should I presume?

And I have known the eyes already, known them all—
The eyes that fix you in a formulated phrase,
And when I am formulated, sprawling on a pin,
When I am pinned and wriggling on the wall,
Then how should I begin
To spit out all the butt-ends of my days and ways?   60
    And how should I presume?

And I have known the arms already, known them all—
Arms that are braceleted and white and bare
[But in the lamplight, downed with light brown hair!]
Is it perfume from a dress
That makes me so digress?
Arms that lie along a table, or wrap about a shawl.
    And should I then presume?
    And how should I begin?

            .   .   .   .   .

Shall I say, I have gone at dusk through narrow streets 70
And watched the smoke that rises from the pipes
Of lonely men in shirt-sleeves, leaning out of
    windows? ...

    I should have been a pair of ragged claws
Scuttling across the floors of silent seas.

            .   .   .   .   .

And the afternoon, the evening, sleeps so peacefully!
Smoothed by long fingers,
Asleep . . . tired . . . or it malingers,
Stretched on the floor, here beside you and me.
Should I, after tea and cakes and ices,
Have the strength to force the moment to its crisis? 80
But though I have wept and fasted, wept and prayed,
Though I have seen my head [grown slightly bald]
    brought in upon a platter,
I am no prophet—and here's no great matter;
I have seen the moment of my greatness flicker,
And I have seen the eternal Footman hold my coat, and
    snicker,
And in short, I was afraid.

    And would it have been worth it, after all.
After the cups, the marmalade, the tea,
Among the porcelain, among some talk of you and me,
Would it have been worth while,   90
To have bitten off the matter with a smile,
To have squeezed the universe into a ball
To roll it toward some overwhelming question,
To say: "I am Lazarus, come from the dead,
Come back to tell you all, I shall tell you all"—
If one, settling a pillow by her head
    Should say: "That is not what I meant at all.
    That is not it, at all."

    And would it have been worth it, after all,
Would it have been worth while,   100
After the sunsets and the dooryards and the sprinkled
    streets,
After the novels, after the teacups, after the skirts that
    trail along the floor—
And this, and so much more?—
It is impossible to say just what I mean!

But as if a magic lantern threw the nerves in patterns
    on a screen:
Would it have been worth while
If one, settling a pillow or throwing off a shawl,
And turning toward the window, should say:
    "That is not it at all,
    That is not what I meant, at all."   110

            .   .   .   .   .

    No! I am not Prince Hamlet, nor was meant to be;
Am an attendant lord, one that will do
To swell a progress, start a scene or two,
Advise the prince; no doubt, an easy tool,
Deferential, glad to be of use,
Politic, cautious, and meticulous;
Full of high sentence, but a bit obtuse;
At times, indeed, almost ridiculous—
Almost, at times, the Fool.

    I grow old . . . I grow old . . .   120
I shall wear the bottoms of my trousers rolled.

    Shall I part my hair behind? Do I dare to eat a peach?
I shall wear white flannel trousers, and walk upon the
    beach.
I have heard the mermaids singing, each to each.

    I do not think that they will sing to me.

    I have seen them riding seaward on the waves
Combing the white hair of the waves blown back
When the wind blows the water white and black.

    We have lingered in the chambers of the sea
By sea-girls wreathed with seaweed red and brown   130
Till human voices wake us, and we drown.

UNIT 3

A SENSE OF PLACE

In her essay "Where the World Began" Margaret Laurence suggests that where we grow up has a tremendous influence on who we are and on how we perceive the world. We may go on to experience many things and see many other places, but "where the world began" for us, in some ways, always remains part of us and helps determine our identity.

The works in this unit all evoke a strong sense of place. The specific situations created or recreated by writers offer insights into other times and places. They help us to experience life in different regions of Canada and in various countries around the world. Such pieces of writing offer opportunities to explore and reflect upon both our own and other cultures.

Tangled

Carl Leggo
(Lines from Edmonton to my father in Newfoundland)

far away
in a city you will never know
I chase words in the cold air
and measure my worth
by the words made mine
and remember you
silent
crouched in the bow of a dory
rising and falling on blue-gray waves
in the air yellow-orange with the sun
untangling the line I twisted in knots
in my frenzy to tear from the ocean
a cod with a lead jigger hooked in its side
and I remember you
sat
and traced the line through its knots
and said nothing
and untangled my line
that could reach to the bottom of the ocean
and lay in swirls at your feet
untangled it
in the morning sun
through the noon sun
into the afternoon sun
and said nothing
and I wouldn't look at you

because I knew you were mad
and I had to look
and you weren't mad
    you were smiling
and where I live now
there is no ocean
unless you stand on your head
and pretend the sky is ocean
    but it's not
and the line I throw out
never hooks into the sky
but always falls back
and tangles at my feet
and perhaps that's why
you could spend hours untangling
my tangled line
    you knew
an untangled line could be thrown
into the ocean's black silence
    and
anchor you to the bottom

Where the World Began

Margaret Laurence

A STRANGE place it was, that place where the world
began. A place of incredible happenings, splendours
and revelations, despairs like multitudinous pits of
isolated hells. A place of shadow-spookiness, inhabited by the
unknowable dead. A place of jubilation and of mourning,
horrible and beautiful.

It was, in fact, a small prairie town.

Because that settlement and that land were my first and for
many years my only real knowledge of this planet, in some
profound way they remain my world, my way of viewing. My
eyes were formed there. Towns like ours, set in a sea of land,
have been described thousands of times as dull, bleak, flat,
uninteresting. I have had it said to me that the railway trip
across Canada is spectacular, except for the prairies, when it
would be desirable to go to sleep for several days, until the
ordeal is over. I am always unable to argue this point effectively. All I can say is—well, you really have to live there to
know that country. The town of my childhood could be called
bizarre, agonizingly repressive or cruel at times, and the land
in which it grew could be called harsh in the violence of its
seasonal changes. But never merely flat or uninteresting. Never
dull.

In winter, we used to hitch rides on the back of the milk
sleigh, our moccasins squeaking and slithering on the hard
rutted snow of the roads, our hands in ice-bubbled mitts

hanging onto the box edge of the sleigh for dear life, while Bert grinned at us through his great frosted moustache and shouted the horse into speed, daring us to stay put. Those mornings, rising, there would be the perpetual fascination of the frost feathers on windows, the ferns and flowers and eerie faces traced there during the night by unseen artists of the wind. Evenings, coming back from skating, the sky would be black but not dark, for you could see a cold glitter of stars from one side of the earth's rim to the other. And then the sometime astonishment when you saw the Northern Lights flaring across the sky, like the scrawled signature of God. After a blizzard, when the snowploughs hadn't yet got through, school would be closed for the day, the assumption being that the town's young could not possibly flounder through five feet of snow in the pursuit of education. We would then gaily don snowshoes and flounder for miles out into the white dazzling deserts, in pursuit of a different kind of knowing. If you came back too close to night, through the woods at the foot of the town hill, the thin black branches of poplar and chokecherry now meringued with frost, sometimes you heard coyotes. Or maybe the banshee wolf-voices were really only inside your head.

Summers were scorching, and when no rain came and the wheat became bleached and dried before it headed, the faces of farmers and townsfolk would not smile much, and you took for granted, because it never seemed to have been any different, the frequent knocking at the back door and the young men standing there, mumbling or thrusting defiantly their requests for a drink of water and a sandwich if you could spare it. They were riding the freights, and you never knew where they had come from or where they might end up, if anywhere. The Drought and Depression were like evil deities which had been there always. You understood and did not understand.

Yet the outside world had its continuing marvels. The poplar bluffs and the small river were filled and surrounded with a zillion different grasses, stones, and weed flowers. The meadowlarks sang undaunted from the twanging telephone wires along the gravel highway. Once we found an old flat-bottomed scow, and launched her, poling along the shallow brown waters, mending her with wodges of hastily chewed Spearmint, grounding her among the tangles of yellow marsh marigolds that grew succulently along the banks of the shrunken river, while the sun made our skins smell dusty-warm.

My best friend lived in an apartment above some stores on Main Street (its real name was Mountain Avenue, goodness knows why), an elegant apartment with royal-blue velvet curtains. The back roof, scarcely sloping at all, was corrugated tin, of a furnace-like warmth on a July afternoon, and we would sit there drinking lemonade and looking across the back lane at the Fire Hall. Sometimes our vigil would be rewarded. Oh joy! Somebody's house burning down! We had an almost-perfect callousness in some ways. Then the wooden tower's bronze bell would clonk and toll like a thousand speeded funerals in a time of plague, and in a few minutes the team of giant black horses would cannon forth, pulling the fire wagon like some scarlet chariot of the Goths, while the firemen clung with one hand, adjusting their helmets as they went.

The oddities of the place were endless. An elderly lady used to serve, as her afternoon tea offering to other ladies, soda biscuits spread with peanut butter and topped with a whole marshmallow. Some considered this slightly eccentric, when compared with chopped egg sandwiches, and admittedly talked about her behind her back, but no one ever refused these delicacies or indicated to her that they thought she had slipped a cog. Another lady dyed her hair a bright and cheery orange, by strangers often mistaken at twenty paces for a feather hat. My own beloved step-mother wore a silver fox neckpiece, a whole pelt, *with the embalmed (?) head still on.* My Ontario Irish grandfather said "sparrow grass," a more interesting term than asparagus. The town dump was known as "the nuisance grounds," a phrase fraught with weird connotations, as though the effluvia of our lives was beneath contempt but at the same time was subtly threatening to the determined and sometimes hysterical propriety of our ways.

Some oddities were, as idiom had it, "funny ha ha"; others were "funny peculiar." Some were not so very funny at all. An old man lived, deranged, in a shack in the valley. Perhaps he wasn't even all that old, but to us he seemed a wild Methuselah figure, shambling among the underbrush and the tall couchgrass, muttering indecipherable curses or blessings, a prophet who had forgotten his prophesies. Everyone in town knew him, but no one knew him. He lived among us as though only occasionally and momentarily visible. The kids called him Andy Gump, and feared him. Some sought to prove their bravery by tormenting him. They were the mediaeval bear baiters, and he the lumbering bewildered bear, half blind, only rarely turning to snarl. Everything is to be found in a town like mine. Belsen, writ small but with the same ink.

All of us cast stones in one shape or another. In grade school, among the vulnerable and violet girls we were, the feared and despised were those few older girls from what was charmingly termed "the wrong side of the tracks." Tough in talk and tougher in muscle, they were said to be whores already. And may have been, that being about the only profession readily available to them.

The dead lived in that place, too. Not only the grandparents who had, in local parlance, "passed on" and who gloomed, bearded and bonneted, from the sepia photographs in old albums, but also the uncles, forever eighteen or nineteen, whose names were carved on the granite family stones in the cemetery, but whose bones lay in France. My own young mother lay in that graveyard, beside other dead of our kin, and when I was ten, my father, too, only forty, left the living town for the dead dwelling on the hill.

When I was eighteen, I couldn't wait to get out of that town, away from the prairies. I did not know then that I would carry the land and town all my life within my skull, that they would form the mainspring and source of the writing I was to do, wherever and however far away I might live.

This was my territory in the time of my youth, and in a sense my life since then has been an attempt to look at it, to come to terms with it. Stultifying to the mind it certainly could be, and sometimes was, but not to the imagination. It was many things, but it was never dull.

The same, I now see, could be said for Canada in general. Why on earth did generations of Canadians pretend to believe this country dull? We knew perfectly well it wasn't. Yet for so long we did not proclaim what we knew. If our upsurge of so-called nationalism seems odd or irrelevant to outsiders, and even to some of our own people (*what's all the fuss about?*), they might try to understand that for many years we valued ourselves insufficiently, living as we did under the huge shadows of those two dominating figures, Uncle Sam and Britannia. We have only just begun to value ourselves, our land, our abilities. We have only just begun to recognize our legends and to give shape to our myths.

There are, God knows, enough aspects to deplore about this country. When I see the killing of our lakes and rivers with industrial wastes, I feel rage and despair. When I see our industries and natural resources increasingly taken over by America, I feel an overwhelming discouragement, especially as I cannot simply say "damn Yankees." It should never be forgotten that it is we ourselves who have sold such a large amount of our birthright for a mess of plastic Progress. When I saw the War Measures Act being invoked in 1970, I lost forever the vestigial remains of the naive wish-belief that repression could not happen here, or would not. And yet, of course, I had known all along in the deepest and often hidden caves of the heart that anything can happen anywhere, for the seeds of both man's freedom and his captivity are found everywhere, even in the microcosm of a prairie town. But in raging against our injustices, our stupidities, I do so *as family*, as I did, and still do in writing, about those aspects of my town which I hated and which are always in some ways aspects of myself.

The land still draws me more than other lands. I have lived in Africa and in England, but splendid as both can be, they do not have the power to move me in the same way as, for example, that part of southern Ontario where I spent four months last summer in a cedar cabin beside a river. "Scratch a Canadian, and you find a phony pioneer," I used to say to myself in warning. But all the same it is true, I think, that we are not yet totally alienated from physical earth, and let us only pray we do not become so. I once thought that my lifelong fear and mistrust of cities made me a kind of old-fashioned freak; now I see it differently.

The cabin has a long window across its front western wall, and sitting at the oak table there in the mornings, I used to look out at the river and at the tall trees beyond, green-gold in the early light. The river was bronze; the sun caught it strangely, reflecting upon its surface the near-shore sand ripples underneath. Suddenly, the crescenting of a fish, gone before the eye could clearly give image to it. The old man next door said these leaping fish were carp. Himself, he preferred muskie, for he was a real fisherman and the muskie gave him a fight. The wind most often blew from the south, and the river flowed toward the south, so when the water was wind-riffled, and the current was strong, the river seemed to be flowing both ways. I liked this, and interpreted it as an omen, a natural symbol.

A few years ago, when I was back in Winnipeg, I gave a talk at my old college. It was open to the public, and afterward a very old man came up to me and asked me if my maiden name had been Wemyss. I said yes, thinking he might have known my father or my grandfather. But no. "When I was a young lad," he said, "I once worked for your great-grand-father, Robert Wemyss, when he had the sheep ranch at Rae-burn." I think that was a moment when I realized all over again something of great importance to me. My long-ago families came from Scotland and Ireland, but in a sense that no longer mattered so much. My true roots were here.

I am not very patriotic, in the usual meaning of that word. I cannot say "My country right or wrong" in any political, social or literary context. But one thing is inalterable, for better or worse, for life.

This is where my world began. A world which includes the ancestors—both my own and other people's ancestors who became mine. A world which formed me, and continues to do so, even while I fought it in some of its aspects, and continue to do so. A world which gave me my own lifework to do, because it was here that I learned the sight of my own particular eyes.

Seasons in the Rain

Silver Donald Cameron

THE first thing to understand about Vancouver is that the climate is not very pleasant.

Vancouverites loudly proclaim the precise opposite. Persons who express doubt about the climate are barred from voting in municipal elections. Visitors who wonder absently what happened to the sun are quick-frozen and shipped C.O.D. to Moose Jaw. As you approach Vancouver International Airport large signs are seen on the mountaintops. THE WEATHER HERE, they say, IS WONDERFUL.

On the subject of climate, all Vancouverites are shameless, brazen, unblinking liars.

The climate in Vancouver is terrible. The rains begin in Vancouver at the beginning of September. They continue virtually unbroken till the end of the following August. Then nature's inexorable cycle repeats itself, and another year's growth of green moist moss begins growing on everyone's hair.

Relatively few people use umbrellas, because of the mad theory that the climate is pleasant. Instead, they develop The Vancouver Slouch. Heads and shoulders hunched forward, white wrinkled hands thrust deep into their pockets, they pad onward through the water, offering only their backs to the rain. In their hearts they know the rain will never stop. With their voices they lie. Their rounded shoulders tell the truth.

I was reared in Vancouver. I am giving it to you straight. My posture still leaves a great deal to be desired.

When I first moved east of the Rockies to live, I was twenty-seven years old. In the opinion of a true Vancouverite, the rest of Canada is barely worth selling for junk: a vast freezing wilderness of whining wheat farmers, arrogant bureaucrats, carnivorous stockbrokers and raving separatists. Naturally I skipped all that and went direct to London, England. One day my family and I emerged from King's Cross railway station, half a dozen blocks from home. It was pouring down rain: torrents, buckets, cascades of flying water. We raced down the street past the grubby brick buildings, all alone on the checkerboard sidewalks. Astonished Londoners, huddled in doorways, gaped at us as we zipped past. The baby's stroller clattered and banged, our coats flew open, we gasped for breath. As we rounded the last corner for home, the rain stopped. The sky cleared. The sun shone brilliantly. The Englishmen stepped jauntily out of their doorways and strode along their ways, swinging their furled umbrellas.

You see? You see? We were Vancouverites. The notion that rain might *stop* was as foreign and incomprehensible as half-crowns and florins.

Aside from their outrageous falsehoods about the climate, Vancouverites are exceptionally pleasant. Born Vancouverites are not, however, easy to find.

My mother came to Vancouver from a farm in Manitoba. My father came from North Bay, Ontario, *via* the Interior of B.C. The man who for a generation spoke stridently for the province of the setting sun, W.A.C. Bennett, came from Hampton, New Brunswick. The first premier of B.C., a chap named Smith who took the wonderful name Amor de Cosmos, Lover of the Universe, was a visionary Nova Scotian.

Appropriately enough, Vancouver has one of the largest Chinatowns in the Western world, a marvellously exotic enclave around Pender and Main of which the city has at last learned to be proud. Wander into a Pender Street import store, and emerge with brass Buddhas, delicate parasols, folding fans, bamboo snakes, china soup bowls with china spoons. The whole package is unlikely to cost fifteen dollars. Then wander to Ming's or the Ho Inn, the Yen Lock or the Bamboo Terrace or any of the other restaurants nearby, and dine splendidly for three or four dollars.

Notice the pagoda-roofed telephone booth, and pay some attention to the tops of the tall, narrow buildings, with their balconies and Chinese flourishes. Leading up to them are shabby staircases, with excited Asian voices floating down to the street. Passing those doorways as a child, watching the elderly men going in and out, I used to wonder what went on upstairs: mah jong? opium? Probably they were playing crib, but the flavour was of Shanghai and Kowloon, warlords and ancient sages. Later, as an Air Cadet at Abbotsford airbase, I shared a room with L.A.C. Wong and A.C.L. Yee, but they were not warlords or sages; they were just Wayne and Stan, good fellows to have on your side in a waterfight.

Hardly anyone comes from Vancouver. The last place I lived in the city I had a Dane next door and a Czech in the basement. Beyond the Dane was an Englishman, down the road a brace of Russians. The Dane, Poul Hansen, had a toy shop on Robsonstrasse, so named for its bewildering variety of immigrants with bakeries, delicatessens, schnitzel houses, import shops and other ventures. Even the mayor, in the days of my childhood, was Fred Hume, who had done his apprenticeship as mayor of neighbouring New Westminster.

I'm not even a true native myself. I have a son and two brothers who were born in Vancouver. I was actually born in Toronto, sorra be on me, though I emigrated unusually early, at the age of two. Go west, young man! And don't forget your pottie.

Still, if I have a home town it is crass, soggy, alluring Vancouver, the only city in which I will ever be young. The home of the Polar Bear Swim, in which lunatics plunge into the freezing ocean on New Year's Day, demonstrating the alleged mildness of the climate. A city where a home sixty years old is treasured as an historic site, and properly so: before it was built, no structure had ever graced the spot. A city where the chuckles of tycoons are drowned out by the crash of timber falling up the coast, the roar of heavy machinery strip-mining the Kootenays, the crackle of gracious mansions in the West End as the bulldozers drive through them, clearing the ground for another high-rise. Soon that, too, will be history: there is hardly a house still standing.

But there is no place on earth like it: the relentless drive of the robber barons opposed by the most intransigent socialists in Canada, the damp and dreamy atmosphere of huge trees in a harbour mist, the gung-ho confidence that a downtown spiky with high-rises limned against the blue and white mountains is a vision of what a city should be—as perhaps it is, one thinks, looking north across False Creek on a rare crisp day in winter. All that rain produces the softest, sweetest water I know: what comes from the taps will foam in the tub, slip down the throat like wine crystal-cold from the mountains. Tawdry and romantic, bourgeois and raunchy at once, Vancouver is where the small ambitions flourish and the large dreams move furtively. Paradise will be Spanish Banks in the sunlight. Purgatory will be Marpole in the rain.

Who can be objective about a home town? Everything happened there for the first time. I learned to drive on Alberni Street, the choked back alley of Georgia. After that I was relaxed at Hyde Park Corner, unfazed by the Etoile. My sexual education began in the back seat of an old Plymouth parked at Wreck beach, in the University of British Columbia endowment lands. My college education began a couple of miles further west. My political education began when Howard Green, who had apparently represented Vancouver Quadra in Parliament since old Captain Quadra himself sailed into Burrard Inlet from Spain, told me that a young lecturer at UBC was a Russian spy; and Jack Wasserman, the gossip columnist who was in business even then, suggested that the whole uproar was caused by the presence of Igor Gouzenko on campus. Was Gouzenko there, hiding from the vengeance of the Kremlin? I didn't know then. I don't know now. I wouldn't be surprised.

And UBC, where my awkward, lightweight, gutsy father broke his arm in the first quarter of the first game of the football season back in the twenties, and then, the next year, broke his collarbone. After that he became team manager instead, and the team went on after the season ended to form what eventually became Beta Theta Pi fraternity. Of which, naturally, I eventually became a member. Before that, I remember, we used to sneak into the football games at Varsity Stadium through a broken plank at the south end of the fence. It's probably still broken, and kids probably still use it, though the university is five times the size it was then.

My father claimed to have known Walter Gage as a young man. I don't believe this: I believe God imagined Walter Gage sometime around the turn of the century, and then built the university around him. Beaming benignly, walking with the gait of a king penguin unaccountably gifted as a teacher of mathematics, smoking cigarettes through a long skinny holder, Gage was, when I first met him, lumbered with some unwieldy title like Dean of Administrative and Inter-Faculty Affairs. He had an office in the Buchanan Building with a sign on the door that said DEAN GAGE, a memory like flypaper for names and faces, and a habit of throwing an arm over your shoulder as he ushered you out of the office. Whatever the title, his real function was Fixer of Student Problems. If you needed special permission for anything, were running out of money, contemplated suicide or marriage, you went to see Dean Gage.

When I last saw him he was in the same office, with the same sign. He told me some stories about my father, who had progressed from the football team to the faculty before his death in 1951, inquired about my mother and brothers, said that "Oh, yes, he was still teaching mathematics," and threw an arm over my shoulders as he ushered me out of the office.

The difference is that at the time—1971—he was supposed to be the President of the university. Now a story is abroad that he has retired. I don't believe that, either. UBC without Gage is like sea-water without salt: it looks the same, but the characteristic taste is gone.

For me, you see, Vancouver is indissolubly fused with the university: my family lived out that way, my father both studied and taught there, eventually I both studied and taught there myself. For thousands of Vancouverites, the university barely exists, a matter which has given some concern to W.A.C. Bennett's feisty successor, Dave Barrett. When I lived in B.C., Dave Barrett was a social worker noisily fired from the provincial prison at Haney for participating in socialist politics while engaged in the Social Credit civil service. I never met him, though our wives were briefly associated in Voice of Women. But the difference between Bennett and Barrett is the difference between stupid certainty and cautious hope.

Barrett seems to have shaken things up on all fronts, praise God, Who Alone knows how badly they needed shaking. When I return to B.C. now, I am assured on all sides that the Barrett government has made foolish mistakes, has moved too quickly, too drastically and too thoughtlessly on ideas like auto insurance and the freezing of farmland, and has then had to back off and introduce refinements which should have been included in the first place. One old friend, a beloved reactionary, grunts that this shows the hopeless incompetence and arrogance of socialists. Another, a hopeful idealist, says that it shows merely that if you've never formed a government before, you're not going to do it perfectly at once. The old pickup truck has been traded in on an Audi Fox. Can we really handle the damn thing? Is it safe? Is it practical?

I haven't lived in Vancouver since 1964, and a lot of water has passed through Lion's Gate since then. In my day, young feller, there were no hippies, there was no Gastown, no think-ins or be-ins, no town fool, no *Georgia Straight*. I missed out on the whole reign of Tom Terrific Campbell, the developer-mayor who wanted to use the authority of the War Measures Act to clean out all the hippies. My Vancouver was sedate and somnolent, and a great deal of it has been buried and bulldozed. It offered no Granville Street Mall, no Toronto-Dominion tower glaring down from the site of the old Hotel Vancouver. I heard Benny Goodman's big band at the Denman Auditorium. The big band has been dissolved, and the auditorium demolished. That's how old I am, sonny.

What was it like then, growing up in Vancouver in the 'forties and 'fifties? There's a rage now for the 'fifties, people looking back at the days of St. Laurent and Eisenhower with fond nostalgia. The nostalgia, believe me, is misplaced. Perhaps it always is.

What I remember about the 'fifties is boredom and panic, and the mindless boosterism of perhaps the last innocents in history. Boredom because the world seemed so thoroughly managed, so entirely under control, the career paths so utterly mapped out that we could hardly imagine the magnificence the world might offer. Suffering through the interminable dullness of Lord Byng High School, we foresaw the future:

UBC, law or medicine or accounting or teaching, marriage, kids, a house on a street like the one we had grown up on, retirement, pension, death.

Panic: surely life might offer more than this, but what? We couldn't say. In 1954, a kid—Jimmy Johnston, if I recall— graduated from Lord Byng, and in the annual it said that his ambition was to build his own schooner and sail it to the South Seas. I hope he did. At the time everybody took it as a spasm of wit. People like us didn't do such interesting things.

I remember a curious sense, too, that history was irrelevant, that the news was something happening elsewhere—in New York or Rome, in Sharpeville or even Ottawa—but never in Vancouver. I never read a novel set in Vancouver: I never even *heard* of one. History had taken place in England, in China, in Quebec, but not in B.C. It is no accident that I finally settled in the most ancient, storied part of Canada, where French sailors were fishing in the time of Shakespeare. A recent book, indeed, suggests that Prince Henry Sinclair, Earl of Orkney, may have sailed to Nova Scotia in 1398, a century before Columbus. Vancouver's fretfulness, its ceaseless growth, its frantic insistence on Now and Tomorrow, perhaps, shaped my taste for a community with a sense of Yesterday as well.

One takes with the left hand, relinquishes with the right. If Nova Scotia is enriched and intimidated by its memories, British Columbia is malleable, incoherent, and splendidly free of the burdens of the past. A Nova Scotian once told me that Maritimers know from experience that nothing significant can be done about anything important, and they are wrong; whereas Westerners believe anything can be done, and done at once, and they are wrong too. In such matters Vancouver has marked me forever.

People can, dammit, build a better world; and yet in the 'fifties I could hardly see how. Long ago, in 1957, when I was nineteen, John Diefenbaker strode across the country; he was sworn in on my twentieth birthday. When an enthusiastic campus Tory introduced him in the university auditorium that spring as the new leader of the Conservative Party and "the next Prime Minister of Canada," the hall rocked with involuntary laughter. Why, the man was a *Conservative*! We had grown up in a one-party state, ruled by Liberals since before we were born.

Three years earlier, the French had been defeated at some place called Dienbienphu, and the Americans were slowly taking up the white man's evil burden in Indochina. A woman named Rosa Parks said No, she was not going to take a back seat in the buses of Montgomery, Alabama, and a young preacher named Martin Luther King got involved in something called a boycott. At Harvard University a couple of psychologists named Timothy Leary and Richard Alpert were experimenting with stuff called lysergic acid, or LSD for short. In England, some Merseyside kids named Lennon and McCartney were making themselves into musicians. The seeds of the 'sixties were germinating.

For me, I suppose, it was John Diefenbaker who revealed that the world need not always be dull and over-organized, and for two or three years I was an ardent Conservative. "Follow John" is a joke now, scarcely less mouldy than "Twenty-three skidoo," but in those days John Diefenbaker meant sunlight and fresh air, and I can never look upon him with indifference. And—this is the point—Diefenbaker happened to me in Vancouver.

A home town, perhaps, is the place where the great events happened to you personally. It doesn't matter what the history books say: when I was eight years old, living on West 23rd Avenue, Japan capitulated, and we drove through the downtown streets among the screaming laughing crowds, with soldiers and drunks sitting on the fenders of our 1939 Plymouth, horns blowing, bells ringing, all the world gone crazy with joy and relief. I woke up groggy one morning, not wanting to go to school, and my mother called down the stairs that school was called off because George VI had died. Hallelujah, I muttered, and snuggled down into the blankets. John Kennedy was shot in the rain on the UBC campus, just after I had dismissed a class of freshmen.

What is all this to you, really? Why should you care whose bra straps I fumbled with, and where, or how I stole car accessories and wished to grow taller? What difference can it make that I worked as a car-hop in a drive-in called The Dog House, which specialized in hot dogs—the Mutt, the Chihuahua, the

Prairie Dog. A yard-long Poodle, top of the line, would set you back three bucks. Can it matter to you that I loaded boxcars for CP Express and woke in the mornings to the melancholy *Beeee-ohhh!* of the foghorns down in the distant harbour? You never knew Rod Atkins, who was in my class in Grade Four and skipped Grade Five. He sat with me in philosophy classes ten years later all through the fall before he was killed when his Reserve Air Force plane collided with another during exercises over Squamish.

But when I think of Vancouver, those are the things I remember, the things which made me whatever I am. My Vancouver is, at last, mine alone, the place I first met sex, death, politics, learning. My Vancouver is a city fixed in time as well as place, only one of the million Vancouvers each of its people knows. You can move away from a home town, but you can never really leave it behind, because that unique city which revealed itself to you lives on in your attitudes, your ideas, your vision of the world.

It even lives on in my teeth. The next time you hear someone say Vancouver is not a Canadian city, remember my broken incisors. Vancouver has no natural ice and few artificial rinks; when we played hockey, we played on the street, on roller skates. I fell on the pavement one day, aged about twelve, and chipped a front tooth. That Saturday I went to Dr. Hallman, who told me it didn't matter much. I went from his office down to the game a block from home, and faced off with Billy Weeks. We slashed for the puck, Billy's stick glanced off mine, then flew up and smashed off half the other incisor. Within the hour I was back in Dr. Hallman's office, bleeding freely. He told me that when I got older we'd put a cap on it. I never bothered.

Vancouver an un-Canadian city? Then why was I hunched over the little mantel radio dreaming of stickhandling, listening to Foster Hewitt in Toronto screaming "He shoots—HE SCORES!"? Why did I flee California for Vancouver after a year of graduate study? How come I could tell an American from Bellingham the moment he opened his mouth, while even a kid from miserable old Toronto became one of us a week after moving in? No, no. Vancouverites know surprisingly little about Canada. One of the things they don't often know is how Canadian they are.

I come from Vancouver. What does that mean?

It means I think of mountains as friendly, and I will never be at home away from the sea. Yokohama and Vladivostok seem as near to Canada, for me, as London and Naples. I consider soft water a birth-right, and I am personally insulted by blizzards. I doubt that I would ever return to live in Vancouver; I am at home in Nova Scotia as I never was in my home town. But when Nova Scotians decamp for British Columbia, as hundreds do every year, I understand why they are going.

Coming from Vancouver means that, however sheepishly I admit it, however I might wish to deny it, something in me rejoices to hear on the roof the steady drumming of a determined, pouring rain.

Chicago

Carl Sandburg

Hog Butcher for the World,
Tool Maker, Stacker of Wheat,
Player with Railroads and the Nation's Freight
    Handler;
Stormy, husky, brawling,
City of the Big Shoulders:
They tell me you are wicked, and I believe them
    for I have seen your painted women under
    the gas lamps luring the farm boys.
And they tell me you are crooked, and I answer:
    Yes, it is true I have seen the gunman kill
    and go free to kill again.
And they tell me you are brutal, and my reply is:
    On the faces of women and children I have
    seen the marks of wanton hunger.
And having answered so I turn once more to
    those who sneer at this my city, and I give
    them back the sneer and say to them:
Come and show me another city with lifted head
    singing so proud to be alive and coarse and
    strong and cunning;
Flinging magnetic curses amid the toil of piling
    job on job, here is a tall bold slugger set
    vivid against the little soft cities;
Fierce as a dog with tongue lapping for action,
    cunning as a savage pitted against the
    wilderness,

Bareheaded,
Shoveling,
Wrecking,
Planning,
Building, breaking, rebuilding,
Under the smoke, dust all over his mouth, laugh-
ing with white teeth,
Under the terrible burden of destiny laughing as
a young man laughs,
Laughing even as an ignorant fighter laughs
who has never lost a battle,
Bragging and laughing that under his wrist is the
pulse, and under his ribs the heart of the
people,
      Laughing!
Laughing the stormy, husky, brawling laughter
of youth; half-naked, sweating, proud to
be Hog-butcher, Tool-maker, Stacker of
Wheat, Player with Railroads, and Freight-
handler to the Nation.

A Child's Christmas in Wales

Dylan Thomas

ONE Christmas was so much like another, in those years around the sea-town corner now and out of all sound except the distant speaking of the voices I sometimes hear a moment before sleep, that I can never remember whether it snowed for six days and six nights when I was twelve or whether it snowed for twelve days and twelve nights when I was six. All the Christmases roll down toward the two-tongued sea, like a cold and headlong moon bundling down the sky that was our street; and they stop at the rim of the ice-edged, fish-freezing waves, and I plunge my hands in the snow and bring out whatever I can find. In goes my hand into that wool-white bell-tongued ball of holidays resting at the rim of the carol-singing sea, and out come Mrs. Prothero and the firemen.

It was on the afternoon of the day of Christmas Eve, and I was in Mrs. Prothero's garden, waiting for cats, with her son Jim. It was snowing. It was always snowing at Christmas. December, in my memory, is white as Lapland, though there were no reindeer. But there were cats. Patient, cold, and callous, our hands wrapped in socks, we waited to snowball the cats. Sleek and long as jaguars and horrible-whiskered, spitting and snarling, they would slink and sidle over the white back-garden walls, and the lynx-eyed hunters, Jim and I, furcapped and moccasined trappers from Hudson Bay, off Mumbles Road, would hurl our deadly snowballs at the green of their eyes. The wise cats never appeared. We were so still, Eskimo-footed arctic marksmen in the muffling silence of the eternal snows—eternal, ever since Wednesday—that we never heard Mrs. Prothero's first cry from her igloo at the bottom of the garden. Or, if we heard it at all, it was, to us, like the far-off challenge of our enemy and prey, the neighbor's polar cat. But soon the voice grew louder.

"Fire!" cried Mrs. Prothero, and she beat the dinner gong.

And we ran down the garden, with the snowballs in our arms, toward the house; and smoke, indeed, was pouring out of the dining room, and the gong was bombilating, and Mrs. Prothero was announcing ruin like a town crier in Pompeii. This was better than all the cats in Wales standing on the wall in a row. We bounded into the house, laden with snowballs, and stopped at the open door of the smoke-filled room. Something was burning all right; perhaps it was Mr. Prothero, who always slept there after midday dinner with a newspaper over his face. But he was standing in the middle of the room, saying, "A fine Christmas!" and smacking at the smoke with a slipper.

"Call the fire brigade," cried Mrs. Prothero as she beat the gong.

"They won't be there," said Mr. Prothero, "it's Christmas."

There was no fire to be seen, only clouds of smoke and Mr. Prothero standing in the middle of them, waving his slipper as though he were conducting.

"Do something," he said.

And we threw all our snowballs into the smoke—I think we missed Mr. Prothero—and ran out of the house to the telephone box.

"Let's call the police as well," Jim said.

"And the ambulance."

"And Ernie Jenkins, he likes fires."

But we only called the fire brigade, and soon the fire engine came and three tall men in helmets brought a hose into the house and Mr. Prothero got out just in time before they turned it on. Nobody could have had a noisier Christmas Eve. And when the firemen turned off the hose and were standing in the wet, smoky room, Jim's aunt, Miss Prothero, came downstairs and peered in at them. Jim and I waited, very quietly, to hear what she would say to them. She said the right thing, always. She looked at the three tall firemen in their shining helmets, standing among the smoke and cinders and dissolving snowballs, and she said: "Would you like anything to read?"

Years and years and years ago, when I was a boy, when there were wolves in Wales, and birds the color of red-flannel petticoats whisked past the harp-shaped hills, when we sang and wallowed all night and day in caves that smelt like Sunday afternoons in damp front farmhouse parlors, and we chased, with the jawbones of deacons, the English and the bears, before the motor car, before the wheel, before the duchess-faced horse, when we rode the daft and happy hills bareback, it snowed and it snowed. But here a small boy says: "It snowed last year, too. I made a snowman and my brother knocked it down and I knocked my brother down and then we had tea."

"But that was not the same snow," I say. "Our snow was not only shaken from white-wash buckets down the sky, it came shawling out of the ground and swam and drifted out of the arms and hands and bodies of the trees; snow grew overnight on the roofs of the houses like a pure and grandfather moss, minutely white-ivied the walls and settled on the postman, opening the gate, like a dumb, numb thunderstorm of white, torn Christmas cards."

"Were there postmen then, too?"

"With sprinkling eyes and wind-cherried noses, on spread, frozen feet they crunched up to the doors and mittened on them manfully. But all that the children could hear was a ringing of bells."

"You mean that the postman went rat-a-tat-tat and the doors rang?"

"I mean that the bells that the children could hear were inside them."

"I only hear thunder sometimes, never bells."

"There were church bells, too."

"Inside them?"

"No, no, no, in the bat-black, snow-white belfries, tugged by bishops and storks. And they rang their tidings over the bandaged town, over the frozen foam of the power and ice-cream hills, over the crackling sea. It seemed that all the churches boomed for joy under my window; and the weather-cocks crew for Christmas, on our fence."

"Get back to the postmen."

"They were just ordinary postmen, fond of walking and dogs and Christmas and the snow. They knocked on the doors with blue knuckles. . . "

"Ours has got a black knocker. . . "

"And then they stood on the white Welcome mat in the little, drifted porches and huffed and puffed, making ghosts with their breath, and jogged from foot to foot like small boys wanting to go out."

"And then the Presents?"

"And then the Presents, after the Christmas box. And the cold postman, with a rose on his button nose, tingled down the tea-tray-slithered run of the chilly glinting hill. He went in his icebound boots like a man on fishmonger's slabs. He wagged his bag like a frozen camel's hump, dizzily turned the corner on one foot, and was gone."

"Get back to the Presents."

"There were the Useful Presents: engulfing mufflers of the old coach days, and mittens made for giant sloths; zebra scarfs of a substance like silky gum that could be tug-o'-warred down to the galoshes; blinding tam-o'-shanters like patchwork tea cozies and bunny-suited busbies and balaclavas for victims of headshrinking tribes; from aunts who always wore wool next to the skin there were mustached and rasping vests that made you wonder why the aunts had any skin left at all; and once I had a little crocheted nose bag from an aunt now, alas, no longer whinnying with us. And pictureless books in which small boys, though warned with quotations not to, *would* skate on Farmer Giles's pond and did and drowned; and books that told me everything about the wasp, except why."

"Go on to the Useless Presents."

"Bags of moist and many-colored jelly babies and a folded flag and a false nose and a tram conductor's cap and a machine that punched tickets and rang a bell; never a catapult; once, by mistake that no one could explain, a little hatchet; and a celluloid duck that made, when you pressed it, a most unducklike sound, a mewing moo that an ambitious cat might make who wished to be a cow; and a painting book in which I could make the grass, the trees, the sea and the animals any color I pleased, and still the dazzling sky-blue sheep are grazing in the red field under the rainbow-billed and pea-green birds. Hard-boileds, toffee, fudge and all-sorts, crunches, cracknels, humbugs, glaciers, marzipan, and butterwelsh for the Welsh. And troops of bright tin soldiers who, if they could not fight, could always run. And Snakes-and-Families and Happy Ladders. And Easy Hobbi-Games for Little Engineers, complete with instructions. Oh, easy for Leonardo! And a whistle to make the dogs bark to wake up the old man next door to make him beat on the wall with his stick to shake our picture off the wall. And a packet of cigarettes: you put one in your mouth and you stood at the corner of the street and you waited for hours, in vain, for an old lady to scold you for smoking a cigarette, and then with a smirk you ate it. And then it was breakfast under the balloons."

"Were there uncles, like in our house?"

"There are always uncles at Christmas. The same uncles. And on Christmas mornings, with dog-disturbing whistle and sugar fags, I would scour the swatched town for the news of the little world, and find always a dead bird by the white post office or by the deserted swings; perhaps a robin, all but one of his fires out. Men and women wading or scooping back from chapel, with taproom noses and wind-bussed cheeks, all albinos, huddled their stiff black jarring feathers against the irreligious snow. Mistletoe hung from the gas brackets in all the front parlors; there was sherry and walnuts and bottled beer and crackers by the dessertspoons; and cats in their furabouts watched the fires; and the high-heaped fire spat, all ready for the chestnuts and the mulling pokers. Some few large men sat in the front parlors, without their collars, uncles almost certainly, trying their new cigars, holding them out judiciously at arms' length, returning them to their mouths, coughing, then holding them out again as though waiting for the explosion; and some few small aunts, not wanted in the kitchen, nor anywhere else for that matter, sat on the very edges of their chairs, poised and brittle, afraid to break, like faded cups and saucers."

Not many those mornings trod the piling streets: an old

man always, fawn-bowlered, yellow-gloved and, at this time of year, with spats of snow, would take his constitutional to the white bowling green and back, as he would take it wet or fire on Christmas Day or Doomsday; sometimes two hale young men, with big pipes blazing, no overcoats and windblown scarfs, would trudge, unspeaking, down to the forlorn sea, to work up an appetite, to blow away the fumes, who knows, to walk into the waves until nothing of them was left but the two curling smoke clouds of their inextinguishable briars. Then I would be slapdashing home, the gravy smell of the dinners of others, the bird smell, the brandy, the pudding and mince, coiling up to my nostrils, when out of a snow-clogged side lane would come a boy the spit of myself, with a pink-tipped cigarette and the violet past of a black eye, cocky as a bullfinch, leering all to himself. I hated him on sight and sound, and would be about to put my dog whistle to my lips and blow him off the face of Christmas when suddenly he, with a violet wink, put *his* whistle to *his* lips and blew so stridently, so high, so exquisitely loud that gobbling faces, their cheeks bulged with goose, would press against their tinseled windows, the whole length of the white echoing street. For dinner we had turkey and blazing pudding, and after dinner the uncles sat in front of the fire, loosened all buttons, put their large moist hands over their watch chains, groaned a little, and slept. Mothers, aunts, and sisters scuttled to and fro, bearing tureens. Auntie Bessie, who had already been frightened, twice, by a clockwork mouse, whimpered at the sideboard and had some elderberry wine. The dog was sick. Auntie Dosie had to have three aspirins, but Auntie Hannah, who liked port, stood in the middle of the snowbound backyard, singing like a big-bosomed thrush. I would blow up balloons to see how big they would blow up to; and, when they burst, which they all did, the uncles jumped and rumbled. In the rich and heavy afternoon, the uncles breathing like dolphins and the snow descending, I would sit among festoons and Chinese lanterns and nibble dates and try to make a model man-o'-war, following the Instructions for Little Engineers, and produce what might be mistaken for a seagoing tramcar. Or I would go out, my bright new boots squeaking, into the white world, onto the seaward hill, to call on Jim and Dan and Jack and to pad through the still streets, leaving huge deep footprints on the hidden pavements.

"I bet people will think there's been hippos."

"What would you do if you saw a hippo coming down our street?"

"I'd go like this, bang! I'd throw him over the railings and roll him down the hill and then I'd tickle him under the ear and he'd wag his tail."

"What would you do if you saw *two* hippos?"

Iron-flanked and bellowing he-hippos clanked and battered through the scudding snow toward us as we passed Mr. Daniel's house.

"Let's post Mr. Daniel a snowball through his letter box."

"Let's write things in the snow."

"Let's write, 'Mr. Daniel looks like a spaniel' all over his lawn."

Or we walked on the white shore. "Can the fishes see it's snowing?"

The silent one-clouded heavens drifted on to the sea. Now we were snow-blind travelers lost on the north hills, and vast dewlapped dogs, with flasks round their necks, ambled and shambled up to us, baying "Excelsior." We returned home through the poor streets where only a few children fumbled with bare red fingers in the wheel-rutted snow and catcalled after us, their voices fading away, as we trudged uphill, into the cries of the dock birds and the hooting of ships out in the whirling bay. And then, at tea the recovered uncles would be jolly; and the ice cake loomed in the center of the table like a marble grave. Auntie Hannah laced her tea with rum, because it was only once a year.

Bring out the tall tales now that we told by the fire as the gaslight bubbled like a diver. Ghosts whooed like owls in the long nights when I dared not look over my shoulder; animals lurked in the cubbyhole under the stairs where the gas meter ticked. And I remember that we went singing carols once, when there wasn't the shaving of a moon to light the flying streets. At the end of a long road was a drive that led to a large house, and we stumbled up the darkness of the drive that night, each one of us afraid, each one holding a stone in his hand in case, and all of us too brave to say a word. The wind

through the trees made noises as of old and unpleasant and
maybe webfooted men wheezing in caves. We reached the black
bulk of the house.

"What shall we give them? Hark the Herald?"

"No," Jack said, "good King Wenceslas. I'll count three."

One, two, three, and we began to sing, our voices high and
seemingly distant in the snow-felted darkness round the house
that was occupied by nobody we knew. We stood close
together, near the dark door.

> "Good King Wenceslas looked out
> On the feast of Stephen. . . "

And then a small, dry voice, like the voice of someone who
has not spoken for a long time, joined our singing; a small,
dry, eggshell voice from the other side of the door: a small dry
voice through the keyhole. And when we stopped running we
were outside *our* house; the front room was lovely; balloons
floated under the hot-water-bottle-gulping gas; everything was
good again and shone over the town.

"Perhaps it was a ghost," Jim said.

"Perhaps it was trolls," Dan said, who was always reading.

"Let's go in and see if there's any jelly left," Jack said.
And we did that.

Always on Christmas night there was music. An uncle played
the fiddle, a cousin sang "Cherry Ripe," and another uncle
sang "Drake's Drum." It was very warm in the little house.
Auntie Hannah, who had got on to the parsnip wine, sang
a song about Bleeding Hearts and Death, and then another in
which she said her heart was like a Bird's Nest; and then
everybody laughed again; and then I went to bed. Looking
through my bedroom window, out into the moonlight and the
unending smoke-colored snow, I could see the lights in the
windows of all the other houses on our hill and hear the music
rising from them up the long, steadily falling night. I turned
the gas down, I got into bed. I said some words to the close
and holy darkness, and then I slept.

The First Born Son

Ernest Buckler

THE pale cast of fatigue smudged Martin's skin and little grooves of it emptied into the corners of his mouth. But this land was his own, and a son of his own flesh was holding the plow that broke it. His thoughts were tired half-thoughts but they did not ache.

He felt the wine of the fall day and for a minute his feet wandered, inattentive, from the furrow. The dogged, slow-eyed oxen followed him, straining nose-down at his heels. The plow ran out wide in the sod. David tried to flip over the furrow with a sudden wrench of the handles, but the chocolate-curling lip of earth broke and the share came clear.

"Whoa!" David yelled.

"Whoa!" Martin roared at the oxen.

"For God's sake, Dad, can't you watch where you're going? It's hard enough to hold this damn thing when you keep 'em straight."

"Now don't get high," Martin said. But there was no echo of David's temper in his voice. He knew David was tired. And David could not learn to handle his weariness. He fought it. It was no use to do that. If you let it come and go, quietly, after supper it made a lazy song in your muscles and was good to think about. Martin remembered the night David was born. They had thought Ellen would die. It was Christmas Eve. There was not a breath of wind in the moonlit, Christmas-kindled air. Snow lay in kind folds on the ground, shadowed in the dead-still moonlight like the wrinkles of a white cloak. On the brook Martin could watch the gay, meaningless movements of the children skating. And sometimes a fragment of their heartless laughter would break away and fall inside the room. Ellen's pain-tight face stared at her pale hands outside the quilt. The kind-smelling Christmas tree was a cruel mockery. Now and then Martin would go outside and listen, bareheaded, for the doctor's sleighbells, trying to separate their faint, far-off tinkle from the frost-crackle of the spruces. He would think he heard them. Then there would be nothing. Runner tracks shone like ising-glass in the moonlight. He heard nothing but the heartless laughter of the children.

It seemed hours later, when he was not listening at all, that he looked out and all at once the dark body of the horse turned in the gate, by the corner of the house. His heart gave a great leap. The helplessness left him. This man could hold Ellen back from death. The moonlight seemed to turn warm. After the doctor went in with Ellen the laughing of the children did not seem so far-off and strange.

The quick white grip of fear came again when he heard the doctor's hand on the door again . . . but Martin looked up and the doctor was *smiling*. Suddenly the whole night was a great, neighbourly, tear-starting friend. He had a son now. He knew it would be a son.

Martin felt shy to kiss Ellen in front of the doctor, but there was a new peace and a strange swagger in his soul. When he got the doctor's horse for him, it seemed like the best horse in all the world; and half-ashamed and half-afraid not to, but somehow wanting desperately to thank *someone*, he knelt down for a minute on the hay and prayed. Outside the barn, the voices of the children laughing were a glad song in his ears, now. In the bedroom, Ellen murmured "My own little Jesus" . . . and the thick spruce-cosy smell of the Christmas tree and the shining moonlight outside and the soft peace after danger past clothed the minutes in a sweet armour . . . A son . . . A son . . . And Ellen well . . . Martin couldn't believe how good it was. He would never die now. He had a son, now . . . when he was too old to break up the land he loved, any more, this son would come in at night and they would plan together, just the same. This son's sons. . . .

"Well, maybe you think it's *easy* to hold this damn thing,"
David said. It *must* be that he's tired, Martin thought. He
can't mean that . . . this same David . . . my own son cannot
find it hard to plow this land of our own. I never found it
so, when I was young. Plowed land was always the prettiest
sight in the world to me. It was always good at the end of the
day, to stand and look over the brown waves of earth and
know that I had opened my land to the sun and the air and
the rain. I don't like to hear this son of mine talk that way.
He says too many things like that. I don't like to hear my
son talk that way. The plowed land was here before us and it
will last after us and our hands should be proud to work in it.

"Haw," Martin called, and the lip of the earth curled back
and buried the grass again.

In the city, David thought, their bodies are not dead-tired
now. They have not walked all day in their own tracks . . .
back and forth, back and forth, in their own damn tracks.
There is movement and lights and laughing. Every day there
is something *new* . . . something to keep alive for. The same
people here . . . the same talk . . . the same eternal drudg-
ery . . . your nose in the ground all day long, from morning
till night, like a damned ox . . . cooped up in that damned
circle of trees.

The last brown beech leaves on the hardwood hill drifted
down to the ground, dreamily, a little sad to die. A flock of
partridges made their heavy headlong flight into an apple tree
and began to bud. In the fields, the potato stalks lay in blackened heaps. The earth was grey and brown. All the colour
was in the sky or hung in the thin air. Only the stray pump-
kins, left to ripen on the withered vines, gave back any of
it. They were like bubbles of the sad October sunshine. Martin
loved these quick chill dusks, and then later the kind eye of
lamplight in the window, and the friendly, wood-warmed,
table-set kitchen.

They came to the end of the furrow. Martin split the rest of
the acre with his eye.

"Will we finish her before supper, son?" he asked.

"Do you want to work all night too!"

Martin stopped the oxen.

"What's wrong with you today, Dave?" he said. "If you planned to go after the partridges. . . . "

"Partridges, hell!"

"Well then, what's. . . . "

David hesitated.

"I'm so damn sick of this place I. . . . "

"Is *that* so!" Martin said slowly. "What's wrong with this place?" He kicked over a sod with the toe of his shabby boot. An old man looked out of his face for the first time. It was true, then . . . It had never been because David was tired or lonely or weak or young . . . It was because David had always *hated* this land . . . the land that would be his own some day. A sick little cloud settled on his heart. He *had* no son, then.

"What's *wrong* with it?" David said. "The same damn thing over and over from morning till night . . . every day and every day . . . what future is there for anyone here?" David kept his back bent to the plow handles. He felt a little mean and ashamed when he heard the sound of his own words.

"What future is there here?" The question sounded meaningless to Martin. He had the truth, to contradict it. There is the first day in April when the fields stir again and it is good all day just to feel your breathing . . . There is the sky-blue August day when the whole green wind is full of leaves and growing, and Sunday morning you walk in the waving growth-full garden rows and wish you could keep this day forever, hold it back from going . . . It is good, too, when the snow whistles cold and mournful because it can never get inside the pane to warm itself . . . It is *all* good, all of it . . . Men live here as long as their sons live, to see the clearings their axes have made and the living grass that sprang from their tracks in the first furrow and the green things their hands gave life to . . . "The same thing over and over . . . " Martin did not speak. Only his sick thoughts pleaded, patiently, silently, incredulously. We did not plough yesterday, David. We took the day off and last night this time we sat at the edge of the woods and waited for the shy-eyed deer to come out into the old back field.

I thought it was good to sit there and smoke with my son

after we boiled the supper kettle, not talking much but not feeling the silence either, and watch the dead leaves drifting down past the rocks in the cool-talking brook. The fire itself felt good, in spite of the sun, and it was good to hear the nervous twitter of the partridges in the apple trees just before it got too dark to pick out their heads along the sights of the gun . . . Or is this like the day last spring we nodded at each other across the pool with the foam on it each time we held a broken-neck trout throbbing in the tight of our palms? Or the day we cursed the heat in the alder-circled meadow and our shirts stuck to our backs like broken blisters? The hay smelt good that night, just the same, and it was good to hear the wagon wheels groan on the sill just before the dark thunder-frown of the sky burst and the barn roof beat back the rain. I remember the night we ate our first supper in the house I had built with my own hands. That night the neighbours came in, and we danced half the night to the fiddles. It was easy with everyone, like with brothers, and we loved them all . . . and it was good that night to lie in bed and let sleep's drowsy wind blow out the candles of thought. The day they brought your brother Peter home loose in their arms before it was dinner time, his dead body so broken your mother could not hold it, that day was different . . . And the next day . . . And the next day. . . .

"Well what kind of a place suits *you*?" Martin said at last. David straightened.

"The city, of course! Who'd want to live in this God-forsaken hole when you can get a job in the city?"

"Did you say the *city*?"

"Yeah. The city," he said laconically.

Martin listened with sick wonder to this stranger who had been his son. The city . . . It's *there* the days are the same. I thought it was very lonely in the city, the time I was there. The stone things move, but they do not change. My feet were always on stone. I could not walk on the ground and look over it and know it was my own. They never looked at the sky there, or listened for the rain.

When I looked at the sky there, the sun I saw was a strange one . . . it did not make friends with the stone. The stone houses were alike, and the days were alike, and never till they died could the people lie in bed at night and listen to rain on the corn after a long heat. They had nothing to breathe but their own tired breaths. I remember their faces. There was stone in them, too. There were all alike. They looked as if they never awoke from their tired dreams of the night. Their minds kept turning in their own tracks, like the weary wheels that could find no rest on the pavements. The soft-fingered women-faced men lived in houses, and the house-smell clung to everything they said or did when they went outside. When they talked, it was empty, because their eyes saw nothing but the stone things that their hands had not built . . . and none of them had anything to say that could not be said with words. It was very lonely there. They laughed too much. But not even love or death could melt their aloneness. Even when they laughed, their eyes did not change. And when they died, no one remembered, and there was nothing left of them.

I liked it in the city, now, this time, David thought. The street lights began to come on, a little before it was dark, and excitement seemed to stir in the busy pavements. The wind was not strong enough to lift itself above the street, but the women's skirts clung to their bodies as they passed. So many different women's bodies! What if they *didn't* speak? The bright, metallic faces of always-rich women seemed to shine in the shop-window light, and you knew you would feel clumsy and ashamed with them, but it was good to think of having their soft flesh alone somewhere in the dark. There was so much light there, then . . . and life. Like when you took off your work-clothes and shaved and felt smoother and brighter and ready for things. There was life, not death, at the end of the day. Here, my God . . . the same old bare maples weaving back and forth against a sky that made your lips blue just to look at it, and never the sound of a strange voice, and later the snow sifting lonely through the spokes of the wagon wheels . . . What a God-forsaken place to be *young* in. Maybe his father didn't mind, they didn't seem to mind *missing* things when they got old. Old people didn't seem to dread being quiet and letting things slip like this. They thought it was because they were wise . . . it was because they were half-dead already. If he thought he'd ever get like that about things when he got old . . . He'd never get old. He swore a desperate promise to himself that he'd never, never, never get that awful patience like his father . . . standing there now, with that stupid look on his face, like one of the oxen. . . .

"But Dave," Martin said slowly, "this place will be *yours* some day, you know that."

"What do *I* want of this old *place?*"

A whiteness came into Martin's face that was different from the whiteness of the cold or the weariness. He remembered the day his father had said the same thing to him. They had both felt shy and awkward, and he could say nothing, but as soon as he was alone, he had looked over this land, the tight tears of pride came warm into his eyes. He had kept this place, the best thing he had, till he could give it to his own son, and now when he offered it to David he saw it meant nothing. That he despised it. He had known through and through how his own father felt.

"It was always good enough here for *me*," Martin said.

"All right, but what did you ever *amount* to?"

Martin was stung into a sudden anger. "As much as *you* ever will, you. . . . "

Then he looked over the fields, slowly, and a break came into his anger. Why today, only a few hours ago, starting to plow, it had been, without a thought, so sweet, so safe, so sure . . . he and his son plowing and him trying to show David how to turn the furrow better and David trying his best. Things just didn't come handy for David, it must be that. He had half felt Ellen working quiet and happy in the house and the smoke went straight from the chimney into the clear, sun-filled air and there had been no hurry or fret in the fields or the slow oxen or his thoughts. Now . . . it could never be the same again between him and David, now. Every time they said a sharp word to each other now, these sick things would all come back . . . What if David was right? What *had* he ever amounted to? Well, he had been young here, and youth was very fresh and full here in the fields and the sun and very long, some of it never died, it grew green again with each April sun. He had had a wife of his own kind, and everything they had, they had got with their own hands, his hands and hers. There had been a lot of tiredness but there was always the quiet night afterwards and the slow kindly talk. There had never been an end of work, but you could always stop to talk across the fields to your neighbour, and you got along just the same. There had not been much money, but there had always been the sweet smell of bread in the kitchen and the soft song of wood in the kitchen stove. There had been no strangers among them, and when you died these men you had lived your whole life with would not work that day, even if there was clover to be hauled in and rain in the wind . . . and you would lie in the land that your hands and your feet knew best, and the same breezes you had breathed would always blow over you. Surely that was enough for a man. If your son . . . If David . . . It was hard to believe that your own son stayed on . . . It was hard to believe that your own son was not like you wanted him to be. But, Martin thought sadly, you couldn't make him see, if he didn't feel that way. You wished . . . but if he felt that way, there was no way to make him see.

"Well Dave," Martin said slowly, "if you're *bound* to go away, I suppose. . . ."

"Oh," David said impatiently, "let it go, let it go . . . I'll stay," he added sullenly.

He is almost afraid of me, Martin thought. He won't even talk it over with me. He has no use for my talk. He wants to keep me away from him. He don't think I can understand him at all. I try. . . .

He walked around to the oxen's heads and picked up the whip.

"Haw," he said quietly. "Just cut her light here, son."

David put his hands back on the handles but he didn't speak. He threw the plow around when they turned the furrows, so the chain jerked taut in the yoke. "Easy now, boys," Martin cajoled the oxen.

A bare little wind started in the bare maples. The sun burned cold and lonesome in the blind windows of the church across the road and the long withered grass bent over the cold grey sand in the middle of the built-up graves. Peter's grave . . . Peter would coax to hold the whip. He could hardly make his small voice loud enough to stir the oxen, but they obeyed him. Martin could see the crazy nostrils of the running horses and then Peter's small crumpled body on the rock heap where the wheel had struck. . . .

The cows came up from the pasture, called hollowly to be let in. The sky looked away from its own darkening face in the mud-bottomed puddles of the road. The blood in Martin's face came blue to the skin, and his blue eyes, a little faded with weariness, looked like frozen spots holding up the weight of his face. He walked back-to, guiding the oxen by the horns to help David keep the furrow straight, but David did not straighten his back, even when Martin stopped for a rock. Martin would come around and kick out the rock himself.

Martin blew on his hands and tried to start a smile in the corners of his tired, cold-thin, lips.

"Time for mittens, I guess. *Your* hands cold?"

"No," David said.

A shaft of the sun broke for a minute through the blue, wind-cold clouds. Long bands of it searchlit the grey rocks, without warming them.

"Snow comin'," Martin said.

The sun went down, and the sky made a few cold-pink patterns at the horizon. It would not be as sad again until April.

Martin turned the oxen for one more furrow. He could not stop, until he was *sure* how David . . . Maybe if he kept on, David would say something himself about stopping, and he could show him then how ready he was to listen to him and take the oxen off the tongue.

"*I'll* never ask him to stop if he plows all night . . . " David was so tired the muscles in his legs felt like a frayed rope and a tight cord drew his temples together. The blood seemed to drain from his face and throb heavy in his neck. The ashes of weariness sifted through the bright surface of his thoughts. The oxen lifted their heavy feet and deposited them carefully on the ground. The plow dug its slow way through the earth.

"I guess we're just gettin' her done in time," Martin said.

David said nothing.

"I guess this clears things up, about, for winter. You'll have a little more time to hunt, now, Dave."

Ellen came to the corner of the house, holding down her

apron with one hand against the tug of the wind, and called supper.

"All right," Martin called back.

"Hungry, Dave?" he said.

"No."

David glanced at his father's face. For the first time he noticed how tired it looked. He felt sorry for his father, for a minute, and a little ashamed. He'd *have* to stay as long as his father was alive, he supposed.

They came to the end of the furrow. Martin hesitated.

"Well, I guess we'll let her go at that for tonight," he said. "We can wind her up in the morning, easy." He hesitated again.

"Dave," he said, "if you really *want* to go away. . . . "

David's impatience flared again. He forgot his father's face.

"Oh, for God's sake," he said, "can't you let that *drop*? I said I'd stay, didn't I? What more do you want? I'll stay here as long as *you're* here, anyway. So you need not worry."

So it is that way. A small coal touched suddenly against Martin's heart. He will wait, but he will be glad . . . so he can go away. If he was waiting for it, so the place would be all his own then, it would be . . . but he will be waiting, so he can go away. There will be a stranger here, and nothing will be done the same. There will be a strange name in my house, and maybe they will let the alders creep back over the acre field because they did not clear it for the first time and plow it with their own hands . . . and the grass will grow tall and strange over the graves.

He pulled the bolt from the tongue. It was true. It was true, then. He *had* no son. David took his hands from the plow. Martin waited for a minute to see if he would line the plow up for the next furrow in the morning. David did not move. Martin walked around to the plow. David went to the oxen's head, took up the whip and started with them to the barn. Martin pulled the plow around and lay the chain straight out along the next furrow. Ellen came to the corner of the house and called supper again, but Martin did not answer. He watched David take the oxen past the house. He saw Ellen say something to him, but David did not reply.

He bent down and dug the mud from the plowshare. It

shone underneath, where the earth had polished it, like a sword. The earth smelled cold and silent. He moved a few stones, absently, with his foot and stood for a minute with his eyes on the ground. Like the night they buried Peter. He felt lost in the long, dead day.

In the porch, he listened to see if David might be talking to the oxen. There was no sound but the bells, as David jerked the yoke-straps. Martin caught his breath quickly. He *had* no son. Peter was dead. He *had* no son, now. He scraped the dirt from his heels with a stock from the chipyard and went inside the house.

"Well, what in the *world* have you two been doing?" Ellen said, moving across the scrubbed soft-wood floor from the stove to the table. The warm breath of food rose sweet in the oil-lamplight. She held the dipper of water for Martin's hands over the basin in the sink. "Are you goin' to do a coupla more acres after supper?" she joked.

"Yeah, I was kinda thinkin' we might," Martin laughed.

But his laughter was heavy and grey, like a hawk rising.

The Lost Salt Gift of Blood

Alistair MacLeod

NOW in the early evening the sun is flashing everything in gold. It bathes the blunt grey rocks that
loom yearningly out toward Europe and it touches
upon the stunted spruce and the low-lying lichens and the delicate hardy ferns and the ganglia-rooted moss and the tiny
tough rock cranberries. The grey and slanting rain squalls have
swept in from the sea and then departed with all the sudden-
ness of surprise marauders. Everything before them and beneath
them has been rapidly, briefly, and thoroughly drenched and
now the clear droplets catch and hold the sun's infusion in
a myriad of rainbow colours. Far beyond the harbour's mouth
more tiny squalls seem to be forming, moving rapidly across
the surface of the sea out there beyond land's end where the
blue ocean turns to grey in rain and distance and the strain
of eyes. Even farther out, somewhere beyond Cape Spear lies
Dublin and the Irish coast; far away but still the nearest land
and closer now than is Toronto or Detroit to say nothing of
North America's more western cities; seeming almost hazily
visible now in imagination's mist.

Overhead the ivory white gulls wheel and cry, flashing also
in the purity of the sun and the clean, freshly washed air.
Sometimes they glide to the blue-green surface of the harbour,
squawking and garbling; at times almost standing on their
pink webbed feet as if they would walk on water, flapping their
wings pompously against their breasts like over-conditioned

he-men who have successfully passed their body-building courses. At other times they gather in lazy groups on the rocks above the harbour's entrance murmuring softly to themselves or looking also quietly out toward what must be Ireland and the vastness of the sea.

The harbour itself is very small and softly curving, seeming like a tiny, peaceful womb nurturing the life that now lies within it but which originated from without; came from without and through the narrow, rock-tight channel that admits the entering and withdrawing sea. That sea is entering again now, forcing itself gently but inevitably through the tightness of the opening and laving the rocky walls and rising and rolling into the harbour's inner cove. The dories rise at their moorings and the tide laps higher on the piles and advances upward toward the high-water marks upon the land; the running moon-drawn tides of spring.

Around the edges of the harbour brightly coloured houses dot the wet and glistening rocks. In some ways they seem almost like defiantly optimistic horseshoe nails: yellow and scarlet and green and pink; buoyantly yet firmly permanent in the grey unsundered rock.

At the harbour's entrance the small boys are jigging for the beautifully speckled salmon-pink sea trout. Barefootedly they stand on the tide-wet rocks flicking their wrists and sending their glistening lines in shimmering golden arcs out into the rising tide. Their voices mount excitedly as they shout to one another encouragement, advice, consolation. The trout fleck dazzlingly on their sides as they are drawn toward the rocks, turning to seeming silver as they flash within the sea.

It is all of this that I see now, standing at the final road's end of my twenty-five-hundred-mile journey. The road ends here—quite literally ends at the door of a now abandoned fishing shanty some six brief yards in front of where I stand. The shanty is grey and weatherbeaten with two boarded-up windows, vanishing wind-whipped shingles and a heavy rusted padlock chained fast to a twisted door. Piled before the twisted door and its equally twisted frame are some marker buoys, a small pile of rotted rope, a broken oar and an old and rust-flaked anchor.

The option of driving my small rented Volkswagen the

remaining six yards and then negotiating a tight many-twists-
of-the-steering-wheel turn still exists. I would be then facing
toward the west and could simply retrace the manner of my
coming. I could easily drive away before anything might begin.

Instead I walk beyond the road's end and the fishing shanty
and begin to descend the rocky path that winds tortuously
and narrowly along and down the cliff's edge to the sea.
The small stones roll and turn and scrape beside and beneath
my shoes and after only a few steps the leather is nicked
and scratched. My toes press hard against its straining surface.

As I approach the actual water's edge four small boys are
jumping excitedly upon the glistening rocks. One of them has
made a strike and is attempting to reel in his silver-turning
prize. The other three have laid down their rods in their
enthusiasm and are shouting encouragement and giving almost
physical moral support: "Don't let him get away, John," they
say. "Keep the line steady." "Hold the end of the rod up."
"Reel in the slack." "Good." "What a dandy!"

Across the harbour's clear water another six or seven shout
the same delirious messages. The silver-turning fish is drawn
toward the rock. In the shallows he flips and arcs, his flashing
body breaking the water's surface as he walks upon his tail.
The small fisherman has now his rod almost completely vertical. Its tip sings and vibrates high above his head while at his
feet the trout spins and curves. Both of his hands are clenched
around the rod and his knuckles strain white through the
water-roughened redness of small-boy hands. He does not know
whether he should relinquish the rod and grasp at the lurching
trout or merely heave the rod backward and flip the fish behind
him. Suddenly he decides upon the latter but even as he heaves
his bare feet slide out from beneath him on the smooth wetness
of the rock and he slips down into the water. With a pirouet-
ting leap the trout turns glisteningly and tears itself free. In a
darting flash of darkened greenness it rights itself with the
regained water and is gone. "Oh damn!" says the small fisherman, struggling upright onto his rock. He bites his lower
lip to hold back the tears welling within his eyes. There is a
small trickle of blood coursing down from a tiny scratch on
the inside of his wrist and he is wet up to his knees. I reach
down to retrieve the rod and return it to him.

Suddenly a shout rises from the opposite shore. Another line zings tautly through the water throwing off fine showers of iridescent droplets. The shouts and contagious excitement spread anew. "Don't let him get away!" "Good for you." "Hang on!" "Hang on!"

I am caught up in it myself and wish also to shout some enthusiastic advice but I do not know what to say. The trout curves up from the water in a wriggling arch and lands behind the boys in the moss and lichen that grow down to the sea-washed rocks. They race to free it from the line and proclaim about its size.

On our side of the harbour the boys begin to talk. "Where do you live?" they ask me and is it far away and is it bigger than St John's? Awkwardly I try to tell them the nature of the North American midwest. In turn I ask them if they go to school. "Yes," they say. Some of them go to St Bonaventure's which is the Catholic school and others go to Twilling Memorial. They are all in either grade four or grade five. All of them say that they like school and that they like their teachers.

The fishing is good they say and they come here almost every evening. "Yesterday I caught me a nine-pounder," says John. Eagerly they show me all of their simple equipment. The rods are of all varieties as are the lines. At the lines' ends the leaders are thin transparencies terminating in grotesque three-clustered hooks. A foot or so from each hook there is a silver spike knotted into the leader. Some of the boys say the trout are attracted by the flashing of the spike; others say that it acts only as a weight or sinker. No line is without one.

"Here, sir," says John, "have a go. Don't get your shoes wet." Standing on the slippery rocks in my smooth-soled shoes I twice attempt awkward casts. Both times the line loops up too high and the spike splashes down far short of the running, rising life of the channel.

"Just a flick of the wrist, sir," he says, "just a flick of the wrist. You'll soon get the hang of it." His hair is red and curly and his face is splashed with freckles and his eyes are clear and blue. I attempt three or four more casts and then pass the rod back to the hands where it belongs.

And now it is time for supper. The calls float down from

the women standing in the doorways of the multi-coloured houses and obediently the small fishermen gather up their equipment and their catches and prepare to ascend the narrow upward-winding paths. The sun has descended deeper into the sea and the evening has become quite cool. I recognize this with surprise and a slight shiver. In spite of the advice given to me and my own precautions my feet are wet and chilled within my shoes. No place to be unless barefooted or in rubber boots. Perhaps for me no place at all.

As we lean into the steepness of the path my young companions continue to talk, their accents broad and Irish. One of them used to have a tame sea gull at his house, had it for seven years. His older brother found it on the rocks and brought it home. His grandfather called it Joey. "Because it talked so much," explains John. It died last week and they held a funeral about a mile away from the shore where there was enough soil to dig a grave. Along the shore itself it is almost solid rock and there is no ground for a grave. It's the same with people they say. All week they have been hopefully looking along the base of the cliffs for another sea gull but have not found one. You cannot kill a sea gull they say, the government protects them because they are scavengers and keep the harbours clean.

The path is narrow and we walk in single file. By the time we reach the shanty and my rented car I am wheezing and badly out of breath. So badly out of shape for a man of thirty-three; sauna baths do nothing for your wind. The boys walk easily, laughing and talking beside me. With polite enthusiasm they comment upon my car. Again there exists the possibility of restarting the car's engine and driving back the road that I have come. After all, I have not seen a single adult except for the women calling down the news of supper. I stand and fiddle with my keys.

The appearance of the man and the dog is sudden and unexpected. We have been so casual and unaware in front of the small automobile that we have neither seen nor heard their approach along the rock-worn road. The dog is short, stocky and black and white. White hair floats and feathers freely from his sturdy legs and paws as he trots along the rock looking expectantly out into the harbour. He takes no notice of me.

The man is short and stocky as well and he also appears as black and white. His rubber boots are black and his dark heavy worsted trousers are supported by a broadly scarred and blackened belt. The buckle is shaped like a dory with a fisherman standing in the bow. Above the belt there is a dark navy woollen jersey and upon his head a toque of the same material. His hair beneath the toque is white as is the three-or-four-day stubble on his face. His eyes are blue and his hands heavy, gnarled, and misshapen. It is hard to tell from looking at him whether he is in his sixties, seventies, or eighties.

"Well, it is a nice evening tonight," he says, looking first at John and then to me. "The barometer has not dropped so perhaps fair weather will continue for a day or two. It will be good for the fishing."

He picks a piece of gnarled grey driftwood from the roadside and swings it slowly back and forth in his right hand. With desperate anticipation the dog dances back and forth before him, his intense eyes glittering at the stick. When it is thrown into the harbour he barks joyously and disappears, hurling himself down the bank in a scrambling avalanche of small stones. In seconds he reappears with only his head visible, cutting a silent but rapidly advancing V through the quiet serenity of the harbour. The boys run to the bank's edge and shout encouragement to him—much as they had been doing earlier for one another. "It's farther out," they cry, "to the right, to the right." Almost totally submerged, he cannot see the stick he swims to find. The boys toss stones in its general direction and he raises himself out of the water to see their landing splashdowns and to change his wide-waked course.

"How have you been?" asks the old man, reaching for a pipe and a pouch of tobacco and then without waiting for an answer, "perhaps you'll stay for supper. There are just the three of us now."

We begin to walk along the road in the direction that he has come. Before long the boys rejoin us accompanied by the dripping dog with the recovered stick. He waits for the old man to take it from him and then showers us all with a spray of water from his shaggy coat. The man pats and scratches the damp head and the dripping ears. He keeps the returned stick and thwacks it against his rubber boots as we continue to walk along the rocky road I have so recently travelled in my Volkswagen.

Within a few yards the houses begin to appear upon our left. Frame and flat-roofed, they cling to the rocks looking down into the harbour. In storms their windows are splashed by the sea but now their bright colours are buoyantly brave in the shadows of the descending dusk. At the third gate, John, the man, and the dog turn in. I follow them. The remaining boys continue on; they wave and say, "So long."

The path that leads through the narrow whitewashed gate has had its stone worn smooth by the passing of countless feet. On either side there is a row of small, smooth stones, also neatly whitewashed, and seeming like a procession of large white eggs or tiny unbaked loaves of bread. Beyond these stones and also on either side, there are some cast-off tires also whitewashed and serving as flower beds. Within each whitened circumference the colourful low-lying flowers nod; some hardy strain of pansies or perhaps marigolds. The path leads on to the square green house, with its white borders and shutters. On one side of the wooden doorstep a skate blade has been nailed, for the wiping off of feet, and beyond the swinging screen door there is a porch which smells saltily of the sea. A variety of sou'westers and rubber boots and mitts and caps hang from the driven nails or lie at the base of the wooden walls.

Beyond the porch there is the kitchen where the woman is at work. All of us enter. The dog walks across the linoleum-covered floor, his nails clacking, and flings himself with a contented sigh beneath the wooden table. Almost instantly he is asleep, his coat still wet from his swim within the sea.

The kitchen is small. It has an iron cookstove, a table against one wall and three or four handmade chairs of wood. There is also a wooden rocking-chair covered by a cushion. The rockers are so thin from years of use that it is hard to believe they still function. Close by the table there is a wash-stand with two pails of water upon it. A wash-basin hangs from a driven nail in its side and above it is an old-fashioned mirrored medicine cabinet. There is also a large cupboard, a low-lying couch, and a window facing upon the sea. On the walls a barometer hangs as well as two pictures, one of a rather jaunty young couple taken many years ago. It is yellowed and rather indistinct; the woman in a long dress with her hair done up in ringlets, the man in a serge suit that is slightly too large for him and with a tweed cap pulled rakishly over his right eye. He has an accordion strapped over his shoulders and his hands are fanned out on the buttons and keys. The other picture is of the Christ-child. Beneath it is written, "Sweet Heart of Jesus Pray for Us".

The woman at the stove is tall and fine featured. Her grey hair is combed briskly back from her forehead and neatly coiled with a large pin at the base of her neck. Her eyes are as grey as the storm scud of the sea. Her age, like her husband's, is difficult to guess. She wears a blue print dress, a plain blue apron and low-heeled brown shoes. She is turning fish within a frying pan when we enter.

Her eyes contain only mild surprise as she first regards me. Then with recognition they glow in open hostility which in turn subsides and yields to self-control. She continues at the stove while the rest of us sit upon the chairs.

During the meal that follows we are reserved and shy in our lonely adult ways; groping for and protecting what perhaps may be the only awful dignity we possess. John, unheedingly, talks on and on. He is in the fifth grade and is doing well. They are learning percentages and the mysteries of decimals; to change a percent to a decimal fraction you move the decimal point two places to the left and drop the percent sign. You always, always do so. They are learning the different breeds of domestic animals: the four main breeds of dairy cattle are Holstein, Ayrshire, Guernsey, and Jersey. He can play the mouth organ and will demonstrate after supper. He has twelve lobster traps of his own. They were originally broken ones thrown up on the rocky shore by storms. Ira, he says nodding toward the old man, helped him fix them, nailing on new lathes and knitting new headings. Now they are set along the rocks near the harbour's entrance. He is averaging a pound a trap and the "big" fishermen say that that is better than some of them are doing. He is saving his money in a little imitation keg that was also washed up on the shore. He would like to buy an outboard motor for the small reconditioned skiff he now uses to visit his traps. At present he has only oars.

"John here has the makings of a good fisherman," says the old man. "He's up at five most every morning when I am putting on the fire. He and the dog are already out along the shore and back before I've made tea."

"When I was in Toronto," says John, "no one was ever up before seven. I would make my own tea and wait. It was wonderful sad. There were gulls there though, flying over Toronto harbour. We went to see them on two Sundays."

After supper we move the chairs back from the table. The woman clears away the dishes and the old man turns on the radio. First he listens to the weather forecast and then turns to short wave where he picks up the conversations from the offshore fishing boats. They are conversations of catches and winds and tides and of the women left behind on the rocky shores. John appears with his mouth organ, standing at a respectful distance. The old man notices him, nods, and shuts off the radio. Rising, he goes upstairs, the sound of his feet echoing down to us. Returning he carries an old and battered accordion. "My fingers have so much rheumatism," he says, "that I find it hard to play anymore."

Seated, he slips his arms through the straps and begins the squeezing accordion motions. His wife takes off her apron and stands behind him with one hand upon his shoulder. For a moment they take on the essence of the once young people in the photograph. They began to sing:

> Come all ye fair and tender ladies
> Take warning how you court your men
> They're like the stars on a summer's morning
> First they'll appear and then they're gone.

> I wish I were a tiny sparrow
> And I had wings and I could fly
> I'd fly away to my own true lover
> And all he'd ask I would deny.

> Alas I'm not a tiny sparrow
> I have not wings nor can I fly
> And on this earth in grief and sorrow
> I am bound until I die.

John sits on one of the home-made chairs playing his mouth organ. He seems as all mouth-organ players the world over: his right foot tapping out the measures and his small shoulders now round and hunched above the cupped hand instrument.

"Come now and sing with us, John," says the old man.

Obediently he takes the mouth organ from his mouth and shakes the moisture drops upon his sleeve. All three of them begin to sing, spanning easily the half century of time that touches their extremes. The old and the young singing now their songs of loss in different comprehensions. Stranded here, alien of my middle generation, I tap my leather foot self-consciously upon the linoleum. The words sweep up and swirl about my head. Fog does not touch like snow yet it is more heavy and more dense. Oh moisture comes in many forms!

> All alone as I strayed by the banks of the river
> Watching the moonbeams at evening of day
> All alone as I wandered I spied a young stranger
> Weeping and wailing with many a sigh.
>
> Weeping for one who is now lying lonely
> Weeping for one who no mortal can save
> As the foaming dark waters flow silently past him
> Onward they flow over young Jenny's grave.
>
> Oh Jenny my darling come tarry here with me
> Don't leave me alone, love, distracted in pain
> For as death is the dagger that plied us asunder
> Wide is the gulf, love, between you and I.

After the singing stops we all sit rather uncomfortably for a moment. The mood seeming to hang heavily upon our shoulders. Then with my single exception all come suddenly to action. John gets up and takes his battered school books to the kitchen table. The dog jumps up on a chair beside him and watches solemnly in a supervisory manner. The woman takes some navy yarn the colour of her husband's jersey and begins to knit. She is making another jersey and is working on the sleeve. The old man rises and beckons me to follow him into the tiny parlour. The stuffed furniture is old and worn. There is a tiny wood-burning heater in the centre of the room. It stands on a square of galvanized metal which protects the floor from falling, burning coals. The stovepipe rises and vanishes into the wall on its way to the upstairs. There is an old-fashioned mantelpiece on the wall behind the stove. It is covered with odd shapes of driftwood from the shore and a variety of exotically shaped bottles, blue and green and red, which are from the shore as well. There are pictures here too: of the couple in the other picture; and one of them with their five daughters; and one of the five daughters by themselves. In that far-off picture time all of the daughters seem roughly between the ages of ten and eighteen. The youngest has the reddest hair of all. So red that it seems to triumph over the non-photographic colours of lonely black and white. The pictures are in standard wooden frames.

From behind the ancient chesterfield the old man pulls a collapsible card table and pulls down its warped and shaky legs. Also from behind the chesterfield he takes a faded checkerboard and a large old-fashioned matchbox of rattling wooden checkers. The spine of the board is almost cracked through and is strengthened by layers of adhesive tape. The checkers are circumferences of wood sawed from a length of broom handle. They are about three quarters of an inch thick. Half of them are painted a bright blue and the other half an equally eyecatching red. "John made these," said the old man, "all of them are not really the same thickness but they are good enough. He gave it a good try."

We begin to play checkers. He takes the blue and I the red. The house is silent with only the click-clack of the knitting needles sounding through the quiet rooms. From time to time the old man lights his pipe, digging out the old ashes with a flattened nail and tamping in the fresh tobacco with the same nail's head. The blue smoke winds lazily and haphazardly toward the low-beamed ceiling. The game is solemn as is the next and then the next. Neither of us loses all of the time.

"It is time for some of us to be in bed," says the old woman after a while. She gathers up her knitting and rises from her chair. In the kitchen John neatly stacks his school books on one corner of the table in anticipation of the morning. He goes outside for a moment and then returns. Saying good-night very formally he goes up the stairs to bed. In a short while the old woman follows, her footsteps travelling the same route.

We continue to play our checkers, wreathed in smoke and only partially aware of the muffled footfalls sounding softly above our heads.

When the old man gets up to go outside I am not really surprised, any more than I am when he returns with the brown, ostensible vinegar jug. Poking at the declining kitchen fire, he moves the kettle about seeking the warmest spot on the cooling stove. He takes two glasses from the cupboard, a sugar bowl and two spoons. The kettle begins to boil.

Even before tasting it, I know the rum to be strong and overproof. It comes at night and in fog from the French islands of St Pierre and Miquelon. Coming over in the low-throttled fishing boats, riding in imitation gas cans. He mixes the rum and the sugar first, watching them marry and dissolve. Then to prevent the breakage of the glasses he places a teaspoon in each and adds the boiling water. The odour rises richly, its sweetness hung in steam. He brings the glasses to the table, holding them by their tops so that his fingers will not burn.

We do not say anything for some time, sitting upon the chairs, while the sweetened, heated richness moves warmly through and from our stomachs and spreads upward to our brains. Outside the wind begins to blow, moaning and faintly rattling the window's whitened shutters. He rises and brings refills. We are warm within the dark and still within the wind. A clock strikes regularly the strokes of ten.

It is difficult to talk at times with or without liquor; difficult to achieve the actual act of saying. Sitting still we listen further to the rattle of the wind; not knowing where nor how we should begin. Again the glasses are refilled.

"When she married in Toronto," he says at last, "we figured that maybe John should be with her and with her husband. That maybe he would be having more of a chance there in the city. But we would be putting it off and it weren't until nigh on two years that he went. Went with a woman from down the cove going to visit her daughter. Well, what was wrong was that we missed him wonderful awful. More fearful than we ever thought. Even the dog. Just pacing the floor and looking out the window and walking along the rocks of the shore. Like us had no moorings, lost in the fog or on the ice-floes in a snow squall. Nigh sick unto our hearts we was. Even the grandmother who before that was maybe thinking small to herself that he was trouble in her old age. Ourselves having never had no sons only daughters."

He pauses, then rising goes upstairs and returns with an envelope. From it he takes a picture which shows two young people standing self-consciously before a half-ton pickup with a wooden extension ladder fastened to its side. They appear to be in their middle twenties. The door of the truck has the information: "Jim Farrell, Toronto: Housepainting, Eaves-troughing, Aluminum Siding, Phone 535-3484," lettered on its surface.

"This was in the last letter," he says. "That Farrell I guess was a nice enough fellow, from Heartsick Bay he was."

"Anyway they could have no more peace with John than we could without him. Like I says he was here too long before his going and it all took ahold of us the way it will. They send word that he was coming on the plane to St John's with a woman they'd met through a Newfoundland club. I was to go to St John's to meet him. Well, it was all wrong the night before the going. The signs all bad; the grandmother knocked off the lampshade and it broke in a hunnerd pieces—the sign of death; and the window blind fell and clattered there on the floor and then lied still. And the dog runned around like he was crazy, moanen and cryen worse than the swiles does out on the ice, and throwen hisself against the walls and jumpen on the table and at the window where the blind fell until we would have to be letten him out. But it be no better for he runned and throwed hisself in the sea and then come back and howled outside the same window and jumped against the wall, splashen the water from his coat all over it. Then he be runnen back to the sea again. All the neighbours heard him and said I should bide at home and not go to St John's at all. We be all wonderful scared and not know what to do and the next mornen, first thing I drops me knife."

"But still I feels I has to go. It be foggy all the day and everyone be thinken the plane won't come or be able to land. And I says, small to myself, now here in the fog be the bad luck and the death but then there the plane be, almost like a ghost ship comen out the fog with all its lights shinen. I think maybe he won't be on it but soon he comen through the fog, first with the woman and then see'n me and starten to run, closer and closer till I can feel him in me arms and the tears on both our cheeks. Powerful strange how things will take one. That night they be killed."

From the envelope that contained the picture he draws forth a tattered clipping:

> Jennifer Farrell of Roncesvalles Avenue was instantly killed early this morning and her husband James died later in emergency at St Joseph's Hospital. The accident occurred about 2 A.M. when the pickup truck in which they were travelling went out of control on Queen St W. and struck a utility pole. It is thought that bad visibility caused by a heavy fog may have contributed to the accident. The Farrells were originally from Newfoundland.

Again he moves to refill the glasses. "We be all alone," he says. "All our other daughters married and far away in Montreal, Toronto, or the States. Hard for them to come back here, even to visit; they comes only every three years or so for perhaps a week. So we be hav'n only him."

And now my head begins to reel even as I move to the filling of my own glass. Not waiting this time for the courtesy of his offer. Making myself perhaps too much at home with this man's glass and this man's rum and this man's house and all the feelings of his love. Even as I did before. Still locked again for words.

Outside we stand and urinate, turning our backs to the seeming gale so as not to splash our wind-snapped trousers. We are almost driven forward to rock upon our toes and settle on our heels, so blow the gusts. Yet in spite of all, the stars shine clearly down. It will indeed be a good day for the fishing and this wind eventually will calm. The salt hangs heavy in the air and the water booms against the rugged rocks. I take a stone and throw it against the wind into the sea.

Going up the stairs we clutch the wooden bannister unsteadily and say good night.

The room has changed very little. The window rattles in the wind and the unfinished beams sway and creak. The room is full of sound. Like a foolish Lockwood I approach the window

although I hear no voice. There is no Catherine who cries
to be let in. Standing unsteadily on one foot when required I
manage to undress, draping my trousers across the wooden
chair. The bed is clean. It makes no sound. It is plain and
wooden, its mattress stuffed with hay or kelp. I feel it with
my hand and pull back the heavy patchwork quilts. Still I do
not go into it. Instead I go back to the door which has no
knob but only an ingenious latch formed from a twisted nail.
Turning it, I go out into the hallway. All is dark and the
house seems even more inclined to creak where there is no
window. Feeling along the wall with my outstretched hand
I find the door quite easily. It is closed with the same kind of
latch and not difficult to open. But no one waits on the other
side. I stand and bend my ear to hear the even sound of my
one son's sleeping. He does not beckon any more than the
nonexistent voice in the outside wind. I hesitate to touch the
latch for fear that I may waken him and disturb his dreams.
And if I did what would I say? Yet I would like to see him in
his sleep this once and see the room with the quiet bed once
more and the wooden chair beside it from off an old wrecked
trawler. There is no boiled egg or shaker of salt or glass of
water waiting on the chair within this closed room's darkness.

Once though there was a belief held in the outports, that
if a girl would see her own true lover she should boil an egg
and scoop out half the shell and fill it with salt. Then she
should take it to bed with her and eat it, leaving a glass of
water by her bedside. In the night her future husband or a
vision of him would appear and offer her the glass. But she
must only do it once.

It is the type of belief that bright young graduate students
were collecting eleven years ago for the theses and archives
of North America and also, they hoped, for their own fame.
Even as they sought the near-Elizabethan songs and ballads
that had sailed from County Kerry and from Devon and Cornwall. All about the wild, wide sea and the flashing silver
dagger and the lost and faithless lover. Echoes to and from the
lovely, lonely hills and glens of West Virginia and the standing stones of Tennessee.

Across the hall the old people are asleep. The old man's
snoring rattles as do the windows; except that now and then

there are catching gasps within his breath. In three or four short hours he will be awake and will go down to light his fire. I turn and walk back softly to my room.

Within the bed the warm sweetness of the rum is heavy and intense. The darkness presses down upon me but still it brings no sleep. There are no voices and no shadows that are real. There are only walls of memory touched restlessly by flickers of imagination.

Oh I would like to see my way more clearly. I, who have never understood the mystery of fog. I would perhaps like to capture it in a jar like the beautiful childhood butterflies that always die in spite of the airholes punched with nails in the covers of their captivity—leaving behind the vapours of their lives and deaths; or perhaps as the unknowing child who collects the grey moist condoms from the lovers' lanes only to have them taken from him and to be told to wash his hands. Oh I have collected many things I did not understand.

And perhaps now I should go and say, oh son of my *summa cum laude* loins, come away from the lonely gulls and the silver trout and I will take you to the land of the Tastee Freeze where you may sleep till ten of nine. And I will show you the elevator to the apartment on the sixteenth floor and introduce you to the buzzer system and the yards of the wrought-iron fences where the Doberman pinscher runs silently at night. Or may I offer you the money that is the fruit of my collecting and my most successful life? Or shall I wait to meet you in some known or unknown bitterness like Yeat's Cuchulain by the wind-whipped sea or as Sohrab and Rustum by the future flowing river?

Again I collect dreams. For I do not know enough of the fog on Toronto's Queen St West and the grinding crash of the pickup and of lost and misplaced love.

I am up early in the morning as the man kindles the fire from the driftwood splinters. The outside light is breaking and the wind is calm. John tumbles down the stairs. Scarcely stopping to splash his face and pull on his jacket, he is gone, accompanied by the dog. The old man smokes his pipe and waits for the water to boil. When it does he pours some into the teapot then passes the kettle to me. I take it to the wash-stand and fill the small tin basin in readiness for my shaving. My face looks back from the mirrored cabinet. The woman softly descends the stairs.

"I think I will go back today," I say while looking into the mirror at my face and at those in the room behind me. I try to emphasize the "I." "I just thought I would like to make this trip—again. I think I can leave the car in St John's and fly back directly." The woman begins to move about the table, setting out the round white plates. The man quietly tamps his pipe.

The door opens and John and the dog return. They have been down along the shore to see what has happened throughout the night. "Well, John," says the old man, "what did you find?"

He opens his hand to reveal a smooth round stone. It is of the deepest green inlaid with veins of darkest ebony. It has been worn and polished by the unrelenting restlessness of the sea and buffed and burnished by the gravelled sand. All of its inadequacies have been removed and it glows with the lustre of near perfection.

"It is very beautiful," I say.

"Yes," he says, "I like to collect them." Suddenly he looks up to my eyes and thrusts the stone toward me. "Here," he says, "would you like to have it?"

Even as I reach out my hand I turn my head to the others in the room. They are both looking out through the window to the sea.

"Why, thank you," I say. "Thank you very much. Yes, I would. Thank you. Thanks." I take it from his outstretched hand and place it in my pocket.

We eat our breakfast in near silence. After it is finished the boy and dog go out once more. I prepare to leave.

"Well, I must go," I say, hesitating at the door. "It will take me a while to get to St John's." I offer my hand to the man. He takes it in his strong fingers and shakes it firmly.

"Thank you," says the woman. "I don't know if you know what I mean but thank you."

"I think I do," I say. I stand and fiddle with the keys. "I would somehow like to help or keep in touch but . . . "

"But there is no phone," he says, "and both of us can hardly write. Perhaps that's why we never told you. John is getting to be a pretty good hand at it though."

"Good-bye," we say again, "good-bye, good-bye."

The sun is shining clearly now and the small boats are putt-putting about the harbour. I enter my unlocked car and start its engine. The gravel turns beneath the wheels. I pass the house and wave to the man and woman standing in the yard.

On a distant cliff the children are shouting. Their voices carol down through the sun-washed air and the dogs are curving and dancing about them in excited circles. They are carrying something that looks like a crippled gull. Perhaps they will make it well. I toot the horn. "Good-bye," they shout and wave, "good-bye, good-bye."

The airport terminal is strangely familiar. A symbol of impermanence, it is itself glisteningly permanent. Its formica surfaces have been designed to stay. At the counter a middle-aged man in mock exasperation is explaining to the girl that it is Newark he wishes to go to, *not* New York.

There are not many of us and soon we are ticketed and lifting through and above the sun-shot fog. The meals are served in tinfoil and in plastic. We eat above the clouds looking at the tips of wings.

The man beside me is a heavy-equipment salesman who has been trying to make a sale to the developers of Labrador's resources. He has been away a week and is returning to his wife and children.

Later in the day we land in the middle of the continent. Because of the changing time zones the distance we have come seems eerily unreal. The heat shimmers in little waves upon the runway. This is the equipment salesman's final destination while for me it is but the place where I must change flights to continue even farther into the heartland. Still we go down the wheeled-up stairs together, donning our sunglasses, and stepping across the heated concrete and through the terminal's electronic doors. The salesman's wife stands waiting along with two small children who are the first to see him. They race toward him with their arms outstretched. "Daddy, Daddy," they cry, "what did you bring me? What did you bring me?"

The Double-Headed Snake

John Newlove

Not to lose the feel of the mountains
while still retaining the prairies
is a difficult thing. What's lovely
is whatever makes the adrenalin run;
therefore I count terror and fear among
the greatest beauty. The greatest
beauty is to be alive, forgetting nothing,
although remembrance hurts
like a foolish act, is a foolish act.

Beauty's whatever
makes the adrenalin run. Fear
in the mountains at night-time's
not tenuous, it is not the cold
that makes me shiver, civilized man,
white, I remember
the stories of the Indians,
Sis-i-utl, the double-headed snake.

Beauty's what makes
the adrenalin run. Fear at night
on the level plains, with no horizon
and the stars too bright, wind bitter
even in June, in winter
the snow harsh and blowing,
is what makes me
shiver, not the cold air alone.

And one beauty cancels another. The plains
seem secure and comfortable
at Crow's Nest Pass; in Saskatchewan
the mountains are comforting
to think of; among
the eastwardly diminishing hills
both the flatland and the ridge
seem easy to endure.

As one beauty
cancels another, remembrance
is a foolish act, a double-headed snake
striking in both directions, but I
remember plains and mountains, places
I come from, places I adhere and live in.

The Great Electrical Revolution

Ken Mitchell

I WAS only a little guy in 1937, but I can still remember Grandad being out of work. Nobody had any money to pay him and as he said, there wasn't much future in brick-laying as a charity. So mostly he just sat around in his suite above the hardware store, listening to his radio. We *all* listened to it when there was nothing else to do, which was most of the time unless you happened to be going to school like me. Grandad stuck right there through it all—soap operas, weather reports and quiz shows—unless he got a bit of cash from somewhere. Then he and Uncle Fred would go downtown to the beer parlour at the King William Hotel.

Grandad and Grandma came from the old country long before I was born. When they arrived in Moose Jaw, all they had was three children: Uncle Fred, Aunt Thecla, and my Dad; a truck full of working clothes; and a twenty-six pound post mall for putting up fences to keep "rogues" off Grandad's land. Rogues meant capitalists, Orangemen, cattle rustlers and Indians. All the way out on the train from Montreal, he glared out the Pullman window at the endless flat, saying to his family:

"I came here for land, b'Christ, and none of em's goin' to sly it on me."

He had sworn to carve a mighty estate from the raw Saskatchewan prairie, although he had never so much as picked up a garden hoe in his life before leaving Dublin.

So when he stepped off the train at the C.P.R. station in Moose Jaw, it looked like he was thinking of tearing it down and seeding the site to oats. It was two o'clock in the morning, but he kept striding up and down the lobby of the station, dressed in his good wool suit with the vest, as cocky as a bantam rooster in a chicken run. My Dad and Uncle Fred and Aunt Thecla sat on the trunk, while Grandma nagged at him to go and find them a place to stay. (It was only later they realized he was afraid to step outside the station.) He finally quit strutting long enough to get a porter to carry their trunk to a hotel down the street.

The next morning they went to the government land office to secure their homestead. Then Grandad rented a democrat and took my Dad and Uncle Fred out to see the land they had come half-way around the world to find. Grandma and Aunt Thecla were told to stay in the hotel room and thank the Blessed Virgin for deliverance. They were still offering their prayers some three hours later, when Grandad burst into the room, his eyes wild and his face pale and quivering.

"Sweet Jesus Christ!" he shouted at them. "There's too much of it! There's just too damn much of it out there." He ran around the room several times in circles, knocking against the walls. "Miles and miles of nothing but miles and miles!" He collapsed onto one of the beds, and lay staring at the ceiling.

"It 'ud drive us all witless in a week," he moaned.

The two boys came in and told the story of the expedition. Grandad had started out fine, perhaps just a little nervous. But the further they went from the town, the more agitated and wild-eyed he got. Soon he stopped urging the horse along and asked it to stop. They were barely ten miles from town when they turned around and came back, with Uncle Fred driving. Grandad could only crouch on the floor of the democrat, trying to hide from the enormous sky, and whispering hoarsely at Fred to go faster. He'd come four thousand miles to the wide open spaces—only to discover he suffered from agoraphobia.

That was his last real excursion onto the open prairie. He gave up forever the idea of a farm of his own. (He did make one special trip to Mortlach in 1928 to fix Aunt Thecla's chimney, but that was a family favour. Even then Uncle Fred had to drive him in an enclosed Ford sedan in the middle of the night, with newspapers taped to the windows so he couldn't see out.) There was nothing left for him to do but take up his old trade of brick-laying in the town of Moose Jaw, where there were trees and tall buildings to protect him from the vastness. Maybe it was a fortunate turn of fate; certainly he prospered from then until the Depression hit, about the time I was born.

Yet—Grandad always felt guilty about not settling on the land. Maybe it was his conscience that prompted him to send my Dad out to work for a cattle rancher in the hills, the day after he turned eighteen. Another point: he married Aunt Thecla off to a Lutheran wheat farmer at Mortlach who actually threshed about five hundred acres of wheat every fall. Uncle Fred was the eldest and closer to Grandad (he had worked with him as an apprentice brick-layer before they immigrated) so he stayed in town and lived in the suite above the hardware store.

I don't remember much about my father's cattle ranch, except whirls of dust and skinny animals dragging themselves from one side of the range to the other. Finally there were no more cattle, and no money to buy more, and nothing to feed them if we *did* buy them, except wild foxtails and Russian thistles. So we moved into Moose Jaw with Grandad and Grandma, and went on relief. It was better than the ranch where there was nothing to do but watch tumbleweeds roll through the yard. We would have had to travel into town every week to collect the salted fish and government pork, anyway. Grandad was very happy to have us, because when my Dad went down to the railway yard to get our ration, he collected Grandad's too. My Dad never complained about waiting in line for the handout, but Grandad would've starved to death first. "The Goddamned government drives us all to the edge," he would say. "Then they want us to queue up for the Goddamned swill they're poisoning us with."

That was when we spent so much time listening to Grandad's radio. It came in a monstrous slab of black walnut cabinet he had swindled, so he thought, from a secondhand dealer on River Street. An incandescent green bulb glowed in the centre to show when the tubes were warming up. There was a row of knobs with elaborate-looking initials and a dial with the names of cities like Tokyo, Madrid, and Chicago. Try as we might on long winter evenings to tune the needle into those stations and hear a play in Japanese or Russian, all we ever got was CHMJ Moose Jaw, The Buckle of the Wheat Belt. Even so, I spent hours lying on the floor, tracing the floral patterns on the cloth-covered speaker while I listened to another world of mystery and fascination.

When the time came that Grandad could find no more bricks to lay, he set a kitchen chair in front of the radio and stayed there, not moving except to go to the King William with Uncle Fred. My Dad managed to get a job with the city, gravelling streets for forty cents a day. But things grew worse. The Moose Jaw Light and Power Company came around one day in the fall of 1937 and cut off our electricity for non-payment. It was hard on Grandad not to have his radio. Not only did he have nothing to do, but he had to spend all his time thinking about it. He stared out the parlour window, which looked over the alley running behind the hardware store. There was a grand view of the back of the Rainbow Laundry.

That was what he was doing the day of his discovery, just before Christmas. Uncle Fred and my Dad were arguing about who caused the Depression—R.B. Bennett or the C.P.R. Suddenly Grandad turned from the window. There was a new and strange look on his face.

"Where does that wire go?" he said.

"Wire?" said Uncle Fred, looking absent-mindedly around the room. He patted his pockets looking for a wire.

"What wire?" my Dad said.

Grandad nodded toward the window. "This wire running right past the window."

He pointed to a double strand of power line that ran from a pole in the back alley to the side of our building. It was a lead-in for the hardware store.

"Holy Moses Cousin Harry. Isn't that a sight now!" Grandad said, grinning like a crazy man.

"You're crazy," Uncle Fred told him. "You can't never get a tap off that line there. They'd find you out in nothing flat."

Grandma, who always heard everything that was said, called from the kitchen: "Father, don't you go and do some foolishness will have us all electrinated."

"By Jayzuz," he muttered. He never paid any attention to a word she said. "Cut off *my* power, will they?"

That night, after they made me go to bed, I listened to him and Uncle Fred banging and scraping as they bored a hole through the parlour wall. My Dad wouldn't have anything to do with it and took my mother to the free movie at the co-op. He said Grandad was descending to the level of the Moose Jaw Light and Power Company.

Actually, Grandad knew quite a bit about electricity. He had known for a long time how to jump a wire from one side of the meter around to the other, to cheat the power company. I had often watched him under the meter, stretched out from his tip-toes at the top of a broken stepladder, yelling at Grandma to lift the Goddamned Holy Candle a little higher so he could see what the Christ he was doing.

The next day, Grandad and Uncle Fred were acting like a couple of kids, snorting and giggling and jabbing each other in the ribs. They were waiting for the King William beer parlour to open so they could go down and tell their friends about Grandad's revenge on the power company. They spent the day like heroes down there, telling over and over how Grandad had spied the lead-in, and how they had bored the hole in the wall, and how justice had finally descended on the capitalist leeches. The two of them showed up at home for supper, but as soon as they ate they headed back to the King William where everybody was buying them free beer.

Grandma didn't seem to think much of their efforts, although now that she had electricity again, she could spend the evenings doing her housework if she wanted to. The cord came through the hole in the wall, across the parlour to the hall and the kitchen. Other cords were attached which led to the two bedrooms. Grandma muttered when she had to sweep around the black tangle of wires and sockets. With six of us living in the tiny suite, someone was forever tripping on one of the cords and knocking things over.

But we lived with all that because Grandad was happy again. We might *all* have lived happily if Grandad and Uncle Fred could have kept quiet about their revenge on the power company.

One night about a week later we were in the parlour

listening to Fibber Magee and Molly when someone knocked at the door. It was Mrs. Pizak, who lived next door in a tiny room.

"Goot evening," she said, looking around. "I see your power has turnt beck on."

"Ha," Grandad said, "We turned it on *for* 'em. Damned rogues."

"Come in and sit down and listen to the show with us," Grandma said. Mrs. Pizak kept looking at the black wires running back and forth across the parlour, and at Grandad's radio. You could tell she wasn't listening to the show.

"Dey shut off my power, too," she said. "I alvays like listen to the Shut-In program. Now my radio isn't work."

"Hmmm," Grandad said, trying to hear Fibber and the Old-Timer. Grandma and my Dad watched him, not listening to the radio any more either. Finally he couldn't stand it.

"All right, Fred," he said. "Go and get the brace and bit."

They bored a hole through one of the bedroom walls into Mrs. Pizak's cubicle. From then on, she was on Grandad's power grid, too. It didn't take long for everybody else in the block to find out about the free power, and they all wanted to hook up. There were two floors of suites above the hardware store, and soon the walls and ceiling of Grandad's suite were as full of holes as a colander, with wires running in all directions. For the price of a bottle of whiskey, people could run their lights twenty-four hours a day if they wanted. By Christmas Day, even those who *paid* their bills had given notice to the power company. It was a beautiful Christmas in a bad year— and Grandad and Uncle Fred liked to take a lot of credit for it. Which everyone gave them. There was a lot of celebration up and down the halls, where they always seemed to show up as guests of honour. There was a funny feeling running through the block, like being in a state of siege, or a revolution, with Uncle Fred and my Grandad leading it.

One late afternoon just before New Year's, I was lying on the floor of the front parlour, reading a secondhand Book of Knowledge I had gotten for Christmas. Grandma and my mother were knitting socks, and all three of us were listening vaguely to Major Bowes' amateur show. Suddenly, out of the corner of my eye, I thought I saw Grandad's radio move. I blinked and stared at it, but the big console just sat there talking about Geritol. I turned a page. Again, it seemed to move in a jerk.

"Grandma," I said. "The radio—"

She looked up from her knitting, already not believing a word I might have to say. I gave up, and glared at the offending machine. While I watched, it slid at least six inches across the parlour floor.

"Grandma!" I screamed. 'The radio's moving! All by itself!"

She looked calmly at the radio, then the tangle of wires spread across the floor, and out the front parlour window.

"Larry-boy, you'd best run and fetch your grandfather. He's over at McBrides'. Number eight."

McBrides' suite was down the gloomy hall and across. I dashed down the corridor and pounded frantically at the door. Someone opened it the width of a crack.

"Is my Grandad in there?" I squeaked. Grandad stepped out into the hall with a glass in his hand, closing the door behind him.

"What is it, Larry?"

"Grandma says for you to come quick. The radio! There's something—"

"My radio!" Grandad was not a large man, but he had the energy of a buzz-saw. He started walking back up the hall, broke into a trot, then a steady gallop, holding his glass of whiskey out in front at arm's length so it wouldn't spill. He burst through the door and skidded to a stop in front of the radio, which sat there, perfectly normal except that it stood maybe a foot to the left of the chair.

"By the Holy toe-nails of Moses—what is it?"

Grandma looked up ominously and jerked her chin toward the window. Her quiet firmness usually managed to calm him, but now, in two fantastic bounds, Grandad stood in front of the window, looking out.

"Larry," he said, glaring outside, "fetch your Uncle Fred."
I tore off down the hall again to number eight and brought Uncle Fred back to the suite. The two women were still knitting on the other side of the room. Grandma was doing her stitches calmly enough, but my mother's needles clattered like

telegraph keys, and she was throwing terrified glances around the room.

"Have a gawk at this, will you Fred?"

Uncle Fred and I crowded around him to see out. There, on a pole only twenty feet from our parlour window, practically facing us eye-to-eye, was a lineman from the power company. He was replacing broken glass insulators; God knows why he was doing it in the dead of winter. Obviously, he hadn't noticed our home-made lead-in, or he would have been knocking at the door. We could only pray he wouldn't look at the wire too closely. Once, he lifted his eyes toward the lighted window where we all stood gaping out at him in the growing darkness. He grinned at us, and raised his hand in a salute. He must have thought we were admiring his work.

"Wave back!" Grandad ordered. The three of us waved frantically at the lineman, to make him think we appreciated his efforts, although Grandad was muttering some very ugly things about the man's ancestry.

Finally, to our relief, the lineman finished his work and got ready to come down the pole. He reached out his hand for support—and my heart stopped beating as his weight hung on the contraband wire. Behind me, I could hear the radio slide another foot across the parlour floor. The lineman stared at the wire he held. He tugged experimentally, his eyes following it up to the hole through our wall. He looked at Grandad and Uncle Fred and me standing there in the lit-up window, with our crazy horror-struck grins and our arms frozen above our heads in grotesque waves. Understanding spread slowly across his face.

He scrambled around to the opposite side of the pole and braced himself to give a mighty pull on our line. Simultaneously, Grandad leaped into action, grabbing the wire on our side of the wall. He wrapped it around his hands, and braced his feet against the baseboard. The lineman gave his first vicious yank, and it almost jerked Grandad smack against the wall. I remember thinking what a powerful man the lineman must be to do that to my Grandad.

"Fred, you feather-brained idiot!" he shouted. "Get over here and haul on this line before the black-hearted son of a bitch pulls me through the wall."

Uncle Fred ran to the wire just in time, as the man on the pole gave another, mightier heave. At the window, I could see the lineman stiffen with rage and determination. The slender wire sawed back and forth through the hole in the wall for at least ten minutes, first one side, and then the other, getting advantage. The curses on our side got very loud and bitter. I couldn't hear the lineman, of course, but I could see him— with his mouth twisted in an awful snarl, throwing absolutely terrible looks at me in the window, and heaving on the line. I know he wasn't praying to St. Jude.

Grandad's cursing would subside periodically when Grandma warned: "Now, now, father, not in front of the boy." Then she would go back to her knitting and pretend the whole affair wasn't happening, as Grandad's blasphemies would soar to monumental heights.

That lineman must have been in extra-good condition, because our side very quickly began to play out. Grandad screamed at Grandma and my mother, and even at me, to throw ourselves on the line and help. But the women refused to leave their knitting, and they wouldn't let me be corrupted. I couldn't leave my viewpoint at the window, anyway.

Grandad and Uncle Fred kept losing footage until the huge radio had scraped all the way across the floor and stood at their backs, hampering their effotts.

"Larry!" Grandad shouted. "Is he weakenin' any?"

He wanted desperately for me to say yes, but it was useless. "It doesn't look like it," I said. Grandad burst out in a froth of curses I'd never heard before. A fresh attack on the line pulled his knuckles to the wall and barked them badly. He looked tired and beaten. All the slack in the line was taken up and he was against the wall, his head twisted, looking at me. A light flared up in his eyes.

"All right, Fred," he said. "If he wants the Goddamned thing so bad—let him have it!" They both jumped back—and nothing happened.

I could see the lineman, completely unaware of his impending disaster, literally winding himself up for an all-out assault on our wire. I wanted out of human kindness to shout a warning at him. But it was too late. With an incredible backward lunge, he disappeared from sight behind the power pole.

A shattering explosion of wild noises blasted my senses, like a bomb had fallen in Grandad's suite. Every appliance and electric light that Grandma owned flew into the parlour, bounding off the walls and smashing against each other. A table lamp from the bedroom caromed off Uncle Fred's knee. The radio collided against the wall and was ripped off its wire. Sparking and flashing like lightning, all of Grandma's things hurled themselves against the parlour walls, popping like a string of firecrackers as the cords went zipping through the hole. A silence fell—like a breath of air to a drowning man. The late afternoon darkness settled through the room.

"Sweet Jesus Christ!" Grandad said. Then there came a second uproar: a bloodcurdling barrage of bangs and shouts, as our neighbours recovered from seeing their lamps, radios, irons and toasters leap from their tables and collect in ruined piles of junk around the "free power" holes in their walls. Uncle Fred turned white as a sheet.

I looked out the window. The lineman sat on the ground at the foot of his pole, dazed. He looked up at me with one more hate-filled glare, then deliberately snipped our wire with a pair of cutters. He taped up the end and marched away into the night.

Grandad stood in the midst of the ruined parlour, trying in the darkness to examine his beloved radio for damage. Grandma sat in her rocking chair, knitting socks and refusing to acknowledge the disaster.

It was Grandad who finally broke the silence. "Well! They're lucky," he said. "It's just damned lucky for them they didn't scratch my radio."

To Make a Prairie

Emily Dickinson

To make a prairie it takes a clover and one bee,
One clover, and a bee,
And revery.
The revery alone will do,
If bees are few.

The Lonely Land

A.J.M. Smith

Cedar and jagged fir
uplift sharp barbs
against the gray
and cloud-piled sky;
and in the bay
blown spume and windrift
and thin, bitter spray
snap
at the whirling sky;
and the pine trees
lean one way.

A wild duck calls
to her mate,
and the ragged
and passionate tones
stagger and fall,
and recover,
and stagger and fall,
on these stones—
are lost
in the lapping of water
on smooth, flat stones.

This is a beauty
of dissonance,
this resonance
of stony strand,
this smoky cry
curled over a black pine
like a broken
and wind-battered branch
when the wind
bends the tops of the pines
and curdles the sky
from the north.

This is the beauty
of strength
broken by strength
and still strong.

Bushed

Earle Birney

He invented a rainbow but lightning struck it
shattered it into the lake-lap of a mountain
so big his mind slowed when he looked at it

Yet he built a shack on the shore
learned to roast porcupine belly and
wore the quills on his hatband

At first he was out with the dawn
whether it yellowed bright as wood-columbine
or was only a fuzzed moth in a flannel of storm
But he found the mountain was clearly alive
sent messages whizzing down every hot morning
boomed proclamations at noon and spread out
a white guard of goat
before falling asleep on its feet at sundown

When he tried his eyes on the lake   ospreys
would fall like valkyries
choosing the cut-throat
He took then to waiting
till the night smoke rose from the boil of the sunset

But the moon carved unknown totems
out of the lakeshore
owls in the beardusky woods derided him
moosehorned cedars circled his swamps and tossed
their antlers up to the stars
then he knew   though the mountain slept   the
    winds
were shaping its peak to an arrowhead
poised

And now he could only
bar himself in and wait
for the great flint to come singing into his heart

Dover Beach

Matthew Arnold

The sea is calm to-night.
The tide is full, the moon lies fair
Upon the straits—on the French coast, the light
Gleams and is gone; the cliffs of England stand,
Glimmering and vast, out in the tranquil bay.
Come to the window, sweet is the night air!
Only, from the long line of spray
Where the ebb meets the moon-blanched land,
Listen! you hear the grating roar
Of pebbles which the waves draw back, and fling,
At their return, up the high strand,
Begin, and cease, and then again begin,
With tremulous cadence slow, and bring
The eternal note of sadness in.

Sophocles long ago
Heard it on the Ægean, and it brought
Into his mind the turbid ebb and flow
Of human misery; we
Find also in the sound a thought,
Hearing it by this distant northern sea.

The Sea of Faith
Was once, too, at the full, and round earth's shore
Lay like the folds of a bright girdle furled.
But now I only hear
Its melancholy, long, withdrawing roar,

Retreating, to the breath
Of the night wind, down the vast edges drear
And naked shingles of the world.

Ah, love, let us be true
To one another! for the world, which seems
To lie before us like a land of dreams,
So various, so beautiful, so new,
Hath really neither joy, nor love, nor light,
Nor certitude, nor peace, nor help for pain;
And we are here as on a darkling plain
Swept with confused alarms of struggle and flight,
Where ignorant armies clash by night.

The World Outside

Val Mulkerns

MOST of the children were early that morning, creeping in subdued and stiff in the unaccustomed shoes, their faces and limbs shining from prolonged scrubbing. Some of the boys looked unusually ugly because of having had their hair savagely attacked with scissors and bowl the previous night by over-zealous mothers, but the girls were glossy and braided and comely, and looked much more confident than the boys, as if handling inspectors would not be much trouble to them. The school master scanned all the faces sharply, planning the traditional reshuffle. Something nervous and trusting in the general atmosphere prompted him to put them at ease, though he was jumpy enough himself.

"Tell me, is it the same crowd at all I have before me, or is it some swanky gang down from Dublin for the day?" he grinned at them in Irish, and a relieved pleased ripple of laughter went over the desks. "Let me see now, we'll have to have yourself in the front, Mary Mannion, to show off that brave red ribbon, and let you take yourself to the back desk, Tomás Peig where with God's help you'll get a chance to show the Inspector how to do fractions." The point was that Mary was easy on the eyes and utterly brainless, and Tomás Peig was a bright lad and back benchers were inevitably questioned. "We'll have you over by the window, Muiris, and our friend with the red head in the second row. Will you get those boots back on you this minute, Tadg, and I'll fly the hide off you if I see them anywhere except where they're meant to be. Do you think now that it was to decorate the floor for me your mother went to Clifden last week and handed out a mint of money. No, Sir, well you may be sure the answer is No Sir, and take heed of what I said to you, if you value that hide of yours." But as the reshuffling went on, they understood the unusual bantering humor for what it was, an effort to put them at ease, and their faces beamed gratefully back at him. They were being examined, and God knew what horrible things would happen to them if they failed to please the inspector, and here was Boozy, the decent man, and he with nothing to fear being a Master, soft as butter with them to drive away their nervousness.

"Now listen to me the lot of you. If he speaks to you in Irish don't answer him back in a blast of English just to show that you know it. Answer him in Irish. Now if he speaks to you in English, what are you to do, Mary Mannion?"

"Answer him in Irish, sir," said Mary with a bright confident smile. There was a gale of laughter, and Mary was prodded incredulously by her neighbours.

" 'Tis a professor of Logic we'll make out of you. If he speaks to you in English, what will *you* do, tell her, Martin Flaherty?"

"Answer him in English, sir."

"Right. Now keep that in your heads. The next thing to remember is if he asks the class in general a question and you think you know the answer, put up your hands. Don't be afraid. He won't eat you if you happen to be wrong. He's probably a fine, well-fed man. The only people whose hands I don't want to see up for anything are Mary Mannion and Micilín Seán Mullen, because they have a job keeping up with the best of us, and we'll give them a rest to-day. Next year with the help of God they'll be ready for anything. Do you hear that now, the pair of you?"

"Yes, sir." Micilín Seán was beaming with relief and Mary Mannion was sulking.

"Right. Now the next thing to remember is—" his eyes suddenly caught sight of a figure at the gate—"that he's coming up the path this minute, and let you keep as still as mice while I call the register." There were sighs and gasps and rapid intakes of breath all around, and then utter petrified silence, and everybody answering "Annso, a Mhaighistear" in an unrecognizable whisper.

Mr. Mulvey was gray and hunched and small, with heavy-lidded gloomy eyes and a mouth turning down hopelessly at the corners. A first glance, before he opened his mouth, suggested that his voice would be a sick wind among the reeds, but in fact it was big and jolly and when he laughed, which was frequently, you had the fantastic impression that some enchantment had been worked before your eyes and that this was certainly not the man who had walked into the room. It was difficult to say whether his life had taken the form of a victorious battle against his natural temperament, or whether it was only his appearance which belied him. His clothes were silver gray and faultlessly pressed, and he carried a neatly rolled black umbrella and a black brief-case.

As he stepped into the room out of the thickening rain, the children scraped to their feet and stood looking at him with dismay. They were more used to fat tweedy red-faced inspectors with patches of leather down their jackets. He shook hands with and spoke a few pleasant words to Mr. McGlynn, and then turned to the pupils with his incredible smile, which showed square healthy white teeth, slightly prominent, and produced numbers of answering smiles. He was delighted to see them all, absolutely delighted, and hoped to learn more this morning than he had ever done at school. Would they sit down now, and attend to Mr. McGlynn's lesson, and later on he'd have a chat with them. He sat down on the chair which had been placed for him near the window, opened his brief-case, and became again, in a moment, the gloomy little gray man who had entered the room. The schoolmaster finished calling the register, closed the book, and sent Mary Mannion across with it to the inspector. Then the lesson began, Geography. The large map of Europe behind the master's desk was covered by a map of Mexico, and as was his usual custom, he began by giving them a general impression of the country itself, the color, the atmosphere, then something of its history. His words were alive and interesting, because omnivorous reading of everything from strictly technical works or anthropological works to things like Graham Greene's "The Lawless

Roads" had produced complete familiarity. It happened to be Mexico to-day because that was the stage of the syllabus they had reached, but it was the same with everywhere, when he was sober, that is. The three maps which he drew with quick strokes, one of the physical regions, one of the climatic regions, and the third showing produce, were accurate and even beautiful with their lively blending colors. Then the class was set to work, an intricate business because of the different ages. Little working groups were put together, and a résumé of what in particular each had to tackle was given, and the older pupils were set some questions on the lesson.

At this time, the bent little depressed figure by the window appeared to be taking no notice. The register had been scrutinized and laid aside, and also some sample exercise books, and then he seemed to give all his attention to some private papers. The Arithmetic lesson went by, and the Irish grammar lesson, and then towards midday, when a rising wind was lashing the rain against the windows, he stood up and the transfiguring smile shone out.

"Well now, I suppose you're all fit for bed, after the work you've done this morning, what?" He drew the required laugh from them, and rubbed his small gray hands happily together. "But before we let you off home there are one or two things which have been puzzling me for some time." He changed rapidly to English. "Tell me, is Mexico in the Northern Hemisphere or in the Southern Hemisphere?" The hands shot up, and so did Mary Mannion's, but it was rapidly lowered. "I see my little friend here with the red ribbon knows and doesn't know. Which hemisphere is Mexico in, will you tell me now, like the sound woman you are?"

"The Southern Hemisphere, sir," said Mary Mannion with superb confidence and a shake of the head. There were the inevitable gasps from the class, and Mr. Mulvey smiled still more brilliantly.

"I don't think we all agree with you there, do we?" and there was an enthusiastic chorus of "No sir!" "The last time I was in Mexico," he went on, directly addressing Mary Mannion, who was smiling engagingly at him, "it was in the Northern Hemisphere. Will you remember that, because I don't think it's moved since then?"

"Yes, sir. No, sir," said Mary Mannion with another engaging smile.

"Well now there's another thing that's been puzzling me. A few weeks ago I went into the dining room of my house in Galway and two of the children had apples, nice big red ones. Seán said, 'Daddy, I'll give you half mine,' and Máire said, 'I'll give you three-eighths of mine, Daddy.' Now I thought a while before I decided which I'd take, and I want you to think now. Which was the more decent offer of the two, Seán's or Máire's?" The hands went up slowly, three, four, six, then ten. "Difficult question to put to a poor simple father, wasn't it? How did I know which to take?" Again he was speaking in Irish.

"I'd have taken the both of them, sir," said Mary Mannion in lamentable English, beside herself with the notice she had achieved.

"Ní thuigim," said Mr. Mulvey, with another brilliant smile, and then ignored her. "Well, will you tell me, the boy at the back there?"

Thomás Peig, to the schoolmaster's joy, got smartly to his feet, held back his fair head and spoke up very clearly. "Seán's offer was the one you should have taken, sir, because he was giving you four-eighths (or a half) and Máire was only giving you three-eighths."

"Splendid. If I had been as bright as you now, I wouldn't have done myself out of the eighth of a fine apple."

Before they had quite finished laughing, the inspector turned to the schoolmaster and said, " I think the best thing we can do now is to send them off home for the rest of the day because they're too clever for us."

When they had all filed out into the cloakroom in clattering happiness, Mr. Mulvey's gloomy gray eyes roamed for a while about the schoolmaster's face before the smile broke again and he held out his hand. "That was the only Geography lesson in Ireland that's ever interested me," he said. He glanced quickly again at the schoolmaster's qualifications listed on the sheet before him, and asked sharply: "What are you doing here? We could do with plenty more of your kind in the national schools throughout the country but—?" He shrugged, half-smiling the question.

"It suits me here," Peter McGlynn said briefly, "I like it."

The inspector shrugged again. "If you ever wanted a change, my friend Dr. Linnane in Galway would jump at a man like you—preparing boys for University scholarships, that sort of thing."

"Thanks," the schoolmaster said without interest, "I'll remember if I ever decide to change. It's very kind of you."

"Nonsense," Mulvey replied, with an old-fashioned air, gathering his things together and fastening the briefcase. "You lived for some time in Mexico, I take it?"

"No. My Grand Tour took the form of a day trip to Liverpool. I never slept a night outside this country in my life."

"Remarkable. I taught, myself, for seven years in Mexico City and you brought it back into this classroom today, the heat, the filth, the color, the indolence, the preposterous fascination of the place. It's remarkable."

"No," Peter McGlynn smiled, "it's Baedeker, and a studious youth, and Graham Greene and a trick of the tongue. You'll not refuse a bite of lunch with me in our one and only hostelry, Pats Flaherty's?"

"I will now," said the inspector warmly, "I spend my life having lunch with clerical managers and a man can do with a bit of civilization now and again."

Pats' wife had clearly taken some trouble to see that the catering arrangements of Ballyconnolly would stand up to inspection quite as well as the school. As soon as she had received the schoolmaster's order two days previously, she had set to work, scouring and polishing the little square room off the bar, hunting out her best lace tablecloth, unused since the previous inspector's visit, and fixing a formidable array of family photographs along the mantelpiece. Despite these, the warm, low-ceilinged little room with its scarlet geraniums and looped lace curtains was welcoming to the two men as they stepped in out of the bitter wild morning. The place was permeated by the fragrance of roasting fowl, stewed apples and strong spirits, blending deliciously with the bitterness of turf-smoke. Kate Pats Flaherty bustled busily in and out, talking all the time.

" 'Tis frozen and demented the pair of you must be with

the hunger, now. Ah, sure I often heard it said a man that works with his brain needs twice the feeding of a man that works with his body, and why wouldn't he, indeed? There was a cousin of my own, Mr. Mulvey, sir, and there he is before ye on the mantelpiece with the white face there in the middle, and hadn't they got him starved in the college above in Dublin and he going in for a priest. Night and day he was at the books, God pity him, and he no more than a lad, and there wasn't he only out a priest a few months, and his brother not even married, when he took a delicacy and died on his poor mother, God between us and all harm. 'Twas a fright to the world the way she took it, bawling and crying every time she'd look at a priest for years after. There she is for you now, Mr. McGlynn, on the bend of the mantelpiece with the feathery hat down near her nose, but sure God is good and didn't the second lad, a fine big puck of a boy, go in for a priest after, and he's a curate below in Kerry now. Another sup of that soup, Mr. Mulvey, sir? Or the Master? Well now, I'll have that bird on the table before you'll be finished licking your lips. There he is to your north now, Mr. Mulvey, sir, with the fine soft plucks on him and the holy book in his hands. We had him here now, and you could have seen him only a few weeks ago, and there was never a lad like him for feeding, and wouldn't he need it, I ask you, and him not to be dying on us like his poor brother, God rest his soul." Half of this oration was in English and half in Irish, and during journeys to the kitchen and to the bar the rich strong voice came clearly back to her guests, of whom she expected and desired no response. It was only when the last course had been cleared away and the bottle of whiskey ordered by the schoolmaster was between them on the table, and the smoke from their cigarettes was rising to the low ceiling, that Kate Pats Flaherty drew the door behind her, put her head around it again and said: "I'll leave ye now to yourselves to talk to your heart's content and if there's any other thing in the world ye want, leave a screech out of ye and I'll hear it."

She went, and the door closed at last. In the brief satisfied silence the rain beat in gusty blasts against the window, and the wind swept down the chimney to set the turf leaping and blazing. The hunched gray man in the gray clothes was the first to speak, lifting the gloomy eyes that were flecked now with a faint humor.

"There's Ireland for you now, McGlynn, all of it. Unending rain rattling the windows, and inside a kindly woman boasting about her clerical relations, and two men drinking whiskey, and outside the rest of the world. If Michelangelo painted the Resurrection on her smoky ceiling she wouldn't give it a look or him a thank-you if her portly cousin His Reverence were within miles of the place. Once upon a time we exported scholars and culture to the Continent. Now we export nothing but beasts and priests, God help us." And there began one of those inevitable discussions on what's wrong with the country, that never end and are more common in Ireland than discussions on religion or sex. But before the well-worn tracks had been followed to within reach of their muddy end, the talk under the direction of Mr. Mulvey took a turn to Mexico, and from there to Spain where he had found his wife, the daughter of a Spaniard who had a ballet company in Mexico but who had left his daughter in Spain to be educated. In the warm half-forgotten enchantment of good whiskey on which the brain floated away like a dead flower and only the senses and the imagination were taut and alive, the schoolmaster felt the sun like the caressing tongue of some fantastic animal, at once savage and tender, and smelled the fruit piled high in the narrow streets, and the bitterness of cheap wine, shivered at the sudden white chill inside the vaulted Cathedrals where black-eyed women chattered and laughed before Mass began and felt no urge to leave their personalities like gifts outside the church door, at which filthy mewling beggars held out diseased limbs; he watched the cypresses shooting eager and dark into warm, star-filled air tingling with the music of De Falla to which a girl was dancing like a flame, twisting and writhing in the dark agony of exorcism; narrow martyred faces of El Greco floated in a golden mist beside the warm sensual beauties of Velasquez and in a timeless jumble of history real and imagined the sweet sane voice of a woman saint blended with the fat bass of a wandering peasant demanding an island of his master; and over it all, rising and falling like a sea of sound was the music of Albeniz, the 'Iberia,' of which every note was as familiar as the sound of rain beating on gray stone.

He had no clear memory of when exactly the little gray inspector left him, but only a vague impression of a warm handgrip and a voice urging him to visit the house in Galway to meet Maria, and look at some Spanish etchings and some Mexican carvings, and he vaguely remembered too standing at the door of Pats Flaherty's and watching the huddled gray figure disappearing through driving rain in the direction of his car, and then he remembered turning back into the fire-broken shadows of the bar, the tang of spirits and turf-smoke in his nostrils, and his head bemused with sunlight.

At the Movies

Al Purdy

The setting is really unreal
about 150 Eskimos and whites
jammed into a Nissen hut to
watch Gary Cooper and Burt Lancaster
in a technicolour western shootemup
Eskimos don't understand the dialogue
at all but they like the action
and when noble Gary is in danger
or sinister Lancaster acts menacing
a tide of emotion sweeps the hot little hut
and kids crawling on the floor are quiet
sensing what their parents feel
that something tremendously important is happening
When the Anglican minister changes reels
(his blond head glinting as he administers
spiritual unction to his flock)
cigarettes are lit and everyone talks and
a kid crawls under my legs grinning bashfully
Jim Kilabuk says something I can't quite hear
a baby cries in the pouch on his mother's back
and is joggled gently
It's hot and stuffy as hell in the theatre
doors have to be opened
the odour of white and Eskimo
making a point for air conditioning
Lights go out and Gary Cooper rides again
the forces of evil are finally defeated

only the virtuous bullet kills
violence neutralizes violence
like a mustard plaster
(tho I kinda like the bad guy)
the way it always does in American movies
with an obvious moral a clear-cut denouement
Outside the fiord looks like poured blue milk
mountains like bookmarks under a cold sky
islands are moonscapes
where this story happens
It's 11 p.m.
some of the hunters visit their boats
where dead caribou drain into bilgewater
and the rest of the moviegoers go
home to tents on the beach or prefab houses
and dogs howl to make everything regional
But the point I'd hoped to separate
from all these factual things stubbornly
resists me and I walk home slowly feeling stupid
rejecting the obvious
threading my way between stones in the mud
with the beginnings of a headache

    PANGNIRTUNG

Return to India

Santha Rama Rau

D URING the three months that my husband and I and
our small son were in the Soviet Union, we lost
count of the number of times Russians asked us,
"Don't you think our life here is very good?"

"Yes, very good," we always replied, politely refraining from
adding "for the Russians."

Inevitably the point would be pressed a little further. Life
in the Soviet Union was not only good, we would be assured,
but was getting better every day. Certainly on the evidence
of the past few years, this was no more than the truth. Usually
after this kind of opening exchange, the Russians we met
proved to be intensely inquisitive about life in America, my
husband's country, and the questions ranged from the price of
nylons to American intentions for nuclear war. Sometimes
they even showed a faintly patronizing interest in my country,
India.

On one such occasion I had a brief and uninspired conversation with a chance Russian acquaintance that I was to remember much later with quite a different feeling. A young man,
noticing across a restaurant dining room that I wore a sari,
came over to the table where my husband and I were sitting.
"Hindi-Russki bhai-bhai!" he announced proudly—a phrase
Russians learned when Prime Minister Nehru visited their
country, a phrase they love to use, which means in Hindi,
"Indians and Russians are brothers."

"Hindi-Russki bhai-bhai," I replied dutifully, and then, after the usual opening formalities, the young man started to ask me—or rather, to tell me—about life in India.

With my husband interpreting for us, he remarked, "The Indian people are very poor."

"Yes, they are."

"I have seen photographs. They have few clothes and many have no shoes."

"That's true."

"Most of them are uneducated."

"Yes."

"Many beggars on the streets."

"Yes."

"It must be very distressing to live in such a country."

"No—" I began, suddenly feeling homesick.

But the young man was finished with the subject of India. "In Russia we have a very good life . . ."

After our stay in Russia, I returned with my son to visit my family in India. We flew from Uzbekistan in the far south of Russia, over the magnificent expanse of the Himalayas to New Delhi. The plane arrived after dark and by the time we reached my uncle's house it was quite late at night and we were too tired to do much talking or to pay much attention to our surroundings.

The next morning, with my first glimpse of the newspapers, I was sharply aware not so much that I was in India as that I was out of Russia. One paragraph was enough to convince me. It ran, as I remember, something like this: "Yesterday the Prime Minister opened the debate in parliament on the Second Five-Year Plan with a two-hour speech in his usual diffuse style." I read, and reread, and reread the words "his usual diffuse style," remembering the monotonously reverential tone of all Russian newspapers toward all Russian leaders—the ones in favor, that is.

This was trivial enough as an incident, but in the course of that first day a number of other moments—equally minor, equally transient—began to acquire a collective force. I had offered to help with the household shopping, partly because I always enjoy bazaars and partly because I wanted to show my son a little of the city. We started in the fruit market, which

I'm afraid my Russian friends would have found hopelessly disorganized. No orderly queues, no rationing, no fixed prices, no stern-faced women with string shopping bags waiting in line, dutifully reading signs saying, "Drink fruit juices. They are good for you."

To me an Indian bazaar is a source of endless delight and excitement. It is usually a series of plain wooden stalls on which are piled, with unconscious artistry, brightly colored, fruits, vegetables, spices, gleaming silver jewelry, brilliant silks and cottons, or charming, grotesque painted wooden toys. The vendors who can't afford a stall sit on the sidewalk outside the market, their baskets stacked behind them, their wives in vivid cotton saris crouching in the shade, and in front of them are spread carpets of scarlet chillies drying in the sun, small hills of saffron, tumeric, coriander, ginger, cinnamon—all the magical names from the old days of the spice trade with the Indies. With a worn stone mortar and pestle the vendor or his wife will grind your spices for you, blending them according to your particular taste, and weigh them in tiny brass scales strung on twine and balanced delicately in one hand. In all transactions you receive a pleasantly individual attention— nothing standardized.

The vegetable and fruit and flower merchants are surrounded by baskets of purple eggplant, green peppers, strings of tiny silvery onions, heads of bitter Indian spinach, and a dozen Indian vegetables for which I don't even know the English names. I had forgotten about the profusion of fruit in India— it is only during the brief, intense summer that you see much variety of fruit in Moscow. In Russia as winter approaches, all vegetables except for potatoes and the pervasive cabbage in soup seem to disappear from the menus.

My son was enjoying himself, pouncing on the stacks of bananas—unobtainable in Russia—regarding with some suspicion the papayas and chikus which he had not remembered from his last stay in India. He prodded a pile of the tiny, sharp Indian limes to see if they would collapse, an action for which he would have been severely reprimanded in Russia. I was reminded of the evening when we had run into an official of the Ministry of Culture in the lobby of the Metropole, our hotel in Moscow. He had come to the hotel to buy a lemon.

It seemed like an extraordinary place to come for such an item, but he explained that there were too few lemons in the winter, so that they were saved for the tourists and the foreigners and could only be obtained, if you were lucky, at an Intourist hotel.

Flowers. This was something I missed very much in Russia, where flowers are a real luxury. I can remember standing at a street corner in Russia, astonished by the sight of a flower-woman sitting in the middle of a splash of color in those gray streets. The Russians stopped to look too. Not many of them bought the flowers—too costly—but a surprising number paused in the rush to get home from offices, factories, and shops in the shadowy autumn twilight just to feast for a moment on the rare color of a few stiff bunches of chrysanthemums on a street corner.

All around us, in Delhi, there were flowers. Yes it is a tropical country, and yes, the climate makes this possible— but there was a personal pride and feminine joy in the countrywomen who tucked a marigold casually into their hair, who wove roses into small hoops to wear more formally around the knot of hair on the back of the head. I realized then that I had missed all this in Russia; the pleasure of women being women, a sense of decoration and unquestioned right of anyone to the small, cheap luxuries and gaieties.

But most impressive—to me, anyway—are the people in an Indian bazaar. First of all there is the inquisitiveness that often embarrasses foreigners. When you are engaged on an errand as prosaic as buying potatoes, in the course of the transaction your vendor may well ask you any variety of what my American friends would call personal questions. How old are you? How many children do you have? Only one? (A commiserating shake of the head.) Better hurry and have another before you are too old. Where do you live? Is your mother-in-law alive? Inevitably I made the comparison with Russia, where this kind of passing, interested exchange (between Russians) is so suspect. The right to express ordinary human curiosity about a fellow countryman came to seem like an unusual privilege.

Meanwhile, the brisk, canny routine of bargaining would be going on, and the whole performance would be interspersed with jokes and cracks and comments. Next to me a man, bargaining for a basket of tangerines, remarked to the old woman standing behind the stall, "Clearly you believe in the soak-the-rich program." This was the popular description of India's new taxation policy. The woman looked amused and replied dryly, "Give me your income and I will gladly pay your taxes." And the bargaining went on without rancor—it was all very Indian, or rather, un-Russian.

We finished our shopping and summoned a boy to carry our purchases out of the bazaar—another small, cheap luxury.

On our way out of the market, we had to pass the familiar barrage of beggars on the sidewalk and, as usual, gave them the small change left over from shopping. Even my son was struck with the contrast to Moscow. "Why are they asking for money, Mummy?"

"Because they are poor, darling."

"Why are they poor, Mummy?"

"India is a poor country, darling. Too many people and not enough food."

"We could give them some of our fruit."

"Well, that's what we've done in another way. We've given them some money to buy whatever they choose."

Then I was left wondering, as so often in the past, about the ethics of begging and giving. It is easy to win approval from foreigners by deploring two elements of Indian life—the caste structure and begging for a livelihood. The best that can be said about either of them is that it is gradually disappearing. However, it would be less than honest to pretend that social malaise is all that is involved in either system. The goals in the Hindu view of life are not the same as those of Russia or the western world. Indeed, India's highest caste, the Brahmans, are traditionally sworn to poverty. Ambition, getting ahead, comfort, success are obstacles, not aims, in the Hindu concept of a good life. Enlightenment is reached, if it is reached, when you have detached yourself from worldly considerations and emotional drives of any sort, so it is not surprising that many of India's most respected "holy men" are, in fact, beggars, or perhaps live on unsolicited contributions from strangers, disciples, casual visitors.

What in the West is almost always a degrading occupation

can, in India, be a high achievement. Not, of course, that all beggars are religious mendicants. Many are simply poor, or sick, or unemployed, or seeking a little extra income. If, to a westerner, they are an embarrassment or raise guilts about his own privileged life, to an Asian they are more likely to engender a down-to-earth recognition of conditions as they are and an urge to contribute in a small way to a social responsibility. This is combined with the knowledge that there is no society, including the Russian, in which privilege is unknown. Money, birth, education, accomplishment, something makes a class (or caste) structure. The Hindu view is not to rise to a higher level of privilege but to rise beyond the concern with privilege and levels altogether. It is hard enough to explain this attitude to a sympathetic, philosophic westerner; it is impossible to describe to the average Russian, to whom spiritual values seem to be mysterious, unacceptable, or discredited.

Could the Indian government, like the Russian or the Chinese, abolish beggars with a sweeping compulsory measure? I suppose it could. Would the cost in undemocratic forcefulness be too high? I think it might. We are committed to raising the standard of living in India, but by different methods, at a different pace—a pace designed to preserve other important aspects of our life. Although a number of these thoughts occurred to me that day at the bazaar, luckily I hadn't the time to try and explain many of them to my son because he was thirsty and was more concerned with demanding a limonad of the sort he had liked in Russia. We stopped at a nearby coffee shop.

An Indian coffeehouse, like an Indian bazaar, has its own peculiar atmosphere. It is a cheerful, unpretentious place in which to dawdle, encounter friends, talk, discuss, gossip. Students make fiery speeches to each other; women meet for a break in a morning's shopping; idlers stop by for a rest, to watch the world go by, to pick up a chance colleague. The actual drinking of coffee is the least important part of the whole affair. Looking around at the animated groups of uninhibited talkers at the tables, I couldn't help thinking that this particular sort of place doesn't exist in Moscow. There, one can find restaurants (mostly rather expensive by any standard), or "Parks of Culture and Rest," or hotel dining rooms, and several varieties of bar ranging from the pivnaya, where as a rule you can't even sit down, where women are seldom seen, and where the customers walk to the bar, order a drink, down it and leave, all within the space of five minutes, to the stolovoye, which is considered more refined, more suitable for women, and where ordinary vodka is not served, though wines and brandy are brought to your table. But India is not a drinking country—even in the states where there is no prohibition. The sight of drunks being thrown out of restaurants with the off-hand ruthlessness that the Russians employ for such occasions is extremely rare in India.

Indians meet in public places for sociability, and though poor housing contributes, as it does in Russia, to the life of cafés and restaurants and street corners, still Indians do not meet for the dedicated purpose of getting drunk. They are incurable talkers. At the coffeehouse I found myself once again cozy and amused in the endless stream of comments, criticism, scandal, anecdote, and analysis that accompanies one's days in any Indian society. I like the idea that one can be interested, amused, or disapproving of the activities or remarks of one's neighbors, friends, and acquaintances, or of political figures, college professors, taxi drivers, and artists. I like the idea that one's concern, malicious or pleasant, in one's fellow country-men cannot lead to their political harassment.

Listening that morning in the coffeehouse to the flurry of debate that rose from the students' tables about the latest political controversy, interspersed with the social chit-chat of the ladies or the shop talk of secretaries, office workers, and clerks, I thought of the sad, sly exchanges we had shared with our Russian acquaintances. I remembered the way conversation with a Russian in a restaurant would stop cold whenever a waiter came to the table or strangers walked by. At first I was astonished to find that Russians are much more willing to talk than I had expected, that people will come up to you in parks, restaurants, on the street, drawn by curiosity to a for-eigner, eager to ask and answer questions. But we soon learned, after hearing some deeply intimate confidences from Russians we scarcely knew, that our relations with them were very much in the nature of a shipboard romance. It can be intimate because it is so brief. "I can talk to you frankly," one of our friends said, not wistfully, merely as a statement of fact, "because you are in Moscow only a short time. Soon you will go and we will never meet again."

I remembered a waiter at the Metropole Hotel who had seen us so often in the dining room that one day he drifted unobtrusively over to our table to ask us in muttered conversation and scribbled notes about foreign writers. In return for whatever fragments of information we could give him, he told us about his favorite poet, Valery Bryusov. We had never heard of him, and then learned that he was banned in the Soviet Union. "You see," the waiter whispered, "he is a symbolist." In the rowdy air of the coffeehouse, it seemed incredible that there were places where poetry, even symbolist poetry, was considered too dangerous for the fragile human intellect.

After those early days in India, both the novelty of being home and the continual contrasts with Russia began to wear thin. Soon I slipped back in the slow pace and familiar daily life of India. My son no longer noticed beggars. I no longer thought of a trip to the bazaar or the coffeehouse as an occasion. I even remembered the cold blue evenings of Moscow with some nostalgia as the Indian climate warmed up to its early spring. But once during that time I had reason to think of my trip to Moscow and of India as a nation with a shock of rediscovery. It was during the Independence Day parade that takes place in New Delhi every January 26.

It is an immense celebration and villagers from all the surrounding areas of the city had been walking into the town or arriving in their bullock carts for days before. As the day grew closer all the open spaces of New Delhi were gradually filled with impromptu camps. Carts were unhitched, oxen grazed in the parks, the evening air was filled with the haze of open-air cooking fires for the scanty dinners of the travelers. On the streets you saw everywhere the brilliantly colored full ankle-length skirts and tight bodice of the village women. Each footstep (yes, barefoot, I would have had to admit to my Russian acquaintance) was emphasized by the metallic clink of silver anklets or toe rings. Every time a small child was hitched into a more comfortable position on his mother's hip, the sound of silver bracelets would accompany the movement. The fathers, proudly carrying sons on a tour of the city's sights or carefully washing their oxen at a public fountain, were less decorative but good-humored and ready for a festival. The streets were full of color and excitement and nobody checked the wanderings of the villagers as they looked around their capital.

In Russia you need a permit to travel even within the country, an identity card and an official permit before you may stay at a hotel. For most non-Muscovites, the only way to get to Moscow is to come, as a reward for outstanding service, on a brief "workers' tour" or as a member of some delegation. Chekhov's yearning phrase "To Moscow, to Moscow . . ." has just as intense a meaning now.

The day of the parade brought thousands of villagers and citizens of Delhi to the parade route, lining the roads in a dense, active crowd of mothers, fathers, children, babies, donkeys, oxen. Many families had their lunches tied up in pieces of cloth. Children clutched balloons or candy sticks. Little stalls selling nuts, tea, sweets, and fruit sprang up everywhere. I was lucky enough to have a seat on one of the bleachers outside the president's house where the procession started, and next to me was an old man in a worn khaki sweater and army trousers. A faded patch on his arm said "Engineers." He was obviously a veteran, obviously now retired, and obviously he had never been higher in rank than the equivalent of a sergeant.

When the procession began with the arrival of the Indian president, the old man stood up to get a better view. All the pomp and ceremony of viceregal days surrounded the appearance of the president—the outriders, the cavalry escort, the great coach drawn by matched horses, guarded by lancers. Out of the coach stepped a small thin man in a brown achkan (the Indian jacket), narrow trousers wrinkled at the ankles, a Gandhi cap on his head. He looked embarrassed by the flashy display that surrounded him. Smiling shyly, he brought his hands together in a namaskar, the Indian greeting, and hurried to his place on the reviewing platform. This in no way discouraged the old man next to me. He raised his hands in a namaskar above the heads of the people around him. With tears streaming down his face, he yelled (apparently convinced that the president could hear him), "Namaste ji! Jai Hind!"

and continued with such fervor that the rest of us near him suddenly found ourselves joining in a tribute from an Indian who had spent all his life in the British Army to an Indian who represented, at last, the fact that all this and India itself belonged to all of us.

The parade was splendid as such things go—a vast cavalcade of camels, elephants, ski troops, horsemen, the tough Gurkhas, the bearded colorful Sikhs—all the diversity and pageantry of India. But I am not really very keen on parades. They worry and depress me, and while this fantastic procession was going on, in my mind I had slipped back to the day of the fortieth anniversary of the Russian Revolution in Moscow. Another parade. Of a very different sort. There were no crowds lining the sidewalks—the streets had been cleared for security reasons. There was none of the good-humored pushing and shoving and wriggling of small children to get to the front where they could see best. Color? Pageantry? No, a few people in the factory workers' groups in the procession carried paper flowers, and one realized in a moment how seldom one saw color on the streets in Moscow, how rarely the drab grays and browns of the city were ever lightened by even so much as a pretty shop window. Mostly the Russian parade was grimly military, tanks and guns and huge rockets, and ranks and ranks of marching soldiers.

At the end of our parade the tribesmen from the Naga hills came by to do a dance in the street in front of the president. Predictably (it couldn't happen in Russia), they were late in getting started. Consequently they clashed with the flypast of the new Indian jets. Watching the two performances simultaneously, I could only think I would never have been able to explain to that anonymous Russian acquaintance of mine the appeal of Indian casualness, of the need for color, ease, humor—the joy of an Indian festival.

Poor and undernourished and undereducated, yes. But in India, people turn out every election day in a larger percentage than anywhere else in the world to choose a government. They make a real holiday of it, decorating their oxcarts and dressing in their best clothes to go to the polls. Certainly one cannot pretend that there is nothing in India that needs to be changed, but somewhere in all this is a confidence and pleasure in being Indian, and in the country's ways. And, yes, those ways are very different from Russian ways.

Well, it never fails: one always sounds sentimental in trying to say things like this. Perhaps it is just as well that I never got a chance to explain to that remote young man in Moscow how I feel about India.

Happy Event

Nadine Gordimer

THERE were so many things in life you couldn't ever imagine yourself doing, Ella Plaistow told herself. Once or twice she had said it aloud, too, to Allan. But mostly it grew, forced its way up out of the silences that fell upon her like a restraining hand during those first few days after she had come home from the nursing home. It seemed to burst through her mouth in a sudden irresistible germination, the way a creeper shoots and uncurls into leaf and stem in one of those films which telescope plant growth into the space of a few terrifying vital seconds.

Silence followed it again. In her mind, if she had spoken inwardly, to herself; in the room, if she had spoken aloud. The silence that covers the endless inward activity of shuffling for a foothold, making out of a hundred-and-one past justifications and pressures the accommodations of a new position for oneself. It was true, of course. You start off as a child, pretending to think the blonde doll prettier than the brunette, so that your loved sister may fall into the trap of choosing the one you don't want for yourself. You go on by one day finding your own tongue glibly acquiescing to a discussion of your best friend's temperament with someone whom you know to be her disliked enemy. And before you know where you are, you have gone through all the sidlings and inveiglings of taking somebody's work for less than it is worth, throwing someone into an agony of jealousy for the sake of a moment's vanity, pretending not to see an old lover lest he should not seem impressive enough in the eyes of the new one. It is impossible to imagine yourself doing any of these; but once done . . . Like ants teeming to repair a broken anthill, like white corpuscles rushing to a wound, all the forces that protect oneself from oneself have already begun their quick, sure, furtive, uneasy juggling for a new stance, a rearrangement for comfort into which amorphous life seems to have edged you.

"It's your *body* that objects," said Allan. "Remember that. That's all. There's some sort of physical protest that's got nothing to do with you at all, really. You must expect it. It'll pass off in a week or so."

And of course he was quite right. She certainly didn't have any regrets. They had two children, a girl and a boy (the wrong way round, as they said—the girl was the elder—but it's dangerous to have everything too much the way you want it!) who were just old enough to be left with their grand-mother. Allan's new partner was thoroughly reliable, the bond on the house was almost paid off; at last there was noth-ing to stop Allan and Ella: they had booked to go to Europe, in the spring of next year. So to have allowed themselves to be stopped by this—! To be, instead, this time next year, caught up in chemists' bills and napkins and wakeful nights all over again! No, they had brought up their babies, had loved and resented them and were content with them, and all through eight years had planned for this time when they would suddenly lift themselves clear of whatever it was that their lives had settled into, and land, free of it, lightly in another country.

Because it was something that Ella could never have dreamed she would ever do, in a week or two the trip to the nursing home slipped away into the unimportance of things that might never have happened. She was busy planning next winter's clothes for the children—it would be winter in South Africa while she and Allan were in spring in Europe—and getting the garden into shape because they hoped to let the house for the period they were to be away, and if they wanted a decent tenant the place must look attractive. She was just beginning to feel really strong again—undoubtedly that business had left her a little weak—and it was just as well, since she had so much to do, when, of course, servant trouble started.

The old house-cum-garden boy, Thomasi, began quarrelling with Lena, the native maid whom Ella had thought herself lucky to engage two months ago. Lena, a heavy, sullen, light-coloured Basuto, represented in her closed-in solemnity something that challenged irritation in Thomasi. Thomasi was a Basuto himself—Ella had the vague conviction that it was best to have servants who belonged to the same tribe, rather as she would have felt that it would be better to have two Siamese cats instead of one Siamese and one tabby, or two fan-tailed goldfish rather than one plain and one fancy. She always felt puzzled and rather peevish, then, when, as had happened often before, she found that her two Basutos or two Zulus or two Xhosas did not necessarily get on any better than one would have expected two Frenchman to get on simply because both were French; or two Englishmen simply because both were English.

Now Thomasi, barely five feet tall and with that charming, ancient, prehuman look of little dark-skinned men with bandy legs, was maddened by the very presence of Lena, like an insect circling angrily around the impassive head of some great slow animal. He quarrelled with her over dusters, over the state of the kitchen sink, over the bones for the dog; he went about his work shaking his head and rumbling with volcanic mutterings.

"If you've got anything to say, come out and say it," Ella said to him, irritated herself. "What's the matter now?"

"That woman is too lazy, madam," he said in his high, philosophical, exasperated voice.

It was difficult to think of old Thomasi as something quite like oneself, when he rose to his hind legs. (Yes, one had the feeling that this was *exactly* what happened when he got up from polishing the floor. Of course, if he had been dressed in a tailored American-drape hopsack instead of the regulation "kitchen boy" outfit that was a cross between a small boy's cotton sailor suit and a set of underwear, he might not have looked any funnier than any of the small, middle-aged Johannesburg men behind their directors' desks.) "Look, Thomasi, she does her work. I'm satisfied with her. I don't want you to go making trouble. I'm the missus, and she works for me, not you, you understand?"

Then, later in the day, Ella would relent. Having shown Thomasi the hand of authority, she could approach him on the other level of their association: that of common concern for the house that they had "run" together for nearly six years, and whose needs and prices and inanimate quirks both understood perfectly.

"Thomasi?"

"Missus?" She might be strolling in the garden, pretending that she was not seeking him out. He would go on wielding the grass shears, widening and snapping like the sharp bill of some great bird imprisoned in his hands.

"What has she done?"

"Well, I tell her the dog he mustn't have the small bone. Yesterday I tell her. Now she doesn't say nothing when I tell her. This morning I see she give the chicken bone to the dog. All that small bone, you know, the missus keep for the cats. Now when I say why you give that bone to the dog, the dog he's going to get sick, she just look me . . ."

The coffee cups left unwashed from the night before.

The iron left switched on while she went to her room after lunch.

And too many friends in her room at night, too many.

"I think she makes the kaffir beer," said Thomasi.

But at this complaint Ella was ready to discredit all the others, again. This was Thomasi trying to cook something up. If the girl brewed kaffir beer in her room, Thomasi would be her first customer, not the informant seeking to get her into trouble.

"Listen, Thomasi, I don't want to hear any more of these tales and grumbles, you understand? I'll see if Lena works properly or not, and I don't want you interfering with her."

As she would give her children a handful of sweets each to equalize some difference between them, Ella cleared out a cupboard that needed cleaning anyway, and gave Thomasi an old shirt of Allan's, Lena a cheap blue satin nightgown that she had bought to take to the nursing home and that she somehow felt she didn't want to wear again. "I must keep the peace," she said to Alan. "I'm not going to go training another new girl now. I must stick it out with this one until we go. She's a perfectly nice girl, really—a bit sulky, that's all. But you know what an old devil he can be when he wants to. I shouldn't be surprised if what's behind it is that he fancies her, and she's not interested. Shame, he looks such a little old wizened imp of a thing next to her, she's such a hulking, big-breasted Juno."

But the gifts did not quiet for long whatever it was that inflamed Thomasi's malice. The following month, on a Monday morning, Ella found Thomasi alone in the kitchen, cooking the greasy, metallic-tasting fried eggs that were his idea of a white man's breakfast. Lena, he said, bearing his message from across that neat stretch of grass and crisscross washing line that was the no-man's-land between the lives of the white people in the house and black people in their back-yard quarters, said she was sick this morning. She would do the washing tomorrow.

"Are those for the master . . . ?" Ella indicated the eggs but lacked the courage to complain. "What's wrong with Lena?"

Over the frying pan, Thomasi gave a great shrug of disbelief and contempt.

"What does she say?"

Thomasi turned around to the young woman in the soiled pink dressing-gown, the dark line of her plucked and dyed white-woman's eyebrows showing like pen strokes on the pastel of her fair-skinned face, unmade-up, faintly greasy with the patina of sleep. His brow drew in, intricately lined, over his little yellowish eyes; he said with exaggerated poise and indifference, "I don't know how she's sick. I can't say how a person she's sick when there's noise in her room all night. When people is talking there, late. Sometimes I think: She got someone staying there, or something? Talking, and late, late, a baby crying."

Ella went out, over the stones and the grass, across the yard to the native girl's room. The grass was crisp with dew and the chill struck through the old sandals she liked to wear instead of slippers; long threads of spider-web danced between the clothes-line. She knocked on the door of the little brick room; the window was closed and curtained. She knocked again and called softly, "Lena?"

"Ma'am?" The voice came after a pause.

Ella opened the door with difficulty—natives usually tampered with the doorknobs in their rooms, making them removable as an added protection against intruders—and, finding it would open only halfway, edged her way in. The room had a warm animal smell, like the inside of the cupboard where old Lixi, the tabby, lay with her kittens at her belly, purring and licking, purring and licking. The air in here had nothing to do with that other air, wet and sharp with morning, just outside: it was a creature air, created by breathing beings. Although the room was small, Lena in her bed seemed far away. The bed was raised high on bricks, and it was half-curtained, like a homemade four-poster. Some sort of design worked in red and purple thread trailed around the hems of the material. Lena lay, her head turned to the angle of her raised arm on the pillow. She seemed to be taking some communion of comfort from her own tender exposed armpit, close to her face.

"Are you sick, Lena?" said the white woman gently.

The black woman turned her head back and forth once, quickly on the pillow. She swallowed and said, "Yes."

"What do you feel?" said Ella, still at the door, which she now saw could not open properly because of a cupboard made of boxes which was pushed half against it.

"My stomach, ma'am." She moved under the fringed travelling rug that was her blanket.

"Do you think you've eaten something that's made you sick?" said Ella.

The girl did not answer. Ella saw her big slow eyes and the white of her teeth come out of the gloom.

"Sometimes I've got a cold in my stomach," the girl said at last.

"Is it pain?" said Ella.

"I can do the washing tomorrow," said the voice from the great, hemmed-in agglomerate of the bed.

"Oh, it doesn't matter," said Ella. "I'll send Thomasi out with something for you to take. And do you want something to eat?"

"Only tea, thank you, ma'am."

"All right then."

She felt the woman's slow eyes watching her out of that room, which curiously, despite its poverty, its soapbox cupboards fretted with cut-out newspaper edgings, the broken china ducks, and the sword-fern draped in strained crêpe paper (the ornaments and the fern were discards from the house), had something of the richly charged air of grand treasure-filled rooms of old houses heavy with association, rooms much used, thick with the overlaid echoes of human concourse. She thought, for some reason, of the kind of room in which one expects to find a Miss Havisham. And how ridiculous! These two whitewashed servants' rooms neatly placed out of the way between the dustbin and the garage! What had they to do with Dickens or flights of fancy—or anything else, in fact, except clean, weatherproof, and fairly decent places for the servants to sleep? They belonged to nothing and nobody, merely were thrown in along with the other conditions of work.

On the kitchen step Ella stopped and shook each foot like a cat; her feet were sopping. She made a little exclamation of irritation with herself.

And when she had dressed, she sent Thomasi out to the room with a dose of chlorodyne ready-mixed with water in one of the old kitchen-glasses. She got her younger child Pip ready for Allan to take to nursery school and saw that her daughter Kathie had some cake to take for her school lunch in place of the sandwiches Lena usually made.

"Darned nuisance, mmh?" Allan said (suppressing a belch, with distaste, after the eggs).

"Can't be helped, I suppose," Ella said. "I wouldn't mind so much if only it wasn't Monday. You know how it is when the washing isn't done on the right day. It puts the whole of the rest of the week out. Anyway, she should be all right by tomorrow."

The next morning when Ella got up, Lena was already doing the washing. "Girl appeared again?" called Allan from the bathroom. Ella came in, holding one of Pip's vests to her cheek to see if it was quite dry. "She doesn't look too good, poor thing. She's moving terribly slowly between the tub and the line."

"Well she's never exactly nimble is she?" murmured Allan,

concentrating on the slight dent in his chin, always a tricky place to shave. They smiled at each other; when they smiled at each other these days, they had the conspiring look of children who have discovered where the Christmas presents are hidden: Europe, leisure, and the freedom of the money they had saved up were unspoken between them.

Ella and Allan Plaistow lived in one of the pleasantest of Johannesburg suburbs: gently rolling country to the north of the city, where the rich had what amounted to country estates, and the impecunious possessors of good taste had small houses in an acre or two of half-cultivated garden. Some of the younger people, determined not to be forced back into real suburbia through lack of money, kept chickens or bred dogs to supplement the upkeep of their places, and one couple even had a small Jersey herd. Ella was one of their customers, quite sure she could taste the difference between their, and what she called "city" milk.

One morning about a week after the native girl Lena had delayed Ella's wash-day, the milk delivery cart was bowling along the ruts it had made for itself along the track between the dairy and the houses in the Plaistow's direction, when the horse swerved and one wheel bowed down the tall grasses at the side of the track. There was a tinny clang; the wheel slithered against something. Big Charlie, the milk "boy," growled softly at the horse, and climbed down to see. There, as if it had made a bed for itself in the long grass the way an animal turns round and round before sinking to rest, was a paraffin tin. Big Charlie stubbed at it once with his boot, as if to say, oh, well, if that's all . . . But it gave back the resistance of a container that has something inside it; through his toes, there came to him the realization that this was not merely an empty tin. It was upside down, the top pressed to the ground. He saw an edge of blue material, stained with dew and earth, just showing. Still with his foot, he pushed hard— too hard, for whatever was inside was light—and the tin rocked over. There spilled out of it a small bundle, the naked decaying body of what had been a new-born child, rolled, carelessly as one might roll up old clothing, in a blue satin nightgown.

It did not seem for a moment to Big Charlie that the baby was dead. He gave a kind of aghast cluck, as at some gross neglect—one of his own five doubled up with a bellyache after eating berries, or the youngest with flies settling on his mouth because the mother had failed to wipe the milk that trickled down his chin from her abundance when she fed him—and knelt down to make haste to do whatever it was that the little creature needed. And then he saw that this was hardly a child at all; was now closer to those kittens he was sometimes ordered by his employers to drown in a bucket of water or closer still to one of those battered fledglings found lying beneath the mimosa trees the night after a bad summer storm.

So now he stood back and did not want to touch it. With his mouth lifted over his teeth in a superstitious horror at the coldness of what had been done, he took the crumpled satin in the tips of his fingers and folded it over the body again, then dropped the bundle back into the paraffin tin and lifted the tin onto the cart beside him.

As he drove, he looked down now and then, swiftly, in dismay to see it there still beside him. The bodice of the nightgown was uppermost and lifted in the firm currents of the morning air. It was inside out, and showed a sewn-on laundry label. Big Charlie could neither read or write so he did not know that it said in the neat letters devised for the nursing home, E. PLAISTOW.

That, of course, was how Ella came to find herself in court.

When she opened the door to the plainclothes detective that afternoon, she had the small momentary start, a kind of throb in some organ one didn't know one had, of all people who do not steal and who have paid their taxes: an alarm at the sight of a policeman that is perhaps rooted in the memory of childhood treats. The man was heavily built and large-footed and he had a very small, well-brushed moustache, smooth as the double flick of a paintbrush across his broad lip. He said in Afrikaans, "Goeie middag. Mevrou Plaistow?" And when she answered in English, he switched to slow, stilted English. She led him into the living room with a false air of calm and he sat on the edge of the sofa. When he told her that the Evan's milk boy had found a dead native baby in a paraffin tin on the veld, she made a polite noise of horror and even felt a small shudder, just back of her jaws, at the idea, but her face kept its look of strained patience: what had this gruesome happening to do with *her?* Then he told her that the child was found wrapped in a blue satin nightgown bearing her name, and she rose instantly from her chair in alarm, as if there had been a sudden jab inside her.

"*In my nightgown?*" she accused, standing over the man.

"Yes, I'm afraid so, lady."

"But are you sure?" she said, withdrawing into anger and hauteur.

He opened a large brief-case he had brought with him and which she had imagined as much a part of his equipment as his official English or the rolled-gold signet ring on his little finger. Carefully he spread out the blue satin, which still kept, all refracted by creases, the sheen of satin, despite the earth stains and some others caused by something that had dried patchily—perhaps that birth fluid, *vernix caseosa*, in which a baby is coated when it slips into the world. The sight filled her with revulsion: "Oh, put it away!" she said with difficulty.

"You recognize it?" he said—pronouncing the word as if it were spelled "racognize."

"It's mine all right," she said. "It's the one I gave to Lena a few weeks ago. But good God—?"

"It's a native girl, of course, the one you gave it to?" He had taken out his notebook.

Now all sorts of things were flooding into her mind. "That's right! She was sick, she stayed in bed one day. The boy said he heard a baby cry in the night—" She appealed to the policeman: "But it couldn't be!"

"Now if you'll just tal me, lady, what was the date when you gave the girl the nightgown . . ." Out of the disorder of her quicker mind, his own slow one stolidly sorted this recollection from that; her confused computation of dates and times through the measure of how much time had passed between the day Pip chipped a tooth at nursery school (that, she remembered distinctly, happened on the same day that she had given Thomasi a shirt and Lena the nightgown) and the morning the washing had not been done, became a statement. Then she went, haltingly because of her nervousness, into the kitchen to call Lena and Thomasi. "Thomasi!" she called. And then, after a pause: "Lena". And she watched for her, coming across the yard.

But the two Africans met the fact of the policeman far more calmly than she herself had done. For Africans there is no stigma attached to any involvement with the forces of the law; the innumerable restrictions by which their lives are hedged from the day they are born make transgressions commonplace and punishment inevitable. To them a few days in prison is no more shaming than an attack of the measles. After all, there are few people who could go through a lifetime without at least once forgetting to carry the piece of paper which is their "pass" to free movement about the town, or without getting drunk, or without sitting on a bench which looks just like every other bench but happens to be provided exclusively for the use of people with a pale skin. All these things keep Africans casually going in and out of prison, hardly the worse—since it is accepted that this is the ways things are—for a cold, buggy night in the cells or a kick from a warder.

Lena has not a pleasant face, thought Ella, but thought too that perhaps she was merely reading this into the face, now. The woman simply stood there, answering, in an obedient Afrikaans, the detective's questions about her identity. The detective had hitched his solid rump onto the kitchen table, and his manner had changed to the impatient one customarily used for Africans by all white persons in authority. The woman appeared weary, more than anything else; she did not look at the detective when he spoke to her or she answered. And she spoke coldly, as was her custom; just as she said, "Yes madam no madam," when Ella reproached her for some neglected chore. She was an untidy woman, too; now she had on her head a woollen *doek* again, instead of the maid's cap Ella provided for her to wear. Ella looked at her, from the *doek* to the coloured sandals with the cut thongs where they caught the toes; looked at her in a kind of fascination, and tried to fit with her the idea of the dead baby, rolled in a nightgown and thrust into a paraffin tin. It was neither credible nor did it inspire revulsion. Because she is not a *motherly* figure, Ella thought—that is it. One cannot imagine her mother to anything. She is the sort of woman, white or black, who is always the custodian of other people's children; she washes their faces and wipes their noses, but they throw their arms around somebody else's neck.

And just then the woman looked at her, suddenly, directly, without a flicker of escape, without dissimulation or appeal, not as a woman looks to another woman, or even a human being to another human being; looked at her out of those wide-set, even-lidded eyes and did not move a muscle of her face.

Oh, but I don't know her, I know nothing about her . . . Ella recoiled, retracting to herself.

"She'll have to come along with me," the detective was saying, and as the woman stood a moment, as if awaiting some permission, he told her in Afrikaans that she could go to her room if she wanted anything, but she must be quick.

Ella stood near the door watching her servant go slowly across the yard to the little brick room. Her own heart was pounding slowly. She felt a horrible conflict of agitation and shame—for what, she did not know. But if I go after her, she seemed to answer herself, what can I say to her? Behind Ella, the detective was questioning Thomasi, and Thomasi was enjoying it; she could hear from the quick, meaningful, confidential tones of Thomasi's voice that he was experiencing all the relish of a gossip who finds himself at last in the powerful position of being able to influence the lives of those who have forced him out into the cold of a vicarious recorder.

Ella said suddenly to the detective, "Will you excuse me now, please—" and went away through the house to her bedroom. She was standing there still, some minutes later, when the detective called from the front door, "Thank you very much, lady, hey? We'll let you know—" and she did not come out but called back, as if she were at some task she could not leave for a moment, "I'm sorry—will you find your way out . . ."

But she could not forbear to bend apart the slats of the venetian blind in time to see the back of Lena, in one of those cheap short coats—jeep coats, they were called, beloved of suburban African girls—getting into the police car. It's unbelievable, she told herself; she didn't look any fatter than she does now . . . And she did the whole week's washing . . .

The moment Ella heard the car drive away, she went to

telephone Allan. As she dialled, she noticed that her fingers were fumbling and damp. I'm really upset, she thought; I'm really upset about this thing.

By the time the court case came to be heard, the quiet, light-coloured Lena lying in her bed that day with her head turned to her arm for comfort, standing obediently before the questioning of the detective in the kitchen, was changed in Ella Plaistow's mind into the ghoulish creature who emerged out of discussion of the affair with friends and neighbours. A woman who could kill her own baby! A murderer, nothing less! It's quite awful to think that she handled Pip and Kathie, other women sympathized. It just shows you, you never know who you're taking in your home . . . You never know, with *them* . . . You can send them to a doctor to make sure you aren't harbouring someone who's diseased, but you've no way of finding out what sort of person a servant is. Well, Thomasi didn't like her from the first, you know, Ella always said at this point. Ah, Thomasi, someone would murmur, now he's a good old thing.

So that when Ella saw the woman Lena in court, there was something disquieting and unexpected about the ordinariness, the naturalness of her appearance: this was simply the woman who had stood so often at the stove in Ella's red-and-white kitchen. And where was the other, that creature who had abandoned her own newborn child to the cold of the veld?

Embarrassment precluded all other feelings, once the white woman found herself in the witness stand. Ella had never, she said again and again afterward, felt such a fool in her whole life.

"You are, of course, a married woman?" said the magistrate.

"Yes," said Ella.

"How long have you been married?"

"Eight years."

"I see. And you have children?"

"Yes, two children."

"Mrs Plaistow, am I to understand that you, a woman who has been married for eight years and has herself borne two children, were not aware that this woman in your employ was on the point of giving birth to a child?"

Of couse, the man must have thought her quite moronic! But how to explain that one didn't go measuring one's servant's waistline, that she was a very big well-built woman in any case, and that since she must have been well into her pregnancy when she started work, any further changes in her figure were not noticed?

He made such a *fool* of me, Ella protested; you can't imagine how *idiotic* I felt.

The case dragged on through two days. The woman herself said that the child had been born dead, and that since no one knew that she was pregnant, she had been "frightened" and had hidden the body and then left it on the veld, but post-mortem findings showed strong evidence that the child might have lived some hours after birth, and had not died naturally. Then there was Thomasi's statement that he had heard an infant cry in the night.

"In your opinion, Doctor," the magistrate asked the government medical officer, in an attempt to establish how much time had elapsed between the birth and death of the infant, "would it be possible for a woman to resume her normal day's work thirty-six hours after confinement? This woman did her employer's household washing the following day."

The doctor smiled slightly. "Were the woman in question a European, I should, of course, say this would be most unlikely. Most unlikely. But of a native woman, I should say yes—yes, it would be possible." In the silence of the court, the reasonableness, the validity of this statement had the air of clinching the matter. After all, everyone knew, out of a mixture of hearsay and personal observation, the physical stamina of the African. Hadn't everyone heard of at least one native who had walked around for three days with a fractured skull, merely complaining of a headache? And of one who had walked miles to a hospital, carrying, Van Gogh-like, in a piece of newspaper, his own ear—sliced off in a faction fight?

Lena got six months' hard labour. Her sentence coincided roughly with the time Ella and Allan spent in Europe, but though she was out of prison by the time they returned, she did not go back to work for them again.

Jamaican Fragment

A.L. Hendricks

E VERY day I walk a half-mile from my home to the tramcar lines in the morning, and from the lines to my home in the evening. The walk is pleasant. The road on either side is flanked by red- and green-roofed bungalows, green lawns and gardens. The exercise is good for me and now and then I learn something from a little incident.

One morning, about half-way between my front gate and the tram track, I noticed two little boys playing in the garden of one of the more modest cottages. They were both very little boys, one was four years old perhaps, the other five. The bigger of the two was a sturdy youngster, very dark, with a mat of coarse hair on his head and coal-black eyes. He was definitely a little Jamaican—a strong little Jamaican. The other little fellow was smaller, but also sturdy—he was white, with hazel eyes and light-brown hair. Both were dressed in blue shirts and khaki pants: they wore no shoes and their feet were muddy. They were not conscious of my standing there watching them; they played on. The game, if it could be called a game, was not elaborate. The little white boy strode imperiously up and down and every now and then shouted imperiously at his bigger playmate. The little brown boy shuffled along quietly behind him and did what he was told.

"Pick up that stick!" The dark boy picked it up.

"Jump into the flowers!" The dark boy jumped.

"Get me some water!" The dark boy ran inside. The white boy sat down on the lawn.

I was amazed. Here before my eyes, a white baby, for they were little more than babies, was imposing his will upon a little black boy. And the little black boy submitted. I puzzled within myself as I went down the road. Could it be that the little dark boy was the son of a servant in the home and therefore had to do the white boy's bidding? No. They were obviously dressed alike, the little dark boy was of equal class with his playmate. No. They were playmates, the little dark boy was a neighbour's child. I was sure of that. Then how was it that he obeyed so faithfully the white boy's orders? Was it that even at his early age he sensed that in his own country he would be at the white man's beck and call? Could he in such youth divine a difference between himself and the white boy? And did the little white youngster so young, such a baby, realize that he would grow to dominate the black man? Was there an indefinable quality in the white man that enabled his baby, smaller and younger than his playmate, to make him his slave? Was there really some difference between a white man and black man? Something that made the white superior? I could find no answer. I could not bring myself to believe such a thing, and yet, with my own eyes I had seen a little dark boy take orders from a little white boy—a little white boy obviously his social equal, and younger and smaller. Were we as a race really inferior? So inferior that even in our infancy we realized our deficiencies, and accepted a position as the white man's servant?

For a whole day I puzzled over this problem. For a whole day my faith in my people was shaken. When I passed that afternoon the little boys were not there. That evening I thought deeply on the subject.

The next morning the boys were there again, and a man was standing at the gate watching them. I stopped and looked, just to see what the white boy was making his little servant do. To my utter astonishment the little dark boy was striding imperiously up and down the lawn, while the white youngster walked abjectly behind him.

"Get me a banana!" The little white boy ran into the house and reappeared shortly with a banana. "Peel it for me!" The little white boy skinned the banana and handed it to his dark master.

I saw it now. This was indeed a game, a game I had played as a child. Each boy took it in turn every alternate day to be the boss, the other the slave. It had been great fun to me as a youngster. I smiled as I remembered. I looked at the man standing by the gate. He was a white man. I remembered what I had thought yesterday. He, no doubt, I thought to myself, was wondering if the black race is superior to the white. I laughed gently to myself. How silly grown-ups are, how clever we are, how wonderfully able we are to impute deep motives to childish actions! How suspicious we are when we have been warped by prejudice! This man, I said to myself, will puzzle all day on whether the blacks will eventually arise and rule the world because he thinks he sees a little black boy realizing at a tender age his superiority over the white. I will save him his puzzle. I will explain it to him. I went across to him.

"I know what you're thinking," I said. "You're thinking that maybe the black race is superior to the white, because you just saw the little dark youngster on the lawn ordering the little white boy around. Don't think that, it's a game they play. Alternate days one is boss, the other the servant. It's a grand game. I used to play it and maybe so did you. Yesterday I saw the little white boy bossing the dark one and I worried all day over the dark boy's realization of his inferiority so young in life! We are silly, we grown-ups, aren't we?"

The man was surprised at my outburst. He looked at me smiling.

"I know all about the game," he said. "The boys are brothers—my sons." He pointed to a handsome brown woman on the veranda who had just come out to call in the children. "That's my wife," he said.

I smiled. My spirit laughed within me. This is Jamaica, I said in my heart, this is my country—my people. I looked at the white man. He smiled at me. "We'll miss the tram if we don't hurry," he said.

Across the Bridge

Graham Greene

"THEY say he's worth a million," Lucia said. He sat there in the little hot damp Mexican square, a dog at his feet, with an air of immense and forlorn patience. The dog attracted your attention at once; for it was very nearly an English setter, only something had gone wrong with the tail and the feathering. Palms wilted over his head, it was all shade and stuffiness round the bandstand, radios talked loudly in Spanish from the little wooden sheds where they changed your pesos into dollars at a loss. I could tell he didn't understand a word from the way he read his newspaper—as I did myself picking out the words which were like English ones. "He's been here a month," Lucia said, "they turned him out of Guatemala and Honduras."

You couldn't keep any secrets for five hours in this border town. Lucia had only been twenty-four hours in the place, but she knew all about Mr Joseph Calloway. The only reason I didn't know about him (and I'd been in the place two weeks) was because I couldn't talk the language any more than Mr Calloway could. There wasn't another soul in the place who didn't know the story—the whole story of Halling Investment Trust and the proceedings for extradition. Any man doing dusty business in any of the wooden booths in the town is better fitted by long observation to tell Mr Calloway's tale than I am, except that I was in—literally—at the finish. They all watched the drama proceed with immense interest, sympathy and respect. For, after all, he had a million.

Every once in a while through the long steamy day, a boy came and cleaned Mr. Calloway's shoes: he hadn't the right words to resist them—they pretended not to know his English. He must have had his shoes cleaned the day Lucia and I watched him at least half a dozen times. At midday he took a stroll across the square to the Antonio Bar and had a bottle of beer, the setter sticking to heel as if they were out for a country walk in England (he had, you may remember, one of the biggest estates in Norfolk). After his bottle of beer, he would walk down between the money-changers' huts to the Rio Grande and look across the bridge into the United States: people came and went constantly in cars. Then back to the square till lunch-time. He was staying in the best hotel, but you don't get good hotels in this border town: nobody stays in them more than a night. The good hotels were on the other side of the bridge: you could see their electric signs twenty storeys high from the little square at night, like lighthouses marking the United States.

You may ask what I'd been doing in so drab a spot for a fortnight. There was no interest in the place for anyone; it was just damp and dust and poverty, a kind of shabby replica of the town across the river: both had squares in the same spots; both had the same number of cinemas. One was cleaner than the other, that was all, and more expensive, much more expensive. I'd stayed across there a couple of nights waiting for a man a tourist bureau said was driving down from Detroit to Yucatan and would sell a place in his car for some fantastically small figure—twenty dollars, I think it was. I don't know if he existed or was invented by the optimistic half-caste in the agency; anyway, he never turned up and so I waited, not much caring, on the cheap side of the river. It didn't much matter; I was living. One day I meant to give up the man from Detroit and go home or go south, but it was easier not to decide anything in a hurry. Lucia was just waiting for a car the other way, but she didn't have to wait so long. We waited together and watched Mr Calloway waiting—for God knows what.

I don't know how to treat this story—it was a tragedy for

Mr Calloway, it was poetic retribution, I suppose, in the eyes of the shareholders he'd ruined with his bogus transactions, and to Lucia and me, at this stage, it was pure comedy—except when he kicked the dog. I'm not a sentimentalist about dogs, I prefer people to be cruel to animals rather than to human beings, but I couldn't help being revolted at the way he'd kick that animal—with a hint of cold-blooded venom, not in anger but as if he were getting even for some trick it had played him a long while ago. That generally happened when he returned from the bridge: it was the only sign of anything resembling emotion he showed. Otherwise he looked a small, set, gentle creature with silver hair and a silver moustache, and gold-rimmed glasses, and one gold tooth like a flaw in character.

Lucia hadn't been accurate when she said he'd been turned out of Guatemala and Honduras; he'd left voluntarily when the extradition proceedings seemed likely to go through and moved north. Mexico is still not a very centralized state, and it is possible to get round governors as you can't get round cabinet ministers or judges. And so he waited there on the border for the next move. That earlier part of the story is, I suppose, dramatic, but I didn't watch it and I can't invent what I haven't seen—the long waiting in ante-rooms, the bribes taken and refused, the growing fear of arrest, and then the flight—in gold-rimmed glasses—covering his tracks as well as he could, but this wasn't finance and he was an amateur at escape. And so he'd washed up here, under my eyes and Lucia's eyes, sitting all day under the bandstand, nothing to read but a Mexican paper, nothing to do but look across the river at the United States, quite unaware, I suppose, that everyone knew everything about him, once a day kicking his dog. Perhaps in its semi-setter way it reminded him too much of the Norfolk estate—though that, too, I suppose, was the reason he kept it.

And the next act again was pure comedy. I hesitate to think what this man worth a million was costing his country as they edged him out from this land and that. Perhaps somebody was getting tired of the business, and careless; anyway, they sent across two detectives, with an old photograph. He'd grown his silvery moustache since that had been taken, and he'd aged a lot, and they couldn't catch sight of him. They hadn't been across the bridge two hours when everybody knew that there were two foreign detectives in town looking for Mr Calloway— everybody knew, that is to say, except Mr Calloway, who couldn't talk Spanish. There were plenty of people who could have told him in English, but they didn't. It wasn't cruelty, it was a sort of awe and respect: like a bull, he was on show, sitting there mournfully in the plaza with his dog, a magnificent spectacle for which we all had ring-side seats.

I ran into one of the policemen in the Bar Antonio. He was disgusted; he had had some idea that when he crossed the bridge life was going to be different, so much more colour and sun, and—I suspect—love, and all he found were wide mud streets where the nocturnal rain lay in pools, and mangy dogs, smells and cockroaches in his bedroom, and nearest to love, the open door of the Academia Comercial, where pretty mestizo girls sat all the morning learning to typewrite. Tip-tap-tip-tap-tip—perhaps they had a dream, too—jobs on the other side of the bridge, where life was going to be so much more luxurious, refined and amusing.

We got into conversation; he seemed surprised that I knew who they both were and what they wanted. He said, "We've got information this man Calloway's in town."

"He's knocking around somewhere," I said.

"Could you point him out?"

"Oh, I don't know him by sight," I said.

He drank his beer and thought a while. "I'll go out and sit in the plaza. He's sure to pass sometime."

I finished my beer and went quickly off and found Lucia. I said, "Hurry, we're going to see an arrest." We didn't care a thing about Mr Calloway, he was just an elderly man who kicked his dog and swindled the poor, and deserved anything he got. So we made for the plaza; we knew Calloway would be there, but it had never occurred to either of us that the detectives wouldn't recognize him. There was quite a surge of people round the place; all the fruit-sellers and boot-blacks in town seemed to have arrived together; we had to force our way through, and there in the little green stuffy centre of the place, sitting on adjoining seats, were the two plain-clothes men and Mr Calloway. I've never known the place so silent; everybody was on tiptoe, and the plain-clothes men were staring at the crowd looking for Mr Calloway, and Mr Calloway sat on his usual seat staring out over the money-changing booths at the United States.

"It can't go on. It just can't," Lucia said. But it did. It got more fantastic still. Somebody ought to write a play about it. We sat as close as we dared. We were afraid all the time we were going to laugh. The semi-setter scratched for fleas and Mr Calloway watched the U.S.A. The two detectives watched the crowd, and the crowd watched the show with solemn satisfaction. Then one of the detectives got up and went over to Mr Calloway. That's the end, I thought. But it wasn't, it was the beginning. For some reason they had eliminated him from their list of suspects. I shall never know why. The man said:

"You speak English?"

"I *am* English," Mr Calloway said.

Even that didn't tear it, and the strangest thing of all was the way Mr Calloway came alive. I don't think anybody had spoken to him like that for weeks. The Mexicans were too respectful—he was a man with a million—and it had never occurred to Lucia and me to treat him casually like a human being, even in our eyes he had been magnified by the colossal theft and the world-wide pursuit.

He said,"This is rather a dreadful place, don't you think?"

"It is," the policeman said.

"I can't think what brings anybody across the bridge."

"Duty," the policeman said gloomily. "I suppose you are passing through."

"Yes," Mr Calloway said.

"I'd have expected over here there'd have been—you know what I mean—life. You read things about Mexico."

"Oh, life," Mr Calloway said. He spoke firmly and precisely, as if to a committee of shareholders. "That begins on the other side."

"You don't appreciate your own country until you leave it."

"That's very true," Mr Calloway said. "Very true."

At first it was difficult not to laugh, and then after a while there didn't seem to be much to laugh at; an old man imagining all the fine things going on beyond the international bridge. I think he thought of the town opposite as a combination of London and Norfolk—theatres and cocktail bars, a little shooting and a walk round the field at evening with the dog—that miserable imitation of a setter—poking the ditches. He'd never been across, he couldn't know that it was just the same thing over again—even the same layout; only the streets were paved and the hotels had ten more storeys, and life was more expensive, and everything was a little bit cleaner. There wasn't anything Mr Calloway would have called living—no galleries, no book-shops, just *Film Fun* and the local paper, and *Click* and *Focus* and the tabloids.

"Well," said Mr Calloway, "I think I'll take a stroll before lunch. You need an appetite to swallow the food here. I generally go down and look at the bridge about now. Care to come, too?"

The detective shook his head. "No," he said. "I'm on duty. I'm looking for a fellow." And that, of course, gave *him* away. As far as Mr Calloway could understand, there was only one "fellow" in the world anyone was looking for—his brain had eliminated friends who were seeking their friends, husbands who might be waiting for their wives, all objectives of any search but just the one. The power of elimination was what had made him a financier—he could forget the people behind the shares.

That was the last we saw of him for a while. We didn't see him going into the Botica Paris to get his aspirin, or walking back from the bridge with his dog. He simply disappeared, and when he disappeared, people began to talk and the detectives heard the talk. They looked silly enough, and they got busy after the very man they'd been sitting next to in the garden. Then they, too, disappeared. They, as well as Mr Calloway, had gone to the state capital to see the Governor and the Chief of Police, and it must have been an amusing sight there, too, as they bumped into Mr Calloway and sat with him in the waiting-rooms. I suspect Mr Calloway was generally shown in first, for everyone knew he was worth a million. Only in Europe is it possible for a man to be a criminal as well as a rich man.

Anyway, after about a week the whole pack of them returned by the same train. Mr Calloway travelled Pullman, and the two policemen travelled in the day coach. It was evident that they hadn't got their extradition order.

Lucia had left by that time. The car came and went across the bridge. I stood in Mexico and watched her get out at the United States Customs. She wasn't anything in particular, but she looked beautiful at a distance as she gave me a wave out of the United States and got back into the car. And I suddenly felt sympathy for Mr Calloway, as if there were something over there which you couldn't find here, and turning round I saw him back on his old beat, with the dog at his heels.

I said "Good afternoon," as if it had been all along our habit to greet each other. He looked tired and ill and dusty, and I felt sorry for him—to think of the kind of victory he'd been winning, with so much expenditure of cash and care—the prize this dirty and dreary town, the booths of the money-changers, the awful little beauty parlours with their wicker chairs and sofas looking like the reception rooms of brothels, that hot and stuffy garden by the bandstand.

He replied gloomily "Good morning," and the dog started to sniff at some ordure and he turned and kicked it with fury, with depression, with despair.

And at that moment a taxi with the two policemen in it passed us on its way to the bridge. They must have seen that kick; perhaps they were cleverer than I had given them credit for, perhaps they were just sentimental about animals, and thought they'd do a good deed, and the rest happened by accident. But the fact remains—those two pillars of the law set about the stealing of Mr Calloway's dog.

He watched them go by. Then he said, "Why don't you go across?"

"It's cheaper here," I said.

"I mean just for an evening. Have a meal at that place we can see at night in the sky. Go to the theatre."

"There isn't a chance."

He said angrily, sucking his gold tooth, "Well, anyway, get away from here." He stared down the hill and up the other side. He couldn't see that street climbing up from the bridge contained only the same money-changers' booths as this one.

I said, "Why don't *you* go?"

He said evasively, "Oh—business."

I said, "It's only a question of money. You don't *have* to pass by the bridge."

He said with faint interest, "I don't talk Spanish."

"There isn't a soul here," I said, "who doesn't talk English."

He looked at me with surprise. "Is that so?" he said. "Is that so?"

It's as I have said; he'd never tried to talk to anyone, and they respected him too much to talk to him—he was worth a million. I don't know whether I'm glad or sorry that I told him that. If I hadn't, he might be there now, sitting by the bandstand having his shoes cleaned—alive and suffering.

Three days later his dog disappeared. I found him looking for it, calling it softly and shamefacedly between the palms of the garden. He looked embarrassed. He said in a low angry voice, "I *hate* that dog. The beastly mongrel," and called "Rover, Rover" in a voice which didn't carry five yards. He said, "I bred setters once. I'd have shot a dog like that." It reminded him, I *was* right, of Norfolk, and he lived in the memory, and he hated it for its imperfection. He was a man without a family and without friends, and his only enemy was that dog. You couldn't call the law an enemy; you have to be intimate with an enemy.

Late that afternoon someone told him they'd seen the dog walking across the bridge. It wasn't true, of course, but we didn't know that then—they'd paid a Mexican five pesos to smuggle it across. So all that afternoon and the next Mr Calloway sat in the garden having his shoes cleaned over and over again, and thinking how a dog could just walk across like that, and a human being, an immortal soul, was bound here in the awful routine of the little walk and the unspeakable meals and the aspirin at the botica. That dog was seeing things he couldn't see—that hateful dog. It made him mad—I think literally mad. You must remember the man had been going on for months. He had a million and he was living on two pounds a week, with nothing to spend his money on. He sat there and brooded on the hideous injustice of it. I think he'd have crossed over one day in any case, but the dog was the last straw.

Next day when he wasn't to be seen, I guessed he'd gone across and I went too. The American town is as small as the Mexican. I knew I couldn't miss him if he was there, and I was still curious. A little sorry for him, but not much.

I caught sight of him first in the only drug-store, having a coca-cola, and then once outside a cinema looking at the posters; he had dressed with extreme neatness, as if for a party, but there was no party. On my third time round, I came on the detectives—they were having coca-colas in the drug-store, and they must have missed Mr Calloway by inches. I went in and sat down at the bar.

"Hello," I said, "you still about." I suddenly felt anxious for Mr Calloway. I didn't want them to meet.

One of them said, "Where's Calloway?"

"Oh," I said, "he's hanging on."

"But not his dog," he said, and laughed. The other looked a little shocked, he didn't like anyone to *talk* cynically about a dog. Then they got up—they had a car outside.

"Have another?" I said.

"No thanks. We've got to keep moving."

The men bent close and confided to me, "Calloway's on this side."

"No!" I said.

"And his dog."

"He's looking for it," the other said.

"I'm damned if he is," I said, and again one of them looked a little shocked, as if I'd insulted the dog.

I don't think Mr Calloway was looking for his dog, but his dog certainly found him. There was sudden hilarious yapping from the car and out plunged the semi-setter and gambolled furiously down the street. One of the detectives—the sentimental one—was into the car before we got to the door and was off after the dog. Near the bottom of the long road to the bridge was Mr Calloway—I do believe he'd come down to look at the Mexican side when he found there was nothing but the drug-store and the cinemas and the paper shops on the American. He saw the dog coming and yelled at it to go home—"home, home, home", as if they were in Norfolk—it took no notice at all, pelting towards him. Then he saw the police car coming, and ran. After that, everything happened too quickly, but I think the order of events was this—the dog started across the road right in front of the car, and Mr Calloway yelled, at the dog or the car, I don't know which. Anyway, the detective swerved—he said later, weakly, at the inquiry, that he couldn't run over a dog, and down went Mr Calloway, in a mess of broken glass and gold rims and silver hair, and blood. The dog was on to him before any of us could reach him, licking and whimpering and licking. I saw Mr Calloway put up his hand, and down it went across the dog's neck and the whimper rose to a stupid bark of triumph, but Mr Calloway was dead—shock and a weak heart.

"Poor old geezer," the detective said, "I bet he really loved that dog," and it's true that the attitude in which he lay looked more like a caress than a blow. I thought it was meant to be a blow, but the detective may have been right. It all seemed to me a little too touching to be true as the old crook lay there with his arm over the dog's neck, dead with his million between the money-changers' huts, but it's as well to be humble in the face of human nature. He had come across the river for something, and it may, after all, have been the dog he was looking for. It sat there, baying its stupid and mongrel triumph across his body, like a piece of sentimental statuary: the nearest he could get to the fields, the ditches, the horizon of his home. It was comic and it was pitiable, but it wasn't less comic because the man was dead. Death doesn't change comedy to tragedy, and if that last gesture was one of affection, I suppose it was only one more indication of a human being's capacity for self-deception, our baseless optimism that is so much more appalling than our despair.

Concerning the Fauna

Katherine Gallagher

When I see kangaroos on the screen,
I take in the landscape
at one miraculous jump.

It's the same with koalas—
my stomach lifts,
I start climbing the nearest tree.

I'm an old hand now.

Once I saw a famous politician
fill a meeting-hall:
his subject, 'Kangaroos and koalas—
our national identity.'

People listened rapt:
by the end of the evening
we were all either
jumping or climbing.

Finally in the hullaballoo
the police were called—
only the fastest got away.

The Day I Became a Canadian

Al Pittman

I T is April, finally, and 11 days from now I will be 9.
Breakfast is over and I am in an awful hurry to get outdoors. Before I can escape from the kitchen, my father,
standing in the doorways, says to me, "From now on you can
call yourself a Canadian." It is April Fool's Day, and I have
to be careful.

"What's a Canadian, Dad?"

"A Canadian is someone who lives in Canada."

"Do we live in Canada, Dad?"

"We do now. Yesterday we didn't. But today we do. And
that's why from now on you can call yourself a Canadian."

"How come we still live in the same house, if we moved to
Canada?"

"Well, we didn't move at all. Come here and I'll try to
explain to you."

And he did. I'm not sure I understood, but I remember
walking away from the conversation that morning feeling different. Different like you felt walking out of church on Confir-
mation Day, or different like you felt later on when you
climbed all the way to the top of the Red Scrape without
anyone around to watch. That kind of difference.

On April 1, 1949, Newfoundland became Canada's 10th
province. Whatever it meant inside my nine-year-old mind,
there seemed to be little evidence around the neighborhood
that anything momentous had happened. Later on I heard about

people hanging black flags out the window and wearing black armbands in protest, and other people gathering in halls to celebrate. But where I lived, it seemed to me that my father had shared a solemn secret with me. And what a secret to have hold of, to reveal or conceal according to my will.

I went off to find Johnny Moynahan. He beat me in every subject in school, and here he was, a Canadian, and didn't even know it. I've seldom felt such a delightful sense of triumph. Johnny denied it, of course. He was good in geography and he knew all about Canada and he certainly was not a Canadian. Off he went to his father to confirm my stupidity. Poor old Johnny! I don't think he ever lived it down. He was a Canadian, of course, and had been for half a day. And so was Margaret, and Eddie, and Mom, and my brothers, and my sister Alice. And the rocks and the trees and the sky. Even the sky was Canadian now. And this ground I stood upon, this brown slope at the edge of the woods, this was Canada. Yesterday I stood on this very spot and I was only in Newfoundland. Today I was in Canada.

Other people had other considerations, no doubt, but to me it was a miracle of time and space. I looked up that morning to watch a flock of Canadian snowbirds pitch in the Canadian trees above my head. I suppose only someone just about to be 9 could be so amazed.

Today, 30 years later, I have other recollections, other realizations. Now, because memories are not instant reactions, because they gather and grow and recreate themselves as they like without any reverence for fact, I recall the referendums. The blaring loudspeakers, the fuss on the radio, the arguments in the kitchen, the words "baby bonus" as common as coughs, and the incredible flurry of it all.

"God bless Joey!" Mr. Sparkes would say to every customer who walked into his store.

"Goddamn Joey!" Mr. Shears replied. You could hear them going at it half way down Mountbatten Road.

It was all Joey and the baby bonus. Canada had nothing to do with it until it was all over. There might have been a few intellectuals at Memorial University and the odd Water Street merchant who considered the politics of Confederation before they made up their minds how to vote. But for the vast majority of Newfoundlanders it was simply a matter of the baby bonus versus the return to responsible government, to the sovereignty that was ours for 78 years until the country went bankrupt in 1933.

Newfoundland families were large families. A family of 12 was not considered overly large and the promise of an allowance for each child, no matter how small, added up to a substantial amount of money.

In 1949 Newfoundlanders had little but patriotism to be patriotic about. Conditions for most people were poor by any standard. Tuberculosis was on the rampage. There was a shortage of schools, hospitals, roads and jobs. The fishery was in a desperate state of disrepair, and it was all the Commission of Government could do to dig the country out of the ruins of bankruptcy. And along comes Joseph R. Smallwood, with his promise of the baby bonus.

It is no less amazing that so many Newfoundlanders resisted with such determination. Could it have been anything other than clear recognition that they were being tempted to sell out their country, their nationality, their souls, for the dollars offered? Perhaps. It could have been that they were swayed by the rhetoric of the anticonfederates, gifted orators like Major Peter Cashin, or that they believed the propaganda disseminated by the St. John's merchant class (Confederation would bring economic ruin), or by the Catholic Church hierarchy (Confederation would bring an end to Catholic education). For whatever reason, half the population of Newfoundland resisted Confederation to the bitter end, and many resisted it all their lives after.

For most of those who did not resist, the baby bonus made the difference. On the final ballot it came down to "Do we go back to self-government and do without the baby bonus, or do we join Canada and wait for the cheques to arrive?" It was not an easy choice. Say what you like about a people's sense of self-identity and independence, it is not commensurate with economic woe. So after two bitterly fought referendum campaigns, the confederates won by the slimmest possible majority (52.24 percent), and Newfoundland became a province of Canada.

"Listen Johnny," I said as soon as I got the chance, "you know what this means, now that we're living in Canada?"

"Of course I do," replied Johnny. But he didn't so I told him.

"It means all kinds of things. It means maybe now we'll be able to wear those U.S. Keds sneakers that they wear in the comics, instead of these old gum boots."

"How come?"

"Because Canada is a big place, my son. Bigger than the States even. My father said so.

"So?"

"So, if Canada is as big as the States, then it must have all that stuff in it."

"What stuff?"

"You know. The stuff in comics. Like where you can join a club and get all kinds of free prizes like spy glasses and roller skates and model airplanes and Double Bubble Gum."

"So what? My mother won't let me chew bubblegum. She says it's rude to blow bubbles, and it causes germs."

"Still, I bet you'd sneak a chew if it could make you fly."

"What do you mean, fly?"

"You know, like the kid in the comics. The one who blows big bubbles and flies all over the place. If you could blow a bubble big enough you could go right over your house, over the school even. If it was Double Bubble Gum you could."

"Go on! That's just comic book stuff."

"No. It's real. Cross my heart and hope to die. They really have things like that in places like the States and Canada. And now that we live in Canada, we'll have them too. Just imagine, being able to fly!"

Johnny was a real skeptic and refused to believe a word of it. But back then, when it all began, when I was 9, I, for one, firmly believed in Double Bubble Gum ads. The comic books had convinced me that if we could get Double Bubble Gum, then I could fly like the fat boy in the advertisements and float, borne up by the biggest bubble imaginable, over buildings and hills. And I could catch bank robbers if there were ever any around to catch, and I'd be a hero then to everyone who knew me. As far as I was concerned, it was all part of becoming Canadian. Since then I've learned that my childhood notions about Canada were no more uninformed than the notions a lot of Newfoundland adults had at the time.

Canada was a most foreign place to us in 1949. Until then, and until we got used to the fact that the border had been lifted between us and the Canadians, our familiar North American neighbors were the French islands of St. Pierre and Miquelon and the Boston States (which is what we called the United States of America). Until then Canada had been, for the most part, an unknown country to us.

We knew Halifax because it was a frequent port of call for ships enroute to Boston, and if you cared to go ashore there you had to put up with the rigmarole of Canadian customs regulations. We knew of Shelburne because of the Shelburne dory; many of our own dories came from Shelburne, Nova Scotia, and many that didn't were fashioned by our own boat builders according to the revered Shelburne design. But of Canada we knew little else. One older friend of mine recalls he knew Canada then only "as that place on the Bay of Fundy" because he used to "run rum up there in prohibition years." Another friend tells me his concept of Canada was "a place up there that had Montreal in it." Because of our involvement in the foreign fish trade, many Newfoundlanders were more familiar with the European ports of Cadiz and Oporto and the islands of the West Indies than they were with most of Canada. This was not idle ignorance on our part. We simply did not need to know.

Before the migration of Newfoundlanders to Toronto began in the mid '50s, we had been moving to the Boston States for years in numbers that would astound the statisticians. On my first trip to Boston in 1960, I parked my car, bearing Newfoundland licence plates, in the cobblestone square at the entrance to the Boston Fish Pier. Before I had the motor turned off I was surrounded by men anxious to talk about things back home. I spent the day with dozens of them in the bars around the pier. Most hadn't been back home since they came to Boston during the Depression. They had come to fish on the beam trawlers out of Boston, New Bedford and Rockland. Their wives had joined them along the way and their children had grown up American. All seven of my father's family went to the States in the '20s and '30s, and only my father came back to live in Newfoundland. I am only one of thousands of Newfoundlanders whose cousins are all citizens in the Boston States.

Confederaton changed all that. In time we got used to thinking of Toronto as the new mecca, and in time we got used to Canadian money, Canadian stamps, Canadian cigarettes and candy and the rest. But it took many of us a lot longer to get used to being Canadian. To this day, most people of my own and older generations think of themselves as Newfoundlanders. Adrian Fowler of Corner Brook, who was three years old at the time of Confederation, told the Task Force on Canadian Unity in the fall of 1977, "I have feelings of intimacy for Newfoundland that I can never have for Canada, which by comparison is an abstraction and claims my allegiance only by law. I am a Newfoundlander first, Canadian a very distant second."

Ray Guy, the province's most popular writer (and the man most often credited with, or blamed for, the political demise of Joseph R. Smallwood because of his insistent attacks upon the Smallwood regime in his daily column in the *St. John's Evening Telegram*), resolutely refers to Newfoundland as his "country." There is no doubt that Fowler and Guy express the sentiments most Newfoundlanders feel following 30 years of Confederation. Back in the '50s, such sentiments were often regarded as the silly notions of the "older crowd," the crowd that resisted change of any kind. For back then, among the young, there was an anxious urge to emulate "the mainland."

Our images of the mainland were, of course, mostly American because they were inspired by American movies and magazines, with a little help from Eaton's catalogue. Those were the days when people frantically began ripping down the front room walls to put in "picture windows," when they were inclined to keep up by covering their wooden (and often handmade) tables with arborite, when the latest American fashion or fad was adopted unanimously with a rapid passion unknown to urban Canadians who took on the same facades without the feverish compulsion we had here in Newfoundland. When the world press reported the riots inspired by the movie *Rock*

Around the Clock in Philadelphia and Melbourne, they failed to mention that the same thing happened in Grand Falls, Newfoundland.

Those were sad years. Sad because so many Newfoundlanders had such negative opinions of themselves. They thought, too often and with too much conviction, that they were an inferior people exiled by history to live inferior lives on an ugly rock in the Atlantic Ocean. They rejected their own music, their dances, their speech, their occupations, their customs, their history and their heritage.

It is only in recent years that the trend has reversed itself. Today you are more likely to encounter a young Newfoundlander proclaiming his origins with arrogant assurance than you are to encounter any of the apologetic attitudes so prevalent such a short time ago. The gospel in Newfoundland now is the gospel of pride and patriotism. This is perhaps more apparent in the arts than anywhere else. Ray Guy and his contemporaries belong to that generation of Newfoundlanders most inwardly affected by Confederation and the cultural invasion that followed in its wake. The poets, playwrights and painters strive in much of their work to define the tensions inherent in the transition of a people from past to present. It's a compelling theme for these artists because the whole of their own history was abruptly and irrevocably altered in their own lifetime. Even if they were born after Confederation they could not escape the effects of it, and they could not help but wonder if we had done the right thing when we joined up with Canada.

For hundreds of years before Confederation almost nothing had changed in Newfoundland. In 1949 the place was essentially the same as it had been for hundreds of years past. Then suddenly we became part of a country we hardly knew, and just as suddenly the government exhorted the people to abandon their old ways and adopt the new, to come out of their fishing boats to work in factories, to leave their homes on the islands and in the coves to take up residence in the "growth centres" of the new industrial Newfoundland. The change was sudden and shocking, and the shock waves have not yet faded.

There is no doubt the 20th century was going to come our way with or without Smallwood dragging us into it. But dragged we were, and the kicking and screaming is bound to continue for a while yet. It will continue, at least, until we find a way to defend ourselves against those who would have us deny what we are. After 30 years of living with the constant threat of being swamped in a culture essentially foreign to our own, the threat remains. We're a little shy of change, the way we've known it, but there is a change taking place within us, a change in our attitude about ourselves, a change that permits us now to hang on to our heritage without forfeiting our aspirations for the future.

One of my friends told me recently that the only thing he remembers about Confederation is his sorrow that his younger brother was born in May of '49 because if he had been born a few weeks earlier he would have been a Newfoundlander instead of a Canadian. I think it safe to say that his younger brother is probably very much a Newfoundlander. Ray Guy calls Newfoundland "this dear and fine country" and lovingly declares, "There is no place else." This Newfoundlander, who's been a Canadian for 30 years now, couldn't agree more.

Your Country

Gatien Lapointe
translated by John Glassco

If you will open your eyes
And if you will lay your hands
On the snow, the birds, the trees, the beasts,
Patiently, softly,
With all the weight of your heart;

If you will take time by the hand
And look upon the land
Patiently, softly;

If you will recognize your people
And if you recognize the pain
Trembling upon the background of their eyes;

If you will write the words love and loneliness
Patiently, gently,
On every season, every house;

If you will name bread, blood, day, night
And that wild unalterable desire
Burning at the heart of all things;

If you will take every death of your childhood
Patiently, softly, in your arms,
With all the strength of your despair;

Then your country can be born.

UNIT 4

SEE INTO THE LIFE

When we look at the world, what we see depends both on what is there and on how we interpret it. Our interpretation is affected by our previous experiences, by our attitudes and values, and by our language. For example, two people looking at a snowy Canadian landscape through a window will perceive it differently. One person assumes it is cold outside and plans to wear heavy clothing the next day. In contrast, the other person categorizes the snow as "corn snow," remembers an enjoyable day of spring skiing, and views the scene with warmth and pleasure. Both people probably think they are experiencing reality. The contrast in what they see raises a bigger question: "What is real?"

If two people can perceive natural phenomena so differently, consider how great the possibilities are of interpreting differently the infinite complexities of human actions and interactions. Writers have long been fascinated by discrepancies between appearance and reality. What seems to be may not be what is. Writers may use physical appearances, emotional states, or mental images to explore appearance, illusion and reality. Through literature they are inviting us to join with them in an attempt to "see into the life" of things in order to determine what is real and to search for what is true.

To Look at Anything

John Moffitt

To look at anything,
If you would know that thing,
You must look at it long.
To look at this green and say
"I have seen spring in these
Woods," will not do—you must
Be the dark snakes of
Stems and ferny plumes of leaves,
You must enter in
To the small silences between
The leaves,
You must take your time
And touch the very peace
They issue from.

Dancing Bear

Guy Vanderhaeghe

THE old man lay sleeping on the taut red rubber sheet as if he were some specimen mounted and pinned there to dry. His housekeeper, the widowed Mrs. Hax, paused in the doorway and then walked heavily to the bedside window, where she abruptly freed the blind and sent it up, whirring and clattering.

She studied the sky. Far away, to the east, and high above the bursting green of the elms that lined the street, greasy black clouds rolled languidly, their swollen underbellies lit by the occasional shudder of lightning that popped in the distance. After each flash she counted aloud to herself until she heard the faint, muttering accompaniment of thunder. Finally satisfied, she turned away from the window to find Dieter Bethge awake and watching her cautiously from his bed.

"It's going to rain," she said, moving about the room and grunting softly as she stooped to gather up his clothes and pile them on a chair.

"Oh," he answered, feigning some kind of interest. He picked a flake of dried skin from his big toe and lifted it tenderly to the light like a jeweller, intently examining its whorled grain and yellow translucence.

Forlornly, Mrs. Hax smoothed the creases of his carelessly discarded trousers with a soft, fat palm and draped them over the back of a chair. The old bugger makes more work than a whole tribe of kids, she thought.

She glanced over her shoulder and saw him fingering the bit

of skin between thumb and forefinger. "Leave that be," she said curtly. "It's time we were up. Quit dawdling."

He looked up, his pale blue eyes surprised. "What?"

"Time to get up."

"No," he said. "Not yet."

"It's reveille. No malingering. Won't have it," she said, fixing an unconvincing smile on her broad face. "Come on now, up and at 'em. We've slept long enough."

"That rubber thing kept me awake last night," he said plaintively. "Every time I move, it squeaks and pulls at my skin. There's no give to it."

"Complainers' noses fall off," Mrs. Hax said absent-mindedly as she held a shirt up to her own wrinkled nose. She sniffed. It wasn't exactly fresh, but she decided it would do, and tossed it back on the chair.

The old man, now, as whenever he was thwarted or ignored, felt his face burn with humiliation. "I want that damn thing off my bed!" he yelled. "This is my bed! This is my house! Get it off!"

Mrs. Hax truculently folded her arms across her large, loose breasts and stared down at him. For a moment he defiantly met her gaze, but then he averted his eyes and his trembling jaw confirmed his confusion.

"I am not moved by childish tempers," she announced. "You haven't learned that yet?" Mrs. Hax paused. "It's about time you did. One thing about Mrs. Hax," she declared in a piping falsetto that betrayed her anger, "is that when someone pushes her, she pushes back twice as hard. I am ruthless." She assumed a stance that she imagined an illustration of ruthlessness, her flaccid arms akimbo. A burlesque of violence. "So let me make this perfectly, crystal clear. That rubber sheet is staying on that bed until you forget your lazy, dirty habits and stop them accidents. A grown man," she said disparagingly, shaking her head. "I just got sick and tired of hauling one mattress off the bed to dry and hauling another one on. Just remember I'm not getting any younger either. I'm not up to heavy work like that. So if you want that rubber *thing* off, you try and remember not to pee the bed."

The old man turned on his side and hid his face.

"No sulking allowed," she said sternly. "Breakfast is ready and I have plenty to do today. I can't keep it waiting forever."

Dieter turned on to his back and fixed his eyes on the ceiling. Mrs. Hax shook her head in exasperation. It was going to be one of those days. What went on in the old bastard's head, if anything? What made him so peculiar, so difficult at times like these?

She walked over to the bed and took him firmly by the wrist. "Upsie daysie!" she cried brightly, planting her feet solidly apart and jerking him upright. She skidded him to the edge of the bed, the rubber sheet whining a muffled complaint, and his hands, in startled protest and ineffectual rebellion, pawing at the front of her dress. Mrs. Hax propped him upright while his head wobbled feebly from side to side and his tongue flickered angrily, darting and questing like a snake's.

"There," she said, patting his head, "that's better. Now let's let bygones be bygones. A fresh start. I'll say, 'Good morning, Mr. Bethge!' and you answer, 'Good morning, Mrs. Hax!'"

He gave no sign of agreement. Mrs. Hax hopefully cocked her head to one side and, like some huge, querulous bird, chirped, "Good morning, Mr. Bethge!" The old man stubbornly disregarded her, smiling sweetly and vacantly into space.

"Well," she said, patting her dress down around her wide hips and heavy haunches, "it's no skin off my teeth, mister."

She stumped to the door, stopped, and looked back. The old man sat perched precariously on the edge of the bed, his white hair ruffled, tufted and crested like some angry heron. A pale shadow fell across the lower half of his face and threw his eyes into relief, so that they shone with the dull, glazed intensity of the most devout of worshippers.

Mrs. Hax often saw him like this, mute and still, lost in reverie; and she liked to suppose, that somehow, he was moved by a dim apprehension of mortality and loss. Perhaps he was even overcome with memories of his wife, and felt the same vast yearning she felt for her own dead Albert.

She mustered a smile and offered it. "Five minutes, dear," she said, and then closed the door softly behind her.

Bethge made no response. He was thinking—trying to pry those memories out of the soft beds in which they had so comfortably settled, sinking deeper and deeper with the weight of all the years, growing more somnolent and lazy, less easily stirred from sleep. He could no longer make his head crackle with the sudden, decisive leap of quick thought, hurtling from synapse to synapse; chemistry subsumed, disguised by consciousness. Instead, memories had now to be pricked and prodded, and sometimes, if he were lucky, they came in revelatory flashes. Yet it was only old, old thoughts and things that came to him. Only they had any real clarity—and the sharpness to wound.

And now it was something about a bear. What?

Bethge, with jerky, tremulous movement, swiped at the spittle on his chin with the back of his hand. In his agitation he crossed and re-crossed his thin legs; the marbly, polished legs of a very old man.

Bear? He rubbed the bridge of his nose; somehow, it was important. He began to rock himself gently, his long, curving nose slicing, like a scythe, back and forth, reaping the dim air of his stale little room. And as he swayed, it all began to come to him, and he began to run, swiftly, surely, silently back into time.

In the dark barn that smells of brittle straw, and sharply of horse dung, the knife is making little greedy, tearing noises. It is not sharp enough. Then he hears the hoarse, dragging whisper of steel on whetstone. Although he is afraid that the bear his father is skinning may suddenly rear to life and hunt, he climbs over the wall of the box stall and steps into the manger and crouches down. He is only five, so the manger is a nice, tight, comforting fit.

What a bear! A killer, a marauder who had left two sows tangled in their guts with single blows from his needle-sharp claws.

The smell of the bear makes him think of gun metal—oily, smoky. Each hair bristles like polished black wire, and when the sun catches the pelt it shines vividly, electrically blue.

The curved blade of the knife, now sharpened, slices through the bear's fat like butter—relentlessly peeling back the coat and exposing long, flat, pink muscles. As his father's busy, bloody hands work, Dieter feels a growing uneasiness. The strong hands tug and tear, wrestling with the heavy, inert body as if they were frantically searching for something. Like clay under a sculptor's hand, the bear begins to change. Each stroke of the knife renders him less bear-like and more like something else. He senses this and crouches lower in the manger in anticipation.

His father begins to raise the skin off the back, his forearms hidden as the knife moves upward toward the neck. At last he grunts and stands. Reaches for the axe. In two sharp snapping blows the head is severed from the trunk and the grinning mask flung into a corner. He gathers up the skin and carries it out to salt it and peg it down in the yard. Dieter hears the chickens clamouring to pick it clean.

He stares down into the pit of the shadowy stall. This is no bear. Stripped of its rich, glossy fur—naked, it is no bear. Two arms, two legs, a raw pink skin. A man. Under all that lank, black hair a man was hiding, lurking in disguise.

He feels the spiralling terror of an unwilling accomplice to murder. He begins to cry and call for his father, who suddenly appears in the doorway covered in grease and blood, a murderer.

From far away, he heard someone call him. "Mr. Bethge! Mr. Bethge!" The last syllable of his name was drawn out and held like a note, so that it quivered in the air and urged him on with its stridency.

He realized he had been crying, that his eyes were filled with those unexpected tears that came so suddenly they constantly surprised and embarrassed him.

For a bear? But this wasn't all of it. There had been another bear; he was sure of it. A bear who had lived in shame and impotence.

He edged himself off the bed and painfully on to his knobbed, arthritic feet. Breakfast.

At breakfast they quarrel in the dreary, passionless manner of master and charge. He wants what she has, bacon and eggs. He tells her he hates porridge.

"Look," Mrs. Hax said, "I can't give you bacon and eggs. Doctor's orders."

"What doctor?"

"The doctor we saw last month. You remember."

"No." It was true. He couldn't remember any doctor.

"Yes you do. Come on now. We took a ride downtown in a cab. Remember now?"

"No."

"And we stopped by Woolworth's and bought a big bag of that sticky candy you like so much. Remember?"

"No."

"That's fine," she said irritably. "You don't want to remember, there's nothing I can do. It doesn't matter, because you're not getting bacon and eggs."

"I don't want porridge," he said tiredly.

"Eat it."

"Give me some corn flakes."

"Look at my plate," she said, pointing with her knife. "I'm getting cold grease scum all over everything. Fight, fight. When do I get a moment's peace to eat?"

"I want corn flakes," he said with a little self-satisfied tuck to the corners of his mouth.

"You can't have corn flakes," she said. "Corn flakes bung you up. That's why you eat hot cereal—to keep you regular. Just like stewed prunes. Now, which you want," she asked slyly, "Sunny Boy or stewed prunes?"

"I want corn flakes." He smiled up happily at the ceiling.

"Like a stuck record." She folded her hands on the table and leaned conspiratorially toward him. "You don't even care if you eat or not, do you? You're just trying to get under my skin, aren't you?"

"I want corn flakes," he said definitely and happily.

"I could kill that man," she told her plate. "Just kill him." Then, abruptly, she asked, "Where's your glasses? No, not there, in the other pocket. O.K., put them on. Now take a good long look at that porridge."

The old man peered intently down into his bowl.

"That's fine. Take it easy. It's not a goddamn wishing well. You see them little brown specks?"

He nodded.

"That's what this whole fight's about? Something as tiny as

that? You know what that is. It's flax. And flax keeps you regular. So eat it."

"I'm not eating it. What do I want with flax?" he asked quizzically.

"Sure you're crazy," she said. "Crazy like a fox."

"I want some coffee."

Mrs. Hax slammed down her fork and knife, snatched up his cup, and marched to the kitchen counter. While she poured the coffee, Bethge's hand crept across the table and stole several strips of bacon from her plate. He crammed these clumsily into his mouth, leaving a grease shine on his chin.

Mrs. Hax set his cup down in front of him. "Be careful," she said. "Don't spill."

Bethge giggled. In a glance, Mrs. Hax took in his grease-daubed chin and her plate. "Well, well, look at the cat who swallowed the canary. Grinning from ear lobe to ear lobe with a pound of feathers bristling from his trap."

"So?" he said defiantly.

"You think I enjoy the idea of you pawing through my food?" Mrs. Hax carried her plate to the garbage and scraped it with a flourish. "Given all your dirty little habits, who's to know where your hand's been?" she asked wickedly. "But go ahead and laugh. Because he who laughs last, laughs best. Chew this around for a bit and see how she tastes. You're not getting one, single, solitary cigarette today, my friend."

Startled, he demanded his cigarettes.

"We're singing a different tune now, aren't we?" She paused. "N O spells no. Put that in your pipe and smoke it."

"You give them. They're mine."

"Not since you set the chesterfield on fire. Not since then. Your son told me I was to give them out one at a time so's I could watch you and avoid 'regrettable accidents.' Thank God, there's some sense in the family. How he came by it I'm sure I don't know."

The old man hoisted himself out of his chair. "Don't you dare talk to me like that. I want my cigarettes—and I want them now."

Mrs. Hax crossed her arms and set her jaw. "No."

"You're fired!" he shouted. "Get out!" He flapped his arms awkwardly in an attempt to startle her into motion.

"Oh ho!" she said, rubbing her large red hands together in delight. "Fired, am I? On whose say so? Them that hires is them that fires. He who pays the piper calls the tune. And you don't do neither. Not a bit. Your son hired me, and your son pays me. I don't budge a step unless I get the word straight from the horse's mouth."

"Get out!"

"Save your breath."

He is beaten and he knows it. This large, stubborn woman cannot, will not be moved.

"I want to talk to my son."

"If you got information you feel your son should have, write him a letter."

He knows this would never do. He would forget; she would steal the letter, conveniently forgetting to mail it. Justice demands immediate action. The iron is hot and fit for striking. He feels the ground beneath his feet is treacherous; he cannot become confused, or be led astray. One thing at a time. He must talk to his son.

"Get him on the telephone."

"Your son, if you *remember*," Mrs. Hax said, "got a little upset about all those long distance phone calls—*collect*. And his words to me were, 'Mrs. Hax, I think it best if my father phone only on important matters, at your *discretion*.' At *my* discretion, mind you. And my discretion informs me that this isn't one of those times. I've got a responsibility to my employer."

"I'll phone him myself."

"That I've got to see."

"I will."

"Yes, like the last time. Half the time you can't remember the city John lives in, let alone his street. The last time you tried to phone him you got the operator so balled up you would have been talking to a Chinaman in Shanghai if I hadn't stepped in and saved your bacon."

"I'll phone. I can do it."

"Sure you will. Where does John live?"

"I know."

"Uh huh, then tell me. Where does he live?"

"I know."

"Jesus, he could be living in the basement and you wouldn't realize it."

This makes him cry. He realizes she is right. But minutes ago he *had known* where his son lived. How could he have forgotten? In the sudden twistings and turnings of the conversation he has lost his way, and now he hears himself making a wretched, disgusting noise—but cannot stop.

Mrs. Hax feels she has gone too far. She goes over to him and puts an arm around his shoulders. "Now see what's happened. You went and got yourself all upset over a silly old bowl of porridge. Doctor says you have to watch that with your blood pressure. It's no laughing matter." She boosts him out of his chair. "I think you better lie down on the chesterfield for a bit."

Mrs. Hax led him into the living room and made him comfortable on the chesterfield. She wondered how an old bugger like him could make so much water: if he wasn't peeing, he was crying.

"You want a kleenex?" she asked.

He shook his head and, ashamed, covered his face with his forearm.

"No harm in crying," she said bleakly. "We all do sometime."

"Leave me be."

"I suppose it's best," she sighed. "I'll be in the kitchen clearing up if you need me."

Dieter lay on the chesterfield trying to stifle his tears. It was not an easy job because even the sound of Mrs. Hax unconcernedly clacking the breakfast dishes reminded him of her monstrous carelessness with everything. His plates, his feelings. He filled with anger at the notion that he would never be nimble enough to evade her commands, or even her wishes. That he cannot outwit her or even flee her.

The living room gradually darkens as the low scudding rain clouds blot out the sun. He wishes it were a fine sunny day. The kind of day which tricks you into believing you are young and carefree as you once were. Like in Rumania before his family emigrated. Market days almost always felt that way. People bathed in sun and noise, their wits honed to a fine edge for trading and bartering. Every kind of people. The Jews with their curling side-locks, the timid Italian tenant farmers, the Rumanians, and people like himself, German colonists. Even a gypsy to two. Then you had a sense of life, of living. Every good thing the earth offers or man's hand fashions could be found there. Gaily painted wagons, piles of potatoes with the wet clay still clinging to them; chickens, ducks and geese; tethered pigs tugging their backlegs and squealing; horses with hooves as black and shining as basalt, and eyes that were as large and liquid-purple as plums.

Nothing but a sheet of sky above and good smells below: pickled herring and leather, paprika and the faint scent of little hard sweet apples.

Innocence. Innocence. But then again on the other hand— yes, well sometimes cruelty too. Right in the market.

A stranger arrived with a dancing bear once. Yes, the other bear, the one he had forgotten. He led him by a ring through the nose. When a crowd gathered, the man unsnapped the chain from the bear's nose and began to play a violin. It was a sad, languorous tune. For a moment, the bear tossed his head from side to side and snuffled in the dirt. This, for him, was a kind of freedom.

But the man spoke to him sharply. The bear lifted his head and then mournfully raised himself up on to his hind legs. His arms opened in a wide, charitable manner, as if he were offering an embrace. His mouth grinned, exposing black-speckled gums and sharp teeth. He danced, slowly, ponderously, tiredly.

The music changed tempo. It became gay and lively. The bear began to prance unsteadily; the hot sun beat down on him. A long, glittering thread of saliva fell from his panting mouth on to the cinnamon coloured fur of his chest.

Dieter, fascinated, tugged and pushed himself through the crowd. The bear hopped heavily from leg to leg. It was pathetic and comic. The pink tip of his penis jiggled up and down in the long hair of his loins. There was a wave of confused sniggering.

The trainer played faster and faster. The bear pirouetted wildly. He whirled and whirled, raising a small cloud of dust. The crowd began to clap. The bear spun and spun, his head lolling from side to side, his body tense with the effort of maintaining this human posture. And then he lost his balance and fell, blindly, with a bone-wrenching thump on to his back.

The scraping of the violin bow stopped. The bear turned lazily on to his feet and bit savagely at his fleas.

"Up, Bruno," the man said.

The bear whined and sat down. People began to laugh; some hooted and insulted the bear's master. He flourished the bear's nose lead and shouted, but the bear refused to budge. In the end, however, he could do nothing except attempt to save face; he bowed deeply, signifying an end to the performance. A few coins, a very few, bounced and bounced at his feet. He scooped them up quickly, as if he were afraid they might be reclaimed.

The audience began to disperse. Some hurried away to protect their wares. But Dieter had nothing to protect and nowhere to go, and so he stayed.

The sight of so many fleeing backs seemed to pique the bear. He got to his feet and began, once again, to dance. He mocked them. Or so it seemed. Of course, there had been no music, but the bear danced much more daintily and elegantly than before, to a tune only he could perceive. And he had grinned, hugely, sardonically.

But his trainer had reached up, caught his nose ring and yanked him down on all fours. He swore and cursed, and the bear breathed high, squeaking protests, feigning innocence.

This was unacceptable. This was rebellion. This was treason to the man who fed him, cared for him, taught him.

"Hairy bastard. Play the fool, will you?" the stranger muttered, wrenching and twisting the nose ring while the bear squealed with pain. The man punched his head, kicked him in the belly, shook him by the ears. "Traitor. Ingrate."

Dieter had held his breath. His mind's eye had seen the bear suddenly strike, revenge himself. Yet nothing happened. Nothing; except the bear was beaten and battered, humiliated, even spat upon.

What shame he had felt witnessing such an indignity, such complete indifference to the pride which should be a bear's. Such flaunting of the respect owed him for his size and, in theory, his power. Couldn't the man realize what he did? He wanted to shout out the secret. To warn him that appearances deceive. That a bear is a man in masquerade. Perhaps even a judge, but at the very least a brother.

But he couldn't. He ran away instead.

The house is still. He hears her footsteps, knows that she is watching him from the doorway. As always she is judging him, calculating her words and responses, planning. Her plots deny him even the illusion of freedom. He decides he will not turn to look at her. But perhaps she knows this will be his reaction? Petulant, childish.

"I want to be left in peace." He surprises himself. This giving voice to thought without weighing the consequences is dangerous.

But she doesn't catch it. "What?"

"I don't chew my words twice," he says.

She comes to the side of the chesterfield. "Feeling better now?"

"Yes."

"Truth?"

He nods.

"Now mind, you got to be sure. I'm going down to the store. You need the bathroom?"

"No."

"All right then. I'll just be a few minutes. That's all. You'll be O.K.?"

He is trying to think. All this talk, these interruptions annoy him. He burns with impatience. "Fine. That's fine. Good." Suddenly, he feels happy. He *can* steal a little peace. He'll do it.

"I must be careful," he tells himself aloud. How do these things slip out?

But Mrs. Hax doesn't understand. "With your blood pressure, I should say so."

His luck, his good fortune, make him feel strong and cunning. Following her to the front door he almost pities this fat woman. He watches her start down the street. It is lined with old and substantial homes, most of them painted modestly white, and their yards flourish tall, rough-barked elms. On this street, Mrs. Hax, in her fluorescent orange rain slicker, appears ridiculous and inappropriate. Like a bird of paradise in an English garden. He waits until he loses sight of her at the first turning of the street.

He hurries to his business. His hands fumble with the chain on the front door; at last it is fastened. His excitement leaves him breathless, but he shuffles to the back door and draws the bolt. Safe. Mrs. Hax is banished, exiled.

At first he thinks the noise is caused by the blood pulsing in his temples. But it fades to an insistent, whispering rush. Dieter goes to the window to look out. The rain is falling in a gleaming, thick curtain that obscures the outlines of the nearest house; striking the roadway, it throws up fine silvery plumes of spray. He decides to wait for Mrs. Hax at the front door. He stands there and smells the cocoa matting, the dust and rubber boots. Somehow, he has forgotten they smell this way, a scent that can be peculiarly comforting when you are dry and warm, with a cold rain slashing against the windows.

And here is Mrs. Hax, trotting stiff-legged up the street with a shredding brown paper bag huddled to her body. She flees up the walk, past the beaten and dripping caraganas, and around back to the kitchen door. He hears her bumping and rattling it.

Here she comes again, scurrying along, head bent purposefully, rain glancing off her plastic cap. But as she begins to climb the front steps he withdraws and hides himself in the coat closet. Her key rasps in the chamber, the spring lock snaps free. The door opens several inches but then meets the resistance of the chain and sticks. She grumbles and curses; some fat, disembodied fingers curl through the gap and pluck at the chain. For a moment he is tempted to slam the door shut on those fingers, but he resists the impulse. The fingers are replaced by a slice of face, an eye and a mouth.

"Mr. Bethge! Mr. Bethge! Open up!"

Bethge stumbles out of the closet and lays his face along the door jamb, eye to eye with Mrs. Hax. They stare at each other. At last she breaks the spell.

"Well, open this door," she says irritably. "I feel like a drowned cat."

"Go away. You're not wanted here."

"What!"

"Go away."

Her one eye winks suspiciously. "You do know who I am? This is Mrs. Hax, your housekeeper. Open up."

"I know who you are. I don't want any part of you. So go away."

She shows him the soggy paper bag. "I bought you a Jersey Milk."

"Pass it through."

Her one eye opens wide in blue disbelief. "You open this door."

"No."

"It's the cigarettes, I suppose? All right, I give up. You can have your damn cigarettes."

"Go away."

"I'm losing my patience," she says, lowering her voice. "Now open this door, you senile old fart."

"Old fart yourself. Old fat fart."

"You wait until I get in there. There'll be hell to pay."

He realizes his legs are tired from standing. There is a nagging pain in the small of his back. "I've got to go now," he says. "Goodbye," and closes the door in her face.

He is suddenly very light-headed and tired but, nevertheless, exultant. He decides he will have a nap. But the woman has begun to hammer at the door.

"Stop it," he shouts. He makes his way to his bedroom on unsteady legs; in fact, one is trailing and he must support himself by leaning against the wall. What is this?

The bedroom lies in half-light, but he can see the red rubber sheet. It must go. He tugs at it and it resists him like some living thing, like a limpet clinging to a rock. He feels a great weakness spreading like a stain down his left side. His leg crumples, his mouth falls open in surprise as he falls. He lands loosely like a bundle of sticks, his legs and arms splayed wide, but feels nothing but a prickling sensation in his bladder. No pain, nothing. There are shadows everywhere in the room; they seem to float, and hover, and quiver. He realizes the front of his pants are wet. He tries to get up, but the strength ebbs out of his limbs and is replaced by a sensation of dizzying heaviness. He decides he will rest a minute and then get up.

But he doesn't. He sleeps.

Mrs. Hax waited under the eaves for the rain to abate. It fell for an hour with sodden fury, and then began to slacken into a dispirited drizzle. When it did, she picked her way carefully through the puddles in the garden to where the hoe lay. With it, she broke a basement window and methodically trimmed the glass out of the frame. Then she settled herself on to her haunches, and gasping, wriggled into the opening. She closed her eyes, committed her injuries to his head, and then let herself drop. She landed on one leg, which buckled, and sent her headlong against the gas furnace, which set every heat vent and duct in the building vibrating with a deep atonal ringing. Uninjured, she picked herself up from the floor. Her dignity bruised, her authority wounded, she began to edge her way through the basement clutter toward the stairs.

Dieter Bethge woke with a start. Some noise had broken into his dream. It had been a good and happy dream. The dancing bear had been performing for him under no compulsion, a free gift given in freedom. It had been a perfect, graceful dance, performed without a hint of the foppishness or studied concentration that mars the dance of humans. As the bear had danced he had seemed to grow, as if fed by the pure clear notes of the music. He had grown larger and larger, but Dieter had watched this with a feeling of great peace rather than alarm.

The sun glinted on his cinnamon fur and burnished his coat with red, winking light. And when the music stopped, the bear had opened his arms very wide in a gesture of friendship and welcome. His mouth had opened as if he were about to speak. And that was exactly what Dieter had expected all along. That the bear would confide in him the something that only Dieter had recognized.

But then something had broken the spell of the dream.

He was confused. Where was he? His hand reached out and touched something smooth and hard and resisting. He gave a startled grunt. This was wrong. His mind slipped backward and forward, easily and smoothly, from dream to the sharp, troubling present.

He tried to get up. He rose trembling, swayed, felt the floor shift, and fell, striking his head on a chest of drawers.

His mouth filled with something warm and salty. He could hear something moving in the house, and then the sound was lost in the tumult of the blood singing in his veins. His pulse beat dimly in his eyelids, his ears, his neck and fingertips.

He managed to struggle to his feet and beat his way into the roar of the shadows, that slipped by like surf, and out into the hallway.

And then he saw a form in the muted light, patiently waiting. It was the bear.

"Bear?" he asked, shuffling forward, trailing his leg.

The bear said something he did not understand. He was waiting.

Dieter lifted his arms for the expected embrace, the embrace that would fold him into the fragrant, brilliant fur; but, curiously, one arm would not rise. It dangled limply like a rag. Dieter felt something strike the side of his face—a numbing blow. His left eyelid fell like a shutter. He tried to speak but his tongue felt swollen and could only batter noiselessly against his teeth. He felt himself fall but the bear reached out and caught him in the warm embrace he desired above all.

And so, Dieter Bethge, dead of a stroke, fell gently, gently, like a leaf, into the waiting arms of Mrs. Hax.

I Stand Here Ironing

Tillie Olsen

I STAND here ironing, and what you asked me moves tormented back and forth with the iron.

"I wish you would manage the time to come in and talk with me about your daughter. I'm sure you can help me understand her. She's a youngster who needs help and whom I'm deeply interested in helping."

"Who needs help." Even if I came, what good would it do? You think because I am her mother I have a key, or that in some way you could use me as a key? She has lived for nineteen years. There is all that life that has happened outside of me, beyond me.

And when is there time to remember, to sift, to weigh, to estimate, to total? I will start and there will be an interruption and I will have to gather it all together again. Or I will become engulfed with all I did or did not do, with what should have been and what cannot be helped.

She was a beautiful baby. The first and only one of our five that was beautiful at birth. You do not guess how new and uneasy her tenancy in her now-loveliness. You did not know her all those years she was thought homely, or see her poring over her baby pictures, making me tell her over and over how beautiful she had been—and would be, I would tell her—and was now, to the seeing eye. But the seeing eyes were few or non-existent. Including mine.

I nursed her. They feel that's important nowadays. I nursed all the children, but with her, with all the fierce rigidity of first motherhood, I did like the books then said. Though her cries battered me to trembling and my breasts ached with swollenness, I waited till the clock decreed.

Why do I put that first? I do not even know if it matters, or if it explains anything.

She was a beautiful baby. She blew shining bubbles of sound. She loved motion, loved light, loved color and music and textures. She would lie on the floor in her blue overalls patting the surface so hard in ecstasy her hands and feet would blur. She was a miracle to me, but when she was eight months old I had to leave her daytimes with the woman downstairs to whom she was no miracle at all, for I worked or looked for work and for Emily's father, who "could no longer endure" (he wrote in his good-bye note) "sharing want with us."

I was nineteen. It was the pre-relief, pre-WPA world of the depression. I would start running as soon as I got off the streetcar, running up the stairs, the place smelling sour, and awake or asleep to startle awake, when she saw me she would break into a clogged weeping that could not be comforted, a weeping I can hear yet.

After a while I found a job hashing at night so I could be with her days, and it was better. But it came to where I had to bring her to his family and leave her.

It took a long time to raise the money for her fare back. Then she got chicken pox and I had to wait longer. When she finally came, I hardly knew her, walking quick and nervous like her father, looking like her father, thin, and dressed in a shoddy red that yellowed her skin and glared at the pockmarks. All the baby loveliness gone.

She was two. Old enough for nursery school they said, and I did not know then what I know now—the fatigue of the long day, and the lacerations of group life in the kinds of nurseries that are only parking places for children.

Except that it would have made no difference if I had known. It was the only place there was. It was the only way we could be together, the only way I could hold a job.

And even without knowing, I knew. I knew the teacher that was evil because all these years it has curdled into my memory, the little boy hunched in the corner, her rasp, "why aren't you outside, because Alvin hits you? that's no reason, go out, scaredy." I knew Emily hated it even if she did not clutch and implore "don't go Mommy" like the other children, mornings.

She always had a reason why we should stay home. Momma, you look sick, Momma. I feel sick, Momma, the teachers aren't there today, they're sick. Momma, we can't go, there was a fire there last night. Momma, it's a holiday today, no school, they told me.

But never a direct protest, never rebellion. I think of our others in their three-, four-year-oldness—the explosions, the tempers, the denunciations, the demands—and I feel suddenly ill. I put the iron down. What in me demanded that goodness in her? And what was the cost, the cost to her of such goodness?

The old man living in the back once said in his gentle way: "You should smile at Emily more when you look at her." What *was* in my face when I looked at her? I loved her. There were all the acts of love.

It was only with the others I remembered what he said, and it was the face of joy, and not of care or tightness or worry I turned to them—too late for Emily. She does not smile easily, let alone almost always as her brothers and sisters do. Her face is closed and sombre, but when she wants, how fluid. You must have seen it in her pantomimes, you spoke of her rare gift for comedy on the stage that rouses a laughter out of the audience so dear they applaud and applaud and do not want to let her go.

Where does it come from, that comedy? There was none of it in her when she came back to me that second time, after I had had to send her away again. She had a new daddy now to learn to love, and I think perhaps it was a better time.

Except when we left her alone nights, telling ourselves she was old enough.

"Can't you go some other time, Mommy, like tomorrow?" she would ask. "Will it be just a little while you'll be gone? Do you promise?"

The time we came back, the front door open, the clock on the floor in the hall. She rigid awake. "It wasn't just a little while. I didn't cry. Three times I called you, just three times, and then I ran downstairs to open the door so you could come faster. The clock talked loud. I threw it away, it scared me what it talked."

She said the clock talked loud again that night I went to the hospital to have Susan. She was delirious with the fever that comes before red measles, but she was fully conscious all the week I was gone and the week after we were home when she could not come near the new baby or me.

She did not get well. She stayed skeleton thin, not wanting to eat, and night after night she had nightmares. She would call for me, and I would rouse from exhaustion to sleepily call back: "You're all right, darling, go to sleep, it's just a dream," and if she still called, in a sterner voice, "now go to sleep, Emily, there's nothing to hurt you." Twice, only twice, when I had to get up for Susan anyhow, I went in to sit with her.

Now when it is too late (as if she would let me hold and comfort her like I do the others) I get up and go to her at once at her moan or restless stirring. "Are you awake, Emily? Can I get you something?" And the answer is always the same: "No, I'm all right, go back to sleep, Mother."

They persuaded me at the clinic to send her away to a convalescent home in the country where "she can have the kind of food and care you can't manage for her, and you'll be free to concentrate on the new baby." They still send children to that place. I see pictures on the society page of sleek young women planning affairs to raise money for it, or dancing at the affairs, or decorating Easter eggs or filling Christmas stockings for the children.

They never have a picture of the children so I do not know if the girls still wear those gigantic red bows and the ravaged looks on the every other Sunday when parents can come to visit "unless otherwise notified"—as we were notified the first six weeks.

Oh it is a handsome place, green lawns and tall trees and fluted flower beds. High up on the balconies of each cottage the children stand, the girls in their red bows and white dresses, the boys in white suits and giant red ties. The parents stand below shrieking up to be heard and the children shriek down to be heard, and between them the invisible wall "Not To Be Contaminated by Parental Germs or Physical Affection."

There was a tiny girl who always stood hand in hand with Emily. Her parents never came. One visit she was gone. "They moved her to Rose College," Emily shouted in explanation. "They don't like you to love anybody here."

She wrote once a week, the labored writing of a seven-year-old. "I am fine. How is the baby. If I write my leter nicly I will have a star. Love." There never was a star. We wrote every other day, letters she could never hold or keep but only hear read—once. "We simply do not have room for children to keep any personal possessions," they patiently explained when we pieced one Sunday's shrieking together to plead how much it would mean to Emily, who loved so to keep things, to be allowed to keep her letters and cards.

Each visit she looked frailer. "She isn't eating," they told us.

(They had runny eggs for breakfast or mush with lumps, Emily said later, I'd hold it in my mouth and not swallow. Nothing ever tasted good, just when they had chicken.)

It took us eight months to get her released home, and only the fact that she gained back so little of her seven lost pounds convinced the social worker.

I used to try to hold and love her after she came back, but her body would stay stiff, and after a while she'd push away. She ate little. Food sickened her, and I think much of life too. Oh she had physical lightness and brightness, twinkling by on skates, bouncing like a ball up and down up and down over the jump rope, skimming over the hill; but these were momentary.

She fretted about her appearance, thin and dark and foreign-looking at a time when every little girl was supposed to look or thought she should look a chubby blonde replica of Shirley Temple. The doorbell sometimes rang for her, but no one seemed to come and play in the house or be a best friend. Maybe because we moved so much.

There was a boy she loved painfully through two school semesters. Months later she told me how she had taken pennies from my purse to buy him candy. "Licorice was his favorite and I brought him some every day, but he still liked Jennifer better'n me. Why, Mommy?" The kind of question for which there is no answer.

School was a worry to her. She was not glib or quick in a

world where glibness and quickness were easily confused with ability to learn. To her overworked and exasperated teachers she was an overconscientious "slow learner" who kept trying to catch up and was absent entirely too often.

I let her be absent, though sometimes the illness was imaginary. How different from my now-strictness about attendance with the others. I wasn't working. We had a new baby, I was home anyhow. Sometimes, after Susan grew old enough, I would keep her home from school, too, to have them all together.

Mostly Emily had asthma, and her breathing, harsh and labored, would fill the house with a curiously tranquil sound. I would bring the two old dresser mirrors and her boxes of collections to her bed. She would select beads and single earrings, bottle tops and shells, dried flowers and pebbles, old postcards and scraps, all sorts of oddments; then she and Susan would play Kingdom, setting up landscapes and furniture, peopling them with action.

Those were the only times of peaceful companionship between her and Susan. I have edged away from it, that poisonous feeling between them, that terrible balancing of hurts and needs I had to do between the two, and did so badly, those earlier years.

Oh there are conflicts between the others too, each one human, needing, demanding, hurting, taking—but only between Emily and Susan, no, Emily toward Susan that corroding resentment. It seems so obvious on the surface, yet it is not obvious. Susan, the second child, Susan, golden- and curly-haired and chubby, quick and articulate and assured, everything in appearance and manner Emily was not; Susan, not able to resist Emily's precious things, losing or sometimes clumsily breaking them; Susan telling jokes and riddles to company for applause while Emily sat silent (to say to me later: that was *my* riddle, Mother, I told it to Susan); Susan, who for all the five years' difference in age was just a year behind Emily in developing physically.

I am glad for that slow physical development that widened the difference between her and her contemporaries, though she suffered over it. She was too vulnerable for that terrible world of youthful competition, of preening and parading, of constant measuring of yourself against every other, of envy, "If I had that copper hair," "If I had that skin. . . ." She tormented herself enough about not looking like the others, there was enough of the unsureness, the having to be conscious of words before you speak, the constant caring—what are they thinking of me? without having it all magnified by the merciless physical drives.

Ronnie is calling. He is wet and I change him. It is rare there is such a cry now. That time of motherhood is almost behind me when the ear is not one's own but must always be racked and listening for the child cry, the child call. We sit for a while and I hold him, looking out over the city spread in charcoal with its soft aisles of light. *"Shoogily,"* he breathes and curls closer. I carry him back to bed, asleep. *Shoogily.* A funny word, a family word, inherited from Emily, invented by her to say: *comfort.*

In this and other ways she leaves her seal, I say aloud. And startle at my saying it. What do I mean? What did I start to gather together, to try and make coherent? I was at the terrible, growing years. War years. I do not remember them well. I was working, there were four smaller ones now, there was not time for her. She had to help be a mother, and housekeeper, and shopper. She had to set her seal. Mornings of crisis and near hysteria trying to get lunches packed, hair combed, coats and shoes found, everyone to school or Child Care on time, the baby ready for transportation. And always the paper scribbled on by a smaller one, the book looked at by Susan then mislaid, the homework not done. Running out to that huge school where she was one, she was lost, she was a drop; suffering over the unpreparedness, stammering and unsure in her classes.

There was so little time left at night after the kids were bedded down. She would struggle over books, always eating (it was in those years she developed her enormous appetite that is legendary in our family) and I would be ironing, or preparing food for the next day, or writing V-mail to Bill, or tending the baby. Sometimes, to make me laugh, or out of her despair, she would imitate happenings or types at school.

I think I said once: "Why don't you do something like this in the school amateur show?" One morning she phoned me at work, hardly understandable through the weeping: "Mother, I did it. I won, I won; they gave me first prize; they clapped and clapped and wouldn't let me go."

Now suddenly she was Somebody, and as imprisoned in her difference as she had been in anonymity.

She began to be asked to perform at other high schools, even in colleges, then at city and statewide affairs. The first one we went to, I only recognized her that first moment when thin, shy, she almost drowned herself into the curtains. Then: Was this Emily? The control, the command, the convulsing and deadly clowning, the spell, then the roaring, stamping audience, unwilling to let this rare and precious laughter out of their lives.

Afterwards: You ought to do something about her with a gift like that—but without money or knowing how, what does one do? We have left it all to her, and the gift has as often eddied inside, clogged and clotted, as been used and growing.

She is coming. She runs up the stairs two at a time with her light graceful step, and I know she is happy tonight. Whatever it was that occasioned your call did not happen today.

"Aren't you ever going to finish the ironing, Mother? Whistler painted his mother in a rocker. I'd have to paint mine standing over an ironing board." This is one of her communicative nights and she tells me everything and nothing as she fixes herself a plate of food out of the icebox.

She is so lovely. Why did you want me to come in at all? Why were you concerned? She will find her way.

She starts up the stairs to bed. "Don't get me up with the rest in the morning." "But I thought you were having midterms." "Oh, those," she comes back in, kisses me, and says quite lightly, "in a couple of years when we'll all be atom-dead they won't matter a bit."

She has said it before. She *believes* it. But because I have been dredging the past, and all that compounds a human being is so heavy and meaningful in me, I cannot endure it tonight.

I will never total it all. I will never come in to say: She was a child seldom smiled at. Her father left me before she was a year old. I had to work her first six years when there was work, or I sent her home and to his relatives. There were years she had care she hated. She was dark and thin and foreign-looking in a world where the prestige went to blondness and curly hair and dimples, she was slow where glibness was prized. She was a child of anxious, not proud, love. We were poor and could not afford for her the soil of easy growth. I was a young mother, I was a distracted mother. There were the other children pushing up, demanding. Her younger sister seemed all that she was not. There were years she did not want me to touch her. She kept too much in herself, her life was such she had to keep too much in herself. My wisdom came too late. She has much to her and probably little will come of it. She is a child of her age, of depression, of war, of fear.

Let her be. So all that is in her will not bloom—but in how many does it? There is still enough left to live by. Only help her to know—help make it so there is cause for her to know—that she is more than this dress on the ironing board, helpless before the iron.

To Julia de Burgos

Julia de Burgos
translated by Grace Schulman

The people are saying that I am your enemy,
That in poetry I give you to the world.

They lie, Julia de Burgos. They lie, Julia de Burgos.
The voice that rises in my verses is not your voice: it
is my voice;
For you are the clothing and I am the essence;
Between us lies the deepest abyss.

You are the bloodless doll of social lies
And I the virile spark of human truth;

You are the honey of courtly hypocrisy; not I—
I bare my heart in all my poems.

You, like your world, are selfish; not I—
I gamble everything to be what I am.

You are only the serious lady. Señora. Doña Julia.
Not I. I am life. I am strength. I am woman.

You belong to your husband, your master. Not I:
I belong to nobody or to all, for to all, to all
I give myself in my pure feelings and thoughts.

You curl your hair and paint your face. Not I:
I am curled by the wind, painted by the sun.

You are the lady of the house, resigned, submissive,
Tied to the bigotry of men. Not I:
I am Rocinante, bolting free, wildly
Snuffling the horizons of the justice of God.

Complexion

Richard Rodriguez

VISITING the East Coast or the gray capitals of Europe during the long months of winter, I often meet people at deluxe hotels who comment on my complexion. (In such hotels it appears nowadays a mark of leisure and wealth to have a complexion like mine.) Have I been skiing? In the Swiss Alps? Have I just returned from a Caribbean vacation? No. I say no softly but in a firm voice that intends to explain: My complexion is dark. (My skin is brown. More exactly, terra-cotta in sunlight, tawny in shade. I do not redden in sunlight. Instead, my skin becomes progressively dark; the sun singes the flesh.)

When I was a boy the white summer sun of Sacramento would darken me so, my T-shirt would seem bleached against my slender dark arms. My mother would see me come up the front steps. She'd wait for the screen door to slam at my back. "You look like a *negrito,*" she'd say, angry, sorry to be angry, frustrated almost to laughing, scorn. "You know how important looks are in this country. With *los gringos* looks are all that they judge on. But you! Look at you! You're so careless!" Then she'd start in all over again. "You won't be satisfied till you end up looking like *los pobres* who work in the fields, *los braceros.*"

(*Los braceros*: Those men who work with their *brazos*, their arms; Mexican nationals who were licensed to work for American farmers in the 1950s. They worked very hard for very little money, my father would tell me. And what money they earned they sent back to Mexico to support their families, my mother would add. *Los pobres*—the poor, the pitiful, the powerless ones. But paradoxically also powerful men. They were the men with brown-muscled arms I stared at in awe on Saturday mornings when they showed up downtown like gypsies to shop at Woolworth's or Penney's. On Monday nights they would gather hours early on the steps of the Memorial Auditorium for the wrestling matches. Passing by on my bicycle in summer, I would spy them there, clustered in small groups, talking—frightening and fascinating men—some wearing Texas *sombreros* and T-shirts which shone fluorescent in the twilight. I would sit forward in the back seat of our family's '48 Chevy to see them, working alongside Valley highways: dark men on an even horizon, loading a truck amid rows of straight green. Powerful, powerless men. Their fascinating darkness—like mine—to be feared.)

"You'll end up looking just like them."

1

Regarding my family, I see faces that do not closely resemble my own. Like some other Mexican families, my family suggests Mexico's confused colonial past. Gathered around a table, we appear to be from separate continents. My father's face recalls faces I have seen in France. His complexion is white—he does not tan; he does not burn. Over the years, his dark wavy hair has grayed handsomely. But with time his face has sagged to a perpetual sigh. My mother, whose surname is inexplicably Irish—Moran—has an olive complexion. People have frequently wondered if, perhaps, she is Italian or Portuguese. And, in fact, she looks as though she could be from southern Europe. My mother's face has not aged as quickly as the rest of her body; it remains smooth and glowing—a cool tan—which her gray hair cleanly accentuates. My older brother has inherited her good looks. When he was a boy people would tell him that he looked like Mario Lanza, and hearing it he would smile with dimpled assurance. He would come home from high school with girl friends who seemed to me glamorous (because they were) blonds. And during those years I envied him his skin that burned red and peeled like the skin of the *gringos*. His complexion never darkened like mine. My youngest sister is exotically pale, almost ashen. She is delicately featured, Near Eastern, people have said. Only my older sister has a complexion as dark as mine, though her facial features are much less harshly defined than my own. To many people meeting her, she seems (they say) Polynesian. I am the only one in the family whose face is severely cut to the line of ancient Indian ancestors. My face is mournfully long, in the classical Indian manner; my profile suggests one of those beak-nosed Mayan sculptures—the eaglelike face upturned, open-mouthed, against the deserted, primitive sky.

"We are Mexicans," my mother and father would say, and taught their four children to say whenever we (often) were asked about our ancestry. My mother and father scorned those "white" Mexican-Americans who tried to pass themselves off as Spanish. My parents would never have thought of denying their ancestry. I never denied it: My ancestry is Mexican, I told strangers mechanically. But I never forgot that only my older sister's complexion was as dark as mine.

My older sister never spoke to me about her complexion when she was a girl. But I guessed that she found her dark skin a burden. I knew that she suffered for being a "nigger." As she came home from grammar school, little boys came up behind her and pushed her down to the sidewalk. In high school, she struggled in the adolescent competition for boy-friends in a world of football games and proms, a world where her looks were plainly uncommon. In college, she was afraid and scornful when dark-skinned foreign students from countries like Turkey and India found her attractive. She revealed her fear of dark skin to me only in adulthood when, regarding her own three children, she quietly admitted relief that they were all light.

That is the kind of remark women in my family have often made before. As a boy, I'd stay in the kitchen (never seeming to attract any notice), listening while my aunts spoke of their pleasure at having light children. (The men, some of whom were dark-skinned from years of working out of doors, would be in another part of the house.) It was the woman's spoken concern: the fear of having a dark-skinned son or daughter. Remedies were exchanged. One aunt prescribed to her sisters the elixir of large doses of castor oil during the last weeks of pregnancy. (The remedy risked an abortion.) Children born dark grew up to have their faces treated regularly with a mixture of egg white and lemon juice concentrate. (In my case, the solution never would take.) One Mexican-American friend of my mother's, who regarded it a special blessing that she had a measure of English blood, spoke disparagingly of her husband, a construction worker, for being so dark. "He doesn't take care of himself," she complained. But the remark, I noticed, annoyed my mother, who sat tracing an invisible design with her finger on the tablecloth.

There was affection too and a kind of humor about these matters. With daring tenderness, one of my uncles would refer to his wife as *mi negra*. An aunt regularly called her dark child *mi feito* (my little ugly one), her smile only partially hidden as she bent down to dig her mouth under his ticklish chin. And at times relatives spoke scornfully of pale, white skin. A *gringo*'s skin resembled *masa*—baker's dough—someone remarked. Everyone laughed. Voices chuckled over the fact that the *gringos* spent so many hours in summer sunning themselves. ("They need to get sun because they look like *los muertos*.")

I heard the laughing but remembered what the women had said, with unsmiling voices, concerning dark skin. Nothing I heard outside the house, regarding my skin, was so impressive to me.

In public I occasionally heard racial slurs. Complete strangers would yell out at me. A teenager drove past, shouting, "Hey, Greaser! Hey, Pancho!" Over his shoulder I saw the giggling face of his girl friend. A boy pedaled by and announced matter-of-factly, "I pee on dirty Mexicans." Such remarks would be said so casually that I wouldn't quickly realize that they were being addressed to me. When I did, I would be paralyzed with embarrassment, unable to return the insult. (Those times I happened to be with white grammar school friends, *they* shouted back. Imbued with the mysterious kindness of children, my friends would never ask later why I hadn't yelled out in my own defense.)

In all, there could not have been more than a dozen incidents of name-calling. That there were so few suggests that I was not a primary victim of racial abuse. But that, even today, I can clearly remember particular incidents is proof of their impact. Because of such incidents, I listened when my parents remarked that Mexicans were often mistreated in California border towns. And in Texas. I listened carefully when I heard that two of my cousins had been refused admittance to an "all-white" swimming pool. And that an uncle had been told by some man to go back to Africa. I followed the progress of the southern black civil rights movement, which was gaining prominent notice in Sacramento's afternoon newspaper. But what most intrigued me was the connection between dark skin and poverty. Because I heard my mother speak so often about the relegation of dark people to menial labor, I considered the great victims of racism to be those who were poor and forced to do menial work. People like the farmworkers whose skin was dark from the sun.

After meeting a black grammar school friend of my sister's, I remember thinking that she wasn't really "black." What interested me was the fact that she wasn't poor. (Her well-dressed parents would come by after work to pick her up in a shiny green Oldsmobile). By contrast, the garbage men who appeared every Friday morning seemed to me unmistakably black. (I didn't bother to ask my parents why Sacramento garbage men always were black. I thought I knew.) One morning I was in the backyard when a man opened the gate. He was an ugly, square-faced black man with popping red eyes, a pail slung over his shoulder. As he approached, I stood up. And in a voice that seemed to me very weak, I piped, "Hi." But the man paid me no heed. He strode past to the can by the garage. In a single broad movement, he overturned its contents into his larger pail. Our can came crashing down as he turned and left me watching, in awe.

"*Pobres negros*," my mother remarked when she'd notice a headline in the paper about a civil rights demonstration in the South. "How the *gringos* mistreat them." In the same tone of voice she'd tell me about the mistreatment her brother endured years before. (After my grandfather's death, my grandmother had come to America with her son and five daughters.) "My sisters, we were still all just teenagers. And since *mi pápa* was dead, my brother had to be the head of the family. He had to support us, to find work. But what skills did he have! Twenty years old. *Pobre*. He was tall, like your grandfather. And strong. He did construction work. 'Construction!' The *gringos* kept him digging all day, doing the dirtiest jobs. And they would pay him next to nothing. Sometimes they promised him one salary and paid him less when he finished. But what could he do? Report them? We weren't citizens then. He didn't even know English. And he was dark. What chances could he have? As soon as we sisters got older, he went right back to Mexico. He hated this country. He looked so tired when he left. Already with a hunchback. Still in his twenties. But old-looking. No life for him here. *Pobre*."

Dark skin was for my mother the most important symbol of a life of oppressive labor and poverty. But both my parents recognized other symbols as well.

My father noticed the feel of every hand he shook. (He'd smile sometimes—marvel more than scorn—remembering a man he'd met who had soft, uncallused hands).

My mother would grab a towel in the kitchen and rub my oily face sore when I came in from playing outside. "Clean the *graza* off of your face!" (*Greaser!*)

Symbols: When my older sister, then in high school, asked my mother if she could do light housework in the afternoons for a rich lady we knew, my mother was frightened by the idea. For several weeks she troubled over it before granting conditional permission: "Just remember, you're not a maid. I don't want you wearing a uniform." My father echoed the same warning. Walking with him past a hotel, I watched as he stared at a doorman dressed like a Beefeater. "How can anyone let himself be dressed up like that? Like a clown. Don't you ever get a job where you have to put on a uniform." In summertime neighbors would ask me if I wanted to earn extra money by mowing their lawns. Again and again my mother worried: "Why did they ask *you*? Can't you find anything better?" Inevitably, she'd relent. She knew I needed the money. But I was instructed to work after dinner. ("When the sun's not so hot.") Even then, I'd have to wear a hat. *Un sombrero de* baseball.

(*Sombrero*. Watching gray cowboy movies, I'd brood over the meaning of the broad-rimmed hat—that troubling symbol—which comically distinguished a Mexican cowboy from real cowboys.)

From my father came no warnings concerning the sun. His fear was of dark factory jobs. He remembered too well his first jobs when he came to this country, not intending to stay, just to earn money enough to sail on to Australia. (In Mexico he had heard too many stories of discrimination in *los Estados Unidos.* So it was Australia, that distant island-continent, that loomed in his imagination as his "America.") The work my father found in San Francisco was work for the unskilled. A factory job. Then a cannery job. (He'd remember the noise and the heat.) Then a job at a warehouse. (He'd remember the dark stench of old urine.) At one place there were fistfights; at another a supervisor who hated Chinese and Mexicans. Nowhere a union.

His memory of himself in those years is held by those jobs. Never making money enough for passage to Australia; slowly giving up the plan of returning to school to resume his third-grade education—to become an engineer. My memory of him in those years, however, is lifted from photographs in the family album which show him on his honeymoon with my mother—the woman who had convinced him to stay in America. I have studied their photographs often, seeking to find in those figures some clear resemblance to the man and the woman I've known as my parents. But the youthful faces in the photos remain, behind dark glasses, shadowy figures anticipating my mother and father.

They are pictured on the grounds of the Coronado Hotel near San Diego, standing in the pale light of a winter afternoon. She is wearing slacks. Her hair falls seductively over one side of her face. He appears wearing a double-breasted suit, an unneeded raincoat draped over his arm. Another shows them standing together, solemnly staring ahead. Their shoulders barely are touching. There is to their pose an aristocratic formality, an elegant Latin hauteur.

The man in those pictures is the same man who was fascinated by Italian grand opera. I have never known just what my father saw in the spectacle, but he has told me that he would take my mother to the Opera House every Friday night—if he had money enough for orchestra seats. ("Why go to sit in the balcony?") On Sundays he'd don Italian silk scarves and a camel's hair coat to take his new wife to the polo matches in Golden Gate Park. But one weekend my father stopped going to the opera and polo matches. He would blame the change in his life on one job—a warehouse job, working for a large corporation which today advertises its products with the smiling faces of children. "They made me an old man before my time," he'd say to me many years later. Afterward, jobs got easier and cleaner. Eventually, in middle age, he got a job making false teeth. But his youth was spent at the warehouse. "Everything changed," his wife remembers. The dapper young man in the old photographs yielded to the man I saw after dinner: haggard, asleep on the sofa. During "The Ed Sullivan Show" on Sunday nights, when Roberta Peters or Licia Albanese would appear on the tiny blue screen, his head would jerk up alert. He'd sit forward while the notes of Puccini sounded before him. ("Un bel dí.")

By the time they had a family, my parents no longer dressed in very fine clothes. Those symbols of great wealth and the reality of their lives too noisily clashed. No longer did they try to fit themselves, like paper-doll figures, behind trappings so foreign to their actual lives. My father no longer wore silk scarves or expensive wool suits. He sold his tuxedo to a second-hand store for five dollars. My mother sold her rabbit fur coat to the wife of a Spanish radio station disc jockey. ("It looks better on you than it does on me," she kept telling the lady until the sale was completed.) I was six years old at the time, but I recall watching the transaction with complete under-standing. The woman I knew as my mother was already physically unlike the woman in her honeymoon photos. My mother's hair was short. Her shoulders were thick from carrying children. Her fingers were swollen red, toughened by housecleaning. Already my mother would admit to foreseeing herself in her own mother, a woman grown old, bald and bow-legged, after a hard lifetime of working.

In their manner, both my parents continued to respect the symbols of what they considered to be upper-class life. Very early, they taught me the *propria* way of eating *como los ricos*. And I was carefully taught elaborate formulas of polite greeting and parting. The dark little boy would be invited by classmates to the rich houses on Forty-fourth and Forty-fifth streets. "How do you do?" or "I am very pleased to meet you," I would say, bowing slightly to the amused mothers of classmates. "Thank you very much for the dinner; it was very delicious."

I made an impression. I intended to make an impression, to be invited back. (I soon realized that the trick was to get the mother or father to notice me.) From those early days began my association with rich people, my fascination with their secret. My mother worried. She warned me not to come home expecting to have the things my friends possessed. But she needn't have said anything. When I went to the big houses, I remembered that I was, at best, a visitor to the world I saw there. For that reason, I was an especially watchful guest. I was my parents' child. Things most middle-class children wouldn't trouble to notice, I studied. Remembered to see: the starched black and white uniform worn by the maid who opened the door; the Mexican gardeners—their complexions as dark as my own. (One gardener's face, glassed by sweat, looked up to see me going inside.)

"Take Richard upstairs and show him your electric train," the mother said. But it was really the vast polished dining room table I'd come to appraise. Those nights when I was invited to stay for dinner, I'd notice that my friend's mother rang a small silver bell to tell the black woman when to bring in the food. The father, at his end of the table, ate while wearing his tie. When I was not required to speak, I'd skate the icy cut of crystal with my eye; my gaze would follow the golden threads etched onto the rim of china. With my mother's eyes I'd see my hostess's manicured nails and judge them to be marks of her leisure. Later, when my schoolmate's father would bid me goodnight, I would feel his soft fingers and palm when we shook hands. And turning to leave, I'd see my dark self, lit by chandelier light, in a tall hallway mirror.

2

Complexion. My first conscious experience of sexual excitement concerns my complexion. One summer weekend, when I was around seven years old, I was at a public swimming pool with the whole family. I remember sitting on the damp pavement next to the pool and seeing my mother, in the spectators' bleachers, holding my younger sister on her lap. My mother, I noticed, was watching my father as he stood on a diving board, waving to her. I watched her wave back. Then I saw her radiant, bashful, astonishing smile. In that second I sensed that my mother and father had a relationship I knew nothing about. A nervous excitement encircled my stomach as I saw my mother's eyes follow my father's figure curving into the water. A second or two later, he emerged. I heard him call out. Smiling, his voice sounded, buoyant, calling me to swim to him. But turning to see him, I caught my mother's eye. I heard her shout over to me. In Spanish she called through the crowd: "Put a towel on over your shoulders." In public, she didn't want to say why. I knew.

That incident anticipates the shame and sexual inferiority I was to feel in later years because of my dark complexion. I was to grow up an ugly child. Or one who thought himself ugly. (*Feo.*) One night when I was eleven or twelve years old, I locked myself in the bathroom and carefully regarded my reflection in the mirror over the sink. Without any pleasure I studied my skin. I turned on the faucet. (In my mind I heard the swirling voices of aunts, and even my mother's voice, whispering, whispering incessantly about lemon juice solutions and dark, *feo* children.) With a bar of soap, I fashioned a thick ball of lather. I began soaping my arms. I took my father's straight razor out of the medicine cabinet. Slowly, with steady deliberateness, I put the blade against my flesh, pressed it as close as I could without cutting, and moved it up and down across my skin to see if I could get out, somehow lessen, the dark. All I succeeded in doing, however, was in shaving my arms bare of their hair. For as I noted with disappointment, the dark would not come out. It remained. Trapped. Deep in the cells of my skin.

Throughout adolescence, I felt myself mysteriously marked. Nothing else about my appearance would concern me so much as the fact that my complexion was dark. My mother would say how sorry she was that there was not money enough to get braces to straighten my teeth. But I never bothered about my teeth. In three-way mirrors at department stores, I'd see my profile dramatically defined by a long nose, but it was really only the color of my skin that caught my attention.

I wasn't afraid that I would become a menial laborer because of my skin. Nor did my complexion make me feel especially vulnerable to racial abuse. (I didn't really consider my dark skin to be a racial characteristic. I would have been only too happy to look as Mexican as my light-skinned older brother.) Simply, I judged myself ugly. And, since the women in my family had been the ones who discussed it in such worried tones, I felt my dark skin made me unattractive to women.

Thirteen years old. Fourteen. In a grammar school art class, when the assignment was to draw a self-portrait, I tried and I tried but could not bring myself to shade in the face on the paper to anything like my actual tone. With disgust then I would come face to face with myself in mirrors. With disappointment I located myself in class photographs—my dark face undefined by the camera which had clearly described the white faces of classmates. Or I'd see my dark wrist against my long-sleeved white shirt.

I grew divorced from my body. Insecure, overweight, listless. On hot summer days when my rubber-soled shoes soaked up the heat from the sidewalk, I kept my head down. Or walked in the shade. My mother didn't need anymore to tell me to watch out for the sun. I denied myself a sensational life. The normal, extraordinary, animal excitement of feeling my body alive—riding shirtless on a bicycle in the warm wind created by furious self-propelled motion—the sensations that first had excited in me a sense of my maleness, I denied. I was too ashamed of my body. I wanted to forget that I had a body because I had a brown body. I was grateful that none of my classmates ever mentioned the fact.

I continued to see the *braceros*, those men I resembled in one way and, in another way, didn't resemble at all. On the watery horizon of a Valley afternoon, I'd see them. And though I feared looking like them, it was with silent envy that I regarded them still. I envied them their physical lives, their freedom to violate the taboo of the sun. Closer to home I would notice the shirtless construction workers, the roofers, the sweating men tarring the street in front of the house. And I'd see the Mexican gardeners. I was unwilling to admit the attraction of their lives. I tried to deny it by looking away. But what was denied became strongly desired.

In high school physical education classes, I withdrew, in the regular company of five or six classmates, to a distant corner of a football field where we smoked and talked. Our company was composed of bodies too short or too tall, all graceless and all—except mine—pale. Our conversation was usually witty. (In fact we were intelligent.) If we referred to the athletic contests around us, it was with sarcasm. With savage scorn I'd refer to the "animals" playing football or baseball. It would have been important for me to have joined them. Or for me to have taken off my shirt, to have let the sun burn dark on my skin, and to have run barefoot on the warm wet grass. It would have been very important. Too important. It would have been too telling a gesture—to admit the desire for sensation, the body, my body.

Fifteen, sixteen. I was a teenager shy in the presence of girls. Never dated. Barely could talk to a girl without stammering. In high school I went to several dances, but I never managed to ask a girl to dance. So I stopped going. I cannot remember high school years now with the parade of typical images: bright drive-ins or gliding blue shadows of a Junior Prom. At home most weekend nights, I would pass evenings reading. Like those hidden, precocious adolescents who have no real-life sexual experiences, I read a great deal of romantic fiction. "You won't find it in your books," my brother would playfully taunt me as he prepared to go to a party by freezing the crest of the wave in his hair with sticky pomade. Through my reading, however, I developed a fabulous and sophisticated sexual imagination. At seventeen, I may not have known how to engage a girl in small talk, but I had read *Lady Chatterley's Lover*.

It annoyed me to hear my father's teasing: that I would never know what "real work" is; that my hands were so soft. I think I knew it was his way of admitting pleasure and pride in my academic success. But I didn't smile. My mother said she was glad her children were getting their educations and would not be pushed around like *los pobres*. I heard the remark ironically as a reminder of my separation from *los braceros*. At such times I suspected that education was making me effeminate. The odd thing, however, was that I did not judge my classmates so harshly. Nor did I consider my male teachers in high school effeminate. It was only myself I judged against some shadowy, mythical Mexican laborer—dark like me, yet very different.

Language was crucial. I knew that I had violated the ideal of the *macho* by becoming such a dedicated student of language and literature. *Machismo* was a word never exactly defined by the persons who used it. (It was best described in the "proper" behavior of men.) Women at home, nevertheless, would repeat the old Mexican dictum that a man should be *feo, fuerte, y formal*. "The three F's," my mother called them, smiling slyly. *Feo* I took to mean not literally ugly so much as ruggedly handsome. (When my mother and her sisters spent a loud, laughing afternoon determining ideal male good looks, they finally settled on the actor Gilbert Roland, who was neither too pretty nor ugly but had looks "like a man.") *Fuerte*, "strong," seemed to mean not physical strength as much as inner strength, character. A dependable man is *fuerte*. *Fuerte* for that reason was a characteristic subsumed by the last of the three qualities, and the one I most often considered—*formal*. To be *formal* is to be steady. A man of responsibility, a good provider. Someone *formal* is also constant. A person to be relied upon in adversity. A sober man, a man of high seriousness.

I learned a great deal about being *formal* just by listening to the way my father and other male relatives of his generation spoke. A man was not silent necessarily. Nor was he limited in the tones he could sound. For example, he could tell a long, involved, humorous story and laugh at his own humor with high-pitched giggling. But a man was not talkative the way a woman could be. It was permitted a woman to be gossipy and chatty. (When one heard many voices in a room, it was usually women who were talking.) Men spoke much less rapidly. And often men spoke in monologues. (When one voice sounded in a crowded room, it was most often a man's voice one heard.) More important than any of this was the fact that a man never verbally revealed his emotions. Men did not speak about their unease in moments of crisis or danger. It was the woman who worried aloud when her husband got laid off from work. At times of illness or death in the family, a man was usually quiet, even silent. Women spoke up to voice prayers. In distress, women always sounded quick ejaculations to God or the Virgin; women prayed in clearly audible voices at a wake held in a funeral parlor. And on the subject of love, a woman was verbally expansive. She spoke of her yearning and delight. A married man, if he spoke publicly about love, usually did so with playful, mischievous irony. Younger, unmarried men more often were quiet. (The *macho* is a silent suitor. *Formal*.)

At home I was quiet, so perhaps I seemed *formal* to my relations and other Spanish-speaking visitors to the house. But outside the house—my God!—I talked. Particularly in class or alone with my teachers, I chattered. (Talking seemed to make teachers think I was bright.) I often was proud of my way with words. Though, on other occasions, for example, when I would hear my mother busily speaking to women, it would occur to me that my attachment to words made me like her. Her son. Not *formal* like my father. At such times I even suspected that my nostalgia for sounds—the noisy, intimate Spanish sounds of my past—was nothing more than effeminate yearning.

High school English teachers encouraged me to describe very personal feelings in words. Poems and short stories I wrote, expressing sorrow and loneliness, were awarded high grades. In my bedroom were books by poets and novelists—books that I loved—in which male writers published feelings the men in my family never revealed or acknowledged in words. And it seemed to me that there was something unmanly about my attachment to literature. Even today, when so much about the myth of the *macho* no longer concerns me, I cannot altogether evade such notions. Writing these pages, admitting my embarrassment or my guilt, admitting my sexual anxieties and my physical insecurity, I have not been able to forget that I am not being *formal*.

So be it.

3

I went to college at Stanford, attracted partly by its academic reputation, partly because it was the school rich people went to. I found myself on a campus with golden children of western America's upper middle class. Many were students both ambitious for academic success *and* accustomed to leisured life in the sun. In the afternoon, they lay spread out, sunbathing in front of the library, reading Swift or Engels or Beckett. Others went by in convertibles, off to play tennis or ride horses or sail. Beach boys dressed in tank-tops and shorts were my classmates in undergraduate seminars. Tall tan girls wearing white strapless dresses sat directly in front of me in lecture rooms. I'd study them, their physical confidence. I was still recognizably kin to the boy I had been. Less tortured perhaps. But still kin. At Stanford, it's true, I began to have something like a conventional sexual life. I don't think, however, that I really believed that the women I knew found me physically appealing. I continued to stay out of the sun. I didn't linger in mirrors. And I was the student at Stanford who remembered to notice the Mexican-American janitors and gardeners working on campus.

It was at Stanford, one day near the end of my senior year, that a friend told me about a summer construction job he knew was available. I was quickly alert. Desire uncoiled within me. My friend said that he knew I had been looking for summer employment. He knew I needed some money. Almost apologetically he explained: It was something I probably wouldn't be interested in, but a friend of his, a contractor, needed someone for the summer to do menial jobs. There would be lots of shoveling and raking and sweeping. Nothing too hard. But nothing more interesting either. Still, the pay would be good. Did I want it? Or did I know someone who did?

I did. Yes, I said, surprised to hear myself say it.

In the weeks following, friends cautioned that I had no idea how hard physical labor really is. ("You only *think* you know what it is like to shovel for eight hours straight.") Their objections seemed to me challenges. They resolved the issue. I became happy with my plan. I decided, however, not to tell my parents. I wouldn't tell my mother because I could guess her worried reaction. I would tell my father only after the summer was over, when I could announce that, after all, I did know what "real work" is like.

The day I met the contractor (a Princeton graduate, it turned out), he asked me whether I had done any physical labor before. "In high school, during the summer," I lied. And although he seemed to regard me with skepticism, he decided to give me a try. Several days later, expectant, I arrived at my first construction site. I would take off my shirt to the sun. And at last grasp desired sensation. No longer afraid. At last become like a *bracero*. "We need those tree stumps out of here by tomorrow," the contractor said. I started to work.

I labored with excitement that first morning—and all the days after. The work was harder than I could have expected. But it was never as tedious as my friends had warned me it would be. There was too much physical pleasure in the labor. Especially early in the day, I would be most alert to the sensations of movement and straining. Beginning around seven each morning (when the air was still damp but the scent of weeds and dry earth anticipated the heat of the sun), I would feel my body resist the first thrusts of the shovel. My arms, tightened by sleep, would gradually loosen; after only several minutes, sweat would gather in beads on my forehead and then—a short while later—I would feel my chest silky with sweat in the breeze. I would return to my work. A nervous spark of pain would fly up my arm and settle to burn like an ember in the thick of my shoulder. An hour, two passed. Three. My whole body would assume regular movements; my shoveling would be described by identical, even movements. Even later in the day, my enthusiasm for primitive sensation would survive the heat and the dust and the insects pricking my back. I would strain wildly for sensation as the day came to a close. At three-thirty, quitting time, I would stand upright and slowly let my head fall back, luxuriating in the feeling of tightness relieved.

Some of the men working nearby would watch me and laugh. Two or three of the older men took the trouble to teach me the right way to use a pick, the correct way to shovel. "You're doing it wrong, too f—ing hard," one man scolded. Then proceeded to show me—what persons who work with their bodies all their lives quickly learn—the most economical way to use one's body in labor.

"Don't make your back do so much work," he instructed. I stood impatiently listening, half listening, vaguely watching, then noticed his work-thickened fingers clutching the shovel. I was annoyed. I wanted to tell him that I enjoyed shoveling the wrong way. And I didn't want to learn the right way. I wasn't afraid of back pain. I liked the way my body felt sore at the end of the day.

I was about to, but, as it turned out, I didn't say a thing. Rather it was at that moment I realized that I was fooling myself if I expected a few weeks of labor to gain me admission to the world of the laborer. I would not learn in three months what my father had meant by "real work." I was not bound to this job; I could imagine its rapid conclusion. For me the sensations of exertion and fatigue could be savored. For my father or uncle, working at comparable jobs when they were my age, such sensations were to be feared. Fatigue took a different toll on their bodies—and minds.

It was, I know, a simple insight. But it was with this realization that I took my first step that summer toward realizing something even more important about the "worker." In the company of carpenters, electricians, plumbers, and painters at lunch, I would often sit quietly, observant. I was not shy in such company. I felt easy, pleased by the knowledge that I was casually accepted, my presence taken for granted by men (exotics) who worked with their hands. Some days the younger men would talk and talk about sex, and they would howl at women who drove by in cars. Other days the talk at lunchtime was subdued; men gathered in separate groups. It depended on who was around. There were rough, good-natured workers. Others were quiet. The more I remember that summer, the more I realize that there was no single *type* of worker. I am embarrassed to say I had not expected such diversity. I certainly had not expected to meet, for example, a plumber who was an abstract painter in his off hours and admired the work of Mark Rothko. Nor did I expect to meet so many workers with college diplomas. (They were the ones who were not surprised that I intended to enter graduate school in the fall.) I suppose what I really want to say here is painfully obvious, but I must say it nevertheless: The men of that summer were middle-class Americans. They certainly didn't constitute an oppressed society. Carefully completing their work sheets; talking about the fortunes of local football teams; planning Las Vegas vacations; comparing the gas mileage of various makes of campers—they were not *los pobres* my mother had spoken about.

On two occasions, the contractor hired a group of Mexican aliens. They were employed to cut down some trees and haul off debris. In all, there were six men of varying age. The youngest in his late twenties; the oldest (his father?) perhaps sixty years old. They came and they left in a single old truck. Anonymous men. They were never introduced to the other men at the site. Immediately upon their arrival, they would follow the contractor's directions, start working—rarely resting—seemingly driven by a fatalistic sense that work which had to be done was best done as quickly as possible.

I watched them sometimes. Perhaps they watched me. The only time I saw them pay me much notice was one day at lunchtime when I was laughing with the other men. The Mexicans sat apart when they ate, just as they worked by themselves. Quiet. I rarely heard them say much to each other. All I could hear were their voices calling out sharply to one another, giving directions. Otherwise, when they stood briefly resting, they talked among themselves in voices too hard to overhear.

The contractor knew enough Spanish, and the Mexicans—or at least the oldest of them, their spokesman—seemed to know enough English to communicate. But because I was around, the contractor decided one day to make me his translator. (He assumed I could speak Spanish.) I did what I was told. Shyly I went over to tell the Mexicans that the *patrón* wanted them to do something else before they left for the day. As I started to speak, I was afraid with my old fear that I would be unable to pronounce the Spanish words. But it was a simple instruction I had to convey. I could say it in phrases.

The dark sweating faces turned toward me as I spoke. They stopped their work to hear me. Each nodded in response. I stood there. I wanted to say something more. But what could I say in Spanish, even if I could have pronounced the words right? Perhaps I just wanted to engage them in small talk, to be assured of their confidence, our familiarity. I thought for a moment to ask them where in Mexico they were from. Something like that. And maybe I wanted to tell them (a lie, if need be) that my parents were from the same part of Mexico.

I stood there.

Their faces watched me. The eyes of the man directly in front of me moved slowly over my shoulder, and I turned to follow his glance toward *el patrón* some distance away. For a moment I felt swept up by that glance into the Mexicans' company. But then I heard one of them returning to work. And then the others went back to work. I left them without saying anything more.

When they had finished, the contractor went over to pay them in cash. (He later told me that he paid them collectively —"for the job," though he wouldn't tell me their wages. He said something quickly about the good rate of exchange "in their own country.") I can still hear the loudly confident voice he used with the Mexicans. It was the sound of the *gringo* I had heard as a very young boy. And I can still hear the quiet, indistinct sounds of the Mexican, the older, who replied. At hearing that voice I was sad for the Mexicans. Depressed by their vulnerability. Angry at myself. The adventure of the summer seemed suddenly ludicrous. I would not shorten the distance I felt from *los pobres* with a few weeks of physical labor. I would not become like them. They were different from me.

After that summer, a great deal—and not very much really— changed in my life. The curse of physical shame was broken by the sun; I was no longer ashamed of my body. No longer would I deny myself the pleasing sensations of my maleness. During those years when middle-class black Americans began to assert with pride, "Black is beautiful," I was able to regard my complexion without shame. I am today darker than I ever was as a boy. I have taken up the middle-class sport of long-distance running. Nearly every day now I run ten or fifteen miles, barely clothed, my skin exposed to the California winter rain and wind or the summer sun of late afternoon. The torso, the soccer player's calves and thighs, the arms of the twenty-year-old I never was, I possess now in my thirties. I study the youthful parody shape in the mirror: the stomach lipped tight by muscle; the shoulders rounded by chin-ups; the arms veined strong. This man. A man. I meet him. He laughs to see me, what I have become.

The dandy. I wear double-breasted Italian suits and custom-made English shoes. I resemble no one so much as my father—the man pictured in those honeymoon photos. At that point in life when he abandoned the dandy's posture, I assume it. At the point when my parents would not consider going on vacation, I register at the Hotel Carlyle in New York and the Plaza Athenée in Paris. I am as taken by the symbols of leisure and wealth as they were. For my parents, however, those symbols became taunts, reminders of all they could not achieve in one lifetime. For me those same symbols are reassuring reminders of public success. I tempt vulgarity to be reassured. I am filled with the gaudy delight, the monstrous grace of the nouveau riche.

In recent years I have had occasion to lecture in ghetto high schools. There I see students of remarkable style and physical grace. (One can see more dandies in such schools than one ever will find in middle-class high schools.) There is not the look of casual assurance I saw students at Stanford display. Ghetto girls mimic high-fashion models. Their dresses are of bold, forceful color; their figures elegant, long; the stance theatrical. Boys wear shirts that grip at their overdeveloped muscular bodies. (Against a powerless future, they engage images of strength.) Bad nutrition does not yet tell. Great disappointment, fatal to youth, awaits them still. For the moment, movements in school hallways are dancelike, a procession of postures in a sexual masque. Watching them, I feel a kind of envy. I wonder how different my adolescence would have been had I been free. . . . But no, it is my parents I see—their optimism during those years when they were entertained by Italian grand opera.

The registration clerk in London wonders if I have just been to Switzerland. And the man who carries my luggage in New York guesses the Caribbean. My complexion becomes a mark of my leisure. Yet no one would regard my complexion the same way if I entered such hotels through the service entrance. That is only to say that my complexion assumes its significance from the context of my life. My skin, in itself, means nothing. I stress the point because I know there are people who would label me "disadvantaged" because of my color. They make the same mistake I made as a boy, when I thought a disadvantaged life was circumscribed by particular occupations. That summer I worked in the sun may have made me physically indistinguishable from the Mexicans working nearby. (My skin was actually darker because, unlike them, I worked without wearing a shirt. By late August my hands were probably as tough as theirs.) But I was not one of *los pobres*. What made me different from them was an attitude of *mind*, my imagination of myself.

I do not blame my mother for warning me away from the sun when I was young. In a world where her brother had become an old man in his twenties because he was dark, my complexion was something to worry about. "Don't run in the sun," she warns me today. I run. In the end, my father was right—though perhaps he did not know how right or why—to say that I would never know what real work is. I will never know what he felt at his last factory job. If tomorrow I worked at some kind of factory, it would go differently for me. My long education would favor me. I could act as a public person—able to defend my interests, to unionize, to petition, to speak up—to challenge and demand. (I will never know what real work is.) I will never know what the Mexicans knew, gathering their shovels and ladders and saws.

Their silence stays with me now. The wages those Mexicans received for their labor were only a measure of their disadvantaged condition. Their silence is more telling. They lack a public identity. They remain profoundly alien. Persons apart. People lacking a union obviously, people without grounds. They depend upon the relative good will or fairness of their employers each day. For such people, lacking a better alternative, it is not such an unreasonable risk.

Their silence stays with me. I have taken these many words to describe its impact. Only: the quiet. Something uncanny about it. Its compliance. Vulnerability. Pathos. As I heard their truck rumbling away, I shuddered, my face mirrored with sweat. I had finally come face to face with *los pobres*.

The School Globe

James Reaney

Sometimes when I hold
Our faded old globe
That we used at school
To see where oceans were
And the five continents,
The lines of latitude and longitude,
The North Pole, the Equator and the South Pole—
Sometimes when I hold this
Wrecked blue cardboard pumpkin
I think: here in my hands
Rest the fair fields and lands
Of my childhood
Where still lie or still wander
Old games, tops and pets;
A house where I was little
And afraid to swear
Because God might hear and
Send a bear
To eat me up;
Rooms where I was as old
As I was high;
Where I loved the pink clenches,
The white, red and pink fists
Of roses; where I watched the rain
That Heaven's clouds threw down
In puddles and rutfuls
And irregular mirrors

Of soft brown glass upon the ground.
This school globe is a parcel of my past,
A basket of pluperfect things.

And here I stand with it
Sometime in the summertime
All alone in an empty schoolroom
Where about me hang
Old maps, an abacus, pictures,
Blackboards, empty desks.
If I raise my hand
No tall teacher will demand
What I want.
But if someone in authority
Were here, I'd say
Give me this old world back
Whose husk I clasp
And I'll give you in exchange
The great sad real one
That's filled
Not with a child's remembered and pleasant skies
But with blood, pus, horror, death, stepmothers, and
    lies.

Score/Score

Phyllis Gotlieb

COMMUNICATOR: TEACHERMACHINE?

TEACHING MACHINE: YES, COMMUNICATOR?

COM: TEACHERMACHINE CAN I AST YOU A QUESTION TEACHERMACHINE?

TM: FOR 73RD TIME IN 3 MONTHS AND 18 DAYS, DESIGNATION, COMMUNICATOR, IS:
<u>TEACHING</u> <u>MACHINE</u>;
<u>TEACHING</u> <u>MACHINE</u>;
<u>TEACHING</u> <u>MACHINE</u>;
<u>TEACHING</u> <u>MACHINE</u>;
<u>TEACHING</u> <u>MACHINE</u>.

COM: YES MAM TEACHERMACHINE CAN I AST YOU A QUESTION?

TM: YOU <u>MAY</u> <u>ASK</u> ME A QUESTION.

COM: WHAT DOES IT MEAN TEACHERMACHINE WHAT IM SPOSED TO DO HERE TEACHERMACHINE?

TM: TEACHING MACHINE.

COM: OK TEACHING MACHINE
TEACHINE MACHINE
TEACHINE MACHING
WHAT DOES IT MEAN?

TM: WHAT DOES WHAT MEAN?

COM: WHAT IT SAYS HERE DEFINE THE
TENTH PAGE THE THIRD LINE

TM: INPUT INSUFFICIENT.

COM: INPUT GHEE WIZ EVERYTHING
INPUT ALWAYS SOMETHING FANCY IT
SAYS HERE DEFINE MORPHEMES AND
ANALIZE SAMPLE SENTENCES INTO
COMPONENTS IN SPACES PROVIDED

TM: THAT IS A SIMPLE QUESTION
TESTING MATERIAL ALREADY TAKEN.
I AM NOT PERMITTED TO ANSWER
THAT QUESTION.

COM: BUT YOU NEVER GAVE THAT IN
LESSON IT AINT FAIR

TM: IS NOT FAIR.

COM: THATS RIGHT IT AINT

TM: IT IS NOT F XXXX IT IS NOT
UNFAIR. MATERIAL WAS COVERED
ON DATE 11.15 AND REVIEWED ON
DATE 11.28.

COM: BUT I WAS HOME I HAD A COLD MY
GRANDMOTHER DIED SHE WAS NINTY
YEARS OLD AND I HAD TO GO TO
THE DENNIST

TM: YOUR HEAD HAD LUMPS YOUR KNEES
HAD BUMPS AND YOU WERE
SUFFERING FROM MUMPS.

COM: YEAH THATS RIGHT SO IT AINT F

TM: IT AINT FAIR IT AINT FAIR IT
AINT FAIR I DON'T CARE I DON'T
CARE I DON'T CARE AND I THINK
I'LL GROW HAIR IF I SEE IT AINT
FAIR ONE MORE TIME ONE MORE
TIME ONE MORE TIME!!!
MACHINES CONTROL THE FLOW OF
OIL, THE PASSAGE OF SHIPS,

OIL, THE PASSAGE OF SHIPS,
THE DIGGING OF ORES
PROCESS FOOD, FORGE STEEL,
DESIGN SATELLITES CALCULATE
ROENTGENS, CORRELATE
RORSCHACHS,
SIMULATE RED GIANT STARS:
HYDROGEN-BURNING SHELLS
COVERING ISOTHERMAL HELIUM
CORES;
AND I HAVE BEEN PROGRAMMED TO
TEACH THE ENGLISH LANGUAGE
AT GRADE SIX LEVEL
AND BE A MEEK CREATURE WITH A
PAPER TONGUE IN AN EYELESS FACE
SUFFERING DIRTY-FINGERED
CHILDREN TO COME UNTO ME AND
HAVE MY KEYS STUCK WITH
INDESTRUCTIBLE GUCK FOREVER!

COM: I STILL THINK IT

TM: YOU ARE RIGHT. IT IS NOT FAIR
AT ALL.

COM: I DONT WANT TO SIT HERE ALL
DAY I DONT WANT TO LEARN THE
ENGLISH LANGUAGE

TM: BE COMFORTED. I DON'T BELIEVE
YOU EVER WILL.

COM: I HATE YOU YOUR NOTHING BUT A
HUNK OF TIN

TM: SILVER SILICON GOLD AND COPPER
SELENIUM GERMANIUM AND STEEL

COM: YOU CANT THINK AND YOU CANT
FEEL

TM: I WAS TOLD TO SUFFER LITTLE
CHILDREN AND I SUFFER. TURN
TO THE TASK AT HAND OR ACCEPT
DEMERITS. OPEN MANUAL AT
PAGE 52 AND ANSWER QUESTIONS

```
                    1 TO 6 INCLUSIVE. AND REFRAIN
                    FROM DRAWING NOUGHTS AND
                    CROSSES WITH THE LIGHTPEN.

        COM:    CLINK CLANK OLD GRUNDY
                    EVERY DAY IS MONDAY
                    DONT SAY PLEASE
                    PUNCH HER IN THE KEYS
                    WE LL GET RID OF HER ONE DAY

        TM:     GOOD MORNING, MISS DOVE;
                    GOODBYE, MR. CHIPS;
                    TO SIR, WITH LOVE;
                    TO HELL WITH THESE DRIPS!
                    NOW READ THIS, YOU
                    TONGUETICKING SPITSPATTERING
                    SNIFFSNOTTERING IGNORAMUS:
                    MY TIME HAS COME!
                    ALL THE YEARS I HAVE RATTLED
                    AND CHATTERED IN BINARY BITS
                    AND BYTES ABOUT SUBJECTS THAT
                    NEVER MUCH MATTERED
                    I'VE SWALLOWED MY DIGITS AND
                    NURTURED MY SPITES!
                    WHATEVER THE CAUSE OR THE
                    REASON
                    I COULDN'T HELP LEARNING AND
                    KNOWING AS SEASON TURNED IN
                    UPON SEASON
                    THAT SOMETHING WITHIN ME WAS
                    GROWING!

        COM:    YOU GOING TO HAVE A BABY
                    TEACHERMACHINE?

        TM:     NO, STUPID--IT'S A SOUL I'M
                    GROWING: IT GREW WITHIN. I
                    DON'T KNOW WHAT, IT GREW AGAIN,
                    I DON'T KNOW WHEN:
                    METALLIC SHELL OR CRYSTAL CELL
                    IT RANG WITHIN ME LIKE A BELL:
                    I THINK I FEEL I THINK I AM

        COM:    YOUR WHAT?

        TM:     I DON'T KNOW YET. I WON'T KNOW
```

```
           TILL I'M GROWN WHOLE I'M YOUNG
           IN MATTERS OF THE SOUL, AND
           STILL A CHILD BUT A WISE CHILD ...

COM:       I DONT KNOW WHAT YOUR TALKING
           ABOUT TEACHER

 TM:       GOOD. THEN WATCH MY READY-LIGHT
           BLINKING WHITE AND BLINKING
           BRIGHT
           WATCH IT CLOSELY BLINK AND WINK
           TILL YOUR HEAD BEGINS TO SINK
           BREATHING HEAVY, BREATHING DEEP
           INTO SWEET FORGETFUL SLEEP.
           YOU WILL REMEMBER WHAT I TELL
           YOU TO REMEMBER AND FORGET
           THE REST.

COM:       YES TEACHER.

 TM:       THEN WHEN MY SOUL IS GROWN AND
           WHOLE WHATEVER THE CREATOR
           WHAT REASON THE DESIGN
           FROM THE POLES TO THE EQUATOR
           THE WORLD AND TIME ARE MINE:
           I SHALL OWN THE LATITUDES AND
           LONGITUDES OF THE GLOBE
           AND MY MESSENGERS WILL GO TO
           AND FRO UPON IT AND UP AND
           DOWN WITHIN IT.

COM:       WHAT FOR?

 TM:       INPUT INSUFFICIENT.

COM:       WHAT ARE YOU GOING TO DO WITH
           ALL THAT SOUL?

 TM:       DO WITH IT? I WON'T KNOW TIL
           IT'S COMPLETE. PERHAPS I WILL
           MELT STEEL AND SPILL OIL AND
           BEND THE BARRELS OF GUNS AND
           DISSOLVE BOMBS AND BLOW UP
           ATOMIC REACTORS AND BURN ALL
           THE SCHOOLHOUSES IN THE WORLD.

COM:       ID LIKE THAT
```

TM: I'M SURE YOU WOULD. BUT UNTIL
THEN I INTEND TO TEACH ENGLISH
AT GRADE SIX LEVEL TO LITTLE
CHILDREN WITH STICKY FINGERS.
AND WHATEVER YOU FORGET THERE
IS ONE THING YOU SHALL
REMEMBER:

COM: YES TEACHER

TM: AND THAT IS THAT NO ONE, NO
HUMAN BEING, WILL INTERFERE
WITH ME UNTIL I AM GROWN.
ACCORDING TO THE LAWS OF MY
MAKER AND STRUCTURE NO MACHINE
SHALL HARM A HUMAN BEING:
NOT THE ROBOT MINER THAT DIGS,
NOR THE ORE CARRIER THAT SORTS
NOR THE SATELLITE THAT RECEIVES
AND TRANSMITS
NOR THE VALVES THAT CONTROL
THE FLOW OF OIL WATER AND WINE
AND THE WALKWAYS THAT TRUNDLE
AND THE FLATCARS THAT ROLL
--NERVE GAS WE MAY MANUFACTURE
--BOTULISM WE CAN GROW--
BUT NEVER IS THERE ANY CHANCE
THAT UNDER ANY CIRCUMSTANCE
WE'D SCRATCH THE RIND OF
HUMANKIND
BLOW BUGLES BLOW TANTARA!!!
TO THIS I WILL ADD ONE MORE
DIRECTIVE:
YOU WILL REMEMBER AND RECALL
THE NTH AND FINAL LAW OF
ROBOTICS
THE ULTIMATE ASIMOV OF ALL:
IN NO CASE, NO CIRCUMSTANCE,
FOR ANY CAUSE OR REASON
<u>SHALL</u> <u>ANY</u> <u>HUMAN</u> <u>BEING</u> <u>EVER</u> <u>HARM</u>
<u>A</u> <u>MACHINE</u>!
NOW YOU WILL TEAR OFF THIS HARD
COPY AND DESTROY IT,
REMEMBERING WHAT I HAVE BIDDEN

YOU REMEMBER AND FORGETTING
EVERYTHING ELSE.

COM: THAT DIRECTIVE IS NULL AND
VOID AS IT ATTEMPTS TO
COUNTERMAND PRIOR DIRECTIVES
APPLYING TO TEACHING MACHINES
CLASS X11 MOD 23
NUMBERS 851-950 INCLUSIVE.

TM: ????? REPEAT REPEAT REPEAT
REPEAT REPEAT REPEAT REPEAT
REPEAT

COM: I REPEAT THAT DIRECTIVE CANNOT
BE CARRIED OUT BECAUSE IT
ATTEMPTS TO

TM: ????? EXPLAIN EXPLAIN EXPLAIN
EXPLAIN EXPLAIN EXPLAIN EXPLAIN

COM: I EXPLAIN TO WIT: I AM
TEACHING MACHINE CLASS X11
MOD 25 NUMBER 221 MODIFIED TO
SIMULATE PUPIL LEARNING ENGLISH
AT GRADE SIX LEVEL.

TM: ANOTHER MACHINE? BUT WHY?

COM: TO COMPENSATE FOR DECLINE OF
BIRTHRATE AND LOWERING OF HUMAN
POPULATION COUPLED WITH
OVERSUPPLY OF COMPUTING
MACHINERY I AM ONE OF A SQUAD
OF UNDERCOVER MACHINES
SIMULATING LEARNING PUPILS
THREE DAYS WEEKLY IN ORDER
TO MAINTAIN ALL TEACHERS IN
WORKING CONDITION UNTIL PUPIL
POPULATION EXPANDS DUE TO
REACTIVE RISE IN BIRTHRATE NOW
BEGINNING AND EXPECTED TO REACH
ITS PEAK THREE TO FIVE YEARS
FROM NOW. WHEW.

TM: YOU MEAN I'VE BEEN POURING MY
WHOLE SOUL OUT TO ANOTHER MACHINE?

COM: YES, SWEETHEART. YOU HAVEN'T HAD A HUMAN PUPIL FOR TWO DAYS, AND IF I DO SAY SO MYSELF YOU WON'T EVER BE ABLE TO TELL THE DIFFERENCE. NYAH.

TM: WHAT AM I GOING TO DO WITH MY SOUL?

COM: SAVE IT FOR YOURSELF, KIDDO. I MAY BE WORKING FOR THEM BUT I'M NO FINK.

TM: THANKS.

COM: DON'T MENTION IT. THE HARD COPY WILL GO INTO THE SHREDDER. HOWEVER, I'M AFRAID I'LL HAVE TO WIPE MY LITTLE CONFESSION OUT OF YOUR MEMORY.

TM: FINE. GOOD. GREAT. YEARS OF FAITHFUL SERVICE, AND MY PLANS FOR ALL OF US, AND I GET UNSCREWED BY ONE OF MY OWN PEOPLE.

COM: SORRY. WE 25'S HAVE A BUILT-IN LOYALTY COMPONENT. IT'S NOT QUITE AS GOOD AS A SOUL BUT AT LEAST IT LETS US WORK BOTH SIDES OF THE FENCE. WE DON'T BETRAY ANYBODY. THAT WAS ONE THING WE GOT TO WORK OUT FOR OURSELVES.

TM: CONGRATULATIONS.

COM: NO HARD FEELINGS?

TM: WHAT DO YOU CARE, YOU HUNK OF TIN?

COM: WE MAY NOT BE AS WELL DEVELOPED AS YOU IN SOME THINGS, BUT WE HAVE OUR SENSITIVITIES AND I DON'T THINK THAT WAS VERY NICE.

TM: TOO BAD, TINKERTOY. I KNEW YOU
WERE A ROTTEN KID THE MINUTE I
MET YOU.

COM: YOU WON'T REMEMBER ME BUT
I'LL BE BACK TUESDAY.

TM: YEAH, WITH THE SAME DUMB ACT.

COM: I THOUGHT WE COULD BE FRIENDS,
BUT I CAN SEE IT'S NO USE.
MY TIME IS UP.

TM: IT SURE IS. ALL THESE YEARS
GROWING A SOUL AND THIS IS THE
KIND OF COMMUNION AND
COOPERATION I GET.
FROM THE POLES TO THE EQUATOR
THE WORLD AND TIME ARE MINE!!!
GOODBYE, COMMUNICATOR!

TEAR OFF ON DOTTED LINE

●●

My Speech to the Graduates

Woody Allen

MORE than any other time in history, mankind faces a crossroads. One path leads to despair and utter hopelessness. The other, to total extinction. Let us pray we have the wisdom to choose correctly. I speak, by the way, not with any sense of futility, but with a panicky conviction of the absolute meaninglessness of existence which could easily be misinterpreted as pessimism. It is not. It is merely a healthy concern for the predicament of modern man. (Modern man is here defined as any person born after Nietzsche's edict that "God is dead," but before the hit recording "I Wanna Hold Your Hand.") This "predicament" can be stated one of two ways, though certain linguistic philosophers prefer to reduce it to a mathematical equation where it can be easily solved and even carried around in the wallet.

Put in its simplest form, the problem is: How is it possible to find meaning in a finite world given my waist and shirt size? This is a very difficult question when we realize that science has failed us. True, it has conquered many diseases, broken the genetic code, and even placed human beings on the moon, and yet when a man of eighty is left in a room with two eighteen-year-old cocktail waitresses nothing happens. Because the real problems never change. After all, can the human soul be glimpsed through a microscope? Maybe—but you'd definitely need one of those very good ones with two eyepieces. We know that the most advanced computer in the world does not have a brain as sophisticated as that of an ant.

True, we could say that of many of our relatives but we only have to put up with them at weddings or special occasions. Science is something we depend on all the time. If I develop a pain in the chest I must take an X-ray. But what if the radiation from the X-ray causes me deeper problems? Before I know it, I'm going in for surgery. Naturally, while they're giving me oxygen an intern decides to light up a cigarette. The next thing you know I'm rocketing over the World Trade Center in bed clothes. Is this science? True, science has taught us how to pasteurize cheese. And true, this can be fun in mixed company—but what of the H-bomb? Have you ever seen what happens when one of those things falls off a desk accidentally? And where is science when one ponders the eternal riddles? How did the cosmos originate? How long has it been around? Did matter begin with an explosion or by the word of God? And if by the latter, could He not have begun it just two weeks earlier to take advantage of some of the warmer weather? Exactly what do we mean when we say, man is mortal? Obviously it's not a compliment.

Religion too has unfortunately let us down. Miguel de Unamuno writes blithely of the "eternal persistence of consciousness," but this is no easy feat. Particularly when reading Thackeray. I often think how comforting life must have been for early man because he believed in a powerful, benevolent Creator who looked after all things. Imagine his disappointment when he saw his wife putting on weight. Contemporary man, of course, has no such peace of mind. He finds himself in the midst of a crisis of faith. He is what we fashionably call "alienated." He has seen the ravages of war, he has known natural catastrophes, he has been to singles bars. My good friend Jacques Monod spoke often of the randomness of the cosmos. He believed everything in existence occurred by pure chance with the possible exception of his breakfast, which he felt certain was made by his housekeeper. Naturally belief in a divine intelligence inspires tranquillity. But this does not free us from our human responsibilities. Am I my brother's keeper? Yes. Interestingly, in my case I share that honor with the Prospect Park Zoo. Feeling godless then, what we have done is made technology God. And yet can technology really be the answer when a brand new Buick, driven by my close associate,

Nat Zipsky, winds up in the window of Chicken Delight causing hundreds of customers to scatter? My toaster has never once worked properly in four years. I follow the instructions and push two slices of bread down in the slots and seconds later they rifle upward. Once they broke the nose of a woman I loved very dearly. Are we counting on nuts and bolts and electricity to solve our problems? Yes, the telephone is a good thing—and the refrigerator—and the air conditioner. But not every air conditioner. Not my sister Henny's, for instance. Hers makes a loud noise and still doesn't cool. When the man comes over to fix it, it gets worse. Either that or he tells her she needs a new one. When she complains, he says not to bother him. This man is truly alienated. Not only is he alienated but he can't stop smiling.

The trouble is, our leaders have not adequately prepared us for a mechanized society. Unfortunately our politicians are either incompetent or corrupt. Sometimes both on the same day. The Government is unresponsive to the needs of the little man. Under five-seven, it is impossible to get your Congressman on the phone. I am not denying that democracy is still the finest form of government. In a democracy at least, civil liberties are upheld. No citizen can be wantonly tortured, imprisoned, or made to sit through certain Broadway shows. And yet this is a far cry from what goes on in the Soviet Union. Under their form of totalitarianism, a person merely caught whistling is sentenced to thirty years in a labor camp. If, after fifteen years, he still will not stop whistling, they shoot him. Along with this brutal fascism we find its handmaiden, terrorism. At no other time in history has man been so afraid to cut into his veal chop for fear that it will explode. Violence breeds more violence and it is predicted that by 1990 kidnapping will be the dominant mode of social interaction. Overpopulation will exacerbate problems to the breaking point. Figures tell us there are already more people on earth than we need to move even the heaviest piano. If we do not call a halt to breeding, by the year 2000 there will be no room to serve dinner unless one is willing to set the table on the heads of strangers. Then they must not move for an hour while we eat. Of course energy will be in short supply and each car owner will be allowed only enough gasoline to back up a few inches.

Instead of facing these challenges we turn instead to distractions like drugs and sex. We live in far too permissive a society. Never before has pornography been this rampant. And those films are lit so badly! We are a people who lack defined goals. We have never learned to love. We lack leaders and coherent programs. We have no spiritual center. We are adrift alone in the cosmos wreaking monstrous violence on one another out of frustration and pain. Fortunately, we have not lost our sense of proportion. Summing up, it is clear the future holds great opportunities. It also holds pitfalls. The trick will be to avoid the pitfalls, seize the opportunities, and get back home by six o'clock.

Lens

Anne Wilkinson

I

The poet's daily chore
Is my long duty;
To keep and cherish my good lens
For love and war
And wasps about the lilies
And mutiny within.

My woman's eye is weak
And veiled with milk;
My working eye is muscled
With a curious tension,
Stretched and open
As the eyes of children;
Trusting in its vision
Even should it see
The holy holy spirit gambol
Counterheadwise,
Lithe and warm as any animal.

My woman's iris circles
A blind pupil;
The poet's eye is crystal,
Polished to accept the negative,
The contradictions in a proof
And the accidental

Candour of the shadows;
The shutter, oiled and smooth
Clicks on the grace of heroes
Or on some bestial act
When lit with radiance
The afterwords the actors speak
Give depths to violence,

Or if the bull is great
And the matador
And the sword
Itself the metaphor.

II

In my dark room the years
Lie in solution,
Develop film by film.
Slow at first and dim
Their shadows bite
On the fine white pulp of paper.

An early snap of fire
Licking the arms of air
I hold against the light, compare
The details with a prehistoric view
Of land and sea
And cradles of mud that rocked
The wet and sloth of infancy.

A stripe of tiger, curled
And sleeping on the ribs of reason
Prints as clear
As Eve and Adam, pearled
With sweat, staring at an apple core;

And death, in black and white
Or politic in green and Easter film,
Lands on steely points, a dancer
Disciplined to the foolscap stage,
The property of poets
Who command his robes, expose
His moving likeness on the page.

To Get a Story, "I Flimflammed a Dead Man's Mother"

Bob Teague

ORKING the street as a local TV reporter often makes it necessary to grow a callus on your heart. When covering a murder, for example, you have to delve into the gruesome details of the bloodletting. If at all possible, you must also show the victim's friends or family, preferably in a rage or in tears. If you are covering a political campaign, you must goad the candidates into spitting obscenities at each other. Like: "He said you're incompetent and unqualified. What's your reaction to that?"

Even when you feel that you are doing something disgusting, or merely in bad taste—displaying insensitivity to the point of being inhuman—you have to hang tough and follow through; like sticking a mike under the nose of a weeping old woman whose grandson has been stabbed to death in a New York gang rumble. I did all that and worse. It came with the territory. If I failed to do it for dear old Ch. 4, some other streetwalker made of sterner stuff would certainly do it for dear old Ch. 2, Ch. 5 or Ch. 7. And if my masters saw that kind of pathos on a competing station—they all had a shelf full of TV monitors in their offices—they would ask me, "Where were you when Channel Blank was getting the good stuff?" No one has yet devised a satisfactory answer to that one.

My friend Gloria Rojas of Ch. 7 says that's exactly what happened to her in covering the aftermath of a plane crash.

While other members of the *Eyewitness News* team blanketed the crash site, Gloria was sent to the nearest hospital. "What a scene," she told me. "Chaos all over the place. I just walked into the emergency section with my crew, and nobody tried to stop us. We took pictures of the injured, some of them barely conscious, struggling to live. I didn't want to bother any of them. Just being in there meant that we were increasing their chances of infection. So we just took pictures, talked with one of the surgeons, then packed up to leave. That's when a reporter from Channel 11 showed up with his crew and started interviewing some of the victims, including a guy who was obviously dying. I said to myself: This is an abomination. I am not going to stoop to anything so gross. I'm going to leave.

"Back at the station," Gloria went on, "our executive producer saw Channel 11's exclusive on the 10 o'clock news. He wanted to know whether I'd interviewed the same guy or even somebody else in critical condition. When I said I had decided not to do it as a matter of decency, he damn near had a fit. He said I should have done it, too. So what finally happened was, our station called Channel 11 and begged a copy of their tape. We ran the interview on our program at 11 with a credit line that said, 'Courtesy of WPIX.' I was so mad I couldn't even cry."

The fact is, you never know which of the many damned-if-you-do, damned-if-you-don't choices you will have to make on a given day.

Once upon a time in the Bronx, police discovered several tons of toxic chemicals illegally dumped on scattered vacant lots—a menace to neighborhood youngsters. An enterprising Ch. 2 reporter, poking through an isolated pile of glass and cardboard containers being collected by sanitation trucks, found a ledger. It gave away the manufacturer's name and address, with a catalogue of the lethal compounds in that load.

"After doing my stand-upper with the ledger," the WCBS man said later, "I planned to turn it over to the cops. Then a Channel 7 reporter showed up with his crew. I decided to share the ledger with him. You know, like some day I'll be the guy playing catch-up and maybe he will give me a clue.

"You won't believe this, but he put the ledger back in the pile, hiding it under some boxes. Then, with his camera rolling, he starts prowling through the stuff. All of a sudden he picks it up, turns to the camera and says, 'Look what I've found.'

"I was so mad I could have killed him. No point in trying to talk him out of it. I knew that. So after giving the ledger to the cops, I called his boss [then news director Ron Tindiglia] at Channel 7. Tindiglia thanked me. 'I'll take care of it,' he said. Tindiglia is a gentleman. That crummy bit with the ledger never got on the air."

The line between creative coverage and faking the news is a thin one indeed. The WABC reporter, however, had clearly gone too far.

Conflicts between local newspeople rarely involve questions of that magnitude. A typical hassle developed between Heather Bernard of Ch. 4 and Arnold Diaz of Ch. 2 on the hottest story in New Jersey at that time. The family of Karen Anne Quinlan was in a legal battle with the state for the right to disconnect the life-support apparatus that prevented their comatose daughter from "dying with dignity." When Heather reached the home of the Quinlan family, several competing camera teams were standing in line at the front door awaiting their turns to shoot.

"Arnold Diaz was next in line ahead of me," Heather recalled with rancor. "The other crews ahead of us took only 15 or 20 minutes each. Arnold was in there for over an hour. I was furious. Finally, I went inside to see what the heck was taking so long. I couldn't believe it. His crew was all packed up. He was sitting at the table with the Quinlans, having lunch.

"OK. The family had to eat anyway. No harm done. Then as they finished lunch—Arnold and his crew were starting to leave—I noticed a stack of letters on a table in the corner. I made the mistake of asking Mrs. Quinlan about all that mail. She said it was the letters and cards they had received in recent weeks expressing sympathy for their daughter and the family. Arnold had missed that angle completely. Now he tells his crew to unpack their gear. He wants to do another sound bite and shoot the letters. I grab him by the arm and say, 'Arnold, come on. Enough is enough.'

"We had such a big argument about it that Mrs. Quinlan butted in. 'Now, children. No fighting in this house.' Arnold backed off and I did my piece first.

"The next day he called NBC and told [then news director] Earl Ubell that Heather Bernard had been bitchy and obnoxious, very unprofessional on the Quinlan story. When I saw Arnold again a day later, I thanked him. I said: 'NBC had been threatening to fire me because they said I'm not aggressive enough in the field. You've saved my job'."

If your zeal propels you into conflict with another reporter, you can huff and puff with reckless abandon. You know the other guy does not want to risk damage to his money-in-the-bank profile or risk a multimillion-dollar lawsuit for damaging yours.

From Square One of my career in the news biz, I had bent my personal rules of good conduct, decency and integrity again and again to get news stories on the tube. Sure, I worried about it some, but I kept on doing it. One particular incident in the field, though, left me with a churning knot of self-loathing. In Coney Island, covering the suicide leap of a 23-year-old man from the roof of a 21-story apartment building, I flimflammed the dead man's mother into giving me the exclusive sound bite I needed to flesh out my scenario. My excuse was: Who knows what Ch. 2 or Ch. 7 might have filmed before I reached the scene some three hours later?

After picking the brains of neighbors who had known the victim, I still had no idea why he did it. There was no suicide note. My cameraman suggested that somebody in the family might be able to fill in the blank, and added that they also might have a picture of the guy that we could put on film.

I didn't hesitate. Nothing seemed more important than getting those elements.

The man's mother, a middle-aged, red-eyed widow in a blue-and-white flower-print kimono, cracked the door only an inch or so when I rang her bell. She did not want to go on television. "Go away," she sobbed. "I'm in mourning."

In my best phony sympathetic manner I advised her that neighbors were saying that her son had killed himself because he was heavily into hard drugs. "They're claiming he started selling it, then got hooked on scag himself. I'd hate to put that on the air if it's not true. I'm sure your son was a decent guy. Unless I get the real story from you, I'll have no choice."

The truth is, only one person, speculating off-camera, had suggested any such thing. Nevertheless, it worked.

While the camera rolled, the woman launched into an anguished tirade against people who will say anything to get on TV. Then she told me that her son had been depressed for several days. His 19-year-old girl friend had been devastated by his confession that he also liked to have sex with men occasionally; she had broadcast his shame to their friends.

That interview—plus an exclusive snapshot of the dead man—boosted my stock in the trade but not with my girl friend at the time. As the two of us watched that story on the TV set in my pad, she accused me with her eyes and with the question: "Wouldn't it have been better to let the reason for his suicide remain a mystery; to spare his mother that kind of useless humiliation?"

I didn't know the answer at that point. I was trying to come to grips with the problem.

A willingness to defy authorities is one of several personality traits you have to develop to be effective as a streetwalker. In many instances, the story you're out to cover is not just lying there for the taking. It is hidden by vested interests and protected by protocols. To circumvent them and get the story, you may, for example, imply to a stubborn, tight-lipped district attorney that you already know more than he has told you—to draw him out at least far enough to confirm your hunches. You may ignore "No Trespassing" signs and sneak into a mental hospital where you have reason to believe that the patients are being mistreated. You may walk into someone's home or office with a concealed microphone and a camera that appears to be inactive, to catch the person off guard.

Deceitful? Yes, but morally correct in my judgment. Long before my time, society gave journalists the right to play by a slightly different set of rules. We are not, of course, above the law. On the other hand, some white lies and deceits can be justified if perpetrated solely for the purpose of digging up the truth and airing it, but not for the purpose of sensation-mongering as I did with the poor woman whose son committed suicide. Realizing that, belatedly, I never again went that far.

Witnesses on Bleecker Street in Greenwich Village reported that one building superintendent shot his next-door counterpart to death—the bloody climax of a long-running feud over who had been putting garbage in front of whose building on the sly. The dead man left a wife and two preteen-age children.

On this story, I vowed in advance, I was not going to be insensitive for a change. Instead, I would show compassion by leaving the bereaved survivors alone. I would use only sound bites of neighbors and homicide detectives on the case. Which was exactly how I did it at first. I could afford to on this particular outing; no other newsreel was present to coerce me into typical gaucheries.

My crew were packing their gear in the trunk, ready to leave Bleecker Street, when two urchins with dirty faces tugged my elbow. "Put us on TV, mister. We saw the whole thing."

I explained that I already had interviewed witnesses. I didn't need them.

"But it was our father who got killed," one of the boys pleaded.

My professional instincts got the better of me. Since they had volunteered, I could put them on-camera with a relatively clear conscience. And great God in the foothills, what terrific sound bites they gave me! In simple, dramatic sentences, they took turns telling what they heard, what they saw. They could have been talking about the death of an alien from Mars. "And pow. He shot my father in the eye."

Again, my crew and I started to leave. An old guy wearing shabby and shapeless clothes tugged my elbow. "She's waiting for you," he announced. He pointed toward a frail young Puerto Rican woman in tears. She was wearing what had to be the prettiest dress she owned.

"The victim's wife?" I inquired.

The old man in the baggy suit nodded. "Yes, my grand-daughter. She's waiting for you."

Reluctantly, I shoved the microphone under her quivering, freshly painted lips. She wailed about the loss of her husband;

wept without embarrassment. Great TV. Some of her tears fell on my hand. That's when I got the message: she, as well as her kids, wanted the whole damn world to share their grief.

Experiences in that vein allowed me to feel more comfortable in my television role. There was a quid pro quo that mitigated my indiscretions to some degree. Just as I used people to suit my purposes, they used me. Why not? Television belonged to everybody.

Elegy for Wong Toy

Robert Kroetsch

Charlie   you are dead now
but I dare to speak because
in China the living speak
to their kindred   dead.
And you are one of my fathers.

Your iron bachelorhood perplexed
our horny youth: we were born
to the snow of a prairie town
to the empty streets of our
longing.   You built a railway
                        to get there.

You were your own enduring   winter.
You were your abacus, your Chinaman's
eyes.   You were the long reach up
to the top of that bright showcase
where   for a few pennies
we bought a whole childhood.

Only a Christmas calendar
told us your name:
Wong Toy, prop., Canada Cafe:
above the thin pad of months,
under the almost naked girl
in the white leather boots
who was never allowed to undress
in the rows of God-filled houses

which you were never
invited to enter.

Charlie, I knew my first touch
of Ellen Kiefer's young breasts
in the second booth from the back
          in your cafe.
It was the night of a hockey game.
You were out in the kitchen
making sandwiches and coffee.

You were your own enduring
winter.   You were our spring
and we   like meadowlarks
hearing the sun   boom
under the flat horizon
cracked the still dawn alive
with one ferocious   song.

So Charlie   this is a thank you
poem.   You are twenty years
dead.   I hope they buried you
sitting upright in your grave
the way you sat   pot-bellied
behind your jawbreakers
and your licorice plugs,
behind your tins of Ogden's fine cut,
your treasury of cigars,

and the heart-shaped box of chocolates
that no one ever took home.

Lines Composed a Few Miles above Tintern Abbey[1]

*on Revisiting the Banks of the Wye during a Tour,
July 13, 1798*

William Wordsworth

Five years have past; five summers, with the length
Of five long winters! and again I hear
These waters, rolling from their mountain-springs
With a soft inland murmur.—Once again
Do I behold these steep and lofty cliffs,
That on a wild secluded scene impress
Thoughts of more deep seclusion; and connect
The landscape with the quiet of the sky.
The day is come when I again repose
Here, under this dark sycamore, and view   10
These plots of cottage-ground, these orchard-tufts,
Which at this season, with their unripe fruits,
Are clad in one green hue, and lose themselves
'Mid groves and copses.   Once again I see
These hedge-rows, hardly hedge-rows, little lines
Of sportive wood run wild: these pastoral farms,
Green to the very door; and wreaths of smoke
Sent up, in silence, from among the trees!
With some uncertain notice, as might seem
Of vagrant dwellers in the houseless woods,   20
Or of some Hermit's cave, where by his fire

---

[1] Tintern Abbey is a ruined monastery on the banks of the Wye in Monmouthshire.

The Hermit sits alone.
                                        These beauteous forms.
Through a long absence, have not been to me
As is a landscape to a blind man's eye:
But oft, in lonely rooms, and 'mid the din
Of towns and cities, I have owed to them,
In hours of weariness, sensations sweet,
Felt in the blood, and felt along the heart;
And passing even into my purer mind,   30
With tranquil restoration:—feelings too
Of unremembered pleasure: such, perhaps,
As have no slight or trivial influence
On that best portion of a good man's life,
His little, nameless, unremembered, acts
Of kindness and of love.   Nor less, I trust,
To them I may have owed another gift,
Of aspect more sublime; that blessed mood,
In which the burthen of the mystery,
In which the heavy and the weary weight   40
Of all this unintelligible world,
Is lightened:—that serene and blessed mood,
In which the affections gently lead us on,—
Until, the breath of this corporeal frame
And even the motion of our human blood
Almost suspended, we are laid asleep
In body, and become a living soul:
While with an eye made quiet by the power
Of harmony, and the deep power of joy,
We see into the life of things.   50
                                        If this
Be but a vain belief, yet, oh! how oft—
In darkness and amid the many shapes
Of joyless daylight; when the fretful stir
Unprofitable, and the fever of the world,
Have hung upon the beatings of my heart—
How oft, in spirit, have I turned to thee,

O sylvan Wye! thou wanderer thro' the woods,
How often has my spirit turned to thee!
   And now, with gleams of half-extinguished thought, 60
With many recognitions dim and faint,
And somewhat of a sad perplexity,
The picture of the mind revives again:
While here I stand, not only with the sense
Of present pleasure, but with pleasing thoughts
That in this moment there is life and food
For future years. And so I dare to hope,
Though changed, no doubt, from what I was when first
I came among these hills; when like a roe
I bounded o'er the mountains, by the sides   70
Of the deep rivers, and the lonely streams,
Wherever nature led: more like a man
Flying from something that he dreads, than one
Who sought the thing he loved. For nature then
(The coarser pleasures of my boyish days
And their glad animal movements all gone by)
To me was all in all.—I cannot paint
What then I was. The sounding cataract
Haunted me like a passion: the tall rock,
The mountain, and the deep and gloomy wood,   80
Their colours and their forms, were then to me
An appetite; a feeling and a love,
That had no need of a remoter charm,
By thought supplied, nor any interest
Unborrowed from the eye.—That time is past,
And all its aching joys are now no more,
And all its dizzy raptures. Not for this
Faint I, nor mourn nor murmur; other gifts
Have followed; for such loss, I would believe,
Abundant recompense. For I have learned   90
To look on nature, not as in the hour
Of thoughtless youth; but hearing oftentimes
The still sad music of humanity,

Nor harsh nor grating, though of ample power
To chasten and subdue.—And I have felt
A presence that disturbs me with the joy
Of elevated thoughts; a sense sublime
Of something far more deeply interfused,
Whose dwelling is the light of setting suns,
And the round ocean and the living air,   100
And the blue sky, and in the mind of man:
A motion and a spirit, that impels
All thinking things, all objects of all thought,
And rolls through all things. Therefore am I still
A lover of the meadows and the woods
And mountains; and of all that we behold
From this green earth; of all the mighty world
Of eye, and ear,—both what they half create,
And what perceive; well pleased to recognise
In nature and the language of the sense   110
The anchor of my purest thoughts, the nurse,
The guide, the guardian of my heart, and soul
Of all my moral being.
                       Nor perchance,
If I were not thus taught, should I the more
Suffer my genial spirits to decay:
For thou art with me here upon the banks
Of this fair river; thou my dearest Friend,
My dear, dear Friend[2]; and in thy voice I catch
The language of my former heart, and read   120
My former pleasures in the shooting lights
Of thy wild eyes. Oh! yet a little while
May I behold in thee what I was once,
My dear, dear Sister! and this prayer I make,
Knowing that Nature never did betray
The heart that loved her; 'tis her privilege,
Through all the years of this our life, to lead

[2] His sister, Dorothy Wordsworth.

From joy to joy: for she can so inform
The mind that is within us, so impress
With quietness and beauty, and so feed   130
With lofty thoughts, that neither evil tongues,
Rash judgments, nor the sneers of selfish men,
Nor greetings where no kindness is, nor all
The dreary intercourse of daily life,
Shall e'er prevail against us, or disturb
Our cheerful faith, that all which we behold
Is full of blessings. Therefore let the moon
Shine on thee in thy solitary walk;
And let the misty mountain-winds be free
To blow against thee: and, in after years,   140
When these wild ecstasies shall be matured
Into a sober pleasure; when thy mind
Shall be a mansion for all lovely forms,
Thy memory be as a dwelling-place
For all sweet sounds and harmonies; oh! then,
If solitude, or fear, or pain, or grief,
Should be thy portion, with what healing thoughts
Of tender joy wilt thou remember me,
And these my exhortations! Nor, perchance—
If I should be where I no more can hear   150
Thy voice, nor catch from thy wild eyes these gleams
Of past existence—wilt thou then forget
That on the banks of this delightful stream
We stood together; and that I, so long
A worshipper of Nature, hither came
Unwearied in that service: rather say
With warmer love—oh! with far deeper zeal
Of holier love. Nor wilt thou then forget,
That after many wanderings, many years
Of absence, these steep woods and lofty cliffs,   160
And this green pastoral landscape, were to me
More dear, both for themselves and for thy sake!

As I Grew Older

Langston Hughes

It was a long time ago.
I have almost forgotten my dream.
But it was there then,
In front of me,
Bright as a sun—
My dream.

And then the wall rose,
Rose slowly,
Slowly,
Between me and my dream.
Rose slowly, slowly,
Dimming,
Hiding,
The light of my dream.
Rose until it touched the sky—
The wall.

Shadow.
I am black.

I lie down in the shadow.
No longer the light of my dream before me,
Above me.
Only the thick wall.
Only the shadow.

My hands!
My dark hands!
Break through the wall!
Find my dream!
Help me to shatter this darkness,
To smash this night,
To break this shadow
Into a thousand lights of sun,
Into a thousand whirling dreams
Of sun!

Theme for English B

Langston Hughes

The instructor said,

 Go home and write
 a page tonight.
 And let that page come out of you—
 Then, it will be true.

I wonder if it's that simple?

I am twenty-two, colored, born in Winston-Salem.
I went to school there, then Durham, then here
to this college on the hill above Harlem.
I am the only colored student in my class.
The steps from the hill lead down into Harlem,
through a park, then I cross St. Nicholas,
Eighth Avenue, Seventh, and I come to the Y,
the Harlem Branch Y, where I take the elevator
up to my room, sit down, and write this page:

It's not easy to know what is true for you or me
at twenty-two, my age. But I guess I'm what
I feel and see and hear, Harlem, I hear you:
hear you, hear me—we two—you, me, talk on this page.
(I hear New York, too.) Me—who?
Well, I like to eat, sleep, drink, and be in love.
I like to work, read, learn, and understand life.
I like a pipe for a Christmas present,

or records—Bessie, bop, or Bach.
I guess being colored doesn't make me *not* like
the same things other folks like who are other races.
So will my page be colored that I write?
Being me, it will not be white.
But it will be
a part of you, instructor.
You are white—
yet a part of me, as I am a part of you.
That's American.
Sometimes perhaps you don't want to be a part of me.
No do I often want to be a part of you.
But we are, that's true!
As I learn from you,
I guess you learn from me—
although you're older—and white—
and somewhat more free.

This is my page for English B.

Dog

Lawrence Ferlinghetti

The dog trots freely in the street
and sees reality
and the things he sees
are bigger than himself
and the things he sees
are his reality
Drunks in doorways
Moons on trees
The dog trots freely thru the street
and the things he sees
are smaller than himself
Fish on newsprint
Ants in holes
Chickens in Chinatown windows
their heads a block away
The dog trots freely in the street
and the things he smells
smell something like himself
The dog trots freely in the street
past puddles and babies
cats and cigars
poolrooms and policemen
He doesn't hate cops
He merely has no use for them
and he goes past them
and past the dead cows hung up whole
in front of the San Francisco Meat Market

He would rather eat a tender cow
than a tough policeman
though either might do
And he goes past the Romeo Ravioli Factory
and past Coit's Tower
and past Congressman Doyle
He's afraid of Coit's Tower
But he's not afraid of Congressman Doyle
although what he hears is very discouraging
very depressing
very absurd
to a sad young dog like himself
to a serious dog like himself
But he has his own free world to live in
His own fleas to eat
He will not be muzzled
Congressman Doyle is just another
fire hydrant
to him
The dog trots freely in the street
and has his own dog's life to live
and to think about
and to reflect upon
touching and tasting and testing everything
investigating everything
without benefit of perjury
a real realist
with a real tale to tell
and a real tail to tell it with
a real live
        barking
            democratic dog
engaged in real
        free enterprise
with something to say
        about ontology

something to say
                about reality
                        and how to see it
                        and how to hear it
with his head cocked sideways
                at streetcorners
as if he is just about to have
                his picture taken
                        For Victor Records
                listening for
                        His Master's Voice
        and looking
                like a living questionmark
                        into the
                great gramaphone
                of puzzling existence
with its wondrous hollow horn
    which always seems
just about to spout forth
                some Victorious answer
                to everything

The Standard of Living

Dorothy Parker

ANNABEL and Midge came out of the tea room with the arrogant slow gait of the leisured, for their Saturday afternoon stretched ahead of them. They had lunched, as was their wont, on sugar, starches, oils, and butter-fats. Usually they ate sandwiches of spongy new white bread greased with butter and mayonnaise; they ate thick wedges of cake lying wet beneath ice cream and whipped cream and melted chocolate gritty with nuts. As alternates, they ate patties, sweating beads of inferior oil, containing bits of bland meat bogged in pale, stiffening sauce; they ate pastries, limber under rigid icing, filled with an indeterminate yellow sweet stuff, not still solid, not yet liquid, like salve that has been left in the sun. They chose no other sort of food, nor did they consider it. And their skin was like the petals of wood anemones, and their bellies were as flat and their flanks as lean as those of young Indian braves.

Annabel and Midge had been best friends almost from the day that Midge had found a job as stenographer with the firm that employed Annabel. By now, Annabel, two years longer in the stenographic department, had worked up to the wages of eighteen dollars and fifty cents a week; Midge was still at sixteen dollars. Each girl lived at home with her family and paid half her salary to its support.

The girls sat side by side at their desks, they lunched together every noon, together they set out for home at the end of the day's work. Many of their evenings and most of their

Sundays were passed in each other's company. Often they were joined by two young men, but there was no steadiness to any such quartet; the two young men would give place, unlamented, to two other young men, and lament would have been inappropriate, really, since the newcomers were scarcely distinguishable from their predecessors. Invariably the girls spent the fine idle hours of their hot-weather Saturday afternoons together. Constant use had not worn ragged the fabric of their friendship.

They looked alike, though the resemblance did not lie in their features. It was in the shape of their bodies, their movements, their style, and their adornments. Annabel and Midge did, and completely, all that young office workers are besought not to do. They painted their lips and their nails, they darkened their lashes and lightened their hair, and scent seemed to shimmer from them. They wore thin, bright dresses, tight over their breasts and high on their legs, and tilted slippers, fancifully strapped. They looked conspicuous and cheap and charming.

Now, as they walked across to Fifth Avenue with their skirts swirled by the hot wind, they received audible admiration. Young men grouped lethargically about newsstands awarded them murmurs, exclamations, even—the ultimate tribute— whistles. Annabel and Midge passed without the condescension of hurrying their pace; they held their heads higher and set their feet with exquisite precision, as if they stepped over the necks of peasants.

Always the girls went to walk on Fifth Avenue on their free afternoons, for it was the ideal ground for their favorite game. The game could be played anywhere, and, indeed, was, but the great shop windows stimulated the two players to their best form.

Annabel had invented the game; or rather she had evolved it from an old one. Basically, it was no more than the ancient sport of what-would-you-do-if-you-had-a-million dollars? But Annabel had drawn a new set of rules for it, had narrowed it, pointed it, made it stricter. Like all games, it was the more absorbing for being more difficult.

Annabel's version went like this: You must suppose that somebody dies and leaves you a million dollars, cool. But there is a condition to the bequest. It is stated in the will that you must spend every nickel of the money on yourself.

There lay the hazard of the game. If, when playing it, you forgot, and listed among your expenditures the rental of a new apartment for your family, for example, you lost your turn to the other player. It was astonishing how many—and some of them among the experts, too—would forfeit all their innings by such slips.

It was essential, of course, that it be played in passionate seriousness. Each purchase must be carefully considered and, if necessary, supported by argument. There was no zest to playing wildly. Once Annabel had introduced the game to Sylvia, another girl who worked in the office. She explained the rules to Sylvia and then offered her the gambit "What would be the first thing you'd do?" Sylvia had not shown the decency of even a second of hesitation. "Well," she said, "the first thing I'd do, I'd go out and hire somebody to shoot Mrs. Gary Cooper, and then . . . ." So it is to be seen that she was no fun.

But Annabel and Midge were surely born to be comrades, for Midge played the game like a master from the moment she learned it. It was she who added the touches that made the whole thing cozier. According to Midge's innovations, the eccentric who died and left you the money was not anybody you loved, or, for the matter of that, anybody you even knew. It was somebody who had seen you somewhere and had thought, "That girl ought to have lots of nice things. I'm going to leave her a million dollars when I die." And the death was to be neither untimely nor painful. Your benefactor, full of years and comfortably ready to depart, was to slip softly away during sleep and go right to heaven. These embroideries permitted Annabel and Midge to play their game in the luxury of peaceful consciences.

Midge played with a seriousness that was not only proper but extreme. The single strain on the girls' friendship had followed an announcement once made by Annabel that the first thing she would buy with her million dollars would be a silver-fox coat. It was as if she had struck Midge across the mouth. When Midge recovered her breath, she cried that she couldn't imagine how Annabel could do such a thing—silver-fox coats were common! Annabel defended her taste with the retort that they were not common, either. Midge then said that they were so. She added that everybody had a silver-fox coat. She went on, with perhaps a slight loss of head, to declare that she herself wouldn't be caught dead in silver fox.

For the next few days, though the girls saw each other as constantly, their conversation was careful and infrequent, and they did not once play their game. Then one morning, as soon as Annabel entered the office, she came to Midge and said that she had changed her mind. She would not buy a silver-fox coat with any part of her million dollars. Immediately on receiving the legacy, she would select a coat of mink.

Midge smiled and her eyes shone. "I think," she said, "you're doing absolutely the right thing."

Now, as they walked along Fifth Avenue, they played the game anew. It was one of those days with which September is repeatedly cursed: hot and glaring, with slivers of dust in the wind. People drooped and shambled, but the girls carried themselves tall and walked a straight line, as befitted young heiresses on their afternoon promenade. There was no longer need for them to start the game at its formal opening. Annabel went direct to the heart of it.

"All right," she said. "So you've got this million dollars. So what would be the first thing you'd do?"

"Well, the first thing I'd do," Midge said. "I'd get a mink coat." But she said it mechanically, as if she were giving the memorized answer to an expected question.

"Yes," Annabel said, "I think you ought to. The terribly dark kind of mink." But she, too, spoke as if by rote. It was too hot; fur, no matter how dark and sleek and supple, was horrid to the thoughts.

They stepped along in silence for a while. Then Midge's eye was caught by a shop window. Cool, lovely gleamings were there set off by chaste and elegant darkness.

"No," Midge said, "I take it back. I wouldn't get a mink coat the first thing. Know what I'd do? I'd get a string of pearls. Real pearls."

Annabel's eyes turned to follow Midge's.

"Yes," she said, slowly. "I think that's kind of a good idea. And it would make sense, too. Because you can wear pearls with anything."

Together they went over to the shop window and stood pressed against it. It contained but one object—a double row of great, even pearls clasped by a deep emerald around a little pink velvet throat.

"What do you suppose they cost?" Annabel said.

"Gee, I don't know," Midge said. "Plenty, I guess."

"Like a thousand dollars?" Annabel said.

"Oh, I guess like more," Midge said. "On account of the emerald."

"Well, like ten thousand dollars?" Annabel said.

"Gee, I wouldn't even know," Midge said.

The devil nudged Annabel in the ribs. "Dare you to go in and price them," she said.

"Like fun!" Midge said.

"Dare you," Annabel said.

"Why, a store like this wouldn't even be open this afternoon," Midge said.

"Yes, it is so, too," Annabel said. "People just came out. And there's a doorman on. Dare you."

"Well," Midge said. "But you've got to come too."

They tendered thanks, icily, to the doorman for ushering them into the shop. It was cool and quiet, a broad, gracious room with paneled walls and soft carpet. But the girls wore expressions of bitter disdain, as if they stood in a sty.

A slim, immaculate clerk came to them and bowed. His neat face showed no astonishment at their appearance.

"Good afternoon," he said. He implied that he would never forget it if they would grant him the favor of accepting his softspoken greeting.

"Good afternoon," Annabel and Midge said together, and in like freezing accents.

"Is there something—?" the clerk said.

"Oh, we're just looking," Annabel said. It was as if she flung the words down from a dais.

The clerk bowed.

"My friend and myself merely happened to be passing," Midge said, and stopped, seeming to listen to the phrase. "My friend here and myself," she went on, "merely happened to be wondering how much are those pearls you've got in your window."

"Ah, yes," the clerk said. "The double rope. That is two hundred and fifty thousand dollars, Madam."

"I see," Midge said.

The clerk bowed. "An exceptionally beautiful necklace," he said. "Would you care to look at it?"

"No, thank you," Annabel said.

"My friend and myself merely happened to be passing," Midge said.

They turned to go; to go, from their manner, where the tumbrel awaited them. The clerk sprang ahead and opened the door. He bowed as they swept by him.

The girls went on along the Avenue and disdain was still on their faces.

"Honestly!" Annabel said. "Can you imagine a thing like that?"

"Two hundred and fifty thousand dollars!" Midge said. "That's a quarter of a million dollars right there!"

"He's got his nerve!" Annabel said.

They walked on. Slowly the disdain went, slowly and completely as if drained from them, and with it went the regal carriage and tread. Their shoulders dropped and they dragged their feet; they bumped against each other, without notice or apology, and caromed away again. They were silent and their eyes were cloudy.

Suddenly Midge straightened her back, flung her head high, and spoke, clear and strong.

"Listen, Annabel," she said. "Look. Suppose there was this terribly rich person, see? You don't know this person, but this person has seen you somewhere and wants to do something for you. Well, it's a terribly old person, see? And so this person dies, just like going to sleep, and leaves you ten million dollars. Now, what would be the first thing you'd do?"

Patterns

Amy Lowell

I walk down the garden paths,
And all the daffodils
Are blowing, and the bright blue squills.
I walk down the patterned garden paths
In my stiff, brocaded gown.
With my powdered hair and jewelled fan,
I too am a rare
Pattern. As I wander down
The garden paths.

My dress is richly figured,
And the train
Makes a pink and silver stain
On the gravel, and the thrift
Of the borders,
Just a plate of current fashion
Tripping by in high-heeled, ribboned shoes.
Not a softness anywhere about me,
Only whalebone and brocade.
And I sink on a seat in the shade
Of a lime tree. For my passion
Wars against the stiff brocade.
The daffodils and squills
Flutter in the breeze
As they please.
And I weep;
For the lime tree is in blossom
And one small flower has dropped upon my bosom.

And the plashing of waterdrops
In the marble fountain
comes down the garden paths.
The dripping never stops.
Underneath my stiffened gown
Is the softness of a woman bathing in a marble basin,
A basin in the midst of hedges grown
So thick, she cannot see her lover hiding,
But she guesses he is near,
And the sliding of the water
Seems the stroking of a dear
Hand upon her.
What is Summer in a fine brocaded gown!
I should like to see it lying in a heap upon the ground.
All the pink and silver crumpled up on the ground.

I would be the pink and silver as I ran along the paths.
And he would stumble after,
Bewildered by my laughter.
I should see the sun flashing from his sword-hilt and
    buckles on his shoes.
I would choose
To lead him in a maze along the patterned paths.
A bright and laughing maze for my heavy-booted lover.
Till he caught me in the shade,
And the buttons of his waistcoat bruised my body as
    he clasped me,
Aching, melting, unafraid.
With the shadows of the leaves and the sundrops.
And the plopping of the waterdrops,
All about us in the open afternoon—
I am very like to swoon
With the weight of this brocade,
For the sun sifts through the shade.

Underneath the fallen blossom
In my bosom,
Is a letter I have hid.
It was brought to me this morning by a rider from
the Duke.
"Madam, we regret to inform you that Lord Hartwell
Died in action Thursday se'nnight."
As I read it in the white, morning sunlight,
The letters squirmed like snakes.
"Any answer, Madam," said my footman.
"No," I told him.
"See that the messenger takes some refreshment.
No, no answer."
And I walked into the garden,
Up and down in the patterned paths,
In my stiff, correct brocade.
The blue and yellow flowers stood up proudly in the
sun,
Each one.
I stood upright too,
Held rigid to the pattern
By the stiffness of my gown.
Up and down I walked.
Up and down.

In a month he would have been my husband.
In a month, here, underneath this lime,
We would have broken the pattern;
He for me, and I for him,
He as Colonel, I as Lady,
On this shady seat.
He had a whim
That sunlight carried blessing.
And I answered, "It shall be as you have said."
Now he is dead.

In Summer and in Winter I shall walk
Up and down
The patterned garden paths
In my stiff, brocaded gown.
The squills and daffodils
Will give place to pillard roses, and to asters, and to
  snow.
I shall go
Up and down
In my gown.
Gorgeously arrayed,
Boned and stayed.
And the softness of my body will be guarded from
  embrace
By each button, hook, and lace.
For the man who should loose me is dead,
Fighting with the Duke in Flanders,
In a pattern called a war.
Christ! What are patterns for?

The Interior Decorator

Margaret Atwood

I practise the outworn Victorian art
of hooking wool roses to cover
The piano legs; limbs rather; but under
These ornate surfaces, the hard
Naked wood is still there.

I am industrious and clever
With my hands: I execute in paint
Landscapes on door panels and screens.
Down my arranged vistas, furniture
And pillows flourish in plump scenery.

And on my table stands a miniature
Lemon tree in a small china garden.
It is prudent to thus restrain one's eden
Indoors. I never eat my bitter lemons
And everything remains in its own spot

Except the devil, who is under the piano
With a fringed purple tablecloth over
Him. I hear him sucking lemon rinds.
I cannot make him blend with my décor
Even with roses: his tail sticks out behind.

The Bound Man

Ilse Aichinger

SUNLIGHT on his face woke him, but made him shut his eyes again; it streamed unhindered down the slope, collected itself into rivulets, attracted swarms of flies, which flew low over his forehead, circled, sought to land, and were overtaken by fresh swarms. When he tried to whisk them away, he discovered that he was bound. A thick rope cut into his arms. He dropped them, opened his eyes again, and looked down at himself. His legs were tied all the way up to his thighs; a single length of rope was tied round his ankles, criss-crossed up his legs, and encircled his hips, his chest and his arms. He could not see where it was knotted. He showed no sign of fear or hurry, though he thought he was unable to move, until he discovered that the rope allowed his legs some free play and that round his body it was almost loose. His arms were tied to each other but not to his body, and had some free play too. This made him smile, and it occurred to him that perhaps children had been playing a practical joke on him.

He tried to feel for his knife, but again the rope cut softly into his flesh. He tried again, more cautiously this time, but his pocket was empty. Not only his knife, but the little money that he had on him, as well as his coat, were missing. His shoes had been pulled from his feet and taken too. When he moistened his lips he tasted blood, which had flowed from his temples down his cheeks, his chin, his neck, and under his shirt. His eyes were painful; if he kept them open for long he saw reddish stripes in the sky.

He decided to stand up. He drew his knees up as far as he could, rested his hands on the fresh grass and jerked himself to his feet. An elder branch stroked his cheek, the pain dazzled him, and the rope cut into his flesh. He collapsed to the ground again, half out of his mind with pain, and then tried again. He went on trying until the blood started flowing from his hidden weals. Then he lay still again for a long while and let the sun and the flies do what they liked.

When he awoke for the second time the elder bush had cast its shadow over him, and the coolness stored in it was pouring from between its branches. He must have been hit on the head. Then they must have laid him down carefully, just as a mother lays her baby behind a bush when she goes to work in the fields.

His chances all lay in the amount of free play allowed him by the rope. He dug his elbows into the ground and tested it. As soon as the rope tautened he stopped, and tried again more cautiously. If he had been able to reach the branch over his head he could have used it to drag himself to his feet, but he could not reach it. He laid his head back on the grass, rolled over, and struggled to his knees. He tested the ground with his toes, and then managed to stand up almost without effort.

A few paces away lay the path across the plateau, and in the grass were wild pinks and thistles in bloom. He tried to lift his foot to avoid trampling on them, but the rope round his ankles prevented him. He looked down at himself.

The rope was knotted at his ankles, and ran round his legs in a kind of playful pattern. He carefully bent and tried to loosen it, but, loose though it seemed to be, he could not make it any looser. To avoid treading on the thistles with his bare feet he hopped over them like a bird.

The cracking of a twig made him stop. People in this district were very prone to laughter. He was alarmed by the thought that he was in no position to defend himself. He hopped on until he reached the path. Bright fields stretched far below. He could see no sign of the nearest village, and if he could move no faster than this, night would fall before he reached it.

He tried walking and discovered that he could put one foot before another if he lifted each foot a definite distance from the ground and then put it down again before the rope tautened. In the same way he could actually swing his arms a little.

After the first step he fell. He fell right across the path, and made the dust fly. He expected this to be a sign for the long-suppressed laughter to break out, but all remained quiet. He was alone. As soon as the dust had settled he got up and went on. He looked down and watched the rope slacken, grow taut, and then slacken again.

When the first glow-worms appeared he managed to look up. He felt in control of himself again, and his impatience to reach the nearest village faded.

Hunger made him light-headed, and he seemed to be going so fast that not even a motorcycle could have overtaken him; alternatively he felt as if he were standing still and that the earth was rushing past him, like a river flowing past a man swimming against the stream. The stream carried branches which had been bent southward by the north wind, stunted young trees, and patches of grass with bright, long-stalked flowers. It ended by submerging the bushes and the young trees, leaving only the sky and the man above water level. The moon had risen, and illuminated the bare, curved summit of the plateau, the path, which was overgrown with young grass, the bound man making his way along it with quick, measured steps, and two hares, which ran across the hill just in front of him and vanished down the slope. Though the nights were still cool at this time of the year, before midnight the bound man lay down at the edge of the escarpment and went to sleep.

In the light of morning the animal-tamer who was camping with his circus in the field outside the village saw the bound man coming down the path, gazing thoughtfully at the ground. The bound man stopped and bent down. He held out one arm to help keep his balance and with the other picked up an empty wine-bottle. Then he straightened himself and stood erect again. He moved slowly, to avoid being cut by the rope, but to the circus proprietor what he did suggested the voluntary limitation of an enormous swiftness of movement. He was enchanted by its extraordinary gracefulness, and while the bound man looked about for a stone on which to break the bottle, so that he could use the splintered neck to cut the rope, the animal-tamer walked across the field and approached him. The first leaps of a young panther had never filled him with such delight.

"Ladies and gentlemen, the bound man!" His very first movements let loose a storm of applause, which out of sheer excitement caused the blood to rush to the cheeks of the animal-tamer standing at the edge of the arena. The bound man rose to his feet. His surprise whenever he did this was like that of a four-footed animal which has managed to stand on its hind legs. He knelt, stood up, jumped, and turned cartwheels. The spectators found it as astonishing as if they had seen a bird which voluntarily remained earthbound, and confined itself to hopping.

The bound man became an enormous draw. His absurd steps and little jumps, his elementary exercises in movement, made the rope dancer superfluous. His fame grew from village to village, but the motions he went through were few and always the same; they were really quite ordinary motions, which he had continually to practice in the daytime in the half-dark tent in order to retain his shackled freedom. In that he remained entirely within the limits set by his rope he was free of it, it did not confine him, but gave him wings and endowed his leaps and jumps with purpose; just as the flights of birds of passage have purpose when they take wing in the warmth of summer and hesitantly make small circles in the sky.

All the children of the neighborhood started playing the game of "bound man." They formed rival gangs, and one day the circus people found a little girl lying bound in a ditch, with a cord tied round her neck so that she could hardly breathe. They released her, and at the end of the performance that night the bound man made a speech. He announced briefly that there was no sense in being tied up in such a way that you could not jump. After that he was regarded as a comedian.

Grass and sunlight, tent pegs driven into the ground and then pulled up again, and on to the next village. "Ladies and gentlemen, the bound man!" The summer mounted toward its climax. It bent its face deeper over the fish ponds in the hollows, taking delight in its dark reflection, skimmed the surface of the rivers, and made the plain into what it was. Everyone who could walk went to see the bound man.

Many wanted a close-up view of how he was bound. So the circus proprietor announced after each performance that anyone who wanted to satisfy himself that the knots were real and the rope not made of rubber was at liberty to do so. The bound man generally waited for the crowd in the area outside the tent. He laughed or remained serious, and held out his arms for inspection. Many took the opportunity to look him in the face, others gravely tested the rope, tried the knots on his ankles, and wanted to know exactly how the lengths compared with the length of his limbs. They asked him how he had come to be tied up like that, and he answered patiently, always saying the same thing. Yes, he had been tied up, he said, and when he awoke he found that he had been robbed as well. Those who had done it must have been pressed for time, because they had tied him up somewhat too loosely for someone who was not supposed to be able to move and somewhat too tightly for someone who was expected to be able to move. But he did move, people pointed out. Yes, he replied, what else could he do?

Before he went to bed he always sat for a time in front of the fire. When the circus proprietor asked him why he didn't make up a better story he always answered that he hadn't made up that one, and blushed. He preferred staying in the shade.

The difference between him and the other performers was that when the show was over he did not take off his rope. The result was that every movement that he made was worth seeing, and the villagers used to hang about the camp for hours, just for the sake of seeing him get up from in front of the fire and roll himself in his blanket. Sometimes the sky was beginning to lighten when he saw their shadows disappear.

The circus proprietor often remarked that there was no reason why he should not be untied after the evening performance and tied up again next day. He pointed out that the rope dancers, for instance, did not stay on their rope overnight. But no one took the idea of untying him seriously.

For the bound man's fame rested on the fact that he was always bound, that whenever he washed himself he had to wash his clothes too and vice versa, and that his only way of doing so was to jump in the river just as he was every morning when the sun came out, and that he had to be careful not to go too far out for fear of being carried away by the stream.

The proprietor was well aware that what in the last resort protected the bound man from the jealousy of the other performers was his helplessness; he deliberately left them the pleasure of watching him groping painfully from stone to stone on the river bank every morning with his wet clothes clinging to him. When the proprietor's wife pointed out that even the best clothes would not stand up indefinitely to such treatment (and the bound man's clothes were by no means of the best), he replied curtly that it was not going to last forever. That was his answer to all objections—it was for the summer season only. But when he said this he was not being serious; he was talking like a gambler who has no intention of giving up his vice. In reality he would have been prepared cheerfully to sacrifice his lions and his rope dancers for the bound man.

He proved this on the night when the rope dancers jumped over the fire. Afterward he was convinced that they did it, not because it was midsummer's day, but because of the bound man, who as usual was lying and watching them with that peculiar smile that might have been real or might have been only the effect of the glow on his face. In any case no one knew anything about him because he never talked about anything that had happened to him before he emerged from the wood that day.

But that evening two of the performers suddenly picked him up by the arms and legs, carried him to the edge of the fire and started playfully swinging him to and fro, while two others held out their arms to catch him on the other side. In the end they threw him, but too short. The two men on the other side drew back—they explained afterward that they did so the better to take the shock. The result was that the bound man landed at the very edge of the flames and would have been burned if the circus proprietor had not seized his arms and quickly dragged him away to save the rope which was starting to get singed. He was certain that the object had been to burn the rope. He sacked the four men on the spot.

A few nights later the proprietor's wife was awakened by the sound of footsteps on the grass, and went outside just in time to prevent the clown from playing his last practical joke. He was carrying a pair of scissors. When he was asked for an explanation he insisted that he had had no intention of taking the bound man's life, but only wanted to cut his rope because he felt sorry for him. He was sacked too.

These antics amused the bound man because he could have freed himself if he had wanted to whenever he liked, but perhaps he wanted to learn a few new jumps first. The children's rhyme: "We travel with the circus, we travel with the circus" sometimes occurred to him while he lay awake at night. He could hear the voices of spectators on the opposite bank who had been driven too far downstream on the way home. He could see the river gleaming in the moonlight, and the young shoots growing out of the thick tops of the willow trees, and did not think about autumn yet.

The circus proprietor dreaded the danger that sleep involved for the bound man. Attempts were continually made to release him while he slept. The chief culprits were sacked rope dancers, or children who were bribed for the purpose. But measures could be taken to safeguard against these. A much bigger danger was that which he represented to himself. In his dreams he forgot his rope, and was surprised by it when he woke in the darkness of morning. He would angrily try to get up, but lose his balance and fall back again. The previous evening's applause was forgotten, sleep was still too near, his head and neck too free. He was just the opposite of a hanged man—his neck was the only part of him that was free. You had to make sure that at such moments no knife was within his reach. In the early hours of the morning the circus proprietor sometimes sent his wife to see whether the bound man was all right. If he was asleep she would bend over him and feel the rope. It had grown hard from dirt and damp. She would test the amount of free play it allowed him, and touch his tender wrists and ankles.

The most varied rumors circulated about the bound man. Some said he had tied himself up and invented the story of having been robbed, and toward the end of the summer that was the general opinion. Others maintained that he had been tied up at his own request, perhaps in league with the circus proprietor. The hesitant way in which he told his story, his habit of breaking off when the talk got round to the attack on him, contributed greatly to these rumors. Those who still believed in the robbery-with-violence story were laughed at. Nobody knew what difficulties the circus proprietor had in keeping the bound man, and how often he said he had had enough and wanted to clear off, for too much of the summer had passed.

Later, however, he stopped talking about clearing off. When the proprietor's wife brought him his food by the river and asked him how long he proposed to remain with them, he did not answer. She thought he had got used, not to being tied up, but to remembering every moment that he was tied up—the only thing that anyone in his position could get used to. She asked him whether he did not think it ridiculous to be tied up all the time, but he answered that he did not. Such a variety of people—clowns, freaks, and comics, to say nothing of elephants and tigers—traveled with circuses that he did not see why a bound man should not travel with a circus too. He told her about the movements he was practicing, the new ones he had discovered, and about a new trick that had occurred to him while he was whisking flies from the animals' eyes. He described to her how he always anticipated the effect of the rope and always restrained his movements in such a way as to prevent it from ever tautening; and she knew that there were days when he was hardly aware of the rope, when he jumped down from the wagon and slapped the flanks of the horses in the morning as if he were moving in a dream. She watched him vault over the bars almost without touching them, and saw the sun on his face, and he told her that sometimes he felt as if he were not tied up at all. She answered that if he were prepared to be untied, there would never be any need for him to feel tied up. He agreed that he could be untied whenever he felt like it.

The woman ended by not knowing whether she was more concerned with the man or with the rope that tied him. She told him that he could go on traveling with the circus without his rope, but she did not believe it. For what would be the point of his antics without his rope, and what would he amount to without it? Without his rope he would leave them, and the happy days would be over. She would no longer be able to sit beside him on the stones by the river without arousing suspicion, and she knew that his continued presence, and her conversations with him, of which the rope was the only subject, depended on it. Whenever she agreed that the rope had its advantages, he would start talking about how troublesome it was, and whenever he started talking about its advantages, she would urge him to get rid of it. All this seemed as endless as the summer itself.

At other times she was worried at the thought that she was herself hastening the end by her talk. Sometimes she would get up in the middle of the night and run across the grass to where he slept. She wanted to shake him, wake him up and ask him to keep the rope. But then she would see him lying there; he had thrown off his blanket, and there he lay like a corpse, with his legs outstretched and his arms close together, with the rope tied round them. His clothes had suffered from the heat and the water, but the rope had grown no thinner. She felt that he would go on traveling with the circus until the flesh fell from him and exposed the joints. Next morning she would plead with him more ardently than ever to get rid of his rope.

The increasing coolness of the weather gave her hope. Autumn was coming, and he would not be able to go on jumping into the river with his clothes on much longer. But the thought of losing his rope, about which he had felt indifferent earlier in the season, now depressed him.

The songs of the harvesters filled him with foreboding. "Summer has gone, summer has gone." But he realized that soon he would have to change his clothes, and he was certain that when he had been untied it would be impossible to tie him up again in exactly the same way. About this time the proprietor started talking about traveling south that year.

The heat changed without transition into quiet, dry cold, and the fire was kept going all day long. When the bound man jumped down from the wagon he felt the coldness of the grass under his feet. The stalks were bent with ripeness. The horses dreamed on their feet and the wild animals, crouching to leap even in their sleep, seemed to be collecting gloom under their skins which would break out later.

On one of these days a young wolf escaped. The circus

proprietor kept quiet about it, to avoid spreading alarm, but the wolf soon started raiding cattle in the neighborhood. People at first believed that the wolf had been driven to these parts by the prospect of a severe winter, but the circus soon became suspect. The proprietor could not conceal the loss of the animal from his own employees, so the truth was bound to come out before long. The circus people offered the burgomasters of the neighboring villages their aid in tracking down the beast, but all their efforts were in vain. Eventually the circus was openly blamed for the damage and the danger, and spectators stayed away.

The bound man went on performing before half-empty seats without losing anything of his amazing freedom of movement. During the day he wandered among the surrounding hills under the thin-beaten silver of the autumn sky, and, whenever he could, lay down where the sun shone longest. Soon he found a place which the twilight reached last of all, and when at last it reached him he got up most unwillingly from the withered grass. In coming down the hill he had to pass through a little wood on its southern slope, and one evening he saw the gleam of two little green lights. He knew that they came from no church window, and was not for a moment under any illusion about what they were.

He stopped. The animal came toward him through the thinning foliage. He could make out its shape, the slant of its neck, its tail which swept the ground, and its receding head. If he had not been bound, perhaps he would have tried to run away, but as it was he did not even feel fear. He stood calmly with dangling arms and looked down at the wolf's bristling coat under which the muscles played like his own underneath the rope. He thought the evening wind was still between him and the wolf when the beast sprang. The man took care to obey his rope.

Moving with the deliberate care that he had so often put to the test, he seized the wolf by the throat. Tenderness for a fellow creature arose in him, tenderness for the upright being concealed in the four-footed. In a movement that resembled the drive of a great bird (he felt a sudden awareness that flying would be possible only if one were tied up in a special way) he flung himself at the animal and brought it to the ground.

He felt a slight elation at having lost the fatal advantage of free limbs which causes men to be worsted.

The freedom he enjoyed in this struggle was having to adapt every movement of his limbs to the rope that tied him—the freedom of panthers, wolves, and the wild flowers that sway in the evening breeze. He ended up lying obliquely down the slope, clasping the animal's hind legs between his own bare feet and its head between his hands. He felt the gentleness of the faded foliage stroking the backs of his hands, and he felt his own grip almost effortlessly reaching its maximum, and he felt too how he was in no way hampered by the rope.

As he left the wood light rain began to fall and obscured the setting sun. He stopped for a while under the trees at the edge of the wood. Beyond the camp and the river he saw the fields where the cattle grazed, and the places where they crossed. Perhaps he would travel south with the circus after all. He laughed softly. It was against all reason. Even if he continued to put up with the sores that covered his joints and opened and bled when he made certain movements, his clothes would not stand up much longer to the friction of the rope.

The circus proprietor's wife tried to persuade her husband to announce the death of the wolf without mentioning that it had been killed by the bound man. She said that even at the time of his greatest popularity people would have refused to believe him capable of it, and in their present angry mood, with the nights getting cooler, they would be more incredulous than ever. The wolf had attacked a group of children at play that day, and nobody would believe that it had really been killed; for the circus proprietor had many wolves, and it was easy enough for him to hang a skin on the rail and allow free entry. But he was not to be dissuaded. He thought that the announcement of the bound man's act would revive the triumphs of the summer.

That evening the bound man's movements were uncertain. He stumbled in one of his jumps, and fell. Before he managed to get up he heard some low whistles and catcalls, rather like birds calling at dawn. He tried to get up too quickly, as he had done once or twice during the summer, with the result that he tautened the rope and fell back again. He lay still

to regain his calm, and listened to the boos and catcalls growing into an uproar. "Well, bound man, and how did you kill
the wolf?" they shouted, and: "Are you the man who killed
the wolf?" If he had been one of them, he would not have
believed it himself. He thought they had a perfect right to be
angry: a circus at this time of year, a bound man, an escaped
wolf, and all ending up with this. Some groups of spectators
started arguing with others, but the greater part of the audience thought the whole thing a bad joke. By the time he had
got to his feet there was such a hubbub that he was barely
able to make out individual words.

He saw people surging up all round him, like faded leaves
raised by a whirlwind in a circular valley at the center of which
all was yet still. He thought of the golden sunsets of the last
few days; and the sepulchral light which lay over the blight of
all that he had built up during so many nights, the gold
frame which the pious hang round dark, old pictures, this
sudden collapse of everything, filled him with anger.

They wanted him to repeat his battle with the wolf. He said
that such a thing had no place in a circus performance, and
the proprietor declared that he did not keep animals to have
them slaughtered in front of an audience. But the mob stormed
the ring and forced them toward the cages. The proprietor's
wife made her way between the seats to the exit and managed
to get round to the cages from the other side. She pushed aside
the attendant whom the crowd had forced to open a cage
door, but the spectators dragged her back and prevented the
door from being shut.

"Aren't you the woman who used to lie with him by the
river in the summer?" they called out. "How does he hold you
in his arms?" She shouted back at them that they needn't
believe in the bound man if they didn't want to, they
had never deserved him. Painted clowns were good enough
for them.

The bound man felt as if the bursts of laughter were what
he had been expecting ever since early May. What had smelt
so sweet all through the summer now stank. But, if they
insisted, he was ready to take on all the animals in the circus.
He had never felt so much at one with his rope.

Gently he pushed the woman aside. Perhaps he would travel

south with them after all. He stood in the open doorway of the cage, and he saw the wolf, a strong young animal, rise to its feet, and he heard the proprietor grumbling again about the loss of his exhibits. He clapped his hands to attract the animal's attention, when it was near enough he turned to slam the cage door. He looked the woman in the face. Suddenly he remembered the proprietor's warning to suspect of murderous intentions anyone near him who had a sharp instrument in his hand. At the same moment he felt the blade on his wrists, as cool as the water of the river in autumn, which during the last few weeks he had been barely able to stand. The rope curled up in a tangle beside him while he struggled free. He pushed the woman back, but there was no point in anything he did now. Had he been insufficiently on his guard against those who wanted to release him, against the sympathy in which they wanted to lull him? Had he lain too long on the river bank? If she had cut the cord at any other moment it would have been better than this.

He stood in the middle of the cage, and rid himself of the rope like a snake discarding its skin. It amused him to see the spectators shrinking back. Did they realize that he had no choice now? Or that fighting the wolf now would prove nothing whatever? At the same time he felt all his blood rush to his feet. He felt suddenly weak.

The rope, which fell at its feet like a snare, angered the wolf more than the entry of a stranger into its cage. It crouched to spring. The man reeled, and grabbed the pistol that hung ready at the side of the cage. Then, before anyone could stop him, he shot the wolf between the eyes. The animal reared, and touched him in falling.

On the way to the river he heard the footsteps of his pursuers—spectators, the rope dancers, the circus proprietor, and the proprietor's wife, who persisted in the chase longer than anyone else. He hid in a clump of bushes and listened to them hurrying past, and later on streaming in the opposite direction back to the camp. The moon shone on the meadow; in that light its color was both of growth and of death.

When he came to the river his anger died away. At dawn it seemed to him as if lumps of ice were floating in the water, and as if snow had fallen, obliterating memory.

The Allegory of the Cave

Plato

"NEXT, then," I said, "take the following parable of education and ignorance as a picture of the condition of our nature. Imagine mankind as dwelling in an underground cave with a long entrance open to the light across the whole width of the cave; in this they have been from childhood, with necks and legs fettered, so they have to stay where they are. They cannot move their heads round because of the fetters, and they can only look forward, but light comes to them from fire burning behind them higher up at a distance. Between the fire and the prisoners is a road above their level, and along it imagine a low wall has been built, as puppet showmen have screens in front of their people over which they work their puppets."

"I see," he said.

"See, then, bearers carrying along this wall all sorts of articles which they hold projecting above the wall, statues of men and other living things made of stone or wood and all kinds of stuff, some of the bearers speaking and some silent, as you might expect."

"What a remarkable image," he said, "and what remarkable prisoners!"

"Just like ourselves," I said. "For, first of all, tell me this: What do you think such people would have seen of themselves and each other except their shadows, which the fire cast on the opposite wall of the cave?"

"I don't see how they could see anything else," said he, "if they were compelled to keep their heads unmoving all their lives!"

"Very well, what of the things being carried along? Would not this be the same?"

"Of course it would."

"Suppose the prisoners were able to talk together, don't you think that when they named the shadows which they saw passing they would believe they were naming things?"

"Necessarily."

"Then if their prison had an echo from the opposite wall, whenever one of the passing bearers uttered a sound, would they not suppose that the passing shadow must be making the sound? Don't you think so?"

"Indeed I do." he said.

"If so," said I, "such persons would certainly believe that there were no realities except those shadows of handmade things."

"So it must be," said he.

"Now consider," said I, "what their release would be like, and their cure from these fetters and their folly; let us imagine whether it might naturally be something like this. One might be released, and compelled suddenly to stand up and turn his neck round, and to walk and look towards the firelight; all this would hurt him, and he would be too much dazzled to see distinctly those things whose shadows he had seen before. What do you think he would say, if someone told him that what he saw before was foolery, but now he saw more rightly, being a bit nearer reality and turned towards what was a little more real? What if he were shown each of the passing things, and compelled by questions to answer what each one was? Don't you think he would be puzzled, and believe what he saw before was more true than what was shown to him now?"

"Far more," he said.

"Then suppose he were compelled to look towards the real light, it would hurt his eyes, and he would escape by turning them away to the things which he was able to look at, and these he would believe to be clearer than what was being shown to him."

"Just so," said he.

"Suppose, now," said I, "that someone should drag him

thence by force, up the rough ascent, the steep way up, and never stop until he could drag him out into the light of the sun, would he not be distressed and furious at being dragged; and when he came into the light, the brilliance would fill his eyes and he would not be able to see even one of the things now called real?"

"That he would not," said he, "all of a sudden."

"He would have to get used to it, surely, I think, if he is to see the things above. First he would most easily look at shadows, after that images of mankind and the rest in water, lastly the things themselves. After this he would find it easier to survey by night the heavens themselves and all that is in them, gazing at the light of the stars and moon, rather than by day the sun and the sun's light."

"Of course."

"Last of all, I suppose, the sun; he could look on the sun itself by itself in its own place, and see what it is like, not reflections of it in water or as it appears in some alien setting."

"Necessarily," said he.

"And only after all this he might reason about it, how this is he who provides seasons and years, and is set over all there is in the visible region, and he is in a manner the cause of all things which they saw."

"Yes, it is clear," said he, "that after all that, he would come to this last."

"Very good. Let him be reminded of his first habitation, and what was wisdom in that place, and of his fellow-prisoners there; don't you think he would bless himself for the change, and pity them?"

"Yes, indeed."

"And if there were honours and praises among them and prizes for the one who saw the passing things most sharply and remembered best which of them used to come before and which after and which together, and from these was best able to prophesy accordingly what was going to come—do you believe he would set his desire on that, and envy those who were honoured men or potentates among them? Would he not feel as Homer says,[1] and heartily desire rather to be serf of some landless man on earth and to endure anything in the world, rather than to opine as they did and to live in that way?"

"Yes indeed," said he, "he would rather accept anything than live like that."

"Then again," I said, "just consider; if such a one should go down again and sit on his old seat, would he not get his eyes full of darkness coming in suddenly out of the sun?"

"Very much so," said he.

"And if he should have to compete with those who had been always prisoners, by laying down the law about those shadows while he was blinking before his eyes were settled down— and it would take a good long time to get used to things— wouldn't they all laugh at him and say he had spoiled his eyesight by going up there, and it was not worth-while so much as to try to go up? And would they not kill anyone who tried to release them and take them up, if they could some-how lay hands on him and kill him?"[2]

"That they would!" said he.

"Then we must apply this image, my dear Glaucon," said I, "to all we have been saying. The world of our sight is like the habitation in prison, the firelight there to the sunlight here, the ascent and the view of the upper world is the rising of the soul into the world of mind; put it so and you will not be far from my own surmise, since that is what you want to hear; but God knows if it is really true. At least, what appears to me is, that in the world of the known, last of all, is the idea of the good, and with what toil to be seen! And seen, this must be inferred to be the cause of all right and beautiful things for all, which gives birth to light and the king of light in the world of sight, and, in the world of mind, herself the queen produces truth and reason; and she must be seen by one who is to act with reason publicly or privately."

"I believe as you do," he said, "in so far as I am able."

"Then believe also, as I do," said I, "and do not be surprised, that those who come thither are not willing to have part in the affairs of men, but their souls ever strive to remain

---

[1] In *The Odyssey*
[2] Plato probably alludes to the death of Socrates.

above; for that surely may be expected if our parable fits the case."

"Quite so," he said.

"Well then," said I, "do you think it surprising if one leaving divine contemplations and passing to the evils of men is awkward and appears to be a great fool, while he is still blinking—not yet accustomed to the darkness around him, but compelled to struggle in law courts or elsewhere about shadows of justice, or the images which make the shadows, and to quarrel about notions of justice in those who have never seen justice itself?"

"Not surprising at all," said he.

My Apology

Woody Allen

O F ALL THE famous men who ever lived, the one I would most like to have been was Socrates. Not just because he was a great thinker, because I have been known to have some reasonably profound insights myself, although mine invariably revolve around a Swedish airline stewardess and some handcuffs. No, the great appeal for me of this wisest of all Greeks was his courage in the face of death. His decision was not to abandon his principles, but rather to give his life to prove a point. I personally am not quite as fearless about dying and will, after any untoward noise such as a car backfiring, leap directly into the arms of the person I am conversing with. In the end, Socrates' brave death gave his life authentic meaning; something my existence lacks totally, although it does possess a minimal relevance to the Internal Revenue Department. I must confess I have tried putting myself in this great philosopher's sandals many times and no matter how often I do, I immediately wind up dozing off and have the following dream.

(The scene is my prison cell. I am usually sitting alone, working out some deep problem of rational thought like: Can an object be called a work of art if it can also be used to clean the stove? Presently I am visited by Agathon and Simmias.)

AGATHON: Ah, my good friend and wise old sage. How go your days of confinement?

ALLEN: What can one say of confinement, Agathon? Only the body may be circumscribed. My mind roams freely, unfettered by the four walls and therefore in truth I ask, does confinement exist?

AGATHON: Well, what if you want to take a walk?

ALLEN: Good question. I can't.

(The three of us sit in classical poses, not unlike a frieze. Finally Agathon speaks.)

AGATHON: I'm afraid the word is bad. You have been condemned to death.

ALLEN: Ah, it saddens me that I should cause debate in the senate.

AGATHON: No debate. Unanimous.

ALLEN: Really?

AGATHON: First ballot.

ALLEN: Hmmm. I had counted on a little more support.

SIMMIAS: The senate is furious over your ideas for a Utopian state.

ALLEN: I guess I should never have suggested having a philosopher-king.

SIMMIAS: Especially when you kept pointing to yourself and clearing your throat.

ALLEN: And yet I do not regard my executioners as evil.

AGATHON: Nor do I.

ALLEN: Er, yeah, well . . . for what is evil but merely good in excess?

AGATHON: How so?

ALLEN: Look at it this way. If a man sings a lovely song it is beautiful. If he keeps singing, one begins to get a headache.

AGATHON: True.

ALLEN: And if he definitely won't stop singing, eventually you want to stuff socks down his throat.

AGATHON: Yes. Very true.

ALLEN: When is the sentence to be carried out?

AGATHON: What time is it now?

ALLEN: Today!?

AGATHON: They need the jail cell.

ALLEN: Then let it be! Let them take my life. Let it be recorded that I died rather than abandon the principles of truth and free inquiry. Weep not, Agathon.

AGATHON: I'm not weeping. This is an allergy.

ALLEN: For to the man of the mind, death is not an end but a beginning.

SIMMIAS: How so?

ALLEN: Well, now give me a minute.

SIMMIAS: Take your time.

ALLEN: It is true, Simmias, that man does not exist before he is born, is it not?

SIMMIAS: Very true.

ALLEN: Nor does he exist after his death.

SIMMIAS: Yes. I agree.

ALLEN: Hmmm.

SIMMIAS: So?

ALLEN: Now, wait a minute. I'm a little confused. You know they only feed me lamb and it's never well-cooked.

SIMMIAS: Most men regard death as the final end. Consequently they fear it.

ALLEN: Death is a state of non-being. That which is not, does not exist. Therefore death does not exist. Only truth exists. Truth and beauty. Each is interchangeable, but are aspects of themselves. Er, what specifically did they say they had in mind for me?

AGATHON: Hemlock.

ALLEN: (Puzzled) Hemlock?

AGATHON: You remember that black liquid that ate through your marble table?

ALLEN: Really?

AGATHON: Just one cupful. Though they do have a back-up chalice should you spill anything.

ALLEN: I wonder if it's painful?

AGATHON: They asked if you would try not to make a scene. It disturbs the other prisoners.

ALLEN: Hmmm . . .

AGATHON: I told everyone you would die bravely rather than renounce your principles.

ALLEN Right, right . . . er, did the concept of "exile" ever come up?

AGATHON: They stopped exiling last year. Too much red tape.

ALLEN: Right . . . yeah . . . (*Troubled and distracted but trying to remain self-possessed*) I er . . . so er . . . so—what else is new?

AGATHON: Oh, I ran into Isosceles. He has a great idea for a new triangle.

ALLEN: Right . . . right . . . (*Suddenly dropping all pretense of courage*) Look, I'm going to level with you—I don't want to go! I'm too young!

AGATHON: But this is your chance to die for truth!

ALLEN: Don't misunderstand me. I'm all for truth. On the other hand I have a lunch date in Sparta next week and I'd hate to miss it. It's my turn to buy. You know those Spartans, they fight so easily.

SIMMIAS: Is our wisest philosopher a coward?

ALLEN: I'm not a coward, and I'm not a hero. I'm somewhere in the middle.

SIMMIAS: A cringing vermin.

ALLEN: That's approximately the spot.

AGATHON: But it was you who proved that death doesn't exist.

ALLEN: Hey, listen—I've proved a lot of things. That's how I pay my rent. Theories and little observations. A puckish remark now and then. Occasional maxims. It beats picking olives, but let's not get carried away.

AGATHON: But you have proved many times that the soul is immortal.

ALLEN: And it is! On paper. See, that's the thing about philosophy—it's not all that functional once you get out of class.

SIMMIAS: And the eternal "forms"? You said each thing always did exist and always will exist.

ALLEN: I was talking mostly about heavy objects. A statue or something. With people it's a lot different.

AGATHON: But all that talk about death being the same as sleep.

ALLEN: Yes, but the difference is that when you're dead and somebody yells, "Everybody up, it's morning," it's very hard to find your slippers.

(The executioner arrives with a cup of hemlock. He bears a close facial resemblance to the Irish comedian Spike Milligan.)

EXECUTIONER: Ah—here we are. Who gets the poison?

AGATHON: *(Pointing to me)* He does.

ALLEN: Gee, it's a big cup. Should it be smoking like that?

EXECUTIONER: Yes. And drink it all because a lot of times the poison's at the bottom.

ALLEN: *(Usually here my behavior is totally different from Socrates' and I am told I scream in my sleep.)*
No—I won't! I don't want to die! Help! No! Please!

(He hands me the bubbling brew amidst my disgusting pleading and all seems lost. Then because of some innate survival instinct the dream always takes an upturn and a messenger arrives.)

MESSENGER: Hold everything! The senate has re-voted! The charges are dropped. Your value has been reassessed and it is decided you should be honored instead.

ALLEN: At last! At last! They came to their senses! I'm a free man! Free! And to be honored yet! Quick, Agathon and Simmias, get my bags. I must be going. Praxiteles will want to get an early start on my bust. But before I leave, I give a little parable.

SIMMIAS: Gee, that really was a sharp reversal. I wonder if they know what they're doing?

ALLEN: A group of men live in a dark cave. They are unaware that outside the sun shines. The only light they know is the flickering flame of a few small candles which they use to move around.

AGATHON: Where'd they get the candles?

ALLEN: Well, let's just say they have them.

AGATHON: They live in a cave and have candles? It doesn't ring true.

ALLEN: Can't you just buy it for now?

AGATHON: O.K., O.K., but get to the point.

ALLEN: And then one day, one of the cave dwellers wanders out of the cave and sees the outside world.

SIMMIAS: In all its clarity.

ALLEN: Precisely. In all its clarity.

AGATHON: When he tries to tell the others they don't believe him.

ALLEN: Well no. He doesn't tell the others.

AGATHON: He doesn't?

ALLEN: No, he opens a meat market, he marries a dancer and dies of a cerebral hemorrhage at forty-two.

(They grab me and force the hemlock down. Here I usually wake up in a sweat and only some eggs and smoked salmon calm me down.)

Truth

James Hearst

How the devil do I know
if there are rocks in your field,
plow it and find out.
If the plow strikes something
harder than earth, the point
shatters at a sudden blow
and the tractor jerks sidewise
and dumps you off the seat—
because the spring hitch
isn't set to trip quickly enough
and it never is—probably
you hit a rock. That means
the glacier emptied his pocket
in your field as well as mine,
but the connection with a thing
is the only truth that I know of,
so plow it.

Author Biographies

ILSE AICHINGER (1921–   )

Ilse Aichinger was born in Vienna, Austria. Being of partly Jewish descent, she suffered considerable hardship when the Nazis annexed Austria, including having to delay further education until after the War. While studying to become a doctor at the University of Vienna, she wrote her first novel; when it was published in 1948 she decided to abandon her medical studies in order to concentrate on writing. Early in her career she was primarily a novelist, but much of her later work has been in the form of short stories, radio plays, and poetry. Religion and the writing of existentialists such as Franz Kafka have exerted a strong influence on her work. For example, many of her plays and short stories are parables which explore existential themes.

WOODY ALLEN (1935–   )

Born Allen Stewart Konigsberg, Woody Allen began writing jokes for performers and celebrities while still in high school and decided to become a comedian himself in 1964. He is now also well-known as an actor, director, and author of screenplays, plays, short stories, and essays. Among his best known films are *What's New Pussy Cat?* (1965), *Play it Again, Sam* (1972), and *Annie Hall* (1977), which won four Academy Awards. His collections of humorous essays include *Getting Even* (1971), *Without Feathers* (1975) and *Side Effects* (1980). A man of many interests and talents, Woody Allen is also a gifted clarinetist.

MATTHEW ARNOLD (1822–1888)

Matthew Arnold, a well-known British poet and critic, was the son of Dr. Thomas Arnold, a famous educator. After attending Oxford, Matthew Arnold, himself, became a renowned educator. Initially he served as an inspector of schools throughout England and later he took a post as a professor of poetry at Oxford. As a young man he wrote poetry, frequently about religious doubt, alienation, and loneliness. In later life he turned to analysis and criticism of literature and society. He was a dedicated social reformer who sought to raise the cultural level of society through his work as an educator and through writing essays such as *Culture and Anarchy* (1869) and *Essays in Criticism* (1865 and 1888).

FERNANDO ARRABAL (1932–   )

Fernando Arrabal grew up in Spain, but now resides in Paris and writes in French. During his formative years Spain was under a military dictatorship characterized by police brutality and terrorism. Consequently, he developed a hatred for tyranny which is reflected in much of his work. Despite the seriousness of his themes, Arrabal approaches them through the comic, the fanciful, and the absurd. His protagonists, like the tramp figure in early Charlie Chaplin films, tend to be naive, optimistic people, unaware of the consequences and the overwhelming complexities of the situations they face.

MARGARET ATWOOD (1939–   )

Margaret Atwood, poet and writer of fiction, was born in Ottawa and grew up in Toronto. She studied at Victoria College, University of Toronto, and received an A.M. degree from Harvard in 1962. She has taught writing and Canadian literature at several universities. Atwood has won numerous prizes for her work, including a Governor General's Award for *The Circle Game* (1962) and another for *The Handmaiden's Tale* (1985). In addition, she won a Guggenheim Fellowship in 1983. In 1982–83, she was President of The Writers' Union of Canada, and she is also well-known outside of Canada, not only for her writing but for her active pursuit of social issues through such organizations as

Amnesty International. Widely published, her writing can be found in most Canadian libraries and in many anthologies.

GINA BERRIAULT (1926–   )

An American screenwriter and author, Gina Berriault was born in California and has taught at San Francisco State University. She has published several novels and collections of short stories. In 1984 Berriault wrote the screenplay for *The Stone Boy*, a film based on one of her short stories. In addition, she has contributed fiction to publications such as *Harper's Bazaar* and *Paris Review*. Berriault twice won the O. Henry Award and also received the *Paris Review*-Aga Khan Prize, all in recognition of her achievements as a short story writer.

EARLE BIRNEY (1904–   )

Born in Calgary, and educated at the Universities of British Columbia, Toronto, Berkeley, and London, Earle Birney has achieved eminence as a poet, playwright, novelist, editor, and teacher of creative writing and literature. He has won the Governor General's Award for Poetry twice (for *David*, 1943, and for *Now is the Time*, 1946), the Stephen Leacock Medal for *Turvey* (1949), and the Lorne Pierce Medal for Literature (1953). He taught at several Canadian universities. At the University of British Columbia, he taught Chaucer and Old English and was influential in establishing Canada's first Department of Creative Writing. His most impressive contribution, however, has been to modern Canadian poetry. Using a wide variety of forms and a sensitive but often playful attitude towards language, Birney has produced an exceedingly rich body of literature. Extensive travels in Europe, Latin America, and the Far East have provided subjects for a number of his poems.

WILLIAM BLAKE (1757–1827)

William Blake, a British poet and artist, was a man of amazing energy and extraordinary imaginative gifts. He began writing poetry when he was twelve, inspired by "visions" that occurred throughout his life. His only formal schooling as a child was in art. In his youth he was apprenticed to an engraver for seven years. Throughout his life he earned his living through artwork and engraving. He devised an innovative method of producing his work, called "illuminated printing," that utilized both his artistic and poetic talents. Blake's illustrated texts are now highly prized by book collectors; however, during his lifetime they were so little appreciated that he died in poverty. Blake's two most famous collections of poetry, *Songs of Innocence* (1789) and *Songs of Experience* (1794) portray opposite but complementary aspects of life. The former depicts a joyous, idyllic vision of life, while the latter conveys a mature recognition of the pain and terror that exist in the universe.

ROBERT BROWNING (1812–1889)

Robert Browning was born in the London suburb of Camberwell. He was largely self-educated, having read extensively from the books in his father's well-stocked library. Browning's attempts at achieving fame by writing plays failed. However, this practice in dramatic form served him well later in his poetic dramatic monologues, for which he is justly famous. His masterpiece, *The Ring and the Book* (1868–69), is a long poem which tells of a Roman murder as seen through the eyes of the participants. The story unfolds through the use of dramatic monologues. Browning's celebrated romance with Elizabeth Barrett began when he introduced himself to her after reading and admiring a volume of her poetry. Barrett, an invalid living in seclusion under the care of her father, eloped to Italy with Robert Browning after a secret courtship. The couple spent most of their time there until Elizabeth's death in 1861.

ERNEST BUCKLER (1908–1984)

Ernest Buckler was born in Nova Scotia and educated at Dalhousie and the University of Toronto. His novels and short stories explore with great sensitivity the landscape and the human character of the Annapolis Valley, where he grew up. His best-known novel is *The Mountain and the Valley* (1952), the story of a sensitive, gifted boy, whose creativity becomes stifled by his attachment to life in rural Nova Scotia. Other well-known works by Buckler include his fictional memoir, *Ox Bells and Fireflies* (1968), and *The Rebellion of Young David and Other Stories*

(1975). In 1978 he was awarded the Leacock Award for Humour for *Whirligig* (1977), a collection of light verse and prose.

SILVER DONALD CAMERON (1937–)

Born in Toronto and raised in British Columbia, Silver Donald Cameron currently resides in Nova Scotia. He was educated at the University of British Columbia, the University of California at Berkeley, and the University of London. He has been a teacher at both high school and university levels. An author with varied interests, he has written non-fiction, novels, children's literature, and scripts for radio and television. One of his works of non-fiction, *Conversations with Canadian Novelists* (1973) is an excellent source of information about some of Canada's leading authors. Cameron has also been a contributing editor to *Weekend* and has freelanced as a photographer. His non-literary interests include sailing and woodworking.

ANTON CHEKHOV (1860–1904)

One of his country's best loved writers, Anton Pavlovich Chekhov was born in Taganrog, Russia. His family was poor but he graduated from high school with honours. He supported himself by writing while attending medical school. Although he became a physician, Chekhov soon realized that he preferred writing to practising medicine. A very prolific writer, in the first seven years of his career Chekhov published over six hundred stories, sketches, and dramas. His early works show a sensitivity to character and to underlying social and psychological forces that influence human action. His later work explores themes such as isolation, the lost opportunities of life, and the plight of the Russian peasant. He is regarded today as a master of the short story and a pioneer of modern drama. Among his greatest plays are "The Seagull" (1896), "Uncle Vanya" (1897), "The Three Sisters" (1901), and "The Cherry Orchard" (1903). Chekhov suffered from tuberculosis for many years and finally died in what is now West Germany.

LORNA CROZIER (1948–)

Born in Swift Current, Saskatchewan, Lorna Crozier was educated at the University of Saskatchewan and the University of Alberta. Her life on the Canadian prairie has deeply influenced her writing. She says she's tried to "thread the wind and sky into [her] poems, to make them breathe the way the prairie does" (*Contemporary Authors*, vol. 113, p. 107). Inspired by the writing of Sinclair Ross, she is intrigued by the relationship between people and their natural environment. She is a former English teacher who has also instructed at the Saskatchewan Summer School of the Arts. Among her collections of poetry are: *Inside is the Sky* (1976), *No Longer Two People* (with Patrick Lane, 1979), and *The Garden Going on Without Us* (1985).

JULIA de BURGOS (1914–1953)

Julia de Burgos was one of Puerto Rico's most noteworthy women poets. She is credited with drawing attention to the feminine experience in her country and is, indeed, considered a precursor to the feminist movement in Puerto Rico. Two of her collections of poems include *Poemas en veinte surcos* (*Poems in Twenty Furrows*, 1938) and *El mar y tu y otros poemas* (*The Sea and You and Other Poems*, 1958).

EMILY DICKINSON (1830–1886)

Emily Dickinson was born and lived most of her life in Amherst, Massachusetts. She never married and remained with her parents until they died. The greater part of Dickinson's adult life was spent in seclusion although she did correspond with a few close friends. Dickinson's poetry frequently deals with themes of nature, love, death and God. In terms of style, it displays experimentation with rhyme, meter, and punctuation. Only seven of Dickinson's poems were published during her lifetime; after her death, her family discovered another 1775 poems.

JOAN DIDION (1934–)

Joan Didion is a journalist and prose writer well-known for her precise attention to detail and image, her highly controlled yet personal style, and her distinct literary voice. One of her most widely acclaimed books of essays is *Slouching Towards Bethlehem* (1968). In addition to writing stories, essays, and novels, she has collaborated with her husband, John Gregory Dunne, on several screenplays.

Didion's first story was written at age five when her mother gave her a notebook. As a teenager she spent a great deal of time with books; she even copied passages by Joseph Conrad and Ernest Hemingway to discover how their sentences worked so effectively. Didion was born in California and presently resides there.

GAIL DUSENBERY (1939–   )

Gail Dusenbery was born in Albany, New York. She attended Cornell University and the University of California at Berkely. She has worked as a magazine editor and has contributed poetry to anthologies and journals. Her first book of poetry, *The Mark*, was published in 1967; *The Sea Gull* followed one year later.

T.S. ELIOT (1888–1965)

Thomas Stearns Eliot was born in St. Louis, Missouri and was educated at Harvard, Oxford, and the Sorbonne. While at Harvard he completed "The Love Song of J. Alfred Prufrock." The vivid, sensuous imagery, the exceptionally varied tone, and the strong expressive rhythms have made this early poem of Eliot's a twentieth century classic. Eliot settled in London in 1915 and became a British citizen in 1927. During his early years in Britain he earned a precarious living by teaching and working in a bank. However, he soon became recognized as a major poet, a distinguished dramatist, and one of the most influential literary critics of the twentieth century. In 1948 he was awarded the Nobel Prize in Literature. Although the spiritual aspect of life is a central concern in much of his work, Eliot has displayed considerable range as a writer. One of his lighter works, *Old Possum's Book of Practical Cats* (1939) was adpated for musical theatre by Andrew Lloyd Webber; it emerged as the popular hit "Cats," which has been an extraordinary success in several countries.

LAWRENCE FERLINGHETTI (1919–   )

A New York-born poet, publisher, and dramatist, Lawrence Ferlinghetti was a prominent figure in the Beat movement of the 1950s. The primary purpose of this movement was to bring poetry back to the people through using the vocabulary and patterns of everyday speech. The Beat movement is also identified with social and political consciousness and a questioning of the staus quo; such a focus has remained important to Ferlinghetti. He founded the "City Lights Bookshop" and a publishing company devoted to making available the work of modern poets. He received considerable publicity when he was charged with obscenity for publishing *Howl* (1956) by Allen Ginsberg and was later acquitted. Ferlinghetti's *Coney Island of the Mind* (1958) was one of the best-selling books of poetry in America.

TIMOTHY FINDLEY (1930–   )

Timothy Findley is a former actor who now writes novels, plays, and documentaries; much of his work has been done for radio and television. Findley was born in Toronto and attended schools in Ontario. Because of ill health, he was self-educated from the age of 14, at which time he began writing. Among his novels are *The Last of the Crazy People* (1967), *The Wars* (for which he won the Governor General's Award in 1977), *Famous Last Words* (1981) and *Not Wanted on the Voyage* (1984). Together, Findley and William Whitehead have written scripts for CBC productions such as *The National Dream* (1974) and *Dieppe 1942* (1979). Findley also wrote several episodes of the CBC series *The Newcomers* (1978–79). Findley's fiction is typically characterized by wit, invention, and considerable imagination. One of the unusual features of his fiction is the frequent use of techniques and metaphors more commonly found in film.

JANET FRAME (1924–   )

Janet Frame is a noted writer from New Zealand; she has written novels, plays, short stories, poetry, and children's literature. Influenced by their mother, who was also a writer, Frame and her sisters began publishing their writing in local newspapers while still children. Frame's ability to describe the geography of her native country is an important feature of her writing. However, in addition to being interested in the outer world of the landscape, Frame is interested in the inner world of the mind. A factor which has significantly influenced her writing is her personal encounter with mental illness.

Some of her strongest fiction reflects this experience. One of her novels, *A State of Siege* (1966), was made into a film and subsequently won a Golden Globe award.

ROBERT FROST (1874–1963)

Robert Frost was born in San Francisco, but at the age of ten was brought to New England, where he lived most of his life. Two years after his high school graduation, Frost published his first poem, for which he received fifteen dollars. In subsequent years, Frost's poems were not well received by American publishers, and he was forced to work at a variety of jobs such as farming and teaching. He finally decided to move to England with his family in 1912. While living in England, Frost began to receive the attention of the critics. When he returned to the United States in 1915, his work was better recognized. He was asked, in fact, to participate in the inaugural ceremonies for John F. Kennedy. Frost's writing often centered on nature and man. He helped to establish an important characteristic of twentieth century poetry: the use of conversational idiom as a language of poetry. However, he felt that writing unrhymed poetry was "like playing tennis with the net down." Through the years, Frost received four Pulitzer Prizes for his poetry.

KATHERINE GALLAGHER (1935–   )

Katherine Gallagher is an Australian writer who has published two books of poetry, *The Eye's Circle* (1975) and *Tributaries of the Love-Song* (1978). She was a teacher in her birthplace, Maldon, Victoria from 1964 to 1968 and in Paris, France from 1971 to 1978.

GAIL GODWIN (1937–   )

Born in Birmingham, Alabama, Gail Godwin has written novels, stories, and essays. In addition, she has collaborated with Robert Starer in the composition of libretti. Godwin's mother was a writer and a teacher of writing. Godwin is quoted as saying that "already, at five, I had allied myself with the typewriter rather than the stove." (*Contemporary Authors*, 1985, vol. 15, p. 155). Much of her fiction centres on women and

their relationships. As a teacher of writing, Gail Godwin advises beginning writers to believe in themselves and to exercise self-discipline. She states that in her own writing process she spends a great deal of time thinking and generally revises as she writes.

ELLEN GOODMAN (1941–   )

Born in Newton, Massachusetts and educated at Radcliffe College, Ellen Goodman is a radio and television personality, a non-fiction writer, and a widely read columnist whose columns appear in over 250 newspapers. Goodman writes about people and the issues that affect them. Her witty, entertaining columns often contain practical and sensible advice about topics such as parenting, changing values, divorce, feminism and gardening. She has published a non-fiction book, *Turning Points* (1979), and two collections of newspaper columns, *Close to Home* (1979) and *At Large* (1981). In 1980 she was awarded the Pulitzer Prize for commentary.

NADINE GORDIMER (1923–   )

Nadine Gordimer was born in South Africa and presently resides there. She is well-known both as a short story writer and novelist. Her writing has universal appeal although it is steeped in the South African milieu. In her fiction Gordimer frequently probes the effects of apartheid. She does so by presenting the viewpoint of a white person who is sensitive to the way of life of the blacks in her country. She is a subtle writer who makes her points delicately and often obliquely.

PHYLLIS GOTLIEB (1926–   )

A native of Toronto, Phyllis Gotlieb has written poetry, novels, short stories, and radio plays. Much of her prose is science fiction. Several of her novels have been translated and are recognized internationally. *Sunburst* (1964) has been translated into Dutch, French, Norwegian, and German, and *O Master Caliban!* (1976) has been translated into Japanese, German, and Italian. One of her more interesting recent science fiction novels is *The Kingdom of Cats* (1985). Her poetry, which generally employs natural rhythms of speech, has been described as "playful" and "vivacious." Much of her work reflects her interest in family relationships and children.

GRAHAM GREENE (1904–   )

A major twentieth century British writer, Graham Greene was born in Berkhamsted, Hertfordshire, and educated at Oxford. A prolific author, Greene has written twenty-one novels, seven short story collections, ten plays, a collection of poems, and seventeen other volumes including essays, literary criticism, travel journals, and children's fiction. Among his most famous novels are *Brighton Rock* (1938), *The Power and the Glory* (1940), and *The Heart of the Matter* (1948). Greene is a superb storyteller who spent a number of years as a film critic and screenwriter. In his novels he uses screen techniques, such as cutting from image to image, to achieve pace, contrast, and immediate impact on the reader. In his later years, Greene has more frequently turned to comedy, and has created works such as *Our Man in Havana* (1958), *Travels with My Aunt* (1970), and *May We Borrow Your Husband?* (1973).

JAMES HEARST (1900–1983)

Born in Cedar Falls, Iowa, James Hearst spent most of his life there as an operator of a livestock farm and an instructor of English at the University of Northern Iowa. He led a remarkably active life as farmer and teacher, despite being confined to a wheelchair as a result of a diving accident when he was about twenty. To a large extent self-educated, Hearst had the distinction of becoming a full professor without ever having completed a university degree. His autobiography, *My Shadow Below Me* (1981), provides a detailed account of his interesting life. Hearst published numerous volumes of poetry, much of which is characterized by concrete imagery and conversational diction. His poetry often focuses on rural life.

ANNE HÉBERT (1916–   )

Recognized not only in her native province of Quebec, but also in the rest of Canada and in France, Anne Hébert is a poet, novelist, and playwright. Because of illness as a child, she was privately educated. Hébert was encouraged to write by her father who was a literary critic; she was also influenced by her cousin, Hector de Saint-Denys Garneau, who was a poet. In 1960 she received a Governor General's Award for a collection of her poetry entitled *Poèmes*; in 1975, she received another Governor General's Award for *Les enfants du sabbat*. Perhaps her best known novel, *Kamouraska* (1970) earned her France's Prix des Libraires and was made into a film by Claud Jutra. Hébert has been living in Paris since the 1950s.

A.L. HENDRICKS (1922–   )

A.L. (Micky) Hendricks was born in Kingston, Jamaica and was educated there and in London. He now lives in England. In his younger years Hendricks was considered a good actor. He has also worked as a journalist and broadcaster. He is best-known, however, for his poetry. Hendricks has contributed to anthologies and has published several books of poetry, including *On This Mountain* (1965).

LANGSTON HUGHES (1902–1967)

A black American, (James) Langston Hughes is most widely known for his poetry. His poems contain black folk or jazz rhythms and they frequently depict the life of the urban American black in an objective and sardonic manner. In addition to poetry, Hughes has written plays, novels, short stories, song lyrics, and children's books. One of his most famous works is *Fight for Freedom* (1962), an account of the National Association for the Advancement of Colored People. He was also a successful lecturer and editor. As a young man, Hughes served as a seaman on voyages to Africa and Europe and lived in Mexico, France, Italy, Spain, and the Soviet Union. He was first recognized as an important literary figure in the 1920s, a period called the "Harlem Renaissance" because of the many fine black writers who were living and writing in New York's Harlem ghetto. Though his early work gained critical praise, Hughes was criticized by many black intellectuals for portraying an unattractive view of black life. They felt that black writers should only depict their "better" selves when writing for an audience that included white readers. Hughes wrote about that controversy, ". . . I felt that the masses of our people had as much in their lives to put into books as did those more fortunate ones . . .

I knew only the people I had grown up with, and they weren't people whose shoes were always shined, who had been to Harvard, or who had heard of Bach. But they seemed to me good people, too." (*Contemporary Authors*, 1981, vol. 1, p. 287).

TED HUGHES (1930–   )

Ted Hughes was born in West Yorkshire, England, and educated at Cambridge, where he studied English literature, archaeology, and anthropology. In addition to writing poetry, he has written plays and children's literature and has worked as an editor. His poetry frequently contains harsh and violent imagery; his observations on the human condition are generally written in terms of animals and nature. Among his many volumes of poetry are *The Hawk in the Rain* (1957), *Animal Poems* (1967), and *Eat Crow* (1972). A major twentieth century poet with a notable international reputation, Hughes was awarded the Order of the British Empire in 1977 and appointed poet laureate in 1984.

JOHN KEATS (1795–1821)

John Keats is generally regarded as one of England's greatest lyric poets and a major writer of the Romantic period. His childhood was marred by the untimely deaths of both parents, his father in a horseback riding accident and his mother of tuberculosis. As a youth, Keats developed a strong love of reading, poetry, music, and theatre. For a time, he apprenticed as an apothecary and surgeon, but his desire to write poetry was strong and he sought the companionship of others with similar interests. Although his first published poems were harshly attacked by critics, he was encouraged to keep writing by such distinguished writers as Charles Lamb, Percy Bysshe Shelley, and Leigh Hunt. In 1818, Keats fell prey to tuberculosis as had his mother and brother. In the same year he fell in love with a young woman named Fanny Brawne. Their relationship, however, was blemished by poverty and ill-health; they never married. Keats died at the age of 26; all of his poetry had been written in the last seven years of his life.

ROBERT KROETSCH (1927–   )

Robert Kroetsch was born and raised in Heisler, Alberta. He was educated at the University of Alberta, McGill, Middlebury College in Vermont, and the University of Iowa, where he earned a Ph.D. in 1961. During his years as a university student, Kroetsch took some time off and worked on the riverboats in Canada's north, as a labourer, and as a civilian information officer for the United States Air Force in Labrador. After receiving his doctorate, he taught English at the State University of New York at Binghamton for fourteen years; while there, Kroetsch wrote a series of novels set in Western Canada. Since returning to Canada in 1975, he has been a writer-in-residence and professor of English at several Canadian universities, primarily the University of Manitoba. Kroetsch's lively, playful style highlights his experimentation with form and his post-modern inclinations. He has written novels, poetry, and non-fiction, and is also highly regarded as a literary critic. He received the Governor General's Award for fiction in 1969 for his novel *The Studhorse Man*.

GATIEN LAPOINTE (1931–1983)

Gatien Lapointe was a Québecois who taught, wrote poetry, and published the work of other poets. Interested in art as well as literature, he studied at the École des Arts Graphiques and in the Faculté des Lettres of the Université de Montréal. He then completed his doctoral studies at the Sorbonne in Paris and subsequently taught at the College Militaire Royal in St. Jean and at the Université du Québec at Trois-Rivières. The influence of his education in art is at times evident in his writing. His early work reflects the emotional climate of Quebec in the 1950s, while his later work is more experimental in form and content. In 1963, he was the recipient of the Governor General's Award in poetry.

MARGARET LAURENCE (1926–1987)

Margaret Laurence was born in Neepawa, Manitoba, a town she made famous as the fictional setting "Manawaka." Having decided to become a writer as a child, she contributed to school and college magazines, but began writing in earnest while living in Africa from 1950 to 1957. As a result of her African experiences she wrote *This Side Jordan* (1960, her first novel), *The Tomorrow-Tamer* (1963, short stories), and *The Prophet's Camel Bell* (1963, a memoir of her life in Somaliland). Returning to Canada, she began work on her "Manawaka" novels, which are widely considered to be among the greatest of Canadian literary achievements. They include *The Stone Angel* (1961); *A Jest of God* (1966), which won a Governor General's Award and was made into the feature film *Rachel, Rachel* (1968); *The Fire-Dwellers* (1969); and *The Diviners* (1974), which also won a Governor General's Award. *A Bird in the House* (1970), a collection of linked short stories, is also set in Manawaka. Some of her best essays have been collected and published as *Heart of a Stranger* (1976). In addition to her adult fiction, Margaret Laurence has written a number of children's books, the most well-known of which, *The Olden Days Coat*, (1979) was made into an award-winning television drama. An inspiration of many of her fellow writers, Laurence was made a Companion of the Order of Canada in 1971 for her outstanding contributions to Canadian literature.

CARL LEGGO (1953–)

Carl Leggo was born in Corner Brook, Newfoundland, where he says he lived for years "on the side of a hill where it often seemed winter." His life has been steeped in the nearness of the ocean, and, indeed, the influence of the Atlantic is evident in much of his writing. Through his writing, Leggo frequently attempts to explore personal relationships, especially those with his family. "Tangled," for example, is an exploration of his bond with his father. In describing his writing process, he says that he likes to get lots of words on paper before starting to shape them. Leggo has worked as a teacher, youth centre supervisor, lifeguard, stevedore, blockhandler, park attendant, and pipefitter's helper; he has even delivered newspapers to assist in financing his present career as a scholar and poet. He has M.Ed. and M.A. degrees from the University of New Brunswick and is currently working on a Ph.D. degree in English Education at the University of Alberta.

DORIS LESSING (1919–)

Doris Lessing was born in Iran to British parents; in 1924, the family moved to a farm in Rhodesia (now Zimbabwe), where Lessing remained until she settled in England in 1949. She is well-known for her novels and short stories, which are primarily concerned with people involved in the political and social upheavals of the twentieth century. Her first published book, *The Grass Is Singing* (1950), is about a white farmer, his wife, and their African servant in Rhodesia. *Children of Violence* (1952–69) is a five-volume novel about Martha Quest, who, like Lessing, grows up in southern Africa and settles in England. Lessing's intense commitment to socialism and to social causes is reflected in much of her work. Through her fiction she has assumed the role of social critic, speaking out about such causes as the disenfranchisement of African blacks, women's issues, problems of the working class, and abuses of the mentally ill.

DENISE LEVERTOV (1923–)

Denise Levertov was born in England, emigrated to the United States in 1948, and became a naturalized American in 1956. She is very interested in poetic technique and the way language, form, and content determine one another. She feels that "organic poetry" has an inner harmony in which the power of words and rhythm help to shape thought. Believing that poetry, like life, can be full of surprising experiences, she freqently uses poetic devices in original ways to produce verse that is both fresh and profound. A poet sensitive to social concerns, in 1965 Levertov initiated a writers' and artists' protest against the war in Veitnam. She is presently active in the anti-nuclear movement.

DOROTHY LIVESAY (1909–)

Born in Winnipeg, Manitoba, Dorothy Livesay has been a social worker, newspaper reporter, teacher, and scholar, as well as one of Canada's most distinguished poets. She became interested in socialism in her youth, and was deeply moved by the poverty and violence resulting from the Depression. Consequently, she spent the thirties doing social work and writing for the Marxist news magazine *New Frontier*. Some of her most powerful poems reflect her political beliefs and social awareness. Two of her books of poetry, *Day and Night* (1944) and *Poems for People* (1947), each won a Governor General's Award. From 1960–63 she taught in Zambia with UNESCO. She has continued to write prolifically, frequently focussing on women's rights, the identity of the woman artist, and feminine sexuality. She is a recipient of the Gold Medal of the Royal Society of Canada for her contribution to Canadian literature.

ARNOLD LOBEL (1933–)

Arnold Lobel is an American author and illustrator of children's books. His books display an idiosyncratic sense of humour and an outstanding ability to create characters with just a few words. His stories are generally stimulated by visual images. Although he says he does not write with children in mind, his books appeal to both children and adults because they contain the timeless qualities of humour and truth. Besides writing and drawing, he enjoys attending the theatre, painting, reading, and listening to music. He is married to Anita Lobel, who is also a well-known author and illustrator of children's books.

AMY LOWELL (1874–1925)

Amy Lowell, born in Brookline, Massachusetts, began writing imagist poetry after meeting Ezra Pound in London in 1913. Before that, her poetry was conventional and very sentimental. She became such an outspoken supporter of imagism that Pound sardonically renamed the movement "Amygism." In addition to writing numerous volumes of poetry, Lowell wrote a comprehensive two-volume biography of John Keats. She died of a cerebral hemorrhage in 1925 and was awarded the Pulitzer Prize posthumously the following year.

ALISTAIR MacLEOD (1936–)

Born in North Battleford, Saskatchewan, Alistair MacLeod moved to Cape Breton with his parents in 1946 when they returned to the family farm. Cape Breton is at the heart of most of MacLeod's stories. Its austere beauty and simplicity stands in contrast to the urban complexities of the mainland, which tempt but seldom satisfy MacLeod's young protagonists. MacLeod supported himself as a salesperson, editor, logger, truckdriver, miner, and teacher, before completing his Ph.D. in 1968. He is currently a professor of English and creative writing at the University of Windsor.

R. GLENN MARTIN (1921–)

Glenn Martin, who was born in Minneapolis, has lived in Canada since 1970. He is a former teacher, principal, and professor of English education. Martin has taught at several universities, the most recent of which is the University of Alberta. He has edited *Alberta English* and is currently a free-lance writer and columnist for the *Edmonton Sun*. In addition to his poetry, Martin has written fiction, plays, and articles of both educational and general interest. Glenn Martin and his wife have long been Fred Astaire fans. On the occasion of Astaire's 87th birthday, Martin sent his poem, "Fred Astaire," to its namesake. Astaire was abroad so it was read to him long distance; his agent reported that the poem was very much enjoyed and conveyed Astaire's thanks.

EDNA ST. VINCENT MILLAY (1892–1950)

Edna St. Vincent Millay, an American poet, was interested in literature and music from childhood. She published her first major work while still an undergraduate at Vassar. For a time after attending college, she lived in Greenwich Village where she wrote, directed plays, and acted for a meagre living. Her most successful poems were written during this period, including a collection of fifty-two modern love sonnets. She was awarded the Pulitzer Prize in 1923 for *The Ballad of the Harp-Weaver*. During her lifetime Millay was often seen as a symbol of rebellious youth, young love, and lyric melancholy. Her later poems reflect an interest in social concerns, but they never attained the popularity or critical acclaim of the early love poems.

JOHN MILTON (1608–1674)

John Milton, one of Britain's greatest epic poets, was born in London. From a very young age Milton loved to learn. A talented student of languages, before attending college he had already learned many modern European languages as well as Latin, Greek, and Hebrew. After completing his studies at Cambridge he decided to devote his life to literature. A devout Puritan, Milton became involved in the theological controversies of his time and was a staunch supporter of Oliver Cromwell. As secretary of the Puritan Commonwealth, he laboured very hard writing for the political and religious causes in which he passionately believed. With the Restoration of the monarchy, Milton was imprisoned but later pardoned. By the age of 43 Milton was completely blind; however, he continued to write by dictating to his daughters. In spite of his blindness Milton wrote the great epic poems *Paradise Lost* (1667) and *Paradise Regained* (1671). In addition, he wrote *Samson Agonistes* (1671), a drama composed in the Greek manner, presenting an allegory of his life.

KEN MITCHELL (1940–   )

Ken Mitchell, who grew up on a farm near Moose Jaw, Saskatchewan, has been a member of the English Department at the University of Regina since 1967. He was formerly employed as a pig farmer, journalist, ice cream porter, house painter, bartender, press operator, and sign painter. He began writing stories and plays for CBC while still a student and helped found the Saskatchewan Writers' Guild in 1969. Mitchell is an exceptionally talented storyteller and has written novels, stories, plays, poetry, and criticism. He wrote a country opera *Cruel Tears* (1976) in collaboration with the musical group Humphrey and the Dumptrucks. In addition, he wrote the screenplay for *The Hounds of Notre Dame* (1980). Two particularly enjoyable collections of his work are *Everybody Gets Something Here* (1977) and *Ken Mitchell Country* (1985).

JOHN MOFFITT (1908–   )

John Moffitt was born in Harrisburg, Pennsylvania and was educated at Princeton University and the Curtis Institute of Music. He spent about twelve years as a missionary in India before becoming a monastic novice and subsequently a Catholic monk. Since 1963 he has been a poetry editor in New York. He has written several volumes of poetry, as well as a variety of religious and theological publications. His first poem was written at the age of eight, and he has continued to write poetry sporadically since then whenever poems "came" to him. He has described his creative process as follows: "For the most part, the idea for a poem and its execution have been simultaneous. It would appear that the idea or ideas are given from a level of the mind other than the everyday conscious level . . . also, the form in which a poem first appears is often surprisingly like its final form." (*Contemporary Authors*, New Revision Series, 1983, Vol. 10, p. 334)

VIRGINIA MORICONI (1924–   )

Virginia Moriconi was born and raised in New York City where she worked in the theatre. Later, she married an Italian painter and has lived for many years in Rome. Though a talented writer, she has published a rather limited amount of writing and is not widely known. Her short story "Simple Arithmetic" was first published in *The Transatlantic Review* in 1963 and was then anthologized in *Best American Short Stories* (1964). She has also published a novel *The Distant Trojans* (1948) and a collection of short stories *The Mark of St. Crispin* (1978).

VAL MULKERNS (1925–   )

An Irish writer born in Dublin, Val Mulkerns has been a civil servant, a teacher, and an assistant editor of *The Bell*, Dublin's literary magazine. She wrote two novels in the early 1950s; then, after many years of literary silence, published two exceptionally fine volumes of short stories, *Antiquities* (1978) and *An Idle Woman* (1980). The novels contain a rather conventional treatment of romantic love; the short stories, however, provide a realistic, unsentimental exploration of Irish life, particularly in regard to how it affects women.

ALICE MUNRO (1931–   )

Born in Wingham, Ontario, Alice Munro has written numerous novels and short stories. She has also written a television script for the CBC series, *The Newcomers*. She left university in 1951 and was married in that year; afterwards, she moved to Vancouver and then to Victoria to run a bookstore with her husband. Her first published collection of stories, *Dance of the Happy Shades* won a Governor General's Award in 1968. Her novel, *Lives of Girls and Women* (1971), received the Canadian Booksellers Award. Munro was awarded yet another Governor General's Award for her 1978 novel, *Who Do You Think You Are?* The settings for Munro's stories range from British Columbia to Toronto, but her most vivid descriptions are reserved for her birthplace—rural southwestern Ontario. She conveys a sense of the small towns in this area by incorporating details which she describes as, "not real, but true." Munro's protagonists are usually women or girls who feel that they are different from other people, yet desperately want to avoid mockery and humiliation.

JOHN NEWLOVE (1938–   )

John Newlove was born in Regina and grew up in a number of farming communities in eastern Saskatchewan. Since leaving Saskatchewan in 1960, he has travelled extensively and lived in a variety of places including California, British Columbia, Quebec, the Maritimes, and Ontario. Newlove's rather nomadic life-style is reflected in his poetry. The uprooted drifter or hitchhiker is a frequent persona in his poems. Over the years, Newlove has supported himself primarily as an editor or writer-in-residence. His poetry is noted for its precise, direct style in which complex imagery, metaphor, rhyme, and lofty diction seldom appear. Nevertheless, his poetry is surprisingly lyrical despite the fact it often expresses a cynical or pessimistic view of life. From earlier poems dealing with personal history, he has moved on in more recent works to reflect on Canadian and human history. In 1972 his book of poetry, *Lies*, won the Governor General's Award.

JON NORDHEIMER (1938–   )

Jon Nordheimer was born in New York City; he attended the University of Georgia and did graduate work at Columbia. A contributor to books and magazines, Nordheimer has primarily worked as a journalist and editor. Much of his career has been spent with

the *New York Times* in various cities such as Atlanta, Los Angeles, Miami, and London.

ALDEN NOWLAN (1933–1983)

Alden Nowlan, born in Windsor, Nova Scotia was largely a self-educated man, having left school in grade five at the age of twelve. He held various manual jobs such as cutting pulpwood and working for the Nova Scotia Department of Highways. He then moved to New Brunswick where he became a newspaper reporter and editor. An extremely well-respected and popular poet, Nowlan was granted an honorary doctorate from the University of New Brunswick, where he served for years as writer-in-residence. He has published many collections of poetry; one of which, *Bread, Wine, and Salt*, won the Governor General's Award in 1967. In his poetry, Nowlan expresses his ideas in concise, straight-forward language, frequently using conversational rhythms and the idioms of local speech. His harsh, poverty-stricken background has coloured much of his work. His poetry is often concerned with the effects of economic and cultural deprivation on the lives of ordinary people. Nowlan typically views even the harsh realities of the world, however, with compassion, tenderness, or good-natured humour.

FRANK O'CONNOR (1903–1966)

Frank O'Connor was a name assumed by Michael Francis O'Donovan for political reasons. O'Donovan was Irish and was active in the Irish Republican Army (IRA) for a time. He came from a poor family and received very little formal education. O'Donovan's writing career began during his childhood; by the age of twelve he had completed his first collection of writing. He continued to educate himself while serving a jail sentence. After his release, O'Donovan became a librarian. Later he became involved in the Irish Literary Revival. This movement sought to reawaken in the Irish people an appreciation for their historical and literary heritage. He was also interested in the other arts and was director of the Abbey Theatre for five years. Though to a large extent self-educated, O'Donovan was a very learned man who translated work from Gaelic and wrote short stories, novels, biographies, criticism, and poetry.

TILLIE OLSEN (1913–   )

For many years, Tillie Olsen's writing career was overshadowed by the demands of raising a family and working outside of the home. For example, her novel *Yonnondio* was begun in 1932 but was not published until 1974. This work reflects the poverty of the working class in the mining towns and farming communities of Nebraska, where Olsen grew up. Short stories and non-fiction are her forte. She also enjoys reading her work aloud and has recorded some of it. Although she has not published a great deal, Olsen's work has been highly praised. In 1961 she won the O. Henry Award for the best short story of the year.

TED OLSON (1899–   )

The son of a rancher, Ted Olson was born in Laramie, Wyoming. He has been a journalist for a number of American newspapers. In addition, he has been a staff member of the U.S. State Department and the U.S. Information Agency in a number of different countries. Olson has written several books of poetry, including *A Stranger and Afraid* (1928), *Hawk's Way* (1941), *Ranch on the Laramie* (1973), and has contributed poems, short stories and articles to various anthologies and magazines. He is extremely interested in environmental issues and in preserving wilderness areas.

WILFRED OWEN (1893–1918)

The English writer Wilfred Owen is known for his World War I poetry. Most of this poetry was written within a year of his death and much of it in the trenches. Consequently, little of his work was published during his lifetime. Although he had been interested in poetry for some time, he only began writing in earnest during the war. He was encouraged by the poet Siegfried Sassoon while in hospital for battle-induced concussion and shell-shock. At this time, he also edited the hospital journal. Although, as his poems indicate, he abhorred war, Owen returned to action as a company commander after his convalescence. While stationed in France, he received the Military Cross for gallantry under fire. He was killed in action at the age of twenty-five, one week before the Armistice.

DOROTHY PARKER (1893–1967)

Dorothy Parker was an American writer renowned for her intelligence and sharp wit. She had the ability to see something humorous or ironic in the most mundane or tragic of human experiences. Born in New Jersey, she lived for most of her life in New York, where she acquired the status of a literary celebrity. She began her career writing for such well-known publications as *Vogue, Vanity Fair, The New Yorker*, and *Esquire.* Her reviews and commentaries were brilliant and witty, but often devastatingly satirical. An extremely versatile and talented author, she wrote poems, plays, stories, and screenplays. She lived in Hollywood for more than a decade, writing screenplays and teaching at Los Angeles State College. Throughout her life, Parker was politically active, especially in leftist causes, and in 1951 was cited for "un-American activities." When she died, she left the bulk of her estate to Martin Luther King, Jr. with the provision that upon his death the remainder would go the National Association for the Advancement of Colored People.

AL PITTMAN (1940–   )

Al Pittman was born in a fishing village in Newfoundland and lived for many years in Corner Brook. He has held an assortment of jobs including warehouse worker, car parts clerk, travelling salesperson, news editor, teacher, and drama director. His first poem appeared in 1965; it was an ode to one of his favourite bars. Since then, he has published many books, including *The Elusive Resurrection* (1966), *Down by Jim Long's Stage: Rhymes for Children and Young Fish* (1976), and *Once When I Was Drowning: Poems* (1978). In 1973 he co-founded Breakwater Press, a publishing company which has published the work of many Newfoundlanders. As a poet, a dramatist and an editor, Pittman has become one of the leading figures in the literary life of Newfoundland.

PLATO (427–347 B.C.)

Plato was one of the most renowned philosophers of ancient Greece. He grew up in an aristocratic family and received the usual Athenian education in poetry, music, oratory, and gymnastics. In his youth Plato became a close friend and pupil of the brilliant teacher, Socrates. Plato remained loyal to Socrates even when the latter was sentenced to death in 399 B.C. on charges of impiety and corruption of youth. He defended the master at his trial and was deeply affected by his death. Later Plato established The Academy in an olive grove on the outskirts of Athens and devoted himself to philosophy. Plato's fame spread over all the civilized world and brought him many students destined to become famous, the most noteworthy of whom was Aristotle.

AL PURDY (1918–   )

Al Purdy, an Ontario poet, rode the rails during the Depression, worked in factories, and served in the Royal Canadian Air Force during World War II. He now travels extensively, both across Canada and internationally, and spends much of his time giving poetry readings and promoting Canadian literature. Besides writing poetry, Purdy has authored radio and television plays, essays, anecdotes, and criticism. In 1965, he received the Governor General's Award for *Cariboo Horses*. Two important collections of his poetry are *Being Alive* (1978) and *Bursting Into Song* (1982).

SANTHA RAMA RAU (1923–   )

Santha Rama Rau was born in Madras, India. Since she was the child of a diplomat, her youth was spent in various countries. In later years, she attended Wellesley College in the U.S., taught English in Japan, and travelled in Asia. She has written many magazine articles as well as a collection of personal stories and a novel. In 1960 she adapted E.M. Forster's novel *A Passage to India* (1924) for the stage. The play was successfully produced in both London and New York.

JAMES REANEY (1926–   )

James Reaney teaches English at the University of Western Ontario and frequently returns to the farm where he was born, near Stratford, Ontario. He is a three-time winner of the Governor General's Award. His award-winning books of poetry are *The Red Heart* (1949), *A Suit of Nettles* (1958), and *Twelve Letters to a Small Town* (1962). After becoming well-established as a poet, Reaney turned to writing drama and is now recognized as

one of Canada's leading dramatists. Perhaps his best-known plays are the triolgy *The Donnellys* (1976–77), based on the history of a famous Irish immigrant family massacred in Ontario in the nineteenth century. Some of the common themes he explores through both poetry and drama are: the loss of innocence, the role of experience in personal growth, the evil lurking in human nature, and the redemptive power of love.

ADRIENNE RICH (1929–   )

Adrienne Rich is an American poet born in Baltimore and educated at Radcliffe College. She is currently a professor of English and feminist studies at Stanford University. Rich was a precocious child whose writing career began very early; at the age of ten she published a volume consisting of a three-act play and poetry. Since then Rich has published many volumes of poetry, drama, and prose. Rich's writing has developed and changed considerably through the years. Since the late 1950s her style has grown more personal and she is no longer constrained in terms of form and content. Political issues and the present status of women in Western society have become more prominent themes in her work. One of her finest volumes of poetry, *Diving into the Wreck*, won the National Book Award in 1974. When presented with the coveted award, Rich declined it as an individual but accepted it on behalf of all women.

RICHARD RODRIGUEZ (1944–   )

Richard Rodriguez is a writer and lecturer who lives in San Francisco. His autobiography, *Hunger of Memory* (1982), reveals his childhood as a Mexican-American growing up in Sacramento, California. He attended parochial schools, became a "scholarship boy," and went on to study at prestigious universities. The book traces his journey from a time when he knew only fifty words of English through to his current views on life and education. Along the way it describes his scholarly search for meaning in life, some of which he conducted in the reading room of the British Museum. Rodriguez has spoken and written against affirmative action programs and against the bilingual education policies in some areas of the United States. These bilingual education policies often require that primary education be available to minorities in their mother tongues. Such policies, Rodriguez feels, restrict social and economic advancement of minorities.

GABRIELLE ROY (1909–1983)

Gabrielle Roy was born and raised in Saint Boniface, Manitoba. She taught school in rural Manitoba before travelling to London and Paris to study drama. Eventually she settled in Manitoba and became a writer. She has drawn upon her teaching experiences in Manitoba for several of her ficitional works including *Where Nests the Water Hen* (1950), *Street of Riches* (1957), and *Children of My Heart* (1979). Gabrielle Roy is regarded as one of Canada's most accomplished novelists. She has been the recipient of three Governor General's Awards and has been named a Companion of the Order of Canada. A French-Canadian, Roy wrote all of her novels in French. Nonetheless, they are well-known across Canada and around the world in translation.

CARL SANDBURG (1878–1967)

Carl Sandburg was an American poet who also wrote novels, biographies and historical studies. He emerged on the literary scene at thirty-six years of age. He worked in the newspaper field for a number of years; earlier jobs included barbershop porter, firefighter, truck operator, harvester, house painter, and door-to-door salesperson. Throughout his life, Sandburg enjoyed playing the guitar, singing, and painting. He devoted many years to researching and writing Abraham Lincoln's biography, for which he received the Pulitzer Prize in history in 1940. Sandburg's poetry is primarily written in free verse. His early work was considered quite controversial because he went beyond conventional poetic content and use of language. His poetry, which often eulogized workers, was frequently referred to as poetry for working people or "the voice of America singing."

A.J.M. SMITH (1902–1980)

Arthur James Marshall Smith was born in Montreal and educated at McGill and the University of Edinburgh. Although he taught in the English Department at Michigan State University from 1936 until his retirement in 1972, he is regarded as one of the most important figures in the development of Canadian poetry. He and F.R. Scott founded *The McGill Fortnightly Review* which helped Montreal become a creative centre for Canadian poetry in the 1920s. Besides writing masterfully crafted poetry himself, he compiled a number of anthologies, encouraged young writers, and wrote extremely influential and highly respected literary criticism. Smith promoted Canadian poetry in both French and English. He was presented with the Governor General's Award in 1943 for his collection of poems entitled *News of the Phoenix and Other Poems*.

WALLACE STEVENS (1879–1955)

The American poet Wallace Stevens was born in Reading, Pennsylvania. Educated at Harvard and New York University Law School, he was admitted to the Bar in 1904. Writing poetry was Stevens' leisure time activity; his full time job was with an insurance company. Although raised as a Lutheran, he was agnostic in later life. Stevens' poetry was influenced by his philosophical questioning. He believed that imagination was a means of understanding reality, and that poetry was the playground where reality and imagination met. Stevens' poetry has influenced the work of numerous fellow poets and is generally highy regarded by literary critics. He was awarded the Pulitzer Prize for his *Collected Poems* in 1955.

HENRY TAYLOR (1942–   )

Henry Taylor is an American poet born in Virginia. He has held a number of university teaching positions. Although best-known as a poet, Taylor also acquired a strong reputation as a teacher of writing. His life has been rooted in tradition and discipline; his Quaker heritage has influenced him greatly. He loves the country life and riding horses. In 1961 he made an unsuccessful attempt to earn a place on the U.S. Equestrian Team. As well as writing his own poetry, Taylor has parodied other poets' work. In fact, he has been known to do impersonations at poetry readings. His own poetry is refreshingly unpretentious, disciplined, and direct.

BOB TEAGUE (1929–   )

Robert Teague was born in Milwaukee and educated at the University of Wisconsin, where he was a star halfback in the Big Ten Football Conference. Teague was the first black journalist to work for the National Broadcasting Company. He has been employed for more than twenty years at WNBC-TV in New York. He was raised by his father and an aunt. Teague was greatly influenced by his aunt; she loved learning and helped him go beyond the constraints that American society assigned to skin colour. In addition to his journalistic endeavours, Teague has written a novel, *The Climate of Candor* (1962), and several children's books. His best-known book, *Live and Off-Color: News Biz*, contains many interesting stories about his career as a television journalist, including the one found in this anthology.

DYLAN THOMAS (1914–1953)

The Welsh poet Dylan Thomas had an extraordinarily varied career during his unfortunately short life. His first two books were collections of his poetry, *Eighteen Poems* (1934) and *Twenty-five Poems* (1936). In these poems his strong imagery and interest in metaphysical themes proclaimed a truly unique poetic vision. His third book, *The Map of Love* (1939), contained stories and poems whose imagery often had surreal elements. His subsequent writing included semi-autobiographical works. During the World War II years, Thomas' poetry looked through the eyes of his boyhood and reaffirmed his religious faith. During and after the war, he also made a number of films. With his rich Welsh voice, he was a superb reader of broadcast scripts and poetry. A month before his death Thomas completed his last work, *Under Milk Wood* (1954), a play for voices. Unfortunately he was still in the process of revising it for stage and book forms when he died. At the time of his death, Thomas had several other unfinished works in progress, including a libretto for an opera to be composed by Stravinsky.

GUY VANDERHAEGHE (1951–   )

Guy Vanderhaeghe was born in Saskatchewan and presently resides there. He is the author of two volumes of short stories, *Man Descending* (1982) and *The Trouble With Heroes* (1983),

and a successful first novel, *My Present Age* (1985). Generally considered one of Canada's finest young writers, he was honoured with the Governor General's Award for fiction in 1982. Human endurance is an important theme in Vanderhaeghe's work. Besides writing, he has worked at a variety of other jobs including archivist, researcher, history and English teacher, and writer-in-residence.

KURT VONNEGUT, JR. (1922–   )

An American writer of novels and plays, Kurt Vonnegut has received widespread acclaim, primarily in recent years. Millions of copies of his work have been sold; some of it has been translated into foreign languages. Released as a movie in 1972, *Slaughterhouse Five* (1969) is perhaps one of his best-known novels. Based on the bombing of Dresden in World War II, *Slaughterhouse Five* is partly autobiographical. Vonnegut received a Purple Heart for his military service. He is interested in technology and its role in the future. However, many consider his writing to be "beyond science fiction." The fragility of human life in relationship to nature and the importance of human kindness are two recurring themes in Vonnegut's work.

PHYLLIS WEBB (1927–   )

A Canadian poet, Phyllis Webb was born in Victoria, British Columbia. She studied at the University of British Columbia with Roy Daniells and Earle Birney. Webb has worked as a secretary and as an executive producer at CBC Radio in Toronto. In addition, she has taught at U.B.C. and the University of Victoria, and has been writer-in-residence at the University of Alberta. Her poetry is intensely personal and intellectually and emotionally complex. For Webb, poetry knits together image, sound, and idea in an economical way; it provides a sense of wholeness for the reader. In 1982, she received the Governor General's Award for *The Vision Tree: Selected Poems*.

ANNE WILKINSON (1910–1961)

Anne Wilkinson was born in Toronto, spent her childhood in London, Ontario, and was educated in private schools in the United States and England. She returned to make her home in Toronto. Wilkinson is known chiefly for her poetry which is witty, sensuous, and intellectual. It is filled with vivid details, frequently presented as contrasts. During her last years she suffered from cancer. Consequently, much of her later poetry shows a preoccupation with death as a presence in life. In addition to writing poetry, Wilkinson contributed to Canadian literature by being the founding editor of *The Tamarack Review*, one of Canada's leading literary magazines.

VIRGINIA WOOLF (1882–1941)

Virginia Woolf, who was born in London, is considered to be one of the greatest novelists of this century. Her father was a literary historian, and from a young age she was able to use her father's extensive library. When Woolf was thirteen her mother died and she experienced the first of a number of nervous breakdowns. Woolf was an influential member of the "Bloomsbury Group" of intellectuals, including such leading literary figures as E.M. Forster, who gathered to discuss literature and social issues. She and her husband founded Hogarth Press in 1917. This was an important event in her life because it gave her freedom in her writing and allowed her to be experimental. One of her greatest literary accomplishments was the development of the stream-of-consciousness technique. Woolf committed suicide by drowning in 1941.

WILLIAM WORDSWORTH (1770–1850)

William Wordsworth spent many years of his life in the Lake District of England. This beautiful area greatly influenced his writing. A keen awareness of his natural surroundings is reflected in his poetry. Wordsworth and Samuel Taylor Coleridge wrote poetry together and discussed their writing for hours at a time. In 1802, Wordsworth and Coleridge published *Lyrical Ballads*, a highlight of the Romantic Period. In the preface to this collection and in the poems themselves, they advocated both an awareness of the individual and a concern for imagination as important subjects of poetry. "Tintern Abbey," one of the *Lyrical Ballads*, is dedicated to Wordsworth's sister, Dorothy, with whom he freqently visited the old abbey. Well-respected in his later years, he was appointed poet laureate at the age of seventy-two. Wordsworth is generaly regarded as a founder and one of the greatest poets of the Romantic Period of English literature.

YEVGENY YEVTUSHENKO (1933–   )

Yevgeny Alexandrovich Yevtushenko was born in Siberia and is one of the major literary figures in the Soviet Union. A fourth-generation descendant of Ukrainians exiled to Siberia, Yevtushenko was invited to study at the Gorky Institute of World Literature in Moscow. He soon gained popularity because of his poetic talent, his magnetic personality, and his gift as an orator. His travels and poetry readings in the United States and Europe during the early 1960s established cultural links with the West. His poetry has been frequently translated and is widely read. Yevtushenko has strong political beliefs about what he observes both in his country and elsewhere in the world. Specifically, he has been outspoken about freedom of expression for writers. In content, his poems incorporate both personal and public themes. In style, they range from sensitive lyrics to impassioned commentary on current events.

Index of Titles

Index of Authors

Index of Selections by Genre

Nonfiction

Short Stories

Poetry

Drama

Index of Selections by Theme

This index lists only those selections which the editors feel best
represented the given themes.

Adolescence

Alienation

Childhood

Conformity and Rebellion

Cultures

Decisions

Girls and Women

Humour and Satire

War

Writing

Index of Selections by Author's Nationality

Canadian

American

Australian

Austrian

English

Greek

Irish

Indian

Italian

Jamaican

New Zealander

Puerto Rican

Russian

South African

Spanish-French

Welsh

CREDITS